BASEBALL
BY THE BOOKS

BASEBALL
BY THE BOOKS

An older boy's or girl's list of baseball tales, being a partially (and at times well-) annotated Bibliography of Baseball Fiction, containing a history of it from the beginning of literature's enchantment with The National Pastime, lists of authors, titles, pseudonyms, genres, diverse other matters, and directions for using same.

Andy McCue

 Wm. C. Brown Publishers

Cover design by Carol V. Hall
Cover photos by Kurt Miller

Copyright ©1991 by Wm. C. Brown Publishers. All rights reserved

Library of Congress Catalog Card Number: 90–82971

ISBN: 0–697–12764–8

Printed in the United States of America by Wm. C. Brown Publishers,
2460 Kerper Boulevard, Dubuque, IA 52001

10 9 8 7 6 5 4 3 2 1

To my Marys
Barden, Bremner, Kenney

Contents

Introduction and Acknowledgments

This project started with a notice I saw in the newsletter of the Society for American Baseball Research. It said Jim O'Donnell had a list of adult baseball fiction that he'd be happy to share with fellow SABR members.

For years, I had bought most baseball fiction I had stumbled across, so I wrote Jim to find out what I had missed. He sent back his list, with a couple of dozen books I'd never heard of. But, to my surprise, I found I had a couple of books that weren't on Jim's list. As we traded correspondence, Jim directed me to the fiction section of Anton Grobani's *Guide to Baseball Literature*. Again, both Jim and I knew of books that weren't there.

In the interests of collecting, I put both lists into a data base program in my computer. And as I expanded and corrected it, I realized that I had something other baseball fiction collectors, or readers, or other fans of the game might be interested in. From that point, it became a four-year search through libraries from here to Cooperstown, through bookstores clean and dusty, in hundreds of letters to dozens of helpful people. I found I wanted to put the books in the context both of baseball and publishing history. That led to more research.

In time, I came to realize that this project really began not with Jim's notice, but with a book I received for my 11th birthday, John Tunis's *Schoolboy Johnson*. At first, I simply was thrilled to read a book set on my favorite team, the Dodgers. In time, as I read his other books, I began to appreciate his broader themes and to read Tunis's imitators nearly as avidly as the man himself. Decker, Scholz, Bowen, Bee, and McCormick bred a love that later fastened on Mark Harris, Robert Coover, and W. P. Kinsella.

Now the bibliography has taken me further, to books I might otherwise not have found—Eliot Asinof's *Man on Spikes*, Ellen Cooney's *All the Way Home*, Owen Johnson's *The Humming Bird*, and a host of juveniles written for my grandfather, my father, and my children.

While much baseball fiction has been written, little has been noted about it. That's what this bibliography attempts to do.

The bibliography includes novels and collections of short stories or cartoons where the majority of stories are about baseball, or where the title story is about baseball. It does not contain individual short stories, poems, or plays. (Grant Burns's *The Sports Pages* has an excellent list of short stories.) It seeks to include the first edition of a book, or the first hardbound edition if a paper version was published earlier.

It includes the "dime novels" that flowered from 1880 to 1910. While they are more the length of a short story than a novel, they have been included for several reasons. At the time, they *were* popular literature. Books were few and expensive. The dime novels served as a spawning ground for writers and characters who were to prove important after the turn of the century, when books became cheaper and more popular. Gilbert Patten and Edward Stratemeyer as writers, Frank and Dick Merriwell as characters, began their careers in dime novels. When the dime novels were collected into books, as the Merriwell stories were, then the bibliography includes only the books.

It seeks to be inclusive. One of the most difficult things in creating this bibliography was deciding what baseball fiction was. Much as I wanted to, I could not find, much less read, all these books and use a uniform set of prejudices about whether a book should be included. There are probably some bad calls in here.

If the book centered on a game won by a bottom-of-the-ninth homer, it was clearly in. The juvenile titles about Little League heroes and minor league struggles also escaped debate.

But what about the murder mysteries where only the victim, the innocent suspect, or the perpetrator were ball players? What about the books that described a boy's year at some prep school or college, running through all the sports and winding up with the big baseball game against State? And what about books about people who used to be ball players? How about softball, or baseball broadcasting, or tabletop baseball games?

The decision was to include them all, and then add annotations to clarify why they were in. You can judge whether the book fits your criteria for a baseball book. Frankly, there was more leeway given to adult books than to juveniles. Baseball in serious fiction has become widespread only recently, and the variations are intriguing.

There are others that were nominated and fell outside even these limits—Hemingway's *The Old Man and the Sea*, Doctorow's *Ragtime*, several of Thomas Wolfe's novels, some P. G. Wodehouse stories. A list of such possible inclusions has been appended to the bibliography.

Acknowledgments

This list is built on the work of earlier bibliographers, especially the fiction and humor sections of Anton Grobani's *Guide to Baseball Literature*, Michael Oriard's *Dreaming of Heroes: American Sports Fiction, 1868–1980*, and Jim O'Donnell and Ralph Graber's "Baseball Fiction for Adults, 1973–1985." There are fuller references in the sources section.

It has benefited immensely from the help of Jim, Frank Phelps, Terry Smith, Patricia Palmer, Eddie Le-Blanc, Deidre Johnson of the Research Center for Childrens' Books at the University of Minnesota, Dave Kelly of the Library of Congress, and other members of SABR's bibliography committee. Bobby Plapinger has been unfailingly helpful. Tom Heitz and Bill Deane of the National Baseball Library in Cooperstown allowed me to spend an extremely fruitful day in their fiction stacks. I have been aided by Rich Arpi, Peter Bjarkman, Nancy Colbert, Sam Fernandez, Cappy Gagnon. Ruth Hadlow of the Cleveland Public Library, Lloyd Johnson, Steve Lehman of the Minneapolis Review of Baseball, Michael Montgomery of The Library at Princeton University, T. Kent Morgan, Gil O'Gara, Bernard Titowsky, and Tom Willman, who among other sterling deeds found a copy of Sheldon's *Captain of the Orient Baseball Nine* and took the pictures.

Still, the category of team errors hasn't been made official. The Es are all mine.

FROM FRANK MERRIWELL TO HENRY WIGGEN: A MODEST HISTORY OF BASEBALL FICTION

On October 15, 1988, with a runner on first, Kirk Gibson of the Los Angeles Dodgers jerked a slider from the Oakland A's Dennis Eckersley into the stands for a 5–4 victory.

Newspaper reports noted that it was the first time a World Series game had been turned to victory from defeat by a final-at-bat home run.

Actually, it wasn't. It had happened tens, dozens, maybe a hundred times before. It had happened in books, books that were implanted in the imagination of every American youngster.

Standing in the backyard, or down at the neighborhood park, it was always the bottom of the ninth. His team was always behind. It was his home run that would save it all.

A boy night never have seen that situation in real life, but he had read about it. Frank Merriwell or Fred Fearnot or Joe Matson or Roy Tucker or Chip Hilton or one of the Blue Sox had banged out that desperation hit, and he could do it, too.

He knew he could because he could recognize in those same stories many things that *had* happened before. Jackie Robinson had rattled many pitchers into balks before Roy Tucker did it. Sal Maglie had shaved a few batters before Speedy Mason. Don Drysdale had come along as a hot-tempered but talented rookie before Schoolboy Johnson. And those characters are from just one book. There are other fictional characters who echo Mike "King" Kelly or Frank Chance, Ralph Branca or Joe Dimaggio.

Baseball's history has been so diverse, and has been recorded so well, that few heroics needed to be imagined. They were there, waiting to be polished.

What was polished changed as the game evolved. Early fictional characters played on town teams, told the pitcher where to throw the ball, and thought the hit and run was the height of skill. With time, they played in domed stadiums, were taught to hit by computers, and waited for the three-run homer.

The first novel that was almost completely about baseball was published in 1884. Noah Brooks's *Our Baseball Club and How It Won the Championship* was a reflection of professional baseball in its formative decades.

Our Baseball Club was an Illinois town team formed from the swells and the mechanics, formed by the city big shots, formed to reflect well on the town and perhaps increase real estate values. Its best players were paid decent salaries by the standards of the time, and its lesser players were paid nothing or next to it. The team traveled, played other teams around the state, and reflected in many ways the career of the Midwestern boy to whom the book was dedicated, Hall of Famer Albert Spalding.

By the first decade of the new century, boys' baseball books were filled with the "inside baseball" of John McGraw and the Giants. Team captains such as Frank Merriwell ran their charges like puppets, with elaborate signs. Professional managers tended to have Irish names, mirroring McGraw, Connie Mack (Cornelius McGillicuddy), Jimmy Collins, and the other famous managers of the era.

In the early 1920s, one of baseball fiction's most popular characters, Baseball Joe Matson, suddenly switched positions. In the teens, Joe had been a pitcher, the dominant position in the dead ball era.

Suddenly, in 1922, just after Babe Ruth had shattered earlier records with consecutive 54-homer and 59-homer seasons, he became *Baseball Joe, Home Run King*.

In the 1950s, black players began to pop up in books, both about neighborhood games (Florence Hayes's *Skid*) and the Big Leagues (Murrell Edmunds's *Behold, Thy Brother*). Little League and its equivalents also became the setting for many a book.

In recent decades, the reliever emerged. No longer merely a way to give a fading starter one last chance for glory, relief pitching produced dominant characters. Television gave authors another possibility, putting the hero in the booth to prolong his connection with the game.

Just as they drew their baseball from the games they watched, writers drew their characters from the players they watched. Sometimes, the debt was acknowledged, as it was to Frank Chance in Hugh Fullerton's *Jimmy Kirkland* series. Sometimes, as in Johnny Madigan (Eddie Stanky) of Duane Decker's *Good Field, No Hit*, it wasn't. Spalding was merely the first of the characters borrowed from life.

George Brett, Charlie Finley, Reggie Jackson, Don Larsen, Connie Mack, Christy Mathewson, Babe Ruth, Eddie Waitkus, and others have all shown up in some form.

If a writer didn't want to borrow wholesale, he could give a baseball figure a bit part using his real name. Babe Ruth has a walk-on in *Spitballs and Holy Water*. Gene Autry has a ride-on in *Johnny Got His Gun*. Shoeless Joe Jackson got a book and a movie from the same bit of imagination.

Some authors took the idea of blending fiction and baseball history to a greater degree of exactness. *Seasons Past*, by the pseudonymous Damon Rice, uses several generations of a family to trace the history of New York City (mostly Brooklyn Dodger) baseball from Bob "Death to Flying Things" Ferguson to Jackie Robinson and Walter O'Malley. Two others, Donald Honig and Frank O'Rourke, built books around transparently disguised versions of the 1941–42 Dodgers and the 1949 Phillies. W. P. Kinsella

imported the 1908 Chicago Cubs for *The Iowa Baseball Confederacy*.

It wasn't only in the writing that baseball fiction reflected the game's history. The illustrations that accompanied the stories are an alternative to photographs. Brooks's book contains drawings of players without gloves and with benches that were exactly that, no roof to shade players from sun or fans.

Since Gilbert Patten's Frank and Dick Merriwell books were reprinted several times from the 1890s to the 1930s, their cover art is a visual history of the period. The pitcher's stage changes from a field-level slab with a path shaved directly to home plate to a raised mound with only a circle of dirt around it. Uniforms, caps, gloves, bats, and stadiums evolve.

FROM THE BEGINNINGS TO 1910

But everything didn't come together at once.

Although forms of baseball were played dating back to colonial times, and some fragments tantalize us, there was nothing recognizable as baseball fiction until after the Civil War made baseball the national game.

In many ways, this was a reflection of the economics of book publishing in the United States. Fewer than 1,000 books were published in the country annually before 1890. Many of these were reprints of popular British authors, whose work American publishers could "borrow" freely because there was no copyright treaty.

Most books were sold for about $2, a substantial sum when $1 a day was a laborer's wage. They were the province of the wealthier classes, a group heavily influenced by English tastes.

In fact, the first substantial appearance of baseball came in a book that was an attempt to capitalize on the popularity of *Tom Brown's School Days*. Thomas Hughes's schoolboy classic had been published in London in 1857. The book has been printed in America as well, and Boston's Lee and Shepard Co. was looking for a way to tap the same market. They snapped up Charles Everett's *Changing Base*, a book of schoolboy adventures with a little more than two chapters devoted to the description of a baseball game. It appeared in 1868.

Between then and the turn of the century, fewer than 20 original novels were published that contained any significant amount of baseball.

Yet, publishers were interested in baseball. In 1887, for example, teams from five publishers had formed a league that played regularly around New York City. The league included teams from Scribner's (which had published Brooks's *Fairport Nine*) and The Century Co. (which would publish its first full baseball novel, Leslie Quirk's *Freshman Dorn, Pitcher*, in 1911). Publisher's Weekly, the bible of the industry since the 1870s, printed box scores of games between publishing house teams.

They also knew there was a market for baseball fiction. For outside the book market, a sizable number of baseball stories were being published.

They were appearing in what we today call story papers and dime novels. Story papers were generally the size of a newspaper and contained several serialized tales. Dime novels were about the size of a comic book and usually contained one or two stories, the main one about the length of a substantial short story. The dime novel story was generally complete in that issue (no heroes were left hanging with the bases loaded), but the characters and general plot lines continued from issue to weekly issue.

The series dime novel had been invented by the Beadle brothers, originally of Cooperstown, New York, in 1860. After the Civil War, the Beadles and their imitators began to publish large amounts of such fiction.

In contrast to the Anglocentric fiction of the rich, dime novels were overtly patriotic. The staples were the American West and heroic moments from American history. In the 1880s, however, faced with a flagging market, dime novel publishers began to cast around for other topics. The major new genre was detective stories. The Beadles tried their share of these, but they also had other ideas.

Since its inception in 1860, the Beadles had published the annual *Beadle's Dime Base-Ball Player* by Henry Chadwick, the inventor of the box score and one of the early codifiers and popularizers of baseball. For example, John McGraw recounted how he established his early baseball reputation in Trux-ton, New York, by purchasing the new edition every year and being the first around to absorb the rules changes and think about their implications.

With this background, it seemed natural for the Beadles to introduce some baseball into their fiction, often in conjunction with detective stories. Their first baseball dime novel, in 1885, was Edward Wheeler's *High Hat Harry, the Baseball Detective*. A couple of years later, they introduced the aptly named Dan Manly as *Double Curve Dan, the Pitcher Detective* by George Jenks. Dan, who made it clear baseball was merely a way to solve crimes and not a career for anyone serious, was the first baseball character to return in multiple dime novels.

At the same time, dime novel publishers were eyeing a younger audience. Dime novels (which usually cost a nickel) were one of the few forms of packaged entertainment a child could afford in the days before movies.

Baseball stories were a natural for this market. They were such a natural that publishers were inclined to fudge a bit in their advertising. Baseball covers became a favorite, even when there was little or no baseball action inside. Book publishers imported the Jack Harkaway boys' adventure series from England and put a picture of Jack on the spine with a baseball bat, even though the Britisher played nothing of the kind. A. L. Burt, one of the large publishers of the day, put out a book called *The Bordentown Story Teller* in 1899. On the cover is a young man sliding into the plate while the catcher reaches for the throw. A crowd watches from a grandstand and the trees behind the outfield fence. Inside is a series of stories about Joseph Bonaparte, brother of Napoleon, after he settled in the United States in the 1820s—not a word of baseball.

Dime novel publishers also learned to jump on current events quickly. In 1890, John Montgomery Ward tried to break the owners' economic stranglehold by creating the Players League, also known as the Brotherhood League. By late April, Street & Smith, which was replacing the Beadles at the top of the dime novel heap, was producing *The Brotherhood Detective, or, Short-Stop Sam*. In May, they had *Brotherhood Buck, or, The Players' League in the South*.

The publishing world's knowledge of baseball's popularity received its greatest confirmation beginning April 18, 1896. On that date appeared *Frank Merriwell's School Days*, the first issue of a new dime novel series, *Tip Top Weekly* from Street & Smith. Frank's creator was Gilbert Patten, a successful dime novel writer from Maine who'd played a lot of baseball as a boy and run a town team as a young man.

From the beginning, Frank played baseball. Oh, he'd stray to football in the fall and a host of lesser sports during the dull winter months (which were often broken by a game of indoor baseball or a trip to some Southern clime for a few winter innings). But Frank's acknowledged favorite was baseball. Baseball tales began with late winter practice, slid into the school team's year, and then stretched into some kind of summer league or barnstorming team. Frank's foreign trips almost always took place during the winter. In all, some 112 of the eventual 245 Merriwell books (Frank spawned a brother, Dick, and later a son, Frank, Jr.) contained baseball, far more than other sports combined.

Frank was a publishing phenomenon, such a phenom that within a year, Street & Smith began to turn the *Tip Top Weekly* episodes into books. They would take three or four of the dime novels, do a little editing for continuity, and put them out with paper covers. A couple of years later, they began putting out hardbound versions.

While no other venture was as successful as Patten/Merriwell, there was no lack of imitators. Fred Fearnot was created by Frank Tousey, Street & Smith's rival, in 1898. He survived into the 1920s and spent many of his summer months playing baseball. Others—Jack Lightfoot, Frank Manley, the Three Chums, Dick Daresome—popped up for a year or so and played baseball.

FROM 1910 TO 1940

But the dime novel was actually on its last legs.

The first blow had hit in the 1890s, with increased postal rates, for most dime novel sales were to subscribers. The publishers were also thrashing around for new genres, new plots, and new characters.

The plots had long ago reached the point where even a 12-year-old reader could recognize a tinge of unreality. 13-year-old heroes regularly out-thought, out-played, and out-fought adults. This came despite these adults trying every known poison, trap, deceit, or disguise imaginable.

And then came the movies. Movies in the early 1910s were much like dime novels. They ran for 15 action-packed minutes. And they just happened to cost a nickel, too. They were such a natural that Gilbert Patten dug up his old dime novels and sold some to moviemakers. (Eventually, in the 1930s, some Merriwell stories would be made into a movie serial.)

Even the perennials like the Merriwell stories began to fade. The last original Merriwell dime novel appeared in 1915, and Patten had bailed out several years before that.

While the dime novel was fading, things were looking up for books. The first impetus was production methods. Cheaper paper and bindings, as well as new, highly automated binding methods, had the potential to cut publishers' costs.

Edward Stratemeyer was one of the first to perceive the potential of lower prices. Stratemeyer was a successful dime novel author and a friend and admirer of Horatio Alger, whose unfinished works he'd completed after Alger's death.

Stratemeyer came up with two successful ideas.

The first, not entirely his own, was to price books at a dollar, or even twenty-five cents. The increased volume would more than make up for the lower profit margin, he reasoned. He turned his pen to producing more of the historical adventure novels he was known for under a variety of pseudonyms. They sold well.

They sold so well they inspired Stratemeyer's second idea, to turn writing into a highly organized, highly profitable enterprise—what a later writer was to call a "fiction factory." Stratemeyer would think of a character and a basic plot outline. This would be turned over to a writer who would produce the book to Stratemeyer's specifications. Stratemeyer would then find a company to publish the book.

In effect, the Stratemeyer Syndicate, as it was known, was a publisher. And thus he put great emphasis on two of a publisher's standard practices of the time—series books and pseudonyms.

The series book was an extension of the most popular publishing ventures in the United States, the mass circulation magazine and the dime novel. Like both of these, the series book sought to interest a broad range of readers rather than a small, upper-class audience. And like the successful dime novels, the series book centered on a character whom the public could identify with. The identity and continuity bred sales.

However, it wasn't a good business practice to attach these potential profits too closely to an author. What if he died, or won the lottery, or decided to write the new *The Scarlet Letter*? Where would the series go? As if they needed another example, American publishers of the 1910s had Sir Arthur Conan Doyle. Sherlock Holmes's creator had decided he wanted to spend his fortune propagating spiritualism rather than write. Harper & Bros. lost the flow of stories from one of its most profitable publishing ventures.

From publishers' nightmares like these arose their penchant for pseudonyms. While they are widely thought of as protecting an author from the immediate consequences of publishing something controversial, in popular fiction they are more often a publisher's device. The character belonged to the publisher, and if it was successful, there was always another hack available.

Stratemeyer made great use of pseudonyms, either the Capt. Ralph Bonehill or Arthur M. Winfield he favored for himself, or the dozens he created for other series. In fact, Stratemeyer made great use of all the tricks of popular fiction. The Syndicate, run by his daughter and others, lasted long after his death in 1930, and still exists as part of Simon & Schuster.

His Syndicate created the Bobbsey Twins, the Hardy Boys, Nancy Drew, the Rover Boys, Tom Swift, Tom Swift, Jr., and a host of less successful series. The books were written over generations by multiple writers, and the Syndicate was so well organized and so secretive that even today the authorship of many of the books has not been established.

Most of the Stratemeyer Syndicate books were not about baseball. Many of the early works were historical. But the next big category Stratemeyer moved into was series featuring a hero or a group of chums having adventures at school, camp, etc., much like the contemporary Merriwell material. And, as with Merriwell, many of these books featured baseball plots or games.

In 1910, having watched the success of the Merriwell series, Stratemeyer created a new pseudonym, Lester Chadwick, specifically to handle baseball books. Stratemeyer was a baseball fan (a krank in the parlance of the time) and chose the name to echo that of Henry Chadwick. The Chadwick pseudonym first appeared on a couple of books about Tom Parsons, a hayseed who goes to college and makes good through baseball.

In 1912, Baseball Joe appeared under the Chadwick name. Joe Matson was an important new type for boys' baseball fiction.

He was the first series hero who was primarily a baseball player. Others had been all-around athletes, such as Jack Lightfoot, or all-around paragons, such as Frank Merriwell. Joe, of course, became a detective, boxer, financial whiz, etc., as the plots demanded, but he sustained none of these.

He was also the first *professional* baseball player in a series. Merriwell, the other dime novel heroes, and the characters springing up in the series books of Ralph Henry Barbour, Albertus True Dudley, and Beth Bradford Gilchrist were amateurs, generally high school or college players. Professionals were faintly disreputable, and frequently beaten by Our Heroes' amateur clubs. Many of the early Baseball Joe books seem to be reacting against this. Joe explains to his mother that he can help more people as a ball player than as a minister, that he can make lots of money, and that he can win the respect of the right people.

Baseball Joe actually began as an amateur, playing as a 15-year-old for the Silver Stars of Riverside, his vaguely New England hometown. In the next books, he moves to prep school and Yale. But by the fourth book, in 1914, he becomes a professional. By the next year, and the next book, he's in the majors. The series eventually ran to 14 books and continued until 1926.

Stratemeyer wasn't the only writer making the transition from dime novels and amateur baseball players.

After Patten begged out of the Merriwell series, Street & Smith made him editor of a new weekly called *Top Notch*. The magazine featured stories of sports and adventure, many written by Patten using the Burt L. Standish pseudonym. He began writing serials for the magazine with baseball themes and characters.

The most popular of these characters was Lefty Locke, and in 1914, the same year Baseball Joe became a pro, the first five books of Patten's "Big League Series" were published. Most of these featured Lefty, but not all, for Patten was breaking even more new ground with this series. They were all set in the same Big League (that's how the books referred to it), and many characters repeated from book to book. But the characters also came and went. Lefty was the central character of the first four books, but in the fifth, *Brick King, Backstop*, he has a cameo at the end, congratulating rival Brick on his play.

Patten, a more skillful and interesting writer than most of his contemporaries, was creating a larger world, one that would give him more freedom to choose characters and plots. The Big League series ran to 16 books and ended in 1928, a run very parallel to Stratemeyer's Baseball Joe. Yet, Patten was never driven to the length of plotting and characterization of the later Baseball Joe books, which reached absurd lengths.

Baseball Joe and Lefty Locke were merely the two most prominent of the series' characters that popped up over these decades.

The writers varied greatly in skill and audience. Some, such as Barbour, Dudley, and William Heyliger, wrote mostly of prep schools. The books were published in nicely bound editions with color illustrations. They chronicled schoolboy high jinks and other sports as well as baseball. They were more expensive and aimed at a "nicer" audience. Barbour worked his way through a large number of series, none of which ran more than 11 books, and none of

which were completely baseball. In all, Barbour published an astounding 135 boys' series books between 1899 and 1943, while writing other works as well. Many consider him, especially in his early works, the most skillful writer of the period. Robert Cantwell maintains Barbour's game descriptions were a major positive influence on sportswriters of the period.

Others, such as Harold Sherman and various pseudonyms from the Stratemeyer stable, were published in cheap editions, with a few black-and-white sketches, paper the first cousin of newsprint, and cardboard covers. Sherman's "Home Run Series" was a series mostly because of its title. Characters didn't carry over from book to book.

Sherman also wrote some of the purpler prose in a mauve era, the kind of prose that has made the era a snicker for modern readers. This is a speech from a chapter called "The Flame of Feeling Grows" in *Fight 'Em, Big Three*. Speaking with "simple directness," the old coach tells the team, "if any of you think that the satisfying of personal grievance means more than victory for Milford, go ahead and betray your fellow team-mates who are giving their all for the finest old high school in the world."

The other notable series of the period was attributed to professional baseball players Christy Mathewson and Everett "Deacon" Scott, but actually written by John Wheeler. The books were linked by their alliterative titles—*Pitcher Pollock, Catcher Craig*—but by little else.

These series went a long way to establishing the characteristics of the baseball series and some of the themes that would stay with it. The characters were positive role models. The books aimed at a moral lesson (teamwork is important, gambling will hurt you). With writers like Barbour and with the greater freedom granted Patten outside the Frank Merriwell stories, the plots and characters improved and became more believable.

FROM 1940 TO 1965—JUVENILES

World War II slowed the production of both babies and baseball fiction. From mid-1942 until 1946, only two baseball novels were published, both by John R. Tunis.

But with the end of the war, the production of baseball fiction shot up, in part to meet the reading habits of the baby explosion that celebrated the end of the war. There were an average of 17.5 baseball novels produced annually during the 1950s, in contrast to the 2.8 of the depression-wracked 1930s or the 4.8 of the booming 1920s.

The traditional series books returned with expanded vigor.

Clair Bee's Chip Hilton and Wilfred McCormick's Bronc Burnett and Rocky McCune re-created the series hero of old. Chip, Bronc, and Rocky carried real-man nicknames and did real-man deeds even though Chip and Bronc were teenagers. They won state and national championships in the big three sports. They defeated bad guys, outwitted gamblers, endured bad umpires, and generally ignored girls. (There was always one on the edge of the story just to let you know our hero's, uh, heart was in the right place.) They mostly played baseball. Even Bee, who before he created Chip was nationally famous as a basketball coach, wrote more baseball stories for Chip than either basketball or football.

Duane Decker's Blue Sox stories were a distinct echo of Gilbert Patten's "Big League Series," which featured the Blue Stockings. Decker's books each follow a player who establishes himself in the Blue Sox lineup, with characters in the later books in the 13-volume series replacing those who had been the heroes of the first books.

Jackson Scholz, Joe Archibald, and Robert Sidney Bowen each cranked out tremendous numbers of boys' sports books between the late 1940s and the early 1970s. As usual, most were about baseball. They were more reminiscent of Harold Sherman's books in that they didn't continue characters from book to book. Bowen, unlike the others, added a touch of extremely proper romance to some of his books.

But new themes were appearing, too.

The most obvious was Little League, which was expanding across the nation in the 1950s. Curtis Bishop and Caary Jackson built series or groups of similar books in Little League settings. Many of the books, especially those from Jackson, included instructional sections to help young players.

Race also was popping up as a topic in the years after Jackie Robinson. The first was *Skid* by Florence Hayes in 1948. Others soon followed, and some of the series book writers took up the theme—Bishop in *Little League Heroes* and Archibald in *Outfield Orphan*.

The pivotal figure in this period was Tunis. Tunis had begun publishing sports books in the 1930s, with stories of Harvard snobbery and track. He wrote them for all ages, but his publisher marketed them as juveniles. Just before World War II, he turned to baseball.

Before Tunis, the values taught in baseball novels were socially very conservative. The themes constantly taught the young readers that the individual had to conform to the group. Individuals could be criminals or cheats, mean or jealous, but society as a whole was fine. These were aberrations. The books showed these evils overcome and society rendered whole again.

Tunis's books rendered a much more liberal view of society. Some evils were broad. *Keystone Kids*, published during World War II, was a story of two brothers who'd fought their way to the big leagues from poverty. It was also a book about anti-Semitism, a social evil that had never served as a theme before. In fact, many turn-of-the-century books were filled with anti-Semitic remarks, and slurs against other ethnic and racial groups, too.

Tunis's themes gained power from his characters, who had many more dimensions than other writers'. Most characters in boys' novels reeked of a nobility unfound in the readers' daily lives. The sneaks and the baddies were easily identifiable. Their "shifty" eyes, or some such thing, would reveal them to the alert reader long before their cowardice or manipulations caused trouble for the hero. Tunis's characters were grayer, and thus their struggles over their own selfishness (*Highpockets*) or insensitivity (*Young Razzle*) carried more weight.

Tunis even had the temerity to challenge that most sacred icon of juvenile baseball book heroes—the former player who is now the main character's coach. In *Buddy and the Old Pro*, Buddy's admiration for his hero turns to disgust when the Stankyish veteran begins to teach him how to cheat.

FROM 1965 TO 1990—JUVENILES

Tunis's work was just one signal of a broader societal change, a greater concern with the rights of the individual than of the society as a whole.

Books about baseball, a team sport, reacted slowly. Even in race, an issue where baseball had been something of a pioneer, the fictional response was slow. Black characters began to appear in books—Matt Christopher's *No Arm in Left Field*, George Shea's *Big Bad Ernie*—but so did a host of groups previously far from the mainstream.

Linnea Due's *High and Outside* looked at alcoholism. Marilyn Levinson's *And Don't Bring Jeremy* was about learning disabilities. Barbara Aiello's *It's Your Turn at Bat* featured a kid with cerebral palsy. In addition to the other themes in these books, each one found society (the baseball team) must come to an understanding of the main character's problem, rather than the character adapting to the group.

To be sure, authors such as Christopher and Bill Knott continued to turn out the more traditional books. But even these authors broke non-traditional ground with Knott's story of a boy who must cope with sitting on the bench while his sister plays or with Christopher's story of a boy struggling while his parents divorce.

The new trend of the post-baby boom years clearly was the role of women, or girls. They were not the non-competitive softball players of earlier books, but rivals. One, R. R. Knudson's Zan Hagen, was even a superwoman of the Frank Merriwell/Chip Hilton ilk, beating all comers at all sports. They also appeared as Little League coaches.

Most of these books came down on the side that girls could and should play with boys. But one, David Klass's *A Different Season*, while accepting the validity of all the feminist arguments, has the main character adamant that there are some things—the high school baseball team, a funky local driving range—that really should be just for boys.

In some ways, these arguments are echoed in a new genre of baseball fiction, one specifically aimed at girls, the juvenile romance. Here, girls are most often cheerleaders, or ball girls, or some other decorative role. Even when they do become players, as in Elaine Harper's *Short Stop for Romance*, they do so to attract the attention of a boy and quit when they get it. He's supposed to be the sweaty sports hero. She's really more into ballet.

Another development of the period was the growth in the number of books designed to be read to children of preschool age. Before 1970, for example, there were only 14 juvenile books of 50 pages or less published. Since then, there have been over 70.

While these books were proliferating, the traditional series had all but disappeared with Bee, McCormick, and Decker in the 1960s. The most prolific writers of the period, notably Christopher, didn't do any series. Throughout the 1970s, no series carried longer than the four books of Clem Philbrook's *Ollie's Team* series.

Very recently, however, the baseball series book appears to be making at least a modest comeback. In 1989 and 1990, four publishers produced paperbound series that echoed many of the traits of the dime novels. They used a recognizable set of characters, were programmed to come out over the course of the baseball season, and focused heavily on the game. The 1989 series, *The Rookies* by Mark Freeman, followed three boys from high school to the World Series in three years.

ADULT BASEBALL NOVELS

While baseball books aimed at teenagers and smaller fry had a long history, the adult baseball novel didn't really flower until the 1950s.

There had been attempts. Some early potboilers were aimed at adults. Heywood Broun wrote a rather interesting novel in the 1920s. And several murder mysteries were published.

The only pre-World War II baseball fiction that was judged to have any literary merit were the Jack Keefe and Danny Warner stories of Ring Lardner. Lardner thought they were simply dialect stories best treated as amusement, but luminaries such as Virginia Woolf thought them interesting. Lardner never pursued the characters, and the literary establishment made it clear they felt baseball and serious literature were incompatible.

This began to change with the publication of Bernard Malamud's *The Natural* in 1952 and Mark Harris's *The Southpaw* in 1953. Both were recognized as literary novels despite their baseball content. But Harris has recalled that at the time he had to do a lot of talking to convince critics that his was a serious book. Harris said he argued this so long that it took him years to acknowledge publicly his debt to the baseball novels he had read as a boy.

That's interesting, because in *The Southpaw* Harris has Henry Wiggen admit to having read Heyliger, Sherman, Tunis, and Lardner, "although Lardner did not seem to me to amount to much, half his stories containing women in them and the other half less about baseball than what was going on in the hotels and trains. He never seemed to care how the games come out. He wouldn't tell you much about the stars but only about bums and punks and second-raters that never had the stuff to begin with. Heyliger and Sherman and some of the others give you a good baseball story that you couldn't lay it down." Henry describes his great delight at a series with strong echoes of Baseball Joe.

While Malamud and Harris were storming the literary gates, the publishing firm of A. S. Barnes was making an effort to create a body of adult baseball fiction in more popular form. In a decade from 1948 to 1957, they published a series of novels by Frank O'Rourke, Jack Weeks, Arnold Hano, and Ed Fitzgerald that took a more adult view of baseball. It wasn't sugarcoated. People lost more than a game at times. Players had trouble (but rarely actual sex) with women.

It was Malamud and Harris, however, who opened the baseball novel to serious literateurs. Novelists began to use baseball to explore established themes and questions in a new way.

From alienation (Robert Coover's *The Universal Baseball Association, Inc., J. Henry Waugh, Prop.*) to magic realism (W. P. Kinsella's *Shoeless Joe*), the themes and styles that dominated American literary writing in the last few decades have appeared in baseball novels.

As the publishing market changed and expanded in the decades following World War II, all the styles and genres threw off baseball novels.

There were the 1950s screwball comedies begging to be movies—H. Allen Smith's *Rhubarb*, Bud Nye's *Stay Loose*, Paul Molloy's *A Pennant for the Kremlin*. Later, the genre went on to the imitators of Dan Jenkins's football book, *Semi-Tough*, adding much more explicit sex.

There were the new types. Romances blossomed, from Lucy Kennedy's *The Sunlit Field* in the 1950s to a host of paperback romances, such as Sheila Paulos's *Wild Roses*, in the 1980s. Interestingly, only the more explicit lines in the romance field used baseball themes. Science fiction produced a couple of baseball books, as did horror novels.

Older genres produced baseball books, too. The detective novel abounded. One of Robert Parker's early Spenser novels had a baseball setting. Richard Rosen turned out several stylish mysteries with a former player as detective. Spy novels, from the grim Cold War seriousness of Robert Wade's *Knave of Eagles* to the spoofs of Ross H. Spencer, used baseball.

The first woman in baseball became a popular theme, ranging from the trashy *A Grand Slam* by Ray Puechner to Barbara Gregorich's *She's on First*. Some in this genre were in sharp contrast to the romances, which for all the statements about independence had women finding their fulfillment in their relationships with men. Books such as Michael Bowen's *Can't Miss* and Gregorich's attempted to take a serious look at the issue and to have the main character be primarily a baseball player rather than a seeker of love.

Graham Greene once noted that literary figures are perfectly happy to acknowledge their debt to writers such as Joseph Conrad, Fyodor Dostoyevsky, and Henry James. But they are, he said, less likely to recognize H. Rider Haggard, the turn-of-the-century writer of fantastic adventures who inspired Greene's own imagination as a boy. Yet, it is writers like Haggard, he said, who bring us to a love of reading when we are young.

The baseball juvenile nurtured many of us in two ways. It created a sense of enjoyment in reading, a joy that we could take to reading of all kinds. It also created a sense of the game, its strategies, its characters, its traditions, the way baseball situations were always the same yet always just a bit different.

The novel may have always brought the winning run to the plate in the bottom of the ninth, but the man at the plate was never quite the same. Maybe he was weak from having escaped gamblers, like Frank Merriwell. Maybe he was tormented by past failures, like Pete Gibbs of the Blue Sox. Maybe he was a man so crippled he had to hit a homer because he couldn't run, like Kirk Gibson.

HOW THE BIBLIOGRAPHY
IS CONSTRUCTED

The most revealing piece of each entry occurs just after the description of the type of book (adult, young adult mystery, juvenile, etc.). If there is nothing after that description, it means I have examined the book myself and noted the publishing data. If I have not, there will be some initials at the end of that line. These were the sources I used not only for publishing information but to decide if a book should be included. A guide to the initials is in the list of sources.

A perfect entry looks like this:

NAME, AUTHOR'S. *The Title of a Wonderful Story about Baseball.* Where it was published: By Whom, When. How it was bound. Number of pages. What type. Source of information.

A description of the book's contents, which seeks to give you some idea why this is judged to be a baseball book. It might also include information about whether the book was part of a series, other exploits of the author or main character, comments about the author's style or knowledge of baseball, or some other cranky thing that has occurred to one of the annotators. TAI (the annotator's initials)

The bibliography is arranged alphabetically by author and includes information about pseudonyms where that is available. If an author used more than one pseudonym, they are listed alphabetically. More background on authors and pseudonyms is sometimes given in the annotation of the first book under the names.

I have included the names of books that were listed in Anton Grobani's *Guide to Baseball Literature*, but which I have concluded should not have

been. A summary of my research is included after these entries.

Titles of many of the early books and dime novels technically are not complete, since many were quite long. Cross-references to republished later versions are included if they had different titles. Many of the dime novels were reprinted with different titles, and an effort has been made to ensure the citation is to the first issuance. More information about series is sometimes given in the annotation of the first entry under the series.

Reprints of a book are generally ignored unless the title was changed or there was a substantial lapse of time (decades, at least) between editions. For a reprint, the number after its title is the year it was published.

The bindings are described as either hardbound, paper, or in one case, spiral. The hardbound label covers a wide range of bindings that aren't paper. It could be either the traditional cloth binding, heavy cardboard, or the more rigid plasticized covers that are described as "library" or "trade" bindings.

The exception to this list of binding descriptions are those labeled "magazines." Actually, this designation was used for what are called dime novels and story papers, dime novels' close cousins. Dime novels were weekly publications, slightly smaller than an 8 1/2-by-11-inch sheet of paper and printed on newsprint with illustrated covers. They contained one story that was complete in that issue, although it was often the further adventures of Our Hero from many earlier episodes. Story papers were printed on larger sheets of paper and contained a number—less than ten—of serialized stories.

Pagination seeks to include only the text of the book. No pagination is given for serials.

The description of the type of book is an attempt to give a reader some idea of what the book is. Most are quite simple. They were clearly aimed at teenagers or were clearly a mystery. Sometimes, however, it can be difficult. The publisher of Quigley's *The Original Colored House of David*, for example, chose to market the book to teenagers. I have classified it as adult because it can be read enjoyably by any age. Also, many of the books written before 1960 were aimed at adults, and yet today would be judged as being for teenagers.

Generally, I have tried to distinguish between juvenile and young adult by cutting things off at about 12 years of age. This is a very fuzzy line. The bibliography might well have benefited from another category that separated books that were designed to be read to a child under seven.

There is plenty of room for argument about many of these classifications, but I think a glance at the number of pages and this description will, in most cases, give a reader a good idea of where the book is aimed. The annotations should help, too.

The annotations were added to the bibliography for one purpose, but they came to include several others.

They were instituted to deal with the question discussed in the introduction—what is a baseball book and why is a given book in this bibliography. Rather than make all these judgments myself, I decided it would be better to give a brief summary of the marginal books and let the readers decide if the book met their expectations of what a baseball novel was. Especially for these books, I have tried to explain not only what the baseball connection is but how much actual baseball playing occurs in the book.

But when I began, I couldn't resist annotating many books, especially juveniles, where there was little doubt they should be included. This allowed me, and subsequently others, to add bits of information. It also allowed us to add a little life to what easily could be just a dull list. Annotations for these books often don't try to detail exactly how much baseball is included.

For collections of stories, the annotation lists the names of authors who are included elsewhere in the bibliography or are famous. If the item in question is an excerpt from a book in the bibliography, that is noted.

In general, I have avoided adjectives that judge whether a given book is good or bad. In a few cases, where I think the books are unquestionably of high, or low, quality, I have said so.

Many of the books were not annotated by myself. Each annotation has a set of initials after it, and information about the annotators is presented in the list of sources.

BIBLIOGRAPHY OF BASEBALL FICTION

A SELF-MADE MAN. (Pseudonym: *See* James P. Tracy.)

AASENG, NATE. *Batting Ninth for the Braves.* Elgin, Il: David C. Cook Publishing Co., 1982. Paper. 129pp. Juvenile.
Little League boys have a coach who emphasizes fun, but then sacrifices some of his principles to keep winning. But he catches himself and draws a Christian moral. Reissued as *A Winning Season for the Braves.* AGM

———. *A Winning Season for the Braves.* (1988) See *Batting Ninth for the Braves.*

———. *Batter Up!* Elgin, Il: David C. Cook Publishing Co., 1990. Paper. 137pp. Juvenile.
Same characters as the earlier book. Unorthodox coach cures our 11-year-old hero's slump with prayer and brings the team together. AGM

ABELS, HARRIETTE S. *A Good Sport.* New York: Tempo Books, 1985. Paper. 149pp. Young adult romance.
The road to romance is rough, but ball girl and rookie third baseman connect. Small amount of game action described from her position down the third-base line. AGM

ADAMS, PHYLLIS, ELEANORE HARTSON, and MARK TAYLOR. *Time Out!* Chicago: Follett Publishing Co., 1982. Hardbound. 32pp. Juvenile.
Cora Cow goes to the rescue when skunks get on the baseball field. One of the Cora Cow series. AGM

ADLER, DAVID A. *Cam Jansen and the Mystery of the Babe Ruth Baseball.* New York: Viking Press, 1982. Hardbound. 57pp. Juvenile mystery.
Cam Jansen uses her photographic memory to help retrieve a baseball signed by Babe Ruth stolen from a hobby show. Some hobby material and attendant history described. One of a series of Cam Jansen stories. AGM

———. *Jeffrey's Ghost and the Leftover Baseball Team.* New York: Holt, Rinehart and Winston, 1984. Hardbound. 58pp. Juvenile.
Neighborhood team made up of kids who were rejected by other teams wins with the help of a ghost. Then they win the big game without him. AGM

———. *Benny, Benny, Baseball Nut.* New York: Scholastic, Inc., 1987. Paper. 46pp. Juvenile.
Benny, who is constantly announcing baseball games in his mind but isn't very good on the field, practices and gets to play in a big local game. AGM

AIELLO, BARBARA, and JEFFREY SHULMAN. *It's Your Turn At Bat.* Frederick, Md: Twenty-First Century Books, 1988. Hardbound. 47pp. Juvenile.
No game action, but much baseball talk. Mark is a fifth grader with cerebral palsy. He's also team manager and designated hitter for a neighborhood team. The plot is moved along by a school project and the missing money for new team jerseys. AGM

ALEXANDER, HOLMES M. *Dust in the Afternoon.* New York: Harper & Bros., 1940. Hardbound. 218pp. Adult.
Rookie pitcher thinks he needs his wife in the stands to win. She wants an acting career. Love triumphs. Many real players of the late 1930s appear by name, and the manager is clearly Leo Durocher. AGM

ALGERMISSEN, JO ANN. (Written as Anna Hudson.) *Fun and Games*. New York: Dell Publishing Co., 1987. Paper. 188pp. Adult romance.
Woman managing a baseball team for young kids gets involved with her male assistant. No. 491 of Candlelight Ecstasy Romance series. AGM

ALLEN, ALEX B. *No Place for Baseball*. Chicago: Albert Whitman & Co., 1973. Hardbound. 64pp. Juvenile.
A neighborhood baseball team works to pay for a window they broke during practice and to find a new place to play. AGM

ALLEN, MERRITT PARMALEE. *Ties in the Ninth*. New York: Century Co., 1930. Hardbound. 251pp. Juvenile. jomo

ALLISON, BOB, and FRANK E. HILL. *The Kid Who Batted 1.000*. Garden City, NY: Doubleday & Co., 1951. Hardbound. 238pp. Juvenile.
Kid with an unflagging ability to hit fouls and raise fowls leads the Chicks to a World Series victory. Many puns. Not THE Bob Allison. AGM

AMARANT, JIGGS. *Tall Baseball Stories*. New York: Association Press, 1948. Hardbound. 128pp. Juvenile collection.
Reissued in 1980 by Todd & Honeywell and marked as a first edition. AGM

ANDERSEN, RICHARD. *Muckaluck*. New York: Delacorte Press, 1980. Hardbound. 206pp. Adult.
Relates events just prior to and during the Muckaluck Indian War of 1873, a war caused in part (fact? fiction?) by a cavalryman's spiking an Indian second baseman. Only one chapter deals with baseball. JO

ANDERSON, CATHERINE CORLEY. *Sister Beatrice Goes to Bat*. Milwaukee: Bruce Publishing Co., 1958. Hardbound. 136pp. Juvenile.
One of a series. Sister Beatrice puts together a junior high school team and helps a refugee from the 1956 Hungarian revolt integrate into the school. AGM

ANDERSON, KEN. *Tom Huntner, Sophomore Pitcher*. Grand Rapids, Mi: Zondervan Publishing, 1947. Hardbound. 72pp. Young adult.

Third of a three-book series about Tom from this publisher of Bibles and other Christian books. Tom fails to heed his college coach's call to turn in teammates who are breaking rules about liquor, gambling, and other sins. AGM

ANDERSON, MARGARET JEAN. *The Brain on Quartz Mountain*. New York: Alfred A. Knopf, Inc., 1982. Hardbound. 114pp. Juvenile.
Boy must spend the summer at a laboratory on an isolated mountain unable to play baseball. He gets involved reading to a chicken brain a scientist is trying to educate and he learns enough to win a ball, a glove, and two tickets to the World Series. No game action. AGM

ARCHIBALD, JOE. *Double Play Rookie*. Philadelphia: Macrae Smith Co., 1955. Hardbound. 208pp. Young adult.
Tough kid who plays the angles as hard as he plays second base must learn to trust. AGM

_____. *Full Count*. Philadelphia: Macrae Smith Co., 1956. Hardbound. 204pp. Young adult.
Pitcher climbs to the Metros (Giants), but his arm has been hurt by an overly ambitious manager. He's released but returns with the Quakers (Phillies) to beat the villain. Much criticism of urban pseudo-sophistication. AGM

_____. *Circus Catch*. Philadelphia: Macrae Smith Co., 1957. Hardbound. 190pp. Young adult.

_____. *Mr. Slingshot*.
Listed by Grobani. This was done by Archibald and published in 1957, but it was a football story. AGM

_____. *Catcher's Choice*. Philadelphia: Macrae Smith Co., 1958. Hardbound. 187pp. Young adult.
Catcher who has been brought up to undervalue himself and shun publicity must turn himself around to realize his potential in the majors. A bit of romance in this one. AGM

_____. *Bonus Kid*. Philadelphia: Macrae Smith Co., 1959. Hardbound. 189pp. Young adult.
Bonus baby pitcher wants revenge for the bad deal his father got at the hands of a manager. Then he must play for the man and learn the truth. AGM

_____. *First Base Hustler*. Philadelphia: Macrae Smith Co., 1960. Hardbound. 190pp. Young adult.

First, he's too nice. Then, he's too selfish. Finally, he strikes a balance, hits .352, and leads Chieftains to World Series. AGM

_____. *Outfield Orphan*. Philadelphia: Macrae Smith Co., 1961. Hardbound. 208pp. Young adult.

Benjie Sadler is the first black player to get a shot with the Boston Pilgrims (read Red Sox). A combination of racism and a chip on his shoulder send him back to the minors, but he returns with another team to win the World Series. AGM

_____. *Shortstop on Wheels*. Philadelphia: Macrae Smith Co., 1962. Hardbound. 205pp. Young adult.

Follows a small, fast SS from Little League up. It's really a paean to the baseball of Cobb and McGraw over Greenberg and Kiner. Our Hero leads an expansion team almost to the pennant in their first year. AGM

_____. *Big League Busher*. Philadelphia: Macrae Smith Co., 1963. Hardbound. 187pp. Young adult.

Million-dollar arm and ten-cent brain college hotshot learns to use his head and heart after being sent to minors. AGM

_____. *Old Iron Glove*. Philadelphia: Macrae Smith Co., 1964. Hardbound. 187pp. Young adult.

Tough guy cum chaw turns into a complete human being (with glasses). AGM

_____. *The Easy Out*. Philadelphia: Macrae Smith Co., 1965. Hardbound. 187pp. Young adult.

Somewhat reminiscent of *First Base Hustler*; a second baseman is too nice. He finally asserts himself. AGM

_____. *Southpaw Speed*. Philadelphia: Macrae Smith Co., 1965. Hardbound. 173pp. Young adult.

A young man discovers that controversial idiosyncrasies, the fast buck, and the cult of youth are not as important as humility, which he begins to learn when his fastball goes bad. TS

_____. *Right Field Rookie*. Philadelphia: Macrae Smith Co., 1967. Hardbound. 179pp. Young adult.

Youth v. age; bonus boy learns he needs seasoning in the minors. TS

_____. *Mitt Maverick*. Philadelphia: Macrae Smith Co., 1968. Hardbound. 186pp. Young adult.

Tracy Radner gets over a swelled head and the notion that everyone is against him. TS

_____. *Two Time Rookie*. Philadelphia: Macrae Smith Co., 1969. Hardbound. 170pp. Young adult.

A rookie outfielder overcomes a sore arm and a too-complacent attitude to become a major league star. TS

_____. *Payoff Pitch*. Philadelphia: Macrae Smith Co., 1971. Hardbound. 191pp. Young adult mystery.

Two plots here; first, a young pitcher works his way on to a major league team; second, the same pitcher solves the mystery of who has been sending him anonymous threatening notes. TS

_____. *Right Field Runt*. Philadelphia: Macrae Smith Co., 1972. Hardbound. 188pp. Young adult.

A young man, small for his age and with a father who does not support his aspirations, makes a place for himself on a professional baseball team. About half the book is concerned with Little League and high school baseball. TS

_____. *The Fifth Base*. Philadelphia: Macrae Smith Co., 1973. Hardbound. 176pp. Young adult.

This book about a young man who makes good in the majors has a religious dimension. Andy Carson's Uncle Lucius, a minister, urges him to be a Christian. He finally makes good in this respect, too. A historical note, he badly hurts his hand and is encouraged with the story of Mordecai "Three Finger" Brown. The fifth base is the boy's values. TS

_____. *Centerfield Rival*. Philadelphia: Macrae Smith Co., 1974. Hardbound. 153pp. Young adult.

A rookie learns the value of seasoning. TS

ARDIZZONE, TONY. *Heart of the Order*. New York: Henry Holt & Co., 1986. Hardbound. 314pp. Adult.

Follows Danny Bacigalupo from Chicago street ball to the high minors. As a kid, he killed a friend with a line drive and that makes him a split-personality hitter. A quite successful example of "magic realism." TS. Ardizzone's *In*

Eliot Asinof, brother of Isaac Asimov and author of Eight Men Out, *the definitive book on the Black Sox scandal. He drew upon his own brief minor league career for* Man on Spikes.

the Name of the Father also contains some baseball material. AGM

ASINOF, ELIOT. *Man on Spikes*. New York: Mc-Graw-Hill Book Co., 1955. Hardbound. 276pp. Adult.

The author of *Eight Men Out* uses his own minor league career as background for the story of a career minor leaguer who finally gets his taste of the bigs. AGM

_____. *The Bedfellow*. New York: Simon and Schuster, Inc., 1967. Hardbound, 223pp. Adult.

A black former major leaguer is the central character, and the book follows him through several days while he undergoes a crisis in his life. Returning to the majors is one of the options he contemplates, and there are several flashbacks to his career and meetings with former teammates, plus a Central Park softball game. AGM

AUMERLE, RICHARD. (Pseudonym: *See* Richard Aumerle Maher.)

AUTHOR UNKNOWN. *Switch-Hitting Big-Leaguer*. New York: Star Distributors, 1986. Paper. 151pp. Adult pornography.

Bisexual pornography. The only baseball connection is that the central character is a professional player. No baseball games described. The author has a real problem with women. AGM

BACHMAN, FRED. *Hang In At the Plate*. New York: Henry Z. Walck, Inc., 1974. Hardbound. 104pp. Juvenile.

First-person tale of a boy's two years of Midget League ball. Author and main character happen to have same name and to grow up in same town, Niles, Michigan. AGM

BAGBY, GEORGE. *The Twin Killing*. Garden City, NY: Doubleday & Co., 1947. Hardbound. 218pp. Adult mystery. jo

BAKER, ETTA ANTHONY. *The Captain of the S.I.G.'s*. Boston: Little, Brown and Co., 1911. Hardbound. 323pp. Young adult. brdnuc

The book's cover identifies it as part of "The Staten Island Giants Series," but no other episodes have been found. Nine boys organized as a baseball team have year-round adventures. AGMBRD

BALL, JOHN. *Johnny Get Your Gun*. Boston: Little, Brown and Co., 1969. Hardbound. 227pp. Adult mystery.

Virgil Tibbs of *In the Heat of the Night* is back in this murder mystery that winds up at Anaheim (Angel) Stadium. Tom Satriano, Ted Bowsfield, and Gene Autry have small speaking parts. One major league game described. Reissued as *Death for a Playmate*. AGM

_____. *Death for a Playmate*. (1972)

See *Johnny Get Your Gun*.

BARBOUR, RALPH HENRY. *Weatherby's Inning*. New York: D. Appleton and Co., 1903. Hardbound. 249pp. Young adult.

Barbour was a frighteningly prolific juvenile fiction writer who created the genre of sports fiction that can be described as the "prep school"

school of writing. Most of his interesting work was done by 1920. Frequently in series that followed a set of chums through several years of school, Barbour's boys are high-spirited, oftentimes financially well-off, and athletically inclined. All sports figure in his fiction, but football and baseball are his two stand-bys. Robert Cantwell has commented that Barbour's books were better written and more entertaining than accounts of actual ballgames of his day, and thus raised the level of American sportswriting as reporters tried to emulate his style. Second of the Erskine series, after a school. PB. After being branded a coward in the first pages of the book, Weatherby makes the baseball team and gives other evidences of being heroic. He has his "inning" in the climactic baseball game and afterwards, when he stops a runaway horse. TS

_____. *The Crimson Sweater.* New York: The Century Co., 1906. Hardbound. 367pp. Young adult.
Year-at-school book winding up with the big baseball game, which occupies just one of 27 chapters. AGM

_____. *Double Play.* New York: D. Appleton and Co., 1909. Hardbound. 315pp. Young adult.
Story of a private school with the big baseball game at the end. Second of eight, mostly football, in the Yardley Hall series. TS

_____. *Finkler's Field.* New York: D. Appleton and Co., 1911. Hardbound. 227pp. Young adult.
Outcast from Kansas at an Eastern boys school wins friends by persuading Finkler the neighboring farmer to let them use his field as a diamond. BRD

_____. *The Lucky Seventh.* New York: D. Appleton and Co., 1915. Hardbound. 311pp. Young adult.
Illustrated by Norman Rockwell. First of three in the Purple Pennant series. Two high school-age boys form a ball club from their school team to play in a summer league. They beat the snobs and take up the exciting new sport of motoring. AGM

_____. *The Purple Pennant.* New York: D. Appleton and Co., 1916. Hardbound. 323pp. Young adult. joagmo

Illustrated by Norman Rockwell. Third of Purple Pennant series. DJ

_____. *Winning His Game.* New York: D. Appleton and Co., 1917. Hardbound. 308pp. Young adult.
Second of three in the Grafton series, named after a school. A shy boy builds confidence by making his prep school team. AGM

_____. *Three-Base Benson.* New York: D. Appleton and Co., 1921. Hardbound. 286pp. Young adult. joagmo
First of three in the North Bank series. DJ

_____. *Tod Hale on the Nine.* New York: Dodd, Mead and Co., 1921. Hardbound. 280 pp. Young adult. joagmo
This and *Tod Hale at Camp* are two of the four in the Tod Hale series. AGM

_____. *Nid and Nod.* New York: D. Appleton and Co., 1923. Hardbound. 360pp. Young adult. joagmo
Second of the two-book Turner Twins series. DJ

_____. *Infield Rivals.* New York: D. Appleton and Co., 1924. Hardbound. 258pp. Young adult. joagmo
"How Tom Landers made the high school team after learning pitching and other things from a most unusual coach." DJ

_____. *Bases Full.* New York: D. Appleton and Co., 1925. Hardbound. 277pp. Young adult.
Second of three in the Wyndham series. DJ

_____. *The Relief Pitcher.* Boston: Little, Brown and Co., 1927. Hardbound. 267pp. Young adult. joagmo
This was third of three in the Channery series, after a school. DJ

_____. *Tod Hale at Camp.* New York: Dodd, Mead and Co., 1927. Hardbound. 280pp. Young adult.
A summer of activities, including several baseball chapters and the foiling of a criminal with the use of a thrown ball. Also see *Tod Hale on the Nine.* AGM

_____. *Lovell Leads Off.* New York: D. Appleton and Co., 1928. Hardbound. 236pp. Young adult.
This is second in the three-book Highwood series. DJ

_____. *Grantham Gets On.* New York: D. Appleton and Co., 1929. Hardbound. 250pp. Young adult. joagmo
Third in the Highwood series. DJ

_____. *Danby's Error*. New York: Cosmopolitan Book Corp., 1931. Hardbound. 239pp. Young adult.

_____. *Squeeze Play*. New York: D. Appleton and Co., 1931. Hardbound. 251pp. Young adult. agmonuc

This was last of three in the Cheltham series, after a school. DJ

_____. *Cub Battery*. New York: D. Appleton and Co., 1932. Hardbound. 276pp. Young adult. joagmo

This is third of six in the Hillfields series. DJ

_____. *Southworth Scores*. New York: D. Appleton and Co., 1934. Hardbound. 269pp. Young adult. joagmo

Sixth in the Hillfields series. DJ

_____. *Merritt Leads the Nine*. New York: D. Appleton-Century Co., 1936. Hardbound. 256pp. Young adult.

This is the first of three books in the Franklin High series. The baseball team captain is hurt in an accident, and his replacement must work against the machinations of the rich kid who caused the accident. Some interesting discussion of the propriety of having professional coaches. TS

_____. *The Score is Tied*. New York: D. Appleton-Century Co., 1937. Hardbound. 277pp. Young adult.

Third in the Franklin High series (the second was the football season of Our Heroes' senior year). The boys must deal with the rivalries that have been the center of earlier books as well as clear the new pitcher they need of suspicions of being a thief. AGM

_____. *Rivals on the Mound*. New York: D. Appleton-Century Co., 1938. Hardbound. 303pp. Young adult. agnuc

First of the three books known as the Cooper Lake series. DJ

_____. *Ninth Inning Rally*. New York: D. Appleton-Century Co., 1940. Hardbound. 265pp. Young adult.

Third in the Cooper Lake series. DJ

_____. *Infield Twins*. New York: D. Appleton-Century Co., 1941. Hardbound. 278pp. Young adult. agmonuc

BARON, NANCY. *Tuesday's Child*. New York: Atheneum, 1984. Hardbound. 112pp. Juvenile.

Grace wants baseball practice; Mom wants ballet lessons. AGM

BARTON, GEORGE. *The Bell Haven Nine*. Philadelphia: John C. Winston Co., 1914. Hardbound. 328pp. Young adult.

First of four Bell Haven books touching on four different sports. Bobby Benson arrives at Bell Haven Academy and is made captain of the nine. With the help of a sensational Indian pitcher, he overcomes various schoolboy problems. AGM

BATTING, JOAN. *Katie and the Very Little League*. Pawtucket, RI: Red Farm Studio Co., 1982. Paper. 24pp. Juvenile.

Katie is too small to play with the other kids, so she forms a team from the animals on her farm and plays teams from other farms. Lots of puns. Book is set up with some pages printed in color and others left for the child to color in. AGM

BEARDSLEE, KEN. *Partners*. Milford, In: Self-published, 1985. Paper. 138pp. Adult.

Beardslee was a former major league scout and executive. AGM

BEAUMONT, GERALD. *Hearts and the Diamond*. New York: Dodd, Mead and Co., 1921. Hardbound. 316pp. Adult collection.

Eleven stories of baseball emphasizing humor and baseball dialect a la Lardner. Grobani says they were based on Beaumont's experiences in the Pacific Coast League. AGM

BECKHAM, BARRY. *Runner Mack*. New York: William Morrow & Co., 1972. Hardbound. 213pp. Adult.

A naive black youth dreams of becoming a major league player until his life is turned around by a charismatic black revolutionary. Constant use of baseball metaphors, some games described, and an interview where the main character tries to convince a big-league team to sign him. AGM

BEE, CLAIR. *Strike Three!* New York: Grosset & Dunlap, Inc., 1949. Hardbound. 212pp. Young adult.

The first of twenty three novels by the former basketball coach whose greatest team was ruined by a gambling scandal. The fabulous and fatherless Chip Hilton plays all three major sports and, of course, excels. In this, the first baseball book, Chip becomes a pitcher, mends a personal rift on the team, and leads Valley Falls High to the state championship as a junior. AGM

_____. *Clutch Hitter!* New York: Grosset & Dunlap, Inc., 1949. Hardbound. 206pp. Young adult.

Chip resists the temptations of professionalism and leads the factory team at his summer job to the league title. AGM

_____. *Pitchers' Duel.* New York: Grosset & Dunlap, Inc., 1950. Hardbound. 212pp. Young adult.

Chip's team loses the state championships in the final but finds that beloved coach Henry Rockwell will be going to State with them. AGM

_____. *Dugout Jinx.* New York: Grosset & Dunlap, Inc., 1952. Hardbound. 210pp. Young adult.

A summer in semipro ball turns out successfully, but Chip's amateur status is nearly ruined by an unscrupulous pro scout. AGM

_____. *Fence Busters.* New York: Grosset & Dunlap, Inc., 1953. Hardbound. 208pp. Young adult.

Frosh ball at State. Chip teaches several resentful teammates the meaning of team play, saves fan's farm from foreclosure, beats varsity with no-hitter, wows them with either arm. . . . AGM

_____. *Pay-Off Pitch.* New York: Grosset & Dunlap, Inc., 1958. Hardbound. 182pp. Young adult.

As a sophomore, Chip leads State to the NCAA championship despite attempts to dupe him into signing a pro contract, thus making him ineligible. AGM

_____. *No-Hitter.* New York: Grosset & Dunlap, Inc., 1959. Hardbound. 182pp. Young adult.

The State team goes to Japan and loses to a team whose ace pitcher has been coached by Chip in a gesture of international friendship. AGM

_____. *Home Run Feud.* New York: Grosset & Dunlap, Inc., 1964. Hardbound. 176pp. Young adult.

A new slugger makes the team home-run happy. Chip, now a junior, makes them team players again. State wins the conference title. AGM

_____. *Hungry Hurler.* New York: Grosset & Dunlap, Inc., 1966. Hardbound. 184pp. Young adult.

State has lost in the NCAA play-offs and Chip goes home to Valley Falls to find the town plagued by juvenile delinquency. The town fathers put him in charge of their youth baseball program, and once again, Chip comes through. AGM

BELL, MARTY. *Breaking Balls.* New York: Signet, 1979. Paper. 249pp. Adult.

A bad imitation of *Semi-Tough* with a baseball setting. Much game and non-game action described. AGM

BENJAMIN, PAUL. *Squeeze Play.* New York: Avon Books, 1984. Paper. 206pp. Adult mystery.

Detective story about the death of a former ball player considering a run for the U.S. Senate. Not much baseball. One game is described. There is thematic use of games and more about the culture of baseball. The narrator's nine-year-old is a fan. TS

BERENSTAIN, STAN and JAN. *The Berenstain Bears Go Out for the Team.* New York: Random House, Inc., 1986. Hardbound. 30pp. Juvenile.

One of a series of books for young children designed to help them cope with new experiences—in this case, Little League. AGM

BERNDT, WALTER. *Smitty at the Ball Game.* New York: Cupples & Leon Co., 1929. Hardbound. 86pp. Young adult cartoons. jtpnuc

BERNSTEIN, JOANNE E., and PAUL COHEN. *Grand Slam Riddles.* Niles, Il: Albert Whitman & Co., 1988. Hardbound. 30pp. Juvenile.

Second graders will love them, two-liners all. No plot. No characters. AGM

BERRA, YOGI, and TIL FERDENZI. *Behind the Plate.* Larchmont, NY: Argonaut Books, Inc., 1962. Hardbound. 190pp. Juvenile.

Unjustly sent to a state farm for juvenile delinquents, Tommy Riggs fights his way to the bigs. Then overconfidence and a scheming rival send him back to the minors, from whence he returns. Catching tips from Yogi in the back. This was one of the projected five-book "All-Star Baseball

Series'' by Argonaut. Others with Ford, Maris, and Mays were published. But *New Blood at First* by Bill Skowron and Jack Lang, while advertised on the covers of others in the series, was never published. AGM

BETHELL, JEAN. *Barney Beagle Plays Baseball*. New York: Grosset & Dunlap, Inc., 1963. Hardbound. 60pp. Juvenile.
Barney gets in trouble with the boys by stealing their ball, but then he wins favor by retrieving it from a difficult spot. AGM

BISHOP, CURTIS K. *Banjo Hitter*. Austin: The Steck Co., 1951. Hardbound. 204pp. Juvenile.
Phenom from University of Texas goes from NCAA champ to overnight sensation. The next year, they find the hole in his swing and he's back in the minors. He matures and converts to pitching. AGM

_____. *Larry of Little League*. Austin: The Steck Co., 1953. Hardbound. 161pp. Juvenile.
The first of a three-book series about Larry and of many books set in the West Austin, Texas, Little League. The coaches basically remain the same through all the rest of Bishop's books, and one, Jim Tracy, is the central character's coach in all but a couple. Very similar to the Bill J. Carol (Bill Knott) books also published by Steck and Steck-Vaughn. At ten, it's Larry's first year. He doesn't play but learns team spirit. AGM

_____. *Larry Leads Off*. Austin: The Steck Co., 1954. Hardbound. 149pp. Juvenile.
Larry's second season finds him earning a starting job as the catcher and lead-off man while helping a boy with delusions about his missing father. Tracy coaches. AGM

_____. *Larry Comes Home*. Austin: The Steck Co., 1955. Hardbound. 202pp. Juvenile.
Larry's third year, Jim Tracy begins to point the boys more toward tournament play. Larry's team wins the league, and then the league all-stars move to the Little League World Series in Williamsport. Tracy also gets married to a woman who has helped coach the boys early in the season when he was tied up with work. (Problem

was he was married in *Larry of Little League*, and we never hear what happened to No. 1.) AGM

_____. *Little Leaguer*. Austin: The Steck Co., 1956. Hardbound. 172pp. Juvenile.
No Tracy in this one, as ex-major leaguer Sneaker Kane manages to help both a budding juvenile delinquent who can hit and an over-protected rich kid who can field. Together, they make a great center fielder. AGM

_____. *The Little League Way*. Austin: The Steck Co., 1957. Hardbound. 159pp. Juvenile.
Fat boy decides he wants to be a catcher. He gets better, but then his drastic weight-loss program catches up with him. He returns to show his cocky teammate about team play. This one features Sneaker Kane, too. AGM

_____. *Lank of the Little League*. Philadelphia: J. B. Lippincott Co., 1958. Hardbound. 190pp. Juvenile.
An orphaned boy is convinced to join Little League and be adopted after leading a very independent life. Tracy manages. AGM

_____. *Little League Heroes*. Philadelphia: J. B. Lippincott Co., 1960. Hardbound. 190pp. Juvenile.
Integration in a Texas Little League. The first black boy to go out for the league improves as a player with the help of his selfless father and Jim Tracy. The boy then helps a white hooligan get into the league and get straightened out. AGM

_____. *Little League Double Play*. Philadelphia: J. B. Lippincott Co., 1962. Hardbound. 189pp. Juvenile.
Ronnie and his buddy Julian Vega form an ace DP combo on Tracy's Giants. Ronnie's aunt, and guardian, doesn't approve of baseball or associating with Mexicans. She is won over. AGM

_____. *The Big Game*. Austin: The Steck Co., 1963. Hardbound. 156pp. Juvenile.

_____. *Little League Amigo*. Philadelphia: J. B. Lippincott Co., 1964. Hardbound. 187pp. Juvenile.
Carlos, a Cuban refugee and a gifted shortstop, must overcome his fear of humiliation to help his Little League team as a pitcher. AGM

_____. *Little League Stepson*. Philadelphia: J. B. Lippincott Co., 1965. Hardbound. 154pp. Juvenile.

Robin and his new stepfather must come to terms not merely as relatives but as coach and player. Features another coach in Jim Tracy's league, Chase Alloway. AGM

_____. *Little League Visitor*. Philadelphia: J. B. Lippincott Co., 1966. Hardbound. 192pp. Juvenile.

Boy drops in for a summer of Little League while traveling with his rock 'n' roll star brother (distinct echoes of Elvis here). When the Big Game comes, the show must move on (but then. . .). Tracy manages. AGM

_____. *Little League Victory*. Philadelphia: J. B. Lippincott Co., 1967. Hardbound. 187pp. Juvenile.

Jim Tracy teaches spoiled and quick-tempered Ed Bogart how to control himself and be a team player, just as he had counseled Bogart's father when they played together in college. AGM

_____. *Little League Little Brother*. Philadelphia: J. B. Lippincott Co., 1968. Hardbound. 185pp. Juvenile.

Younger brother resists catching for his older brother, citing a bum leg (same injury as *Little League Stepson*). Tracy perseveres. AGM

BJARKMAN, PETER C., ed. *Baseball & the Game of Life—Stories for the Thinking Fan*. Otisville, NY: Birch Brook Press, 1990. Hardbound. 230pp. Adult collection.

A collection of interesting baseball stories not seen elsewhere, including pieces by Robert Coover, W. P. Kinsella, Jay Neugeboren, and Merritt Clifton. AGM

BLASSINGAME, WYATT. *John Henry and Paul Bunyan Play Baseball*. Champaign, Il: Garrard Publishing Co., 1971. Hardbound. 36pp. Juvenile.

The two folk legends meet as John Henry pitches and Paul Bunyan bats. Lots of tall-tale wrinkles. AGM

BLISS, RONALD G. *Indian Softball Summer*. New York: Dodd, Mead & Co., 1974. Hardbound. 127pp. Juvenile.

New York teen goes to Kansas for the summer and picks up slow-pitch softball. His team gains a girl Indian shortstop and goes to the finals of the state tournament. AGM

BONEHILL, CAPT. RALPH. (Pseudonym: *See* Edward Stratemeyer.)

BONNER, MARY G. *Out to Win*. New York: Alfred A. Knopf, Inc., 1947. Hardbound. 168pp. Juvenile.

A group of boys grows up as they play summer baseball. AGM

_____. *The Base-Stealer*. New York: Alfred A. Knopf, Inc., 1951. Hardbound. 173pp. Juvenile.

A Police Athletic League baseball team saves a boy from a boring summer. AGM

_____. *Dugout Mystery*. New York: Alfred A. Knopf, Inc., 1953. Hardbound. 209pp. Juvenile mystery.

Little League-age boys' team must discover who has stolen the money they've saved for uniforms plus win the right to play in a regional championship. AGM

_____. *Two-Way Pitcher*. New York: Lantern Press, Inc., 1958. Hardbound. 191pp. Juvenile.

Chronicles a summer league of town boys v. camp boys. Reliever turns into an effective starter. AGM

_____. *Spray Hitter*. New York: Lantern Press, Inc., 1959. Hardbound. 189pp. Juvenile.

Characters from *Two-Way Pitcher* reappear the following summer. Punch-and-Judy hitter loses and gains confidence. Illustrator couldn't decide if he's right or left-handed. AGM

BOOTH, ALBERT J. *The White Nine*. New York: Happy Days Nos. 253–60, Aug. 19 to Oct. 7, 1899. Magazine. Young adult. el

BOWEN, MICHAEL. *Can't Miss*. New York: Harper & Row, 1987. Hardbound. 378pp. Adult.

First woman in the majors. She struggles with teammates and falls for a reporter. Nice moments of clubhouse humor. AGM

BOWEN, ROBERT SIDNEY. *The Winning Pitch*. New York: Lothrop, Lee & Shepard Co., 1948. Hardbound. 206pp. Young adult.

Bowen was a prolific writer, first of air adventures during World War II and then of boys' books after the war. He had a real penchant for vague injuries and improbable plots, some of which he repeated. In this, a rich kid must learn not to be self-centered. He misses a whole season, but returns to pitch a complete game in the 7th game of the World Series. AGM

_____. *Player-Manager*. New York: Lothrop, Lee & Shepard Co., 1949. Hardbound. 187pp. Young adult.

Chuck Lacey's injury stops his career as a big-league catcher, but he starts another one as a manager. AGM

_____. *Ball Hawk*. New York: Lothrop, Lee & Shepard Co., 1950. Hardbound. 180pp. Young adult. agmobrd

College hotshot can't make it in the bigs and has to go to the Texas League to learn how to play ball. DJ

_____. *Hot Corner*. New York: Lothrop, Lee & Shepard Co., 1951. Hardbound. 167pp. Young adult.

Third baseman is offered a bribe to throw the World Series. He refuses but is the goat anyway. He panics, flees, winds up in the Korean War, and returns to vindication. AGM

_____. *Pitcher of the Year*. New York: Lothrop, Lee & Shepard Co., 1952. Hardbound. 183pp. Young adult.

You've got your phenom, you've got your no-hitter, you've got your bad accident, you've got your amnesia, you've got your. . . . All you don't have is an appendectomy performed over the radio. AGM

_____. *Behind the Bat*. New York: Lothrop, Lee & Shepard Co., 1953. Hardbound. 158pp. Young adult.

Another soap opera plot. In the opening chapter, Johnny Morse is hurt in a car accident rushing to the hospital to see his newborn son just after establishing himself in the majors. He's hurt and loses his memory. Worse, he's jailed as a bank robber. Years later, that son makes it to the majors with the help of Pop Smith. And, guess what, it turns out Pop is Johnny. AGM

_____. *Infield Spark*. New York: Lothrop, Lee & Shepard Co., 1954. Hardbound. 187pp. Young adult.

A hard-to-believe story about a second baseman who gets spooked by spikes and runs away from his team. He proves his courage to himself as he rescues an old lady from a fire. He returns to the majors in the heat of the pennant race and must prove his mettle to his teammates. AGM

_____. *The Big Inning*. New York: Lothrop, Lee & Shepard Co., 1955. Hardbound. 183pp. Young adult.

He's gonna be a big-league player-manager. Then a car accident, then a boys-home coaching job and a return to the major league bench after various villains are vanquished. AGM

_____. *The Fourth Out*. New York: Lothrop, Lee & Shepard Co., 1956. Hardbound. 190pp. Young adult.

Boy whose father, a big-league manager, ruined his career crashing into outfield walls makes the majors against his father's wishes. He challenges the fence and becomes wall-shy. But his father obtains him for his own team and cures him. AGM

_____. *No Hitter*. New York: Lothrop, Lee & Shepard Co., 1957. Hardbound. 187pp. Young adult. agmonuc

_____. *The Big Hit*. New York: Lothrop, Lee & Shepard Co., 1958. Hardbound. 188pp. Young adult.

Johnny Price can't be consistent and looks scared to his manager. It turns out Johnny's running from an escaped killer Johnny's testimony had put in jail. Attempted shooting while Johnny's at the plate. AGM

_____. *Triple Play*. New York: Lothrop, Lee & Shepard Co., 1959. Hardbound. 184pp. Young adult.

_____. *Pennant Fever*. New York: Lothrop, Lee & Shepard Co., 1960. Hardbound. 186pp. Young adult.

Rookie is released by big-league Boston Eagles. He takes over as player-manager in the low minors, gets the team going, and after winning an exhibition game against the Eagles, is named their player-manager. AGM

_____. *Million-Dollar Rookie*. New York: Lothrop, Lee & Shepard Co., 1961. Hardbound. 189pp. Young adult.

Millionaire makes bet with friend that he can walk out of the stands and make a major league team. He does and then must prove his real worth to his teammates once he is exposed. AGM

_____. *Bat Boy*. New York: Lothrop, Lee & Shepard Co., 1962. Hardbound. 192pp. Young adult.

_____. *Perfect Game*. New York: Lothrop, Lee & Shepard Co., 1963. Hardbound. 190pp. Young adult.

Unjustly convicted, a young pitcher runs away after serving his time. He connects with a semi-pro team and regains the interest of major league scouts. AGM

_____. *Hot Corner Blues*. New York: Lothrop, Lee & Shepard Co., 1964. Hardbound. 181pp. Young adult.

_____. *Rebel Rookie*. New York: Lothrop, Lee & Shepard Co., 1965. Hardbound. 186pp. Young adult. agmots

A runaway orphan not only makes the roster of a minor league team but finds a father. TS

_____. *Man on First*. New York: Lothrop, Lee & Shepard Co., 1966. Hardbound. 158pp. Young adult.

Marine joins AAA team in Hawaii and succeeds. AGM

_____. *Lightning Southpaw*. New York: Lothrop, Lee & Shepard Co., 1967. Hardbound. 160pp. Young adult.

Pitcher of the Year, Part II: A young pitching phenom, a plane crash, amnesia. New twist: Starts in Vietnam. AGM

_____. *Infield Flash*. New York: Lothrop, Lee & Shepard Co., 1969. Hardbound. 158pp. Young adult.

Story of high school baseball; a transfer student makes the team and leads it to the league championship. TS

(Written as JAMES R. RICHARD.) *The Club Team.* New York: Lothrop, Lee & Shepard Co., 1950. Hardbound. 168pp. Young adult.

A newcomer to the Boys' Club becomes the team's top pitcher. AGM

BOWERING, GEORGE, ed. *Taking the Field: The Best of Baseball Fiction.* Red Deer, Alberta, Canada: Red Deer College Press, 1990. Paper. 296pp. Adult collection.

This collection includes Ring Lardner, Damon Runyon, James Thurber, Nelson Algren, Jack Kerouac, David Carkeet, W. P. Kinsella, Fielding Dawson, Jerry Klinkowitz and Richard Wilbur. It also includes a couple of stories translated into English. JO

BOXER, BILLY, the Referee. (Pseudonym: *See* Frank J. Earll.)

BOYS LIFE, EDITORS OF. *The Boys Life Book of Baseball Stories.* New York: Random House, Inc., 1964. Hardbound. 182pp. Juvenile collection.

Includes stories by William Heuman and William MacKellar. AGM

BRADBURY, BIANCA. *Andy's Mountain.* Boston: Houghton Mifflin Co., 1969. Hardbound. 150pp. Juvenile.

It's a story about a boy and his grandparents whose farm is threatened by a new highway. Subplot that boy is also a pitcher with pro prospects who must deal with his grandfather's wish he be a farmer. AGM

BRADDOCK, GORDON. (Pseudonym: *See* Gilbert Patten.)

BRADY, CHARLES. *Seven Games in October.* Boston: Little, Brown and Co., 1979. Hardbound. 252pp. Adult mystery.

Star player's kids are kidnapped to force him to throw the World Series. Small amount of game action. AGM

BRAINERD, NORMAN. (Pseudonym: *See* Samuel R. Fuller.)

BRANDT, KEITH. *Case of the Missing Dinosaur.* Mahwah, NJ: Troll Associates, 1982. Hardbound. 48pp. Juvenile mystery.

Irving the dinosaur, the team's mascot, gets lost. AGM

BRASHLER, WILLIAM. *The Bingo Long Traveling All-Stars and Motor Kings.* New York: Harper & Row, 1973. Hardbound. 244pp. Adult.

A well-written re-creation of the world of the black barnstorming teams. A fair amount of game action. More on the organization and problems of black barnstormers. Made into a 1976 movie directed by John Badham and starring Billy Dee Williams and James Earl Jones. AGM

BRESLIN, HOWARD. *Autumn Comes Early*. New York: Thomas Y. Crowell Co., 1956. Hardbound. 293pp. Adult.

A romance of old family v. immigrant, town v. city leading to a climactic flood. He's a semi-pro ball player, and several games are described. AGM

BRIER, HOWARD M. *Shortstop Shadow*. New York: Random House, Inc., 1950. Hardbound. 246pp. Juvenile mystery.

College player solves the mystery of why his teammate/hero isn't defending himself against a charge of professionalism. AGM

BROCK, DARRYL. *If I Never Get Back*. New York: Crown Publishers, Inc., 1990. Hardbound. 424pp. Adult.

After traveling back in time, the narrator chronicles the achievements of the 1869 Cincinnati Red Stockings, generally recognized as the first professional team. He becomes involved with both the team and a young Civil War widow with a connection to a militant Irish freedom group. JO

BROEKEL, RAY. *The Mystery of the Stolen Base*. Minneapolis: Carolrhoda Books, 1980. Hardbound. 32pp. Juvenile mystery. nucbip

After an important game, second base is missing. NUC

BROOKS, NOAH. *The Fairport Nine*. New York: Charles Scribner's Sons, 1880. Hardbound. 188pp. Young adult.

The second and last chapters are devoted to games between the Fairport Nine, from the right side of the tracks, and working-class kids who were fishermen and such. The "nice" kids lose the first one, win the second. Other chapters devoted to various summer boys' adventures. One game continues to bottom of ninth even after home team has won. The best friend of the main character, Billy Hetherington, is Sam Black, who is black and also the team's star left fielder. The book was serialized in the popular magazine St. Nicholas from May to October of 1880. AGM

"IDA BOARDMAN SO FAR FORGOT HERSELF AS TO CRY OUT AT THIS CRITICAL JUNCTURE: 'CATCH IT! CATCH IT!'"—Page 136.

Noah Brooks's Our Base Ball Club and How It Won the Championship, *published in 1884, was the first novel that was completely centered on baseball. The unknown artist of this picture was as unfamiliar with the game as other Americans of the era. The layout of the diamond (home plate is at the upper right) bears no relationship to the stands. The left fielder apparently had lined up in foul territory and is pursuing the fly into fair ground and an imminent collision with a center fielder who looks like he lined up in left field. However, other details ring true. The umpire (black coat, white pants) is lined up to the side of the plate, the second baseman is playing on top of the bag, and the fielders wear no gloves.*
Illustration on page 137 of *Our Baseball Club and How It Won the Championship* by Noah Brooks, 1884.

——. *Our Base Ball Club and How It Won the Championship*. New York: E. P. Dutton & Co., 1884. Hardbound. 202pp. Young adult.

This is the first novel completely about baseball. It has an introduction by Albert G. Spalding, recently a player and manager and now with his own sporting goods company, which ran an ad for "baseball supplies" in the back of the book.

Again, two teams from different sides of the tracks start with a game. But the plot then becomes an interesting picture of baseball a decade or so before the book was published. The town fathers decide to sponsor a team, putting together the best players from both the teams that open the book. They bring in some others, begin to pay them on a scale so that most of them are professionals. The Catalpa town team eventually wins the state championship, and the star from the wrong side of the tracks makes it as a lawyer on the good side of town. This was also serialized in St. Nicholas. AGM

_____. *The Boys of Fairport.* New York: Charles Scribner's Sons, 1898. Hardbound. 266pp. Young adult.

This is basically *The Fairport Nine,* with some additional chapters. The baseball parts, however, are unchanged. AGM

BROOKS, WALTER R. *Freddy and the Baseball Team from Mars.* New York: Alfred A. Knopf, Inc., 1955. Hardbound. 241pp. Juvenile.

Freddy is a pig detective who starred in over 20 books. Solving the kidnapping of a Martian introduced in an earlier book is Freddy's main task here, but he also helps organize and coach a town team that includes the Martians. AGM

BROUN, HEYWOOD. *The Sun Field.* New York: G. P. Putnam's Sons, 1923. Hardbound. 204pp. Adult.

The first novel with serious baseball content aimed at an adult audience. The book is narrated by a former sportswriter, as Broun was, in love with a free-spirited, intellectual feminist, as was Broun's wife, while she falls for a baseball player who clearly is modeled on Babe Ruth. Numerous players of the early 1920s appear by name. Several scenes of game action. AGM

BROUN, HOB. *Odditorium.* New York: Harper & Row, 1983. Hardbound. 282pp. Adult.

One of the most marginal books in the bibliography, this concerns three characters on the fringes of society and their eventual flight. One of the characters is a professional woman softball player, and we see her in a couple of game scenes. She also uses her baseball throwing skills at a couple of other points. Author is grandson of Heywood Broun (author of previous entry) and son of TV sportscaster Heywood Hale Broun. AGM

BROWNE, ROBERT. *The New AToms Bombshell.* New York: Ballantine Books, 1980. Paper. 212pp. Adult science fiction.

This is a rewrite of Karlins's *The Last Man Is Out* under a pseudonym. Much of the book is identical, but many details have been altered and the ending has been made much more upbeat. AGM

BUNTING, A. E. *Pitcher to Center Field.* Chicago: Childrens Press, 1974. Hardbound. 59pp. Juvenile.

Steve wants to play center field, but his father pushes him to be a pitcher. A new pitcher in the league solves the problem. AGM

BURCH, MARK H. *Road Game: A Summer's Tale.* New York: Vanguard Press, 1986. Hardbound. 258pp. Adult.

An academic-turned-sports reporter follows the fortunes of a minor league team through a Southern summer. Fair amount of game action. AGM

BURCHARD, MARSHALL and SUE. *I Know a Baseball Player.* New York: G. P. Putnam's Sons, 1975. Hardbound. 47pp. Juvenile.

BURKSAZE, PHIL F. *A Special Season.* San Diego: Budget Book Manufacturing Co., 1980. Paper. 136pp. Juvenile.

Follows a Little League team through a season. Very stiffly written. AGM

BURLEIGH, CECIL. B. *Raymond Benson at Krampton.* Boston: Lothrop, Lee & Shepard Co., 1907. Hardbound. 432pp. Young Adult.

Second of three in the Raymond Benson series. The first, *The Camp on Letter K,* followed Raymond and his friends at a summer camp. This takes the gang to a New England prep school. DJ

_____. *The Kenton Pines.* Boston: Lothrop, Lee & Shepard Co., 1907. Hardbound. 382pp. Young adult.

Third in the Raymond Benson series. The dust jacket assures us Kenton College is modeled after Bowdoin. DJ

(Written as TOM TEASER.) *Muldoon's Base Ball Club*. New York: Five Cent Wide Awake Library No. 959, April 26, 1890. Magazine. 24pp. Young adult. djel

Muldoon was a stock comic character of Five Cent Wide Awake, who had three baseball adventures. In dialect and habits, he was the stereotype of what WASPs thought of Irish immigrants, who dominated baseball at the time. Some of the Tom Teaser stories were written by Edward Ten Eyck. AGM

_____. *Muldoon's Base Ball Club in Boston*. New York: Five Cent Wide Awake Library No. 963, May 10, 1890. Magazine. 24pp. Young adult. modj

_____. *Muldoon's Base Ball Club in Philadelphia*. New York: Five Cent Wide Awake Library No. 971, June 7, 1890. Magazine. 24pp. Young adult

BURROUGH, RUTH J. *Mystery House*. New York: Longmans, Green and Co., 1933. Hardbound. 228pp. Young adult mystery. jo

BUTTERWORTH, WILLIAM. (Written as Edmund O. Scholefield.) *Tiger Rookie*. Cleveland: World Publishing Co., 1966. Hardbound. 159pp. Juvenile.

Matt Lukens moves up quickly but must decide between college and pro ball. Introduction of Russell "The Muscle" Pool, the Minneapolis Tigers' star pitcher, hitter, and befriender of rookies. The author really doesn't know how the game is played. AGM

_____. *L'il Wildcat*. Cleveland: World Publishing Co., 1967. Hardbound. 160pp. Juvenile.

A small guy battles his way to the bigs and then hurts his shoulder. He becomes a minor league manager. Pool becomes his friend, too. AGM

_____. *Maverick on the Mound*. Cleveland: World Publishing Co., 1968. Hardbound. 158pp. Juvenile.

This book returns to Russell Pool's first years as a pro. He must learn to channel his spirit and sense of humor. AGM

CAIRNS, BOB. *The Comeback Kids*. New York: St. Martin's Press, 1989. Hardbound. 317pp. Adult.

A Little League championship game, postponed for 30 years because of racial prejudice, is played as a series of five games from Wrigley Field to Yankee Stadium. AGM

CALHOUN, B. B. (*See* Lucy Ellis.)

CAMP, WALTER. *Captain Danny*. New York: D. Appleton and Co., 1914. Hardbound. 302pp. Juvenile.

Fifth of six Danny books, mostly about football, as might be expected from its first publicist. But this one finds Danny as captain of the prep school baseball team who must deal with a new coach who has professional experience and doesn't appreciate the differences between prep school and pro ball. AGM

(Written as MATTHEW COLTON.) *Frank Armstrong's Second Term*. New York: Hurst & Co., 1911. Hardbound. 318pp. Juvenile.

Third of six books on Frank Armstrong's athletic career. DJ

_____. *Frank Armstrong, Captain of the Nine*. New York: Hurst & Co., 1913. Hardbound. 313pp. Juvenile.

Fifth of the Frank Armstrong series. DJ

CARKEET, DAVID. *The Greatest Slump of All Time*. New York: Harper & Row, 1984. Hardbound. 232pp. Adult.

Novel about a baseball team afflicted with depression. BP

CARLEY, WAYNE. *Percy the Parrot Strikes Out*. Champaign, Il: Garrard Publishing Co., 1971. Hardbound. 37pp. Juvenile. nuc

The White Sox and the Jets have trouble at the game with their mascots—a noisy parrot and a large dog. NUC

CARLIN, STEVE. *Rootie Kazootie, Baseball Star*. New York: Simon and Schuster, Inc., 1954. Hardbound. 26pp. Juvenile.

Gosharootie! I can't believe we read stuff this bad when we were kids, even if it was a Little Golden Book. One of the early TV cartoon heroes, Rootie pitches for the Yankapups, starring outfielder Joe DiPuppio, in this epic. AGM

CARMONA, AL. *Andy: The First Switch-Pitcher*. Los Angeles: Self-published, 1982. Hardbound. 165pp. Adult.

Boy from way out in the sticks has never heard of baseball, but he's been taught to throw rocks with both hands and around corners. He leads a major league team to the World Series title. AGM

CAROL, BILL J. (Pseudonym: *See* Bill Knott.)

CAROSELLI, REMUS F. *The Mystery Cottage in Left Field.* New York: G. P. Putnam's Sons, 1979. Hardbound. 140pp. Juvenile mystery.

CEBULASH, MEL. *Ruth Marini of the Dodgers.* Minneapolis: Lerner Publications Co., 1983. Hardbound. 141pp. Young adult.

The first in a series of books filled with improbable success for teenage Ruth Marini, baseball's first woman pitcher. They're written with a nice realism about young emotions. In this book, Ruth makes it to AAA ball her first year out of high school. AGM

_____. *Ruth Marini, Dodger Ace.* Minneapolis: Lerner Publications Co., 1983. Hardbound. 137pp. Young adult.

Ruth makes the all-star team in her rookie year. AGM

_____. *Ruth Marini, World Series Star.* Minneapolis: Lerner Publications Co., 1985. Hardbound. 144pp. Young adult.

Ruth wins seventh game of the World Series to cap her rookie year. AGM

CHADWICK, GEORGE B. *Chuck Blue of Sterling.* New York: Century Co., 1927. Hardbound. 285pp. Young adult. agmonuc

CHADWICK, LESTER. (Pseudonym: *See* Edward Stratemeyer.)

CHANCE, FRANK. *The Bride and the Pennant.* Chicago: Laird & Lee, 1910. Hardbound. 182pp. Young adult.

Contains a foreword by Charles Comiskey and a short biography of Chance. I suspect Hugh Fullerton was the ghostwriter for this book. He dedicated his own first boys' baseball novel to Chance and ended his last with the toast, "To the bride, the groom and another pennant." AGM

CHANDLER, EDNA WALKER. *The Missing Mitt.* Toronto, Canada: Ginn & Co., 1955. Hardbound. 155pp. Juvenile. nucpub

CHAPMAN, ALLEN. (Pseudonym: *See* Edward Stratemeyer.)

CHARYN, JEROME. *The Seventh Babe.* New York: Arbor House, 1979. Hardbound. 347pp. Adult.

A left-handed third baseman, named Babe Ragland, goes from the major leagues to a black, barnstorming team where he's the only white player. JO

CHRISTIAN, MARY BLOUNT. *The Sand Lot.* New York: Harvey House, 1978. Hardbound. 23pp. Juvenile.

Kids having fun in a sandlot game are organized by adults. When the game gets too formalized and competitive among the parents, they go find a new sandlot. AGM

CHRISTIAN SCIENCE PUBLISHING SOCIETY. *Bats, Bullies and Buddies.* Boston: The Christian Science Publishing Society, 1972. Paper. 89pp. Juvenile.

Despite title, only one of 12 short stories in this tract-like book is about baseball. Also only one of nine testimonies from young Christian Scientists about situations in their lives is baseball. The cover illustration shows baseball. AGM

CHRISTOPHER, MATTHEW F. *The Lucky Baseball Bat.* Boston: Little, Brown and Co., 1954. Hardbound. 124pp. Juvenile.

Youngster gains his own bat, and some confidence. AGM

_____. *Baseball Pals.* Boston: Little, Brown and Co., 1956. Hardbound. 117pp. Juvenile.

Just because he's captain, Johnnie has to learn, doesn't mean he's the pitcher. AGM

_____. *Slide, Danny, Slide.* Austin: The Steck Co., 1958. Hardbound. 130pp. Juvenile.

Danny Masters moves to a new town with no organized baseball. He helps start a Little League. AGM

_____. *Two Strikes on Johnny.* Boston: Little, Brown and Co., 1958. Hardbound. 136pp. Juvenile.

Johnny talks bigger than he plays, until he learns. AGM

_____. *Little Lefty.* Boston: Little, Brown and Co., 1959. Hardbound. 136pp. Juvenile.

Matt Christopher, who wrote children's sports books from the 1950s into the 1990s, thirty-one of them about baseball.
Little, Brown

Bill is determined to succeed as a pitcher, despite his size. AGM

_____. *Long Stretch at First Base*. Boston: Little, Brown and Co., 1960. Hardbound. 149pp. Juvenile.
SS must decide what his role will be when his brother competes against another boy for the 1B job. AGM

_____. *Challenge at Second Base*. Boston: Little, Brown and Co., 1962. Hardbound. 130pp. Juvenile.
Boy is easily discouraged by his mistakes in Little League. He thinks of quitting just as his brother has quit the minors. Both take heart. AGM

_____. *Baseball Flyhawk*. Boston: Little, Brown and Co., 1963. Hardbound. 127pp. Juvenile.

Chico has moved to the U.S. from Puerto Rico. He can play ball, but he makes mistakes through inattention or carelessness. AGM

_____. *Catcher with a Glass Arm*. Boston: Little, Brown and Co., 1964. Hardbound. 137pp. Juvenile.
Young catcher is afraid to throw to second, then he gets beaned and gets jellyleg at the plate, too. AGM

_____. *Too Hot to Handle*. Boston: Little, Brown and Co., 1965. Hardbound. 127pp. Juvenile.
Boy struggles to live up to his family's reputation for baseball. He improves. AGM

_____. *The Reluctant Pitcher*. Boston: Little, Brown and Co., 1966. Hardbound. 131pp. Juvenile.
Little Leaguer must convince his coach he's a better right fielder than pitcher. AGM

_____. *Miracle at the Plate*. Boston: Little, Brown and Co., 1967. Hardbound. 129pp. Juvenile.
Skeeter Miracle is very clumsy, especially in the field, but he's a sensational hitter. His teammates come to accept this. AGM

_____. *The Year Mom Won the Pennant*. Boston: Little, Brown and Co., 1968. Hardbound. 147pp. Juvenile.
Nick is teased, and mortified, when Mom takes over coaching his team, but the Thunderbirds start to win. AGM

_____. *Hard Drive to Short*. Boston: Little, Brown and Co., 1969. Hardbound. 145pp. Juvenile.
Boy won't tell teammates why he leaves games early. AGM

_____. *Shortstop from Tokyo*. Boston: Little, Brown and Co., 1970. Hardbound. 121pp. Juvenile.
Stogie Crane is challenged by Sam Suzuki for the shortstop job. AGM

_____. *Lucky Seven*. Boston: Little, Brown and Co., 1970. Hardbound. 194pp. Juvenile collection.
Three of the seven stories are about baseball. Cover has baseball illustration. AGM

_____. *Look Who's Playing First Base*. Boston: Little, Brown and Co., 1971. Hardbound. 131pp. Juvenile.
Yuri the Russian refugee learns the American game. AGM

_____. *The Kid Who Only Hit Homers*. Boston: Little, Brown and Co., 1972. Hardbound. 151pp. Juvenile.

A boy mysteriously starts to hit nothing but homers. AGM

_____. *Mystery Coach*. Boston: Little, Brown and Co., 1973. Hardbound. 120pp. Juvenile.

A Little League coach is only going through the motions but then the boys start getting mysterious phone calls with playing tips. AGM

_____. *No Arm in Left Field*. Boston: Little, Brown and Co., 1974. Hardbound. 131pp. Juvenile.

Terry can hit and run, but he has trouble throwing to add to his troubles as one of the few black kids in town. AGM

_____. *Jinx Glove*. Boston: Little, Brown and Co., 1974. Hardbound. 47pp. Juvenile.

Chip spends his savings on a new glove and throws the one his father gave him away. Then he starts making errors. AGM

_____. *The Team that Stopped Moving*. Boston: Little, Brown and Co., 1975. Hardbound. 127pp. Juvenile.

A fantasy set in Little League. Stan Wanda, a wizard, stops time to lecture the players on skills and sportsmanship. TS

_____. *The Submarine Pitch*. Boston: Little, Brown and Co., 1976. Hardbound. 137pp. Juvenile.

A Little League setting. A seriously ill central character gives this book some bite. The sick boy teaches Our Hero the submarine pitch he uses to gain his first Little League success. TS

_____. *Johnny No Hit*. Boston: Little, Brown and Co., 1977. Hardbound. 43pp. Juvenile.

Boy must overcome fear of a postgame beating by a rival. AGM

_____. *The Diamond Champs*. Boston: Little, Brown and Co., 1977. Hardbound. 120pp. Juvenile.

Kids wonder why their strange coach insists on certain kids from all over town and then insists they play certain positions. Christopher's first book with girl players. At one time, this had a projected title of *Championship Team*, which appeared on some other Christopher books. AGM

_____. *The Fox Steals Home*. Boston: Little, Brown and Co., 1978. Hardbound. 178pp. Juvenile.

Bobby soothes the pain of his parents' divorce by immersing himself in becoming a base stealer. AGM

_____. *Wild Pitch*. Boston: Little, Brown and Co., 1980. Hardbound. 137pp. Juvenile.

Eddie doesn't like having girls in his Little League. But then he beans one and winds up reconsidering. AGM

_____. *Supercharged Infield*. Boston: Little, Brown and Co., 1985. Hardbound. 120pp. Juvenile.

Team captain is surprised when two of her softball teammates turn into stars. Then she finds they've been hypnotized. AGM

_____. *The Hit-Away Kid*. Boston: Little, Brown and Co., 1988. Hardbound. 60pp. Juvenile.

Little Leaguer bends rules to win until he meets up with a kid who bends them more. Both reform. This and *The Spy on Third Base* are set on a team called the Peach St. Mudders. AGM

_____. *The Dog That Pitched a No-Hitter*. Boston: Little, Brown and Co., 1988. Hardbound. 42pp. Juvenile.

Mike relies on his ESP-powered dog to help him pitch until the big moment of the big game. AGM

_____. *The Spy on Third Base*. Boston: Little, Brown and Co., 1988. Hardbound. 62pp. Juvenile.

Back to the Peach St. Mudders. T.V. Adams studies the game so closely he becomes able to predict what pitch will be thrown and where it will be hit. His teammates become irritated when he tries to position them, and a television report makes it appear he has psychic powers. Much game description. AGM

CLIFTON, MERRITT. *A Baseball Classic*. Richford, Vt: Samisdat, 1978. Paper. 49pp. Adult.

A millhand, a top woman softball player fresh out of the Army, and a long-retired slugger all take a shot at baseball again through a tryout with the Portland Mavericks. AGM

_____. *Baseball Stories for Girls and Boys (Past Puberty)*. Richford, Vt: Samisdat, 1982. Paper. 20pp. Adult collection.

This booklet contains four stories and four poems, the last under the name P. J. Kemp. TS

CLYMER, ELEANOR. *Treasure at First Base.* New York: Dodd, Mead & Co., 1950. Hardbound. 248pp. Young adult. mobrd

A combination of baseball, buried treasure, and history. BRD

COHEN, BARBARA. *Thank You, Jackie Robinson.* New York: Lothrop, Lee & Shepard Co., 1974. Hardbound. 125pp. Juvenile.

Fatherless boy finds growth in his relationship with an old black man who also loves the Dodgers. No games played by main character, but several Ebbets Field games described. AGM

COHEN, DAN. *The Case of the Battling Ball Clubs.* Minneapolis: Carolrhoda Books, 1979. Hardbound. 32pp. Juvenile mystery.

The Growlers' and the Warriors' big game is coming and the Warriors' manager's autographed picture of Babe Ruth is stolen. Ruthann helps solve the mystery. AGM

COHLER, DAVID KEITH. *Gamemaker.* Garden City, NY: Doubleday & Co., 1980. Hardbound. 279pp. Adult mystery.

A madman murders pro athletes because they make too much money, starting with Yankee Willie Bush as he plays center field at Yankee Stadium. Cohler's obviously spent some time there as he knows the park. BP

COLTON, MATTHEW. (Pseudonym: *See* Walter Camp.)

CONTE, SAL. *Child's Play.* New York: Leisure Books, 1986. Paper. 400pp. Adult horror.

Family moves to a town that has just won two Little League World Series titles and finds some evil geniuses are using mind control to program the kids. AGM

COOMBS, CHARLES. *Young Readers Baseball Stories.* New York: Lantern Press Inc., 1950. Hardbound. 190pp. Juvenile collection.

A collection of five of his own stories of boys in the 11–13 range. AGM

_____. *Young Readers Stories of the Diamond.* New York: Lantern Press, Inc., 1951. Hardbound. 194pp. Juvenile collection.

The ball plopped into the catcher's mitt

This illustration accompanied a short story titled "You Just Never Know" in Charles Coombs's Young Readers Stories of the Diamond. *The young woman in the background is Sally Morgan. Sally is, I believe, the first girl or woman to be accorded a major on-the-field role in baseball fiction as she is named the coach of a town team after proving her knowledge of the game. She had soaked it up from her brother Bobo, a major league pitcher. The artist is Charles Geer.*

Illustration on page 78 of *Young Readers Stories of the Diamond* by Charles Coombs, 1951.

A collection of seven of his own stories from Little League to the bigs, including one of the earlier stories of girls playing with boys and another with a girl managing. AGM

_____. *Young Infield Rookie.* New York: Lantern Press, Inc., 1954. Hardbound. 188pp. Juvenile.

This book has two plots. In one, a boy who had his jaw broken by a pitch in a sandlot game must learn to stand in against Little League pitching. In the second, his black friend must win over his teammates and win a place for himself in the league. Both are aided by a big leaguer who's quit after badly beaning a teammate, and they help him regain his willingness to pitch. The big leaguer is named Lefty, and the illustrations show him throwing right-handed. AGM

_____. *Sleuth at Shortstop.* New York: Lantern Press, Inc., 1955. Hardbound. 190pp. Juvenile mystery.

Babe Ruth League shortstop must win over competitors put off by his aggressive style. He also catches the gamblers who are trying to trip the AAA team for which he is the batboy. Reissued as *Young Readers Baseball Mystery.* AGM

_____. *Young Readers Baseball Mystery.* (1959) See *Sleuth at Shortstop.*

COOMER, JOE. *A Flatland Fable.* Austin: Texas Monthly Press, Inc., 1986. Hardbound. 167pp. Adult.

A day in the life of a small town Texas firefighter ends at the ballpark where he coaches Little League. The passing of generations takes place within this brief compass. JO

COONEY, ELLEN. *All the Way Home.* New York: G. P. Putnam's Sons, 1984. Hardbound. 207pp. Adult.

Group of women discover themselves as they learn to play softball. AGM

COONEY, NANCY EVANS. *The Wobbly Tooth.* New York: G. P. Putnam's Sons, 1978. Hardbound. 28pp. Juvenile.

Girl can't seem to lose a loose tooth until she slides in the middle of a neighborhood pickup game. First two-thirds are her failed attempts to lose the tooth, last third is the game where she does. AGM

COOPER, JOHN R. (Pseudonym: *See* Edward Stratemeyer.)

COOVER, ROBERT. *The Universal Baseball Association, Inc., J. Henry Waugh, Prop.* New York: Random House, Inc., 1968. Hardbound. 242pp. Adult.

A marvelous novel of an accountant who creates his own world of a baseball league and its players, all played out with dice on a tabletop in his apartment. AGM

CORBERT, MACK. *Play the Game.* New York: Frederick A. Stokes Co., 1940. Hardbound. 47pp. Juvenile. agmonuc

Created by the reading materials program of the New Deal's Works Progress Administration, AG

CORBETT, SCOTT. *The Baseball Trick.* Boston: Little, Brown and Co., 1965. Hardbound. 105pp. Juvenile.

This and *The Home Run Trick* are two of a 12-book series of Trick books. Sandlot team tries to use chemistry to win the big game, but the potion spreads and the other team gets some, too. AGM

_____. *The Baseball Bargain.* Boston: Little, Brown and Co., 1970. Hardbound. 140pp. Juvenile.

Sixth grader agrees to a pair of bargains to play on a team. The first calls for the theft of a glove, and the second for acts of redemption. He learns many lessons, including that he's a pitcher and can hit better than he thought. AGM

_____. *The Home Run Trick.* Boston: Little, Brown and Co., 1973. Hardbound. 101pp. Juvenile.

See *The Baseball Trick.* The same two teams use numerous methods, including chemistry and lots of inept play, to lose a game so they won't have to play a girls' team. AGM

_____. *The Great McGonigle Switches Pitches.* Boston: Little, Brown and Co., 1980. Hardbound. 56pp. Juvenile.

Second-string catcher makes a heady call in Kilroy High's big game. First of four McGonigle books. AGM

CORCORAN, BARBARA. *"Me and You and a Dog Named Blue."* New York: Atheneum, 1979. Hardbound. 179pp. Young adult.

Follows a teenager through a summer of maturing. She is an outfielder/pitcher on her high school baseball team and dreams of running away to a camp for women pros. Some game description. AGM

CORCORAN, BREWER. *The Barbarian.* Boston: L. C. Page & Co., 1917. Hardbound. 305pp. Juvenile. jonuc

COSGROVE, STEPHEN. *Popp Fly.* Los Angeles: Price Stern Sloan, Inc., 1987. Hardbound. 29pp. Juvenile.
These bugs play baseball, but the plot concerns the conflict between school work and bugball practice. AGM

COX, S. A. D. (Written as Harry Moore.) *Three Chums' ''Fun.''* New York: Three Chums No. 31, June 8, 1900. Magazine. 32pp. Young adult. dj
This dime novel series from Frank Tousey lasted barely over a year, and one baseball season. One of the chums was female. AGM

_____. *Three Chums' Great Game.* New York: Three Chums No. 32, June 15, 1900. Magazine. 32pp. Young adult. dj

_____. *Three Chums' Venture.* New York: Three Chums No. 33, June 22, 1900. Magazine. 32pp. Young adult.

_____. *Three Chums' Great Task.* New York: Three Chums No. 34, June 29, 1900. Magazine. 32pp. Young adult.

_____. *Three Chums Succeeding.* New York: Three Chums No. 35, July 6, 1900. Magazine. 32pp. Young adult.

_____. *Three Chums' Fine Work.* New York: Three Chums No. 36, July 13, 1900. Magazine. 32pp. Young adult.

_____. *Three Chums Still Winning.* New York: Three Chums No. 37, July 20. 1900. Magazine. 32pp. Young adult

_____. *Three Chums' Great ''Form.''* New York: Three Chums No. 38, July 27, 1900. Magazine. 32pp. Young adult.

_____. *Three Chums' Endurance.* New York: Three Chums No. 39, August 3, 1900. Magazine. 32pp. Young adult.

_____. *Three Chums' Double Win.* New York: Three Chums No. 40, August 10, 1900. Magazine. 32pp. Young adult.

COX, WILLIAM R. *The Wild Pitch.* New York: Dodd, Mead & Co., 1963. Hardbound. 208pp. Juvenile.

_____. *Big League Rookie.* New York: Dodd, Mead & Co., 1965. Hardbound. 147pp. Juvenile.
Raw rookie and contentious veteran team up to spark perennial losers to the first division. AGM

_____. *Trouble at Second Base.* New York: Dodd, Mead & Co., 1966. Hardbound. 181pp. Juvenile.
High school outfielder and captain tries to solve racial and baseball problems in his team's double play combo. AGM

_____. *Big League Sandlotters.* New York: Dodd, Mead & Co., 1971. Hardbound. 183pp. Juvenile.
Promising big leaguer is hurt and goes home to recuperate. He helps his former big-leaguer father run a semipro team. AGM

_____. *Chicano Cruz.* New York: Bantam Books, 1972. Paper. 216pp. Juvenile.
Cox deals with the issues of race and class in this book about four young men trying to make the big leagues. TS

_____. *Battery Mates.* New York: Dodd, Mead & Co., 1978. Hardbound. 190pp. Young adult.
Youth league baseball in California. It concerns itself with many typical teenage problems such as getting along with one's peers, growing up, and dating. Also, some debate on having fun v. winning, which they do. TS

CRAIG, JOHN. *All G.O.D.'s Children.* New York: William Morrow & Co., 1975. Hardbound. 210pp. Adult.
An owner who is a mixture of Charlie Finley and a heartless corporate accountant buys a terrible major league team, which proceeds to win the pennant. AGM

_____. *Chappie and Me.* New York: Dodd, Mead & Co., 1979. Hardbound. 247pp. Adult.
A young white man plays in black face with a barnstorming black baseball team in 1939. JO

CREIGHTON, DON. *Little League Giant.* Austin: Steck-Vaughn Co., 1965. Hardbound. 170pp. Juvenile.
First of four books set in the Millbrook Little League, although characters don't repeat from book to book. Extremely tall 12-year-old with little

talent except power learns to play the game. AGM

_____. *The Secret Little Leaguer.* Austin: Steck-Vaughn Co., 1966. Hardbound. 170pp. Juvenile.
Charley, the average student, feels he must keep his ball playing secret from his brainy family. Then, the statistics help him in arithmetic. TS

_____. *Little League Old-Timers.* Austin: Steck-Vaughn Co., 1967. Hardbound. 152pp. Juvenile.
Town loses its Little League field to a shopping center, and the league is forced to move to the grounds of a retirement home. The oldsters take an interest, and the boys reciprocate. AGM

_____. *Little League Ball Hawk.* Austin: Steck-Vaughn Co., 1968. Hardbound. 163pp. Juvenile.
A Little Leaguer has a successful learning season. Title and major subplot concern his dog, who hides all the balls hit into an adjacent woods. Our Hero eventually teaches his dog to bring them back. TS

CRETAN, GLADYS YESSAYAN. *All Except Sammy.* Boston: Little, Brown and Co., 1966. Hardbound. 42pp. Juvenile.
No game action. Sammy is part of a highly musical family but can't play an instrument or sing. He only wants to play baseball, but is convinced to take up art, to teammates' derision. AGM

CRONLEY, JAY. *Screwballs.* Garden City, NY: Doubleday & Co., 1980. Hardbound. 256pp. Adult.
A team of losers turns into winners with an old-time ball player at the helm. JO

CRUTCHER, CHRIS. *The Crazy Horse Electric Game.* New York: William Morrow & Co., 1987. Hardbound. 215pp. Young adult.
A high school baseball player, frustrated at being handicapped after an accident, runs away from home and is helped back to mental and physical health by a black benefactor and the people in the special school where he enrolls. One game described at beginning. AGM

CUMMINGS, PARKE, ed. *Baseball Stories.* New York: Hill and Wang, 1959. Hardbound. 210pp. Juvenile collection.
Includes fictional pieces by Shirley Jackson, Mary Bonner (from *The Base Stealer),* Max Shul-man, Owen Johnson (from *The Varmint,)* Mark Harris (from *The Southpaw).* Also nonfiction by John R. Tunis and Bob Feller. AGM

CURTIS, GAVIN. *Grandma's Baseball.* New York: Crown Publishers, Inc., 1990. Hardbound. 29pp. Juvenile.
Boy's widowed grandmother comes to live with him, bringing a ball signed by members of the (Kansas City?) Monarchs, for whom her husband had played. It helps smooth a difficult relationship between the two. AGM

CURTIS, RICHARD. *The Pro #3: Strike Zone.* New York: Warner Paperback, 1975. Paper. 191pp. Adult mystery.
The third in a series about player agent Dave Bolt, who also works undercover for sports organizations. Here, he is trying to find out who beat up Met prospect Willie Hesketh for crossing a players' union picket line. AGM

CURTISS, PHILIP. *The Ladder: The Story of a Casual Man.* New York: Harper & Bros., 1915. Hardbound. 307pp. Adult.
Only one at-bat is described, but Franklin Connor's baseball talents help him take several steps up the ladder to success. AGM

DAGAVARIAN, DEBRA, ed. *A Century of Children's Baseball Stories.* New York: Stadium Books, 1990. Paper. 192pp. Juvenile collection.

DAVIES, VALENTINE. *It Happens Every Spring.* New York: Farrar, Straus and Co., 1949. Hardbound. 224pp. Adult.
A fantasy involving a chemistry teacher who accidentally discovers a substance allergic to wood. He becomes a pitcher. TS. The plot harks back to an early story by Ralph Henry Barbour. Made into a 1949 movie starring Ray Milland and Jean Peters and directed by Lloyd Bacon. AGM

DAVIS, CAROLINE E. KELLY. *The Yachtville Boys.* Boston: Henry Hoyt, 1869. Hardbound. 148pp. Young adult.
This is the second oldest book I have found with strong baseball content. Two chapters (of 11) cover a game between two town teams. However, the book has a much higher purpose. The star of the game regrets tearing his pants during the ac-

Frontispiece. — Page 83.

This is the earliest illustration of baseball in fiction that I have been able to find, from Caroline E. Kelly Davis's The Yachtville Boys *of 1869. A bat, with no taper between the barrel and handle, has penetrated the umbrella (left) of a spectator. Notice the other bats, on the ground and with the central figures, resemble cricket bats. The artist's name appears to be something like Kilburn.*
Frontispiece from Caroline Davis's *The Yachtville Boys*, 1869.

tion and forfeiting a chance to earn money to help his poor but hardworking mother. He thus gives up baseball, becomes a true Christian, and in the afterword, winds up a missionary in Hindostan. AGM

DAVIS, CLYDE BRION. *Northend Wildcats.* New York: Farrar & Rinehart, Inc., 1938. Hardbound. 306pp. Juvenile.

Two boys form a sandlot team and play other local clubs, winning the final v. their arch rival. A Tom Sawyer-like atmosphere, many racial and ethnic slurs, and many adventures trying to raise money for uniforms. AGM

DAWSON, ELMER. (Pseudonym: *See* Edward Stratemeyer.)

DAWSON, FIELDING. *A Great Day for a Ballgame.* Indianapolis: Bobbs-Merrill Co., 1973. Hardbound. 151pp. Adult.

A very artsy-craftsy romance about literary types. Many baseball references and a couple of game scenes—playing with a child in Central Park and flashing back to high school. But baseball is pretty minimal. AGM

DAY, ALEXANDRA. *Frank and Ernest Play Ball.* New York: Scholastic, Inc., 1990. Hardbound. 36pp. Juvenile.

A bear and an elephant take over running a minor league team for a day. The emphasis is on baseball slang. Very nice illustrations. AGM

DeANDREA, WILLIAM L. *Five O'Clock Lightning.* New York: St. Martin's Press, 1982. Hardbound. 247pp. Adult mystery.

Some baseball games described in the beginning, but primarily a fast-paced action story with former AAA catcher Russ Garrett as the sleuth. The year is 1953, and he brings his friend, Mickey Mantle, into the plot obliquely (he's a suspect). Yankee Stadium is a sometime setting. FP

DECKER, DUANE. *Good Field, No Hit.* New York: M. S. Mill Co., 1947. Hardbound. 208pp. Young adult.

The first of 13 books about the perennially contending Blue Sox. In each book, Decker introduced a new player at a different position and has him work his way into the lineup. By the later books, rookies were coming up to replace players we'd met early in the series. Each story is different, but the players and manager Jug Slavin continue from book to book. From the similarity of the names (Blue Sox and Blue Stockings), I am tempted to believe Decker read Patten's Big League Series as a boy. Players from opposing teams mirror recognizable major league lineups of the day. In this book, Johnny Madigan is a Stankyish third baseman—short on talent, long on the ability to do what is needed. AGM

_____. *Starting Pitcher*. New York: Mill & Morrow, 1948. Hardbound. 187pp. Young adult.

A leg injury ruins Eddie Lasky's career as the Blue Sox' shortstop. He comes back as a starting pitcher. AGM

_____. *Hit and Run*. New York: Mill & Morrow, 1949. Hardbound. 188pp. Young adult.

Chip Fiske has a chip on his shoulder because of his size, and it becomes worse when his slap hitting is put into right field to replace slugging hero Augie Marshall. One frequent element in Decker's books is how the ignorant fans will root against the home team because the new player doesn't have the same skills as the old one or because one rival for a job is flashy rather than a team player. AGM

_____. *The Catcher from Double-A*. New York: William Morrow & Co., 1950. Hardbound. 188pp. Young adult.

Pete Gibbs must learn to have confidence in himself before his teammates will trust him. AGM

_____. *Fast Man on a Pivot*. New York: William Morrow & Co., 1951. Hardbound. 221pp. Young adult.

Like many books in the series, this contrasts a player with small-ball skills against a power hitter. And once again, the team player wins out. Decker never explains why the loser, who is acknowledged to be a much better hitter simply lacking the second baseman's skills, couldn't be moved to another position. AGM

_____. *The Big Stretch*. New York: William Morrow & Co., 1952. Hardbound. 191pp. Young adult.

Former batboy Stretch Stookey takes the first-base job from his hero, Marty "Beef Trust" Blake. Stretch's skills are defense and speed while Blake was a prototype Dick Stuart. As a batboy, Stretch (then known as "Buster") was right-handed but now returns as a lefty. AGM

_____. *Switch Hitter*. New York: William Morrow & Co., 1953. Hardbound. 218pp. Young adult.

Like Madigan as Stanky, Russ Woodward's baseball skills are clearly those of Mickey Mantle. But he won't be a team player until Jug Slavin teaches him the hard way. AGM

_____. *Mister Shortstop*. New York: William Morrow & Co., 1954. Hardbound. 185pp. Young adult.

Andy Pearson must live down his reputation as nothing more than a good utility man to win the shortstop job. AGM

_____. *Long Ball to Left Field*. New York: William Morrow & Co., 1958. Hardbound. 217pp. Young adult.

He thinks he's a pitcher. Jug Slavin knows he's a slugger. AGM

_____. *Third-Base Rookie*. New York: William Morrow & Co., 1959. Hardbound. 186pp. Young adult.

The first changing of the guard. A young player with a tainted past wrests the third-base job from Johnny Madigan, who joined us in *Good Field, No Hit*. AGM

_____. *Showboat Southpaw*. New York: William Morrow & Co., 1960. Hardbound. 188pp. Young adult.

Cocky left-hander loses his fastball and has to learn to pitch. Also the crafty left-hander of the archrival Clippers, who has been Blondy and Wilcy Lord in earlier books, becomes Whitey. In one case, probably a typo, he becomes Ford. AGM

_____. *Rebel in Right Field*. New York: William Morrow & Co., 1961. Hardbound. 190pp. Young adult.

Danny Redd's brother had ruined a promising career with injuries, and he wasn't going to do it too, no matter what Jug Slavin wanted. A cameo appearance by Thornboro, who confirms he is a masked version of Marvellous Marv Throneberry by making an error in his only mention. AGM

_____. *The Grand-Slam Kid*. New York: William Morrow & Co., 1964. Hardbound. 189pp. Young adult.

Bucky O'Brian comes along to replace Pete Gibbs, and his first major league at bat is a pennant-winning grand slam. He then has to learn he's not Frank Merriwell. AGM

(Written as RICHARD WAYNE.) *Clutch Hitter*. Philadelphia: Macrae Smith Co., 1951. Hardbound. 201pp. Young adult.

Mike Tracy has Tony Gwynn's bat, Al Kaline's glove, and Dave Kingman's attitude. AGM

———. *Wrong-Way Rookie.* Philadelphia: Macrae Smith Co., 1952. Hardbound. 189pp. Young adult. He's a catcher with enthusiasm and no talent. They're a team with talent and no hustle. The combination makes the first division. Several echoes of Decker's Blue Sox books. This team's shortstop is Slick Hammill. The same name would duel Andy Pearson for the Blue Sox SS job in a book published two years later. A team named the Clippers is again recognizable as the Yankees. And there's even a sportswriter named Decker. AGM

DEFORD, FRANK. *Casey on the Loose.* New York: Viking Press, 1989. Hardbound. 106pp. Adult. Based on a Sports Illustrated story by Deford, a meringue of a rewrite of Casey at the Bat with a new ending. Deford slips John L. Sullivan, James Naismith, Amos Alonzo Stagg, Kenesaw Mountain Landis, and Babe Ruth into the story as well as some nonsports figures. AGM

DELANEY, NED. *Two Strikes, Four Eyes.* Boston: Houghton Mifflin Co., 1976. Hardbound. 32pp. Juvenile. Toby is torn between the embarrassments of wearing glasses or striking out all the time. AGM

DeMARCO, GORDON. *Frisco Blues.* London: Pluto Press, 1985. Hardbound. 124pp. Adult mystery. Murkily plotted mystery set in 1947. A black ball player is murdered just as it appears he might follow Jackie Robinson to the majors. One game between the Satchel Paige and Bob Feller All-Stars described. AGM

DeMORGAN, JOHN. (Written as Frank Sheridan.) *Jack, the Pride of the Nine.* New York: Golden Hours Nos. 128–37, July 12 to Sept. 13, 1890. Magazine. Young adult. modej

DESSENT, MICHAEL. *Baseball Becky.* San Diego: Oak Tree Publications, 1982. Paper. 150pp. Juvenile. nuc

When clumsy Becky joins a softball team, she learns a great deal about coordination. NUC

DeVRIES, JULIAN. *The Strike-Out King.* Cleveland: World Publishing Co., 1940. Hardbound. 248pp. Juvenile. Pitcher battles rival who flips out. Various other adventures and a pro contract. Pretty mundane. It was republished with a glossy picture-cover edition in 1948, with that date incorrectly indicated as the copyright date. AGM

DEWS, ROBERT P. (Written as Trebor Swed.) *Whichaway.* New York: Rebel Books, 1977. Hardbound. 153pp. Adult. A one-time chain gang escapee, prominent politician, and former baseball player sets out to re-create his escape from prison while recalling his life. Much time spent thinking on the baseball career. Author is a former minor leaguer and father of minor leaguer and Atlanta Braves coach Bobby Dews. AGM

DICKMEYER, LOWELL. *Baseball is for Me.* Minneapolis: Lerner Publications Co., 1978. Hardbound. 46pp. Juvenile. A book that introduces young players to the rules and skills of baseball told through the eyes of a fictional Little Leaguer. AGM

WALT DISNEY PRODUCTIONS. *Mickey Mouse and the Great Lot Plot.* Racine, Wi: Western Publishing Co., 1974. Hardbound. 24pp. Juvenile. In this Little Golden Book, Scrooge McDuck is set to buy up the only lot left in town for the kids to play baseball on. The kids lure him into a game and he learns to love it, turning the lot into a nice ballpark. AGM

DIXON, FRANKLIN W. (Pseudonym: *See* Edward Stratemeyer.)

DIXON, MICHAEL B., and VALERIE SMITH. *Striking Out!* New Orleans: Anchorage Press, 1984. Paper. 38pp. Juvenile. A play for kids set on a Little League team. The team clowns are Cheech and Chong. The umpire is Darth. AGM

DOLAN, ELLEN M. *Casey at the Bat.* St. Louis: Milliken Publishing Co., 1987. Hardbound. 30pp. Juvenile.

A retelling in story form of the poem. AGM

DOLINER, ROY. *The Orange Air.* New York: Charles Scribner's Sons, 1961. Hardbound. 242pp. Adult.

The main character in this improbable thriller has Ralph Branca's past if not his name. No game action but several descriptions of The Pitch and The Game, plus other baseball references. Otherwise we have plotting in Cuba soon after Castro's takeover. AGM

DONOHUE, JAMES F. *Spitballs and Holy Water.* New York: Avon Books, 1977. Paper. 204pp. Adult.

A black nun pitches against the 1927 Yankees, striking out Babe Ruth and later the devil himself. JO

DOUGLAS, CAPTAIN ALAN. *Fast Nine, or, A Challenge from Fairfield.* New York: New York Book Co., 1913. Hardbound. 178pp. Juvenile.

Baseball is the latest challenge in this, the fourth book in the 10-book Hickory Ridge Boy Scouts series. In keeping with its uplifting message, the book also contains extensive information on fish. AGM

DRAPER, ALLYN. (Pseudonym: *See* Harvey K. Shackleford under Col. Ralph Fenton.)

DRDEK, RICHARD. *Lefty's Boy.* Garden City, NY: Doubleday & Co., 1969. Hardbound. 204pp. Juvenile.

Lefty used to pitch for the Cleveland Indians. Now, he's a drunk. Barnaby is also a promising pitcher, but he must learn to deal with his father's neglect. No game action, but much baseball discussion. AGM

DRURY, MAXINE. *Glory for Gil.* New York: David McKay Co., 1964. Hardbound. 184pp. Juvenile. jomo

DUBROVIN, VIVIAN. *Baseball Just for Fun.* St. Paul, Mn: EMC Corp., 1974. Hardbound. 30pp. Juvenile. nucbip

Not good at baseball skills, Pete dreads team practices. Then the coach gives him a chance at something different. NUC

DUDLEY, ALBERTUS TRUE. *Making the Nine.* Boston: Lee and Shepard, 1904. Hardbound. 332pp. Juvenile.

Second of the nine-book Phillips Exeter series, named after the famous prep school. Strangely, the school in the text is called Seaton. The books cover a wide range of schoolboy activities. *Making the Nine* focuses on an underclassman working his way on to the team and winning the big game. AGM

_____. *With Mask and Mitt.* Boston: Lothrop, Lee & Shepard Co., 1906. Hardbound. 300pp. Juvenile.

The underclassman of the preceding book is now a senior and captain, but the book focuses on another underclassman who strives to win the catcher's job. Fourth in the Phillips Exeter series. AGM

_____. *The Great Year.* Boston: Lothrop, Lee & Shepard Co., 1907. Hardbound. 302pp. Juvenile.

In turn, the catcher of *With Mask and Mitt* becomes captain. Much of this book is football although the climax is a baseball game. Fifth of the Phillips Exeter series. AGM

_____. *At the Home Plate.* Boston: Lothrop, Lee & Shepard Co., 1910. Hardbound. 316pp. Juvenile.

Second of three books in the Triangular League series. Despite the title, only the last quarter of the book is about baseball. It follows a group of boys through a year at Newbury Latin School, winding up with a triumph in baseball. AGM

DUE, LINNEA A. *High and Outside.* New York: Harper & Row, 1980. Hardbound. 195pp. Young adult.

High school softball star battles with her alcoholism. Much game and tournament action. AGM

DUFFIELD, J. W. *Bert Wilson's Fadeaway Ball.* New York: Sully and Kleinteich, 1913. Hardbound. 205pp. Young adult.

Second in an eight-book series about the heroic Bert. In this one, he wins a thinly disguised Harvard-Yale game. AGM

DUNHAM, MONTREW. *Abner Doubleday: Young Baseball Pioneer.* Indianapolis: Bobbs-Merrill Co., 1965. Hardbound. 192pp. Juvenile.

A vastly hoked up account of Doubleday's youth and his "invention" of baseball. Description of games of one ol' cat, three ol' cat and town ball. AGM

DYGARD, THOMAS. *The Rookie Arrives.* New York: William Morrow & Co., 1988. Hardbound. 197pp. Young adult.
Ted Bell convinces the Royals to bring him directly from high school to the majors despite the presence of a (slowing) perennial all star. He wins the 3B job in a couple of months and learns baseball can be a hard world. AGM

EARL, JOHN PRESCOTT. (Pseudonym: *See* Beth Bradford Gilchrist.)

EARLL, FRANK J. (Written as Billy Boxer, the Referee.) *King Kelly, the Famous Catcher.* New York: New York Five Cent Library No. 85, June 16, 1894. Magazine. 16pp. Young adult. moel
First of three profiles with oblique relationships to the reality of these players' careers. Kelly is a Hall of Famer and the game's first superstar. AGM

_____. *Captain Billy Nash of the Boston Team.* New York: New York Five Cent Library No. 86, June 23, 1894. Magazine. 16pp. Young adult. moel
Although not well remembered now, Nash spent 15 years in the majors, mostly as a third baseman for the Braves. AGM

_____. *Yale Murphy, the Great Short-Stop.* New York: New York Five Cent Library No. 87, June 30, 1894. Magazine. 16pp. Young adult. agmoel
The "great" Yale managed only 60 major league games at SS. Fortunately for him, they were with the Giants, and then, as now, NY players got the exposure. AGM

_____. *Amos Rusie, Prince of Pitchers.* New York: Golden Hours Nos. 549–53, Aug. 6 to Sept. 3, 1898. Magazine. Young adult. mo
An apt title. Rusie is also a Hall of Famer. AGM

ECONOMOS, CHRIS. *The New Kid.* Milwaukee, Wi: Raintree Publishers, 1989. Hardbound. 32pp. Juvenile.
Chimpanzee subs for a sick baseball player on a neighborhood team. AGM

EDMUNDS, MURRELL. *Behold, Thy Brother.* New York: Beechhurst Press, 1950. Hardbound. 80pp. Adult.
Team with a failing pitching staff late in the 1945 pennant race has a black pitcher thrust on them by the owner's liberal son. The manager tries to avoid using him, but eventually must. He wins the pennant clincher. AGM

EINSTEIN, CHARLES. *The Only Game in Town.* New York: Dell Publishing Co., 1955. Paper. 191pp. Adult.
An aged player-manager returns for one last shot at the bigs. Some nice touches of realism from the compiler of the *Fireside Books of Baseball* and numerous books on Willie Mays. AGM

(Written as D. J. MICHAEL.) *Win–or Else!* New York: Lurton Blassingame, 1954. Paper. 128pp. Adult.

ELISH, DAN. *Jason and the Baseball Bear.* New York: Franklin Watts, Inc., 1990. Hardbound. 147pp. Juvenile.
Jason brings Whitney, the polar bear from the zoo, to coach his Little League team. AGM

ELLER, SCOTT. *Short Season.* New York: Scholastic Inc., 1985. Paper. 154pp. Juvenile.
Two Little League brothers: One can hit, one can field. Though a year apart, they've been inseparable. Then the older quits the team, and the younger must adjust. AGM

ELLIOTT, DON. *Lust League.* San Diego: Corinth Publishing, n.d. Paper. 190pp. Adult pornography.

ELLIS, EDWARD S. *Our Jim.* Boston: Estes & Co., 1901. Hardbound. 327pp. Young adult.
Ellis was one of the most prolific children's writers of the turn of the century, but this is his only known baseball work. The book actually covers growing up in a variety of ways. There are several baseball chapters in the middle. AGM

ELLIS, LUCY. *The Girls Strike Back: The Making of the Pink Parrots.* New York: Sports Illustrated for Kids, 1990. Paper. 119pp. Juvenile.
First of the Pink Parrot series, "created by Lucy Ellis," but written by various others. Girls mistreated in Little League form their own team.

Kathilyn Solomon Proboz and Leah Jerome wrote the book and have some trouble describing the game. AGM

_____. *All That Jazz.* New York: Sports Illustrated for Kids, 1990. Paper. 120pp. Juvenile.
One of the girls must decide between the false friendship of budding socialites and her teammates. Second in the series, written by B. B. Calhoun. Two other titles, *Mixed Signals* by Crystal DiMeo and *Fielder's Choice* by Calhoun, are planned for 1991. AGM

EMERY, RUSSELL G. *High, Inside!* Philadelphia: Macrae Smith Co., 1948. Hardbound. 208pp. Young adult.
Phenom who's only in it for the money comes to the light. AGM

_____. *Relief Pitcher.* Philadelphia: Macrae Smith Co., 1953. Hardbound. 189pp. Young adult.
Johnny Hyland must gain confidence in himself and his knuckleball to make the majors. First of three books on Johnny. AGM

_____. *Hyland of the Hawks.* Philadelphia: Macrae Smith Co., 1955. Hardbound 208pp. Young adult.
Early in his second year in the bigs, Johnny is unjustly sent back to the minors, where he develops into a catcher. AGM

_____. *Action at Third.* Philadelphia: Macrae Smith Co., 1957. Hardbound. 190pp. Young adult.
Hyland returns from two years in the Army to be moved to third base. He leads the Hawks to a World Series win. The illustrations on the cover and title page were drawn by an artist who doesn't have the remotest idea how to make a backhand stop. AGM

EMMETT, R. T. *The Rival Nines.* New York: Happy Days Nos. 41–48, July 27 to Sept. 14, 1895. Magazine. Young adult. el

ENGLEMAN, PAUL. *Dead in Centerfield.* New York: Ballantine Books, 1983. Paper. 213pp. Adult mystery.
A blond, a slugger chasing Ruth's record, and an imitation Philip Marlowe. Little game action, but most of the characters have baseball connections and the denouement comes in CF at Yankee Stadium. AGM

ETHRIDGE, KENNETH. *Viola, Furgy, Bobbi, and Me.* New York: Holiday House, 1989. Hardbound. 164pp. Juvenile.
Three teenage friends try to protect Viola, a wealthy, 78-year-old baseball fan, from her abusive daughters. They want to commit Viola to a nursing home. No game action, but the characters come together because of their shared love for the Detroit Tigers; a fair amount of time is spent listening to or watching games. AGM

ETTER, LES. *Bull Pen Hero.* Indianapolis: Bobbs-Merrill Co., 1966. Hardbound. 212pp. Juvenile.
Kid with a fastball meets his hero in the minors. The hero, thoughtfully provided with a beautiful daughter, has only his curve left. Do not despair! The inevitable move from competition to friendship occurs. AGM

EVERETT, PERCIVAL L. *Suder.* New York: Viking Press, 1983. Hardbound. 171pp. Adult.
A Seattle Mariner who's fearful he may be losing it goes off on an offbeat, entertaining series of adventures. Very little baseball. AGM

EVERETT, WILLIAM. *Changing Base.* Boston: Lee & Shepard, 1868. Hardbound. 282pp. Young adult. agmonuc
The first known novel incorporating baseball activity. Two and one-half chapters devoted to a boys' baseball match, remainder of the book to schoolboy adventures. AG

_____. *Double Play.* Boston: Lee & Shepard, 1871. Hardbound. 244pp. Young adult.
Two lengthy game descriptions plus one shorter description of a baseball variant called scrub interspersed with boys' adventures. Scrub appears to be similar to what we called work-up as boys. The scrub description also shows the lingering influence of cricket as the boys argue whether a batter must run after he hits the ball. In the regular games, we see the rules and the haphazard umpiring of the time come to life. There are no limits to balls or strikes; outs could be run up if a ball was caught on one bounce as well as on the fly. One copy of this book that I have seen gives a copyright date of 1868, but no other sources or copies that I know of list it this way. This

copy is also a reprint from approximately 1900 raising the possibility of a misprint. AGM

_____. *Thine Not Mine.* Boston: Roberts Brothers, 1891. Hardbound. 297pp. Young adult. agmonuc
Several chapters devoted to baseball. AG. Sequel to *Changing Base.* NUC

EYSTER, RICHARD H. *Barefoot Bear Plays Ball.* Bridgehampton, NY: Tern Enterprises, Inc., 1985. Hardbound. 48pp. Juvenile.
BB learns to make friends. The whole book takes place on a series of baseball fields. AGM

FELDSPAR, WALTER. *Squeeze Play.* Manhasset, NY: Kozy Books, 1961. Paper. 150pp. Adult Pornography.

FELSEN, HENRY GREGOR. *Bertie Takes Care.* New York: E. P. Dutton & Co., 1948. Hardbound. 184pp. Juvenile.
Bertie's too fat to be a camp counselor, so he organizes his own camp. His campers wind up beating the snobs at baseball to end the summer. AGM

FENNER, PHYLLIS R., ed. *Crack of the Bat.* New York: Alfred A. Knopf, Inc., 1952. Hardbound. 160pp. Juvenile collection.
Includes stories by John R. Tunis, Jackson Scholz, Frank Graham, Stephen Meader, R. G. Emery, Harold Sherman, and Bob Considine. Several are nonfiction. AGM

FENTON, COL. RALPH. (Pseudonym: *See* Harvey K. Shackleford.)

FERGUSON, DONALD. *Chums of Scranton High Out for the Pennant.* Cleveland: World Syndicate Publishing Co., 1919. Hardbound. 187pp. Juvenile.
Second of four in the Scranton High series. The chums win their league and solve the mystery of an apparent hobo. Dust jacket has an ice hockey illustration, although no hockey in the book. AGM

FERGUSON, WILLIAM BLAIR MORTON. *A Man's Code.* New York: G. W. Dillingham Co., 1915. Hardbound. 305pp. Adult.
Melodrama starring Scrappy Steele, shortstop of the Badgers. Involves bribery, liquor, ladies, and lessons learned from same. AGM

FISH, ROBERT L., and HENRY ROTHBLATT. *A Handy Death.* New York: Simon and Schuster, Inc., 1973. Hardbound. 221pp. Adult mystery.
Former phenom is already doing time but is charged with murder and inciting a riot during a prison ball game. Our (attorney/detective) Hero figures it all out. Little game action. AGM

FISHEL, DICK, and CLAIR HARE. *Terry and Bunky Play Baseball.* New York: G. P. Putnam's Sons, 1947. Hardbound. 90pp. Juvenile.

FISHER, LEONARD EVERETT. *Noonan: A Novel About Baseball, ESP and Time Warps.* Garden City, NY: Doubleday & Co., 1978. Hardbound. 125pp. Juvenile science fiction.
Star pitcher for the 1896 Brooklyn Dutchmen is hit by a foul ball and wakes up in 1996 with the ability to make the ball do strange things. AGM

FITZGERALD, ED. *The Turning Point.* New York: A. S. Barnes and Co., 1948. Hardbound. 236pp. Adult.
The first of three books about Marty Ferris, which follow him from his high school senior year through his first year with the Yankees. In this, he must decide whether to turn pro after high school or go to college. Among other things, he's named MVP of a New York-area high school all-star game and wins a road trip with the Yanks. Fitzgerald was a well-known sportswriter of the era, especially for Sport magazine. AGM

_____. *College Slugger.* New York: A. S. Barnes and Co., 1950. Hardbound. 180pp. Adult.
Now at Fordham, Marty must deal with fraternity rivalries that threaten the team and with the question of jeopardizing his eligibility by taking money in summer ball. AGM

_____. *Yankee Rookie.* New York: A. S. Barnes and Co., 1952. Hardbound. 192pp. Adult.
Ferris joins the Yankees and makes a success after some early troubles. Interestingly, the Yankee second baseman in all these books is named Bobby Richardson. The real Bobby Richardson turned 17 the year this was published. AGM

_____. *The Ballplayer*. New York: A. S. Barnes and Co., 1957. Hardbound. 336pp. Adult.

Follows the rise of Vinnie Burns from poor kid from a broken home to successful American League center fielder and manager. AGM

FITZPATRICK, BURGESS. *Casey's Redemption*. New York: Greenwich Book Publishers, 1958. Hardbound. 40pp. Adult.

Prose sequel to original poem "Casey at the Bat," in which the family name is redeemed by the original's grandson, a college player. AGM

FITZSIMMONS, CORTLAND. *Death on the Diamond*. New York: Frederick A. Stokes Co., 1934. Hardbound. 332pp. Adult mystery.

Probably the first adult baseball murder mystery. There were football and hockey mysteries in the series, too. A number of major league players are murdered or maimed, and Our Reporter-Hero must figure out how it is happening. A smattering of game descriptions and much off-the-field conversation with players. Several of the murders are committed on the field. AGM

FLOOD, RICHARD T. *The Fighting Southpaw*. Boston: Houghton Mifflin Co., 1949. Hardbound. 180pp. Juvenile.

Prep school's star hurler breaks his wrist and the pepper-pot catcher must find a new one. He comes up with a studious left-handed pianist who has quit pitching because he had beaned someone a couple of years earlier. AGM

FOLEY, LOUISE M. *Somebody Stole Second*. New York: Delacorte Press, 1972. Hardbound. 45pp. Juvenile.

The Jets second base disappears before the big game. It's found. AGM

FORBES, GRAHAM. (Pseudonym: *See* Edward Stratemeyer.)

FORD, WHITEY, and JACK LANG. *The Fighting Southpaw*. Larchmont, NY: Argonaut Books, Inc., 1962. Hardbound. 189pp. Juvenile.

Young left-hander learns he needs self-control, too. Echoes of Casey Stengel, Ralph Houk, Jim Turner, and Johnny Sain in some of the characters. Tips from Whitey and biographies of left-handed pitchers who are in the Hall of Fame in the back. See also the Berra/Ferdenzi book. AGM

FOREMAN, HARVEY. *Awk*. Philadelphia: Westminster Press, 1970. Hardbound. 36pp. Juvenile.

After he learns some Spanish, Bob has less trouble organizing a Little League team in Mexico. NUC

FORREST, FRANK. (Pseudonym: *See* H. Irving Hancock.)

FOSTER, ALAN S. *Goodbye, Bobby Thompson! Goodbye, John Wayne!* New York: Simon and Schuster, Inc., 1973. Hardbound. 190pp. Adult.

1951 play-off game between the Dodgers and the Giants is the backdrop for the first three chapters. Baseball is barely mentioned thereafter. JO

FRANK, MORRY. *Every Young Man's Dream: Confessions of a Southern League Shortstop*. Chicago: Silverback Books, 1984. Hardbound. 556pp. Adult.

A struggling minor league shortstop reflects on his checkered past as he tries to redeem himself. He doesn't. AGM

FRANKLIN, LANCE. *Double Play*. New York: Bantam Books, 1987. Paper. 135pp. Juvenile.

One of a series of books about a variety of sports, called the Varsity Coach series. In this, the only baseball volume, Tom Keenan must choose between the high school baseball team and a rising rock band for which he's writer/guitarist. AGM

FREDERIC, MIKE. *Frank Merriwell Returns*. New York: Award Books, 1965. Paper. 157pp. Juvenile.

It's actually the fictional legend's son being heroic, too. Apparently, Frederic didn't realize Frank Merriwell, Jr., had been created back in the 1910s (*see* Gilbert Patten). Volume two of this projected series had a football story, and volume three auto racing. This Frank, Jr., is a student at Danford on the West Coast rather than Yale, but otherwise just as heroic. He does allow a hurt ankle to be shot up with novocaine so he can pitch the second game of a double header, which I'm sure Frank or the real Frank, Jr., would never have done. AGM

FREEMAN, MARK. *Play Ball!* New York: Ballantine Books, 1989. Paper. 134pp. Juvenile.

Introducing David Green (CF), Glen Mitchell (2B), and Roberto Ramirez (RHP), who lead Rosemont High to the Illinois State championship and then are all picked in the first round of the June amateur draft. First of the six-book The Rookies Series. AGM

_____. *Squeeze Play*. New York: Ballantine Books, 1989. Paper. 134pp. Juvenile.
Green (Red Sox), Mitchell (White Sox), and Ramirez (Dodgers) all have excellent first years in rookie ball. Second of The Rookies Series. AGM

_____. *Spring Training*. New York: Ballantine Books, 1989. Paper. 136pp. Juvenile.
All three have strong spring training camps and, one year out of high school, are assigned to AAA. Third of The Rookies Series. AGM

_____. *Big-League Break*. New York: Ballantine Books, 1989. Paper. 134pp. Juvenile.
Within a couple of months, they are all called up to the bigs. The author has begun to lose track of incidents in early books, and mistakes about baseball matters begin to show up. Fourth of The Rookies Series. AGM

_____. *Play-off Pressure*. New York: Ballantine Books, 1989. Paper. 135pp. Juvenile.
All three make the play-offs. Green's Red Sox beat Mitchell's White Sox while Ramirez beats Cards. Tommy Lasorda and Joe Morgan (Red Sox manager) appear by name. Other major leaguers are recognizable by name (Jim Ross for Rice, Roger Cowans for Clemens). Fifth of The Rookies Series. AGM

_____. *Series Showdown*. New York: Ballantine Books, 1989. Paper. 135pp. Juvenile.
Last-at-bat homer by Green beats Dodgers (but not Ramirez) in seventh game of the World Series. Sixth, and last, of The Rookies Series. AGM

FRENCH, ALLEN. *The Junior Cup*. New York: Century Co., 1901. Hardbound. 246pp. Juvenile. jo

FRIEND, DAVID. *Baseball, Football, Daddy, and Me*. New York: Viking Press, 1990. Hardbound. 29pp. Juvenile.

Boy's father takes him to many sporting events beginning with baseball and ending with the boy's favorite—catch. AGM

FRIENDLICH, DICK. *Baron of the Bullpen*. Philadelphia: Westminster Press, 1954. Hardbound. 184pp. Young adult.
Fireballer makes a big splash as a reliever, but then gives up a pennant-losing homer. He must regain his confidence. AGM

_____. *Clean Up Hitter*. Philadelphia: Westminster Press, 1956. Hardbound. 176pp. Young adult.
Clay Norris thinks of himself as a slugging center fielder, and it takes a hard year in the minors for him to learn that he's actually a contact-hitting first baseman. AGM

_____. *Lead-off Man*. Philadelphia: Westminster Press, 1959. Hardbound. 190pp. Young adult.
Short player must learn when to be aggressive. AGM

_____. *Backstop Ace*. Philadelphia: Westminster Press, 1961. Hardbound. 186pp. Young adult.
Ace Elwood, catcher of the National League Eagles, tries to discover what's wrong with the on-mound performance of rookie pitcher Mike North. FP

_____. *Relief Pitcher*. Philadelphia: Westminster Press, 1964. Hardbound. 176pp. Young adult.
Utility infielder's injury sends him back to the minors as a player-manager. He'd rather play than manage and turns himself into a major league reliever. AGM

_____. *Pinch Hitter*. Philadelphia: Westminster Press, 1965. Hardbound. 186pp. Young adult.
Rookie must prove he can hit the curve. Interesting use of newspaper reporters. Their press box comments serve as a Greek chorus to the manager, general manager, and players. AGM

_____. *The Sweet Swing*. Garden City, NY: Doubleday & Co., 1968. Hardbound. 225pp. Young adult.
Born to DH, a minor leaguer must decide if he wants to be a complete player. Breaking all tradition for the genre, he decides to go to college instead. AGM

"How Can I Be a Professional?"

Hugh Fullerton was the premiere baseball reporter of his day. He made his reputation by being the only major journalist to predict the "Hitless Wonders" White Sox would beat the Cubs in the 1906 World Series. He cemented it by being the reporter who broke the story of the Black Sox scandal during the 1919 World Series. In between, he wrote the Jimmy Kirkland series and an instructional with Johnny Evers. I suspect he also wrote the piece of fiction attributed to Frank Chance. This nice illustration by Charles Paxson Gray finds Jimmy trying to worm his way out of a plot to make him ineligible for his college team.
Illustration from page 159 of *Jimmy Kirkland of the Cascade College Team* by Hugh Fullerton, 1915. Plus mugshot of Fullerton from his column in the Chicago Herald and Examiner.

FULLER, SAMUEL R. (Written as Norman Brainerd.) *Winning the Junior Cup.* Boston: Lothrop, Lee & Shepard Co., 1911. Hardbound. 358pp. Juvenile.
Much ado about honor during a freshman year at college. The cover has a nice illustration of a catcher settling under a pop fly and baseball occupies several chapters. Third in the four-book Five Chums series. AGM

FULLERTON, HUGH. *Jimmy Kirkland of the Shasta Boys' Team.* Philadelphia: John C. Winston Co., 1915. Hardbound. 270pp. Young adult.

Fullerton was a reporter for a Chicago paper whose stories were instrumental in breaking open the Black Sox scandal. This is the tale of an orphan sent West to be raised by an old friend of his father's. The boy organizes a team on the friend's ranch. Interesting twist of "All-American racism." Fullerton paints a very positive picture of the polyglot nature of the team, but the villain's sneakiness and cowardice are attributed to his mixed (Mexican and Anglo) blood. Dedicated to Frank Chance with a note that it is "in part reminiscent of (Chance's) own early life." AGM

_____. *Jimmy Kirkland of the Cascade College Team.* Philadelphia: John C. Winston Co., 1915. Hardbound. 265pp. Young adult.
This one, dedicated to Amos Alonzo Stagg, finds Jimmy, now called Larry, moved on to college. He encounters the scheming villain from the earlier book who keeps him off the team till his third year. And, at the end of a successful third year, Larry finds himself caught between a scheming girl and his blustery guardian. The book leaves us hanging as Jimmy goes off to make his fortune. AGM

_____. *Jimmy Kirkland and the Plot for a Pennant.* Philadelphia: John C. Winston Co., 1915. Hardbound. 341pp. Young adult.
Since college has trained him only for baseball, Larry hooks on with a pro team but plays under an assumed name. The team is involved in a pennant fight, old villains from the earlier books surface, and Larry finds true love and thwarts a group of gamblers intent on fixing the pennant race (interesting given Fullerton's reporting a few years later and this book's dedication to Charles Comiskey). AGM

FULTON, REED. *Rookie Coach.* Garden City, NY: Doubleday & Co., 1955. Hardbound. 222pp. Young adult.
This "attack is just another symptom from the real disease this school and community are suffering from—rotten sportsmanship." This quote sums up this extremely high-minded book. The

coach handles all major sports. The last third of the book is the baseball season. AGM

GANTOS, JACK, and NICOLE RUBEL. *Willy's Raiders*. New York: Parents Magazine Press, 1980. Hardbound. 30pp. Juvenile.

Willy's team of raccoons, who always play fair, must overcome Willy's kidnapping by the rival Weasels as well as assorted other tricks to win a league championship. AGM

GARDNER, LILLIAN. *Somebody Called Booie*. New York: Franklin Watts, Inc., 1955. Hardbound. 56pp. Juvenile.

Booie finds glasses help him play baseball. AGM

GARIS, HOWARD ROGER. *Those Smith Boys on the Diamond*. Chicago: M. A. Donohue & Co., 1912. Hardbound. 273pp. Juvenile.

Under the Lester Chadwick pseudonym, Garis also worked on the Baseball Joe series. He also used the Stratemeyer-stable Clarence Young pseudonym. And he wrote all the Uncle Wiggily stories. This is the second of two Smith Boys books. AGM

GARTNER, JOHN. *Ace Pitcher*. New York: Dodd, Mead & Co., 1953. Hardbound. 215pp. Juvenile.

New high school baseball coach has no experience in organized baseball. He wins state championship. AGM

GAULT, CLARE and FRANK. *Norman Plays Second Base*. New York: Scholastic Book Service, 1973. Paper. 30pp. Juvenile.

Norman, a tortoise who has sat on the bench all season, uses his shell to ward off spikes and to help get a hit in the last game. AGM

GAULT, WILLIAM C. *The Lonely Mound*. New York: E. P. Dutton & Co., 1967. Hardbound. 158pp. Young adult.

Young pitcher learns to handle pressure with humor as he moves from high school to the majors in a year and a half. AGM

_____. *Stubborn Sam*. New York: E. P. Dutton & Co., 1969. Hardbound. 158pp. Young adult.

A three-year rise from Class A to the majors for several ball players and their manager. TS

_____. *Trouble at Second*. New York: E. P. Dutton & Co., 1973. Hardbound. 148pp. Young adult.

This deals with racism on a championship baseball team—conflict between a Hispanic and blacks. TS

_____. *The Underground Skipper*. New York: E. P. Dutton & Co., 1975. Hardbound. 134pp. Young adult.

Some of the characters in *Trouble at Second* reappear. The focus is on the manager, who has trouble handling younger players and senses that the game has changed. TS

GELLER, MARK. *My Life in the 7th Grade*. New York: Harper & Row, 1986. Hardbound. 121pp. Juvenile.

He's captain of the class team and must make some tough decisions about who will play. AGM

GELLER, MICHAEL. *Major League Murder*. New York: St. Martin's Press, 1988. Hardbound. 215pp. Adult Mystery.

Private investigator Slots Resnick is asked to clear the name of a lone wolf, black major league pitcher expelled from baseball for allegedly doctoring pitches. As a minor leaguer, Resnick was beaned by this same pitcher. JO

GELMAN, MITCH. *Can You Win the Pennant?* New York: Pocket Books, 1983. Paper. 118pp. Juvenile.

A book where your decisions send you to alternate pages seeking to win the game for the pennant. AGM

_____. *Opening Day*. New York: Pocket Books, 1985. Paper. 118pp. Juvenile.

See previous entry, but win on opening day. AGM

GELMAN, STEVE. *Baseball Bonus Kid*. Garden City, NY: Doubleday & Co., 1961. Hardbound. 141pp. Juvenile.

A year out of high school, a center fielder must mature in the big leagues. AGM

GERBERG, MORT. *Bear-ly Bear-able Baseball*. New York: Scholastic, Inc., 1989. Paper. 32pp. Juvenile.

Jokes, many very bad, but highly humorous to the seven to ten set. AGM

GETHERS, PETER. *Getting Blue*. New York: Delacorte Press, 1987. Hardbound. 346pp. Adult.

A 30-year career from minors to majors teaches a ball player that nothing perfect lasts. Few signs of nostalgia surface here. JO

GIFF, PATRICIA. *Left-Handed Shortstop.* New York: Delacorte Press, 1980. Hardbound. 116pp. Juvenile.
Walter is drafted for a class baseball game because the student coach has the erroneous impression he's a good shortstop even though he's left-handed. Walter puts a fake cast on his arm to avoid the game. A friend gets to play, and everyone lives happily ever after. AGM

_____. *Ronald Morgan Goes to Bat.* New York: Viking Penguin Inc., 1988. Hardbound. 32pp. Juvenile.
Terrible Ronald learns to keep his eyes open when he swings. AGM

GILCHRIST, BETH BRADFORD. (Written as John P. Earl.) *The School Team in Camp.* Philadelphia: Penn Publishing Co., 1909. Hardbound. 331pp. Juvenile.
A group of prep school boys moves to the Maine woods for the summer. The adventures include a baseball game. Second of the four-book School Team series. AGM

_____. *Captain of the School Team.* Philadelphia: Penn Publishing Co., 1910. Hardbound. 324pp. Juvenile.
Third in the School Team series. DJ

_____. *The School Team on the Diamond.* Philadelphia: Penn Publishing Co., 1911. Hardbound. 339pp. Juvenile.
Fourth in the School Team series. DJ

GILCHRIST, GUY. *Tiny Dinos Playing Together.* New York: Warner Books, 1988. Hardbound. 16pp. Juvenile.
What they play together is baseball, although rendered with pink, turquoise, and yellow dinosaurs of the cute persuasion, it's occasionally hard to recognize. AGM

GILL, CHARLES. *The Boozer Challenge.* New York: E. P. Dutton & Co., 1987. Hardbound. 276pp. Adult.
Within this comic novel of implausible characters and events, a major league ball player is one of several siblings competing to inherit a fortune from a ballpark-mustard tycoon. JO

GLENN, MEL. *Squeeze Play.* New York: Clarion Books, 1989. Hardbound. 135pp. Juvenile.
A militaristic coach who has trouble controlling himself and a sixth grader who's been hit in the eye by a line drive are helped by a wise old Holocaust survivor. AGM

GOLD, R. C. *Memoirs of a Pussycad.* Los Angeles: Echelon, 1967. Paper. Adult pornography. jtp

GOLDENBAUM, SALLY, and ADRIENNE STAFF. (Written as Natalie Stone.) *Double Play.* New York: Dell Publishing Co., 1983. Paper. 190pp. Adult romance.
Sally, a sports broadcaster, loves and knows baseball. But she's reduced to doing a cooking show when Kansas City Royals stud hunk third baseman P. J. Decker's (*see* George Brett) shoulder is hurt and he's drafted to boost ratings. Sally must fight to get her job back while the romance blossoms. Several games described as well as many team members and activities off the field. AGM

GOLDFRANK, HELEN C. (Written as Helen Kay.) *The Magic Mitt.* New York: Hastings House, 1959. Hardbound. 54pp. Juvenile.
Lewis gains confidence with a new mitt that he earns the money for. AGM

GOLLOMB, JOSEPH. *That Year at Lincoln High.* New York: The Macmillan Co., 1918. Hardbound. 290pp. Young adult.
Year at school winds up with The Big Game. Underlying theme of anti-Semitism. About 25% baseball. AGM

GOODE, GEORGE W. (*See* Harvey K. Shackleford.)

GORDON, ALISON. *The Dead Pull Hitter.* Toronto: McClelland and Stewart, 1988. Hardbound. 222pp. Adult mystery.
Gordon spent five years covering the Blue Jays for a Toronto paper, and this is a mystery about a female sportswriter covering a major league team. This book has the strongest baseball ambiance and content of any of the baseball mysteries, although the actual mystery is a bit formulaic. BP

GORDON, SHARON. *Play Ball, Kate!* Mahwah, NJ: Troll Associates, 1981. Hardbound. 28pp. Juvenile.
Kate plays baseball with her team in the park. AGM

GRABER, RALPH S., ed. *The Baseball Reader*. New York: A. S. Barnes and Co., 1951. Hardbound. 302pp. Adult collection.

Includes pieces by Valentine Davies (from *It Happens Every Spring*), James T. Farrell, Thomas Wolfe, Paul Gallico, James Thurber, Robert Benchley, Heywood Broun (from *The Sun Field*), Gerald Beaumont (from *Hearts and the Diamond*), Sinclair Lewis, Ring Lardner (from *You Know Me Al*), Damon Runyon, Charles Van Loan (from *Score By Innings*), Zane Grey (from *The Redheaded Outfield*), Burt L. Standish (from *Frank Merriwell at Yale*), and Mark Twain. AGM

GRAHAM, JOHN ALEXANDER. *Babe Ruth Caught in a Snowstorm*. Boston: Houghton Mifflin Co., 1973. Hardbound. 280pp. Adult.

A team consisting of amateurs who desire to play baseball for joy only is invited to join the National League. JO

GRANT, J. JASON. *Dugout Brother*. Los Angeles: Holloway House Publishing, 1978. Paper. 224pp. Juvenile.

Young player in the wake of Jackie Robinson must struggle to become the first black Yankee. His son follows later in the book. Much mention of the great players of the Negro Leagues. AGM

GRANT, ROBERT. *Jack Hall, or, The School Days of an American Boy*. Boston: Jordan, Marsh & Co., 1887. Hardbound. 394pp. Young adult.

Only two baseball games described in this chronicle of Jack's four years at Utopia School. It was a time when it took six balls for a walk and when a prep school star would turn down a professional offer to work for a railroad. AGM

GRANTHAM, KENNETH L. *Baseball's Darkest Days*. New York: Exposition Press, 1965. Hardbound. 103pp. Adult mystery.

Looking for the big score, a businessman organizes a scheme to control baseballs in flight. He makes his million gambling and helps the Cubs to pennant and World Series victories before being discovered. AGM

GRAY, GENEVIEVE. *Stand-Off*. St. Paul, Mn: EMC Corp., 1973. Hardbound. 39pp. Juvenile.

Josie takes on teachers, school board, and others to force them to let her grade school's best softball player—a girl—compete in the city softball tourney. AGM

GREEN, GERALD. *To Brooklyn With Love*. New York: Trident Press, 1967. Hardbound. 305pp. Adult.

This account of one day of a boy's life in Brooklyn in 1934 features street versions of baseball. JO

GREEN, PHYLLIS. *The Fastest Quitter in Town*. Reading, Ma: Addison-Wesley Publishing Co., 1972. Hardbound. 62pp. Juvenile.

Johnny quits the neighborhood ball games as soon as something goes against him. But when his beloved great grandfather loses his wedding ring, Johnny persists. He eventually finds the ring and learns to persist in baseball, too. AGM

GREENBERG, ERIC ROLFE. *The Celebrant*. New York: Everest House, 1983. Hardbound. 272pp. Adult.

Christy Mathewson's career is celebrated by the narrator, a jeweler who makes Matty rings, while the narrator's brother descends through gambling to madness. JOTS

GREENBERG, MARTIN H., ed. *On the Diamond*. New York: Bonanza Books, 1987. Hardbound. 576pp. Adult collection.

Contains stories by Ring Lardner (from *Lose with a Smile*), Thomas Wolfe, Arnold Hano, Ray Bradbury, Rod Serling, Owen Johnson (from *The Humming Bird*), Zane Grey (from *The Redheaded Outfield*), William R. Cox, P. G. Wodehouse, John O'Hara, John D. MacDonald, Paul Gallico, and Jay Neugeboren. It also contains a complete version of Jerome Charyn's *The Seventh Babe*. AGM

GREENE, CARLA. *I Want to be a Baseball Player*. Chicago: Childrens Press, 1961. Hardbound. 28pp. Juvenile.

Introduction to baseball told through eyes of Benny, who's learning the game. AGM

GREENE, LAURA. *I Am Somebody*. Chicago: Childrens Press, 1980. Hardbound. 30pp. Juvenile.

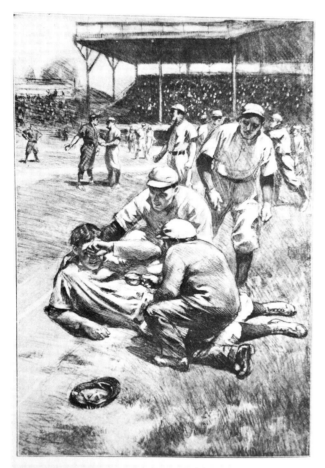

"I'm Not Hurt Much, I Guess," Said Chase. "I'm Only Dizzy"

Before he concentrated on westerns, Zane Grey wrote two baseball novels and a book of short stories. His work reflected the themes other authors of his day chose, too, including the gallant but injured player in this drawing by H. S. DeLay.

Frontispiece illustration of *The Short-Stop* by Zane Grey, 1909.

Boy feels bad about being a Little League failure but then decides he likes being himself. AGM

GREGORICH, BARBARA. *She's On First.* Chicago: Contemporary Books, Inc., 1987. Hardbound. 288pp. Adult.

Linda Sunshine struggles to establish herself as the first woman in the majors. Then, a tangled past comes to light, and she doubts whether she should be there. AGM

GREY, ZANE. *The Short-stop.* Chicago: A. C. McClurg Co., 1909. Hardbound. 310pp. Young adult.

Grey wrote several baseball books before he settled on westerns. He had played briefly as a minor leaguer. This is a classic rags-to-riches story in which Our Hero makes his way up to Detroit. Along the way, he reforms a drunk, argues passionately in favor of Sunday baseball, meets and woos a genteel lady, adopts a hunchback, and engages in a peculiar kind of baseball vengeance when he spikes (with a nail) a third baseman who has given him the hip. TS

_____. *The Young Pitcher.* New York: Harper & Bros., 1911. Hardbound. 249pp. Young adult.

One of a series of books Grey wrote about Ken Ward, who has various adventures around the globe. In this, Ken goes to college to become a forest ranger and finds he must battle to win respect. He does so on the ball field as he leads the college team to the league championship as a freshman. (The upperclassmen have been ruled ineligible for playing professionally during the summer.) AGM

_____. *The Redheaded Outfield and Other Baseball Stories.* New York: McClure Newspaper Syndicate, 1915. Hardbound. 238pp. Young adult collection.

Eleven stories, each with a baseball setting. Five feature the same character, Whitaker "The Rube" Hurtle, who moves from Worcester of the Eastern League to the White Sox. TS. Another features Old Well, Well, the Giants fans also chronicled in a Fred Fearnot dime novel; *see* Harvey K. Shackleford. AGM

GRIFFITH, PEGGY. *The New Klondike.* New York: Jacobsen-Hodgkinson, 1926. Paper. 135pp. Adult. agmonuc

From a movie of the same name. It's set in a Southern spring-training camp. During the 1920s boom in Florida land values, a baseball player is double-crossed in a real estate deal, but comes out a winner. Directed by Lewis Milestone and starring Thomas Meighan, Paul Kelly, and Lila Lee. TPS

GROSSER, MORTON. *The Fabulous Fifty*. New York: Atheneum, 1990. Hardbound. 233pp. Young adult.
In 1921, a 14-year-old gets involved with his friends' scheme to get to the World Series by clipping newspaper coupons. NUC

GUTHRIE, A. B., Jr. *Wild Pitch*. Boston: Houghton Mifflin Co., 1973. Hardbound. 224pp. Adult mystery.
Very little baseball in this one. The narrator is a 17-year-old who pitches for the town team and helps the sheriff. His "wild pitch," aimed at the head of a murderer, hits his gun instead. One game briefly described. TS

GUY, DAVID. *Second Brother*. New York: New American Library, 1985. Hardbound. 264pp. Adult. Richly textured story of friendships and family relationships from 13 to 15. Couple of early baseball scenes establish the relationship between two of the main characters. AGM

HAINES, DONAL HAMILTON. *The Southpaw*. New York: Rinehart & Co., 1931. Hardbound. 272pp. Young adult.
Lefty fights for justice and baseball at a prep school. AGM

HALE, HARRY. *Jack Race's Baseball Nine*. New York: Hearst's International Library Co., 1915. Hardbound. 248pp. Juvenile. agmogo
Second of five in the Jack Race series. Half of the book's ten chapters cover baseball material. GO

HALLOWELL, TOMMY. *Duel on the Diamond*. New York: Viking, 1990. Paper. 122pp. Juvenile.
Second in the Alden All Stars series about junior high school boys. In this, they learn about cliques on the seventh grade team. AGM

HANCOCK, H. IRVING. *The High School Pitcher*. Philadelphia: Henry Altemus Co., 1910. Hardbound. 248pp. Juvenile.
Second of four in the High School Boys series. This was one of eight series that followed the adventures of a group of boys from grammar school

(see the following entry) into careers. The books, which weren't published in the chronological order of the characters' lives, came out between 1910 and 1920. Here, the boys take over the high school baseball team and lead it to victory. AGM

_____. *The Grammar School Boys in Summer Athletics*. Philadelphia: Henry Altemus Co., 1911. Hardbound. 255pp. Juvenile.
Last of four in the Grammar School Boys series. See also the previous entry. About a third of the chapters contain game descriptions. The boys battle for the town's eighth-grade championship. Also, swimming and "adventures." AGM

(Written as FRANK FORREST.) *Dick Daresome's Champion Pitching*. New York: Wide Awake Weekly No. 158, April 23, 1909. Magazine. 32pp. Young adult. jel
It is not actually certain that Hancock wrote all of the Dick Daresome books, although Leithead indicates he wrote the first. AGM

_____. *Dick Daresome's Mistake*. New York: Wide Awake Weekly No. 160, May 7, 1909. Magazine. 32pp. Young adult. djdej

_____. *Dick Daresome's Summer Baseball Nine*. New York: Wide Awake Weekly No. 164, June 4, 1909. Magazine. 32pp. Young adult. jel

(Written as PHYSICAL DIRECTOR.) *Frank Manley on Deck*. New York: The Young Athlete's Weekly No. 11, April 7, 1905. Magazine. 36pp. Young adult. dj
Alfred Trumble also wrote some of the Frank Manley stories. AGM

_____. *Frank Manley at the Bat*. New York: The Young Athlete's Weekly No. 12, April 14, 1905. Magazine. 36pp. Young adult. dj

_____. *Frank Manley's Hard Home Hit*. New York: The Young Athlete's Weekly No. 13, April 21, 1905. Magazine. 36pp. Young adult.

_____. *Frank Manley in the Box*. New York: The Young Athlete's Weekly No. 14, April 28, 1905. Magazine. 36pp. Young adult. dj

_____. *Frank Manley's Scratch Hit*. New York: The Young Athlete's Weekly No. 15, May 5, 1905. Magazine. 36pp. Young adult. el

_____. *Frank Manley's Double Play.* New York: The Young Athlete's Weekly No. 16, May 12, 1905. Magazine. 36pp. Young adult. el

_____. *Frank Manley's All-around Game.* New York: The Young Athlete's Weekly No. 17, May 19, 1905. Magazine. 36pp. Young adult. el

_____. *Frank Manley's Earned Run.* New York: The Young Athlete's Weekly No. 19, June 2, 1905. Magazine. 36pp. Young adult. el

_____. *Frank Manley's Triple Play.* New York: The Young Athlete's Weekly No. 20, June 9, 1905. Magazine. 36pp. Young adult. el

_____. *Frank Manley's Training Table.* New York: The Young Athlete's Weekly No. 21, June 16, 1905. Magazine. 36pp. Young adult. el

_____. *Frank Manley's Coaching.* New York: The Young Athlete's Weekly No. 22, June 23, 1905. Magazine. 36pp. Young adult. el

_____. *Frank Manley's First League Game.* New York: The Young Athlete's Weekly No. 23, June 30, 1905. Magazine. 36pp. Young adult. el

_____. *Frank Manley's March with Giants.* New York: The Young Athlete's Weekly No. 24, July 7, 1905. Magazine. 36pp. Young adult. el

_____. *Frank Manley's Training Camp.* New York: The Young Athlete's Weekly No. 25, July 14, 1905. Magazine. 36pp. Young adult. el

_____. *Frank Manley's Substitute Nine.* New York: The Young Athlete's Weekly No. 26, July 21, 1905. Magazine. 36pp. Young adult. el

_____. *Frank Manley's Bunch of Hits.* New York: The Young Athlete's Weekly No. 28, August 4, 1905. Magazine. 36pp. Young adult. el

_____. *Frank Manley's Double Game.* New York: The Young Athlete's Weekly No. 29, August 11, 1905. Magazine. 36pp. Young adult. djdej

_____. *Frank Manley at His Wits End.* New York: The Young Athlete's Weekly No. 31, August 25, 1905. Magazine. 36pp. Young adult. el

_____. *Frank Manley's Last Ball Game.* New York: The Young Athlete's Weekly No. 32, September 1, 1905. Magazine. 36pp. Young adult. el

_____. *Frank Manley in Yale's Cage.* New York: Frank Manley Weekly No. 29, March 23, 1906. Magazine. 32pp. Young adult. el

After issue No. 32, *Young Athlete's Weekly's* name was changed to *Frank Manley Weekly.* This is the only baseball story in that weekly, and publication expired three weeks later. AGM

HANO, ARNOLD. *The Big Out.* New York: A. S. Barnes and Co., 1951. Hardbound. 181pp. Adult. Brick Palmer is run out of organized ball when he appears to have been throwing games. He comes back morally in an outlaw league. AGM

HARKINS, PHILIP. *Southpaw from San Francisco.* New York: William Morrow & Co., 1948. Hardbound. 247pp. Juvenile.
Ten years before The Move, a lefty from SF (actually Oakland) pitches for the Giants. He's scorned as cocky, gets hit in the face a la Herb Score, but returns to pitch a no-hitter. AGM

_____. *Double Play.* New York: Holiday House, 1951. Hardbound. 249pp. Juvenile.
City boy moves to upstate New York resort and must learn to curb some of his rough competitive edges in semipro play. AGM

HARMON, A. W. *Base Hit.* Philadelphia: J. B. Lippincott Co., 1970. Hardbound. 157pp. Juvenile.
Boy opts out of Little League because he's had too much pressure from his father, the ex-major leaguer. Both he and dad come around. AGM

HARPER, ELAINE. *Short Stop for Romance.* New York: Simon and Schuster, Inc., 1983. Paper. 186pp. Juvenile romance.
Teenager, chasing boy, goes out for softball, does well, and then quits when she gets boy. No. 73 of the First Love from Silhouette series. AGM

HARRIS, MARK. *The Southpaw.* Indianapolis: Bobbs-Merrill Co., 1953. Hardbound. 350pp. Adult.
The first of four outstanding books told in the voice of Henry "Author" Wiggen, a left-hander with the New York Mammoths. In this, Henry leaves Mt. Vernon, NY (coincidentally Harris's birthplace) and wends his way to the majors, learning as he goes. The first three books of the Wiggen series were published in paperback as *Henry Wiggen's Books.* AGM

_____. *Bang the Drum Slowly.* New York: Alfred A. Knopf, Inc., 1956. Hardbound. 243pp. Adult.

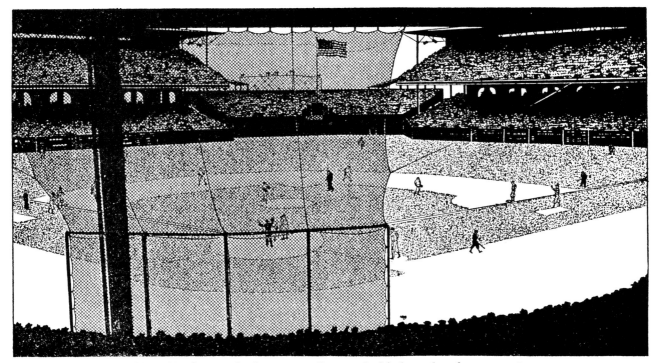

New York now had men on first and third, and only one out.

(Page 208)

Charles Copeland's arresting line drawing of Comiskey Park was the frontispiece to Frank J. Hart's The Speed Boy.
Frontispiece illustration from Frank J. Hart's *The Speed Boy,* 1938.

Henry helps his friend Bruce Pearson die. Made into a 1973 movie directed by John Hancock and starring Robert DeNiro and Michael Moriarty. AGM

_____. *Ticket for a Seamstitch.* New York: Alfred A. Knopf, Inc., 1956. Hardbound. 143pp. Adult.
Henry sends a ticket to a seamstress and in the words of the dust jacket, words that might stand as a summary of the whole Wiggen series, "She had numerous adventures, hitting town just in time, none the worse for wear, though probably smarter than she had been. She learned. We all learned." AGM

_____. *It Looked Like For Ever.* New York: Mc-Graw-Hill Book Co., 1979. Hardbound. 276pp. Adult.
Two hundred forty-seven victories after the beginning, Henry is released. He tries broadcast-

ing "Friday Night Baseball" and coming back as a reliever for another team. He can still pitch a bit, but he can't field. AGM

HARRIS, ROBIE H. *Rosie's Double Dare.* New York: Alfred A. Knopf, Inc., 1980. Hardbound. 112pp. Juvenile.
Rosie takes a dare to get into the neighborhood ball game and winds up on the field at Fenway Park. About half the book involves baseball action. AGM

HART, FRANK J. *The Speed Boy.* Chicago: Lakewood House, 1938. Hardbound. 226pp. Young adult.
An interesting paean to professionalism. Speedy center fielder leaves campus unsure of upright-ness of professional game but becomes con-vinced. What makes this plot historically

interesting is that the team Our Hero joins is the White Sox. And from the names of the players on the other teams (Ty Carr of Detroit, Christy Madison of the Giants), it is apparent the book is set in the years just before the Black Sox scandal. Anyway, Our Hero leads the Sox to a World Series title. Very nice drawings by Charles Copeland. AGM

HAYES, FLORENCE. *Skid*. Boston: Houghton Mifflin Co., 1948. Hardbound. 216pp. Juvenile.

The first baseball juvenile to deal with integration. Skid, the captain of his school team in Georgia, moves to Connecticut, where he's the only black kid in school. He eventually wins friends and begins to form a baseball team there. Games are described in early and late chapters. AGM

HAYNES, MARY. *The Great Pretenders*. New York: Bradbury Press, 1990. Hardbound. 135pp. Juvenile.

Eleven-year-old Molly has gotten off on the wrong foot in her new town by insulting the mayor's daughter, but with the help of her baseball prowess and two friends, she hopes to redeem herself during the Fourth of July parade. NUC

HAYS, DONALD. *The Dixie Association*. New York: Simon and Schuster, Inc., 1984. Hardbound. 384pp. Adult.

An ex-con leads a team of free spirits through a successful season in a Southern baseball league. JO

HEAVILIN, JAY. *Fast Ball Pitcher*. Garden City, NY: Doubleday & Co., 1965. Hardbound. 143pp. Young adult.

Scotty has the best fastball in his high school league, so why does the new coach want to change his style? AGM

HEGNER, WILLIAM. *The Idolaters*. New York: Trident Press, 1973. Hardbound. 445pp. Adult.

Poorly disguised, fictionalized version of the Marilyn Monroe story with "Tommy Amazon" (he's a pitcher here) playing the Joe Dimaggio part. WARNING—Those offended by "copious dollops of sex" (that's what the quote from Publisher's Weekly says, if they'd added "horribly

written" they'd have been dead on target) should pass on this one. BP

HELLER, PETE. *Peppy Learns to Play Baseball*. Thousand Oaks, Ca: Summa Publishing Co., 1985. Paper. 29pp. Juvenile.

An introduction to how the game is played as we follow Peppy's introduction to Little League. AGM

HEMMINGS, T. J. *Fish Strikes Out*. New York: Tempo Books, 1977. Paper. 156pp. Juvenile.

A "novelization" of the TV series "Fish." Detective Phil Fish reluctantly manages a softball team put together from neighborhood kids and the wards of the court who live with him. A terribly written "book." AGM

HEMPHILL, PAUL. *Long Gone*. New York: Viking Press, 1979. Hardbound 213pp. Adult.

A coming-of-age novel set on a Southern minor league team. Made into a 1984 cable TV movie directed by Martin Davidson and starring William Petersen. AGM

HENDERSON, LEGRAND. (Written as Le Grand.) *How Baseball Began in Brooklyn*. New York: Abingdon Press, 1958. Hardbound. 63pp. Juvenile.

A group of Dutch boys and Indians invents baseball, and a game is then played to determine the fate of the Dutch boys' farm. AGM

HERRIN, LAMAR. *The Rio Loja Ringmaster*. New York: Viking Press, 1977. Hardbound. 305pp. Adult.

Former Cincy Brewmasters relief ace finds self, peace, etc., after much psychological maundering and some baseball in Mexico. AGM

HERSKOWITZ, MICKEY. *Letters from Lefty*. Houston: The Houston Post Co., 1966. Spiral. 82pp. Adult collection.

A collection of columns written for the Houston Post. The columns are frankly imitative of Lardner. The central character, Lefty the busher pitcher, is fictional. But many of the incidents and anecdotes of the Colt 45s and early Astros are real. AGM

HEUMAN, WILLIAM. *Wonder Boy*. New York: William Morrow & Co., 1951. Hardbound. 186pp. Juvenile.

Frank Malloy had a promising career cut short when a beaning left him hopelessly frightened at the plate. He finds a wonderful pitcher in the bushes, but the boy only has confidence in him, and Frank must overcome his fears to be the boy's catcher with Frank's old team. AGM

_____. *Little League Champs.* Philadelphia: J. B. Lippincott Co., 1953. Hardbound. 174pp. Juvenile. Team wins Little League World Series with a mix of races, ethnicity, and economic classes. AGM

_____. *Strictly from Brooklyn.* New York: William Morrow & Co., 1956. Hardbound. 191pp. Juvenile. agmobrd Family life with a Dodger fan. BRD

_____. *Rookie Backstop.* New York: Dodd, Mead & Co., 1962. Hardbound. 179pp. Juvenile.

_____. *The Horse That Played the Outfield.* New York: Dodd, Mead & Co., 1964. Hardbound. 145pp. Juvenile. Well, he can't hit or run the bases, but he can catch anything hit to the outfield and that's what this team needs. As with the later *Home Run Henri,* this contains a power-hitting French Canadian lumberjack. AGM

_____. *Hillbilly Hurler.* New York: Dodd, Mead & Co., 1966. Hardbound. 171pp. Juvenile. A hick from the sticks with an unbelievably rubbish collection of friends and relatives leads the Suburbans to a pennant. AGM

_____. *Horace Higby and the Scientific Pitch.* New York: Dodd, Mead & Co., 1968. Hardbound. 180pp. Juvenile. When a prep school baseball team gets into pitching trouble, it turns to Horace Higby, brain of the campus, whose experiments with triple curves and liquid bat magnetizers save the season. AGM

_____. *The Goofer Pitch.* New York: Dodd, Mead & Co., 1969. Hardbound. 123pp. Juvenile. When Andy makes friends with the new rich boy on the Midget League baseball team, he begins to neglect his longtime poorer friend and his responsibilities as the team manager. NUC

_____. *Home Run Henri.* New York: Dodd, Mead & Co., 1970. Hardbound. 146pp. Juvenile.

See *Hillbilly Hurler* for basic plot. This one has a French-Canadian twist. AGM

_____. *Little League Hotshots.* New York: Dodd, Mead & Co., 1972. Hardbound. 107pp. Juvenile. Boys from a camp of Puerto Rican migrant workers form a Little League team and win the county title. AGM

HEYLIGER, WILLIAM. *Bartley, Freshman Pitcher.* New York: D. Appleton and Co., 1911. Hardbound. 235pp. Young adult. The first of six books in the St. Mary's series. A conflict between freshman and sophomore pitchers for the first string job. TS

_____. *The Captain of the Nine.* New York: D. Appleton and Co., 1912. Hardbound. 281pp. Young adult. Third in the St. Mary's series. DJ

_____. *Strike Three!* New York: D. Appleton and Co., 1913. Hardbound. 297pp. Young adult. agmonuc Fourth in the St. Mary's series. DJ

_____. *Against Odds.* New York: D. Appleton and Co., 1915. Hardbound. 310pp. Young adult. School outcast is taken in hand by the team's star pitcher and then reveals such an intimate knowledge of baseball that he becomes the team's "advisor." Sixth in the St. Mary's series. BRD

_____. *Captain Fair-and-Square.* New York: D. Appleton and Co., 1916. Hardbound. 312pp. Young adult. agmonuc First of three in the Fairview High School series. DJ

_____. *The County Pennant.* New York: D. Appleton and Co., 1917. Hardbound. 285pp. Young adult. agmonuc Second in the Fairview High School series. DJ

_____. *Fighting for Fairview.* New York: D. Appleton and Co., 1918. Hardbound. 291pp. Young adult. Third in the Fairview High School series. DJ

_____. *Bean-Ball Bill and Other Stories.* New York: D. Appleton and Co., 1920. Hardbound. 213pp. Young adult collection. Two of the seven stories are baseball. A high school boy learns to eschew the beanball. A high school captain decides he must sacrifice some games this year to gain experience for next season. AGM

_____. *The Spirit of the Leader.* New York: D. Appleton & Co., 1923. Hardbound. 271pp. Young adult.

Eight stories following a group of students through a year of high school. Two stories, including the climactic one, concern baseball. AGM

_____. *Batter Up!* (1923)

See same title under the Hawley Williams pseudonym. AGM

_____. *Dorset's Twister.* New York: D. Appleton & Co., 1926. Hardbound. 241pp. Young adult. monuc

_____. *The Macklin Brothers.* New York: D. Appleton & Co., 1928. Hardbound. 234pp. Young adult. agmonuc

_____. *The Gallant Crosby.* New York: D. Appleton & Co., 1933. Hardbound. 257pp. Young adult. agmonuc

_____. *The Big Leaguer.* Chicago: Goldsmith Publishing Co., 1936. Hardbound. 250pp. Young adult.

Marty Gage returns to prep school with divisive advice from a player on the major league team his father manages. He destroys his pitcher's confidence and must learn to rebuild it. AGM

_____. *The Loser's End.* Chicago: Goldsmith Publishing Co., 1937. Hardbound. 252pp. Young adult.

Hard-bitten Horatio Alger. Our Hero's pitching ability helps on several steps to success. AGM

_____. *Three-Finger Joe.* Akron, Oh: Saalfield Publishing Co., 1937. Hardbound. 155pp. Young adult.

Joe loses a finger to a slugger's foul ball. His missing digit enables him to develop some fearsome pitches and eventually duel the slugger in a big prep school rivalry. This and Sherman's *Last Man Out* are the two baseball books in the four-book Saalfield Sports Books series. AGM

(Written as HAWLEY WILLIAMS.) *Batter Up!* New York: D. Appleton and Co., 1912. Hardbound. 303pp. Young adult.

Prep school baseball with much emphasis on math professor/coach Billy Phillips, the former Princeton pitcher. Reissued under Heyliger's own name in 1923. Second of the seven-book Lansing series, named after the prep school. AGM

_____. *The Winning Hit.* New York: D. Appleton and Co., 1914. Hardbound. 282pp. Young adult.

Two boys duel for the varsity first base job. Fourth of the Lansing series. AGM

_____. *Johnson of Lansing.* New York: D. Appleton and Co., 1914. Hardbound. 332pp. Young adult. agmonuc

Fifth of the Lansing series. DJ

HIDGON, HAL. *The Horse that Played Center Field.* New York: Holt, Rinehart and Winston, 1969. Hardbound. 118pp. Juvenile.

Horse leads New York Goats (Mets) and manager Casey Balloo (Stengel) to the World Series. He's horse-napped before the seventh game. AGM

_____. *The Last Series.* New York: E. P. Dutton & Co., 1974. Hardbound. 138pp. Juvenile.

The worst team in the majors and its loyal fans fight to save its historic stadium with echoes of Wrigley pre-1988 (grass, no lights). At one point, the author allows Our Heroes' opponents four outs in an inning. TS

HIRSHBERG, AL. *The Battery for Madison High.* Boston: Little, Brown and Co., 1956. Hardbound. 245pp. Young adult.

Hirshberg was a longtime Boston sportswriter who wrote *Fear Strikes Out* and numerous other books on the Red Sox, Boston Braves, and Boston sports personalities. The Drake twins play their way to a state high school championship that Barry wins 4–3 with a bottom-of-the-ninth, two-out grand slam homer. AGM

_____. *Varsity Double Play.* Boston: Little, Brown and Co., 1956. Hardbound. 246pp. Young adult.

A sequel to *Battery for Madison High*. It follows the Drakes through four years at Yale and their ultimate signing with the Red Sox. Despite Hirshberg's experience, he does allow Yale four outs in one inning.

HOFF, SYD. *Who Will Be My Friends?* New York: Harper & Row, 1960. Hardbound. 32pp. Juvenile.

New kid in town makes friends playing ball. AGM

_____. *The Witch, the Cat and the Baseball Bat.* New York: Grosset & Dunlap, Inc., 1968. Hardbound. 39pp. Juvenile.
Witch who hates baseball makes a bat with a hole in it and gives it to a major league team. AGM

_____. *Baseball Mouse.* New York: G. P. Putnam's Sons, 1969. Hardbound. 48pp. Juvenile. agmonuc
Bernard was field mouse—an infield mouse—who more than anything else wanted to help the losing team win the pennant. NUC

_____. *The Littlest Leaguer.* New York: E. P. Dutton & Co., 1976. Hardbound. 48pp. Juvenile.
Harold, the littlest player in Little League, comes through. AGM

_____. *Slugger Sal's Slump.* New York: E. P. Dutton & Co., 1979. Hardbound. 48pp. Juvenile.
Sal lets a horrendous slump affect his fielding, too. He comes around. AGM

HOLLAND, MARION. *Billy's Clubhouse.* New York: Alfred A. Knopf, Inc., 1955. Hardbound. 182pp. Juvenile.
Boys who use a vacant lot to play baseball are dismayed when it goes up for sale. Various plots to discourage buyers ensue. AGM

HOLTON, LEONARD. *The Devil to Play.* New York: Dodd, Mead & Co., 1974. Hardbound. 154pp. Adult mystery.
Ninth of the Father Bredder mysteries. Los Angeles Miners' player is shot in the leg while rounding third. A complicated plot and the suicide of the Miners' manager are solved. Couple of game scenes described and other action at what is clearly Dodger Stadium. AGM

HOLTZMAN, JEROME, ed. *Fielder's Choice.* New York: Harcourt Brace Jovanovich, Inc., 1979. Hardbound. 395pp. Adult collection.
The most famous of the fiction collections. It has pieces from Robert Coover (*Universal Baseball Association*), Ring Lardner, Mark Harris (*Bang the Drum Slowly*), H. Allen Smith (*Rhubarb*), James Thurber, Chaim Potok (*The Chosen*), William Brashler (*Bingo Long*), Damon Runyon, Philip Roth (*Great American Novel*), Paul Gallico, John Sayles (*Pride of the Bimbos*), Mordecai Richler (*St. Urbain's Horseman*), Eliot Asinof, Irwin Shaw (*Voices of a Summer's Day*), Valentine Davies (*It Happens Every Spring*), P. G. Wodehouse, Arnold Hano, Charles Einstein, and Bernard Malamud (*The Natural*). AGM

HONIG, DONALD. *Johnny Lee.* New York: McCall Publishing Co., 1971. Hardbound. 115pp. Juvenile.
17-year-old black is sent to the South for his first year of minor league ball. AGM

_____. *Way to Go, Teddy.* New York: Franklin Watts, Inc., 1973. Hardbound. 147pp. Juvenile.
Boy has quick success in the low minors but falters when promoted. Set against the background of his relationship with his father. AGM

_____. *The Professional.* New York: Educational Services, 1974. Hardbound. 47pp. Juvenile.
Follows a talented rookie through spring training to his first appearance in a game. Book contains much baseball slang and definitions of it. Also, many color pictures of real Mets and other teams at spring-training sites. AGM

_____. *Hurry Home.* Reading, Ma: Addison-Wesley Publishing Co., 1976. Hardbound. 30pp. Juvenile.
Worried over his father's illness, Tommy rushes home from a crucial ball game without finding out which team has won. NUC

_____. *Winter Always Comes.* New York: Four Winds Press, 1977. Hardbound. 136pp. Young adult.
Bonus baby learns that while professional baseball is a job, it's a job that's best done with joy, even in the minors. AGM

_____. *The Last Great Season.* New York: Simon and Schuster, Inc., 1979. Hardbound. 384pp. Adult.
This prolific baseball writer's only fiction aimed at adults. It's an extremely thinly disguised rendering of the 1941–42 Dodgers. AGM

HOOD, ROBERT. *Let's Go to a Baseball Game.* New York: G. P. Putnam's Sons, 1973. Hardbound. 47pp. Juvenile.

HOPPER, JAMES. *Coming Back with the Spitball: A Pitcher's Romance.* New York: Harper & Bros., 1914. Hardbound. 70pp. Young adult.

Before the spitter was made illegal, a pitcher falls from the Giants to the low minors before discovering the pitch and returning in triumph. John McGraw appears as John McGrath. AGM

HOPPER, NANCY J. *Ape Ears and Beaky*. New York: E. P. Dutton & Co., 1984. Hardbound. 102pp. Juvenile.
Scott's bad temper gets him kicked off two teams and put into counseling. Then he and archenemy Beaky Norton get together. They solve a mystery and find a team as Scott learns self-control. AGM

HOUGH, JOHN, Jr. *The Conduct of the Game*. New York: Harcourt Brace Jovanovich, Inc., 1986. Hardbound. 340pp. Adult.
Follows the brief career of an umpire who spends three years in the minors and one in the majors before being forced to resign for protecting the reputation of a colleague who's gay. AGM

HUDSON, ANNA. (Pseudonym: *See* Jo Ann Algermissen.)

HUGHES, DEAN. *Hooper Haller*. Salt Lake City: Deseret Book Co., 1981. Hardbound. 129pp. Juvenile.
17-year-old boy from a small town moves directly from high school to the Kansas City Royals. He has rough moments on the field and off but eventually comes to a sense of peace about his life. Much reference to the Mormon religion. AGM

_____. *Making the Team*. New York: Alfred A. Knopf, Inc., 1990. Paper. 93pp. Juvenile.
Kenny, Harlan, and Jacob are third graders starting out in Little League. They make the team but then must win the respect of their teammates. Kenny's father is a former major leaguer. First in the eight-book Angel Park All-Stars series. AGM

_____. *Big Base Hit*. New York: Alfred A. Knopf, Inc., 1990. Paper. 94pp. Juvenile.
Harlan finally learns to hit. Second in the Angel Park All-Stars series. AGM

_____. *Winning Streak*. New York: Alfred A. Knopf, Inc., 1990. Paper. 90pp. Juvenile.
Kenny slumps and Jacob thinks up all kinds of wacky ways to break it. Practice and relaxing work. Third in the Angel Park All-Stars series. AGM

_____. *What a Catch!* New York: Alfred A. Knopf, Inc., 1990. Paper. 84pp. Juvenile.
It's Brian's last year in Little League. He wants to do well, but is too nervous. Our Hero trio helps. Fourth in the Angel Park All-Stars series. AGM

_____. *Rookie Star*. New York: Alfred A. Knopf, Inc., 1990. Paper. 80pp. Juvenile.
Kenny gets a writeup in the local paper. His buddies think he's gotten a swollen head and he starts pressing. Fifth in the Angel Park All-Stars series. AGM

_____. *Pressure Play*. New York: Alfred A. Knopf, Inc., 1990. Paper. 84pp. Juvenile.
The Dodgers, Our Heroes' team, must learn to ignore bench jockeying. Sixth in the Angel Park All-Stars series. AGM

_____. *Line Drive*. New York: Alfred A. Knopf, Inc., 1990. Paper. 87pp. Juvenile.
A new boy from Taiwan joins the team near the end of the season. Seventh in the Angel Park All-Stars series. AGM

_____. *Championship Game*. New York: Alfred A. Knopf, Inc., 1990. Paper. 94pp. Juvenile.
Last in the Angel Park All-Stars series.

HUGHES, RUPERT. *The Lakerim Athletic Club*. New York: St. Nicholas, Nov. 1897 to Oct. 1898. Magazine. Young adult. el

HURWITZ, JOHANNA. *Baseball Fever*. New York: William Morrow & Co., 1981. Hardbound. 128pp. Juvenile.
A father and son story. Son is a fan, but his intellectual father sees no sense in it. Father wises up after meeting peer who is a fan. TS

IRVINE, ROBERT. *Gone to Glory*. New York: St. Martin's Press, 1990. Hardbound. 231pp. Adult mystery.
Salt Lake City detective solves murder involving two boyhood heroes, the former shortstop and manager of the Salt Lake City Bees. Third in a series. AGM

ISADORA, RACHEL. *Max*. New York: Macmillan Publishing Co., 1976. Hardbound. 26pp. Juvenile.

Max finds he can warm up for Saturday neighborhood baseball games at his sister's ballet class. AGM

JACKSON, C. PAUL. *Rookie First Baseman*. New York: Thomas Y. Crowell Co., 1950. Hardbound. 266pp. Young adult.
Immature young man moves from high school to the Detroit Tigers. AGM

_____. *Clown at Second Base*. New York: Thomas Y. Crowell Co., 1952. Hardbound. 250pp. Juvenile.
Rookie second baseman with the Detroit Tigers must learn when to make jokes. AGM

_____. *Little Leaguer's First Uniform*. New York: Thomas Y. Crowell Co., 1952. Hardbound. 99pp. Juvenile.
Big brother gets sick, and little brother is added to the local Little League team as it heads off to Williamsport with him at shortstop. They win. AGM

_____. *Giant in the Midget League*. New York: Thomas Y. Crowell Co., 1953. Hardbound. 90pp. Juvenile.
Too big, too awkward, he gets help from a cat. AGM

_____. *Little League Tournament*. New York: Hastings House, 1959. Hardbound. 117pp. Juvenile.
Follows a team through a postseason tournament as they try to build the confidence of their pitcher. AGM

_____. *World Series Rookie*. New York: Hastings House, 1960. Hardbound. 148pp. Juvenile.
Immodest 18-year-old needles over-the-hill veterans to a World Series victory. AGM

_____. *Bullpen Bargain*. New York: Hastings House, 1961. Hardbound. 157pp. Juvenile.
Bob Thomas survives a trade, a catcher who hates him, and accusations he's throwing games. AGM

_____. *Little Major Leaguer*. New York: Hastings House, 1963. Hardbound. 119pp. Juvenile.
Little League-age boy overcomes the disappointment of not pitching. AGM

_____. *Pee Wee Cook of the Midget League*. New York: Hastings House, 1964. Hardbound. 123pp. Juvenile.

Small boy battles for the SS job. Instructional in back. AGM

_____. *Minor League Shortstop*. New York: Hastings House, 1965. Hardbound. 128pp. Juvenile.
Follows Dan Whitman through his first year in organized baseball, with much background on how the minors work. AGM

_____. *Rookie Catcher with the Atlanta Braves*. New York: Hastings House, 1966. Hardbound. 159pp. Juvenile.
Through the minors with Zeke Pender. Very similar to *Minor League Shortstop* in its emphasis on how the minors work. Instructional in back. AGM

_____. *Bud Baker, High School Pitcher*. New York: Hastings House, 1967. Hardbound. 125pp. Juvenile.
Bud Baker starred in half a dozen books on a variety of sports. In this he's persuaded to go out for baseball as a high school senior and develops into his team's best pitcher. AGM

_____. *Big Play in the Small League*. New York: Hastings House, 1968. Hardbound. 93pp. Juvenile.
Mark wants to move up to the highest levels of Small (read Little) League baseball, but he's very erratic. He grows more consistent, partly by watching a rookie go through similar experiences at the nearby New York Yankees spring-training camp. AGM

_____. *Second Time Around Rookie*. New York: Hastings House, 1968. Hardbound. 157pp. Juvenile.
Signed as a pitcher, he can't throw hard enough. So he becomes an outfielder but has fielding problems. It's solvable. Instructional in back. AGM

_____. *Pennant Stretch Drive*. New York: Hastings House, 1969. Hardbound. 126pp. Juvenile.
Marty Martin tries to juggle his big-league comeback and the expansion of his fast-food business at the same time. AGM

_____. *Bud Baker, College Pitcher*. New York: Hastings House, 1970 Hardbound. 128pp. Juvenile.
Bud finds he needs to adjust to both studies and a stiffer level of competition. He does so and signs with the Dodgers at the end of his freshman year. AGM

_____. *Tom Mosely—Midget Leaguer.* New York: Hastings House, 1971. Hardbound. 128pp. Juvenile.

Tom must adjust to a new town, to being the son of a former big leaguer, and to the fact that his coach is interested in his now-widowed mother. AGM

_____. *Fifth Inning Fade-Out.* New York: Hastings House, 1972. Hardbound. 124pp. Juvenile.

Joe can't seem to pitch through the fifth, until he learns not to let others' mistakes bother him and to concentrate. AGM

(Written as CAARY JACKSON.) *Shorty at Shortstop.* Chicago: Wilcox & Follett Co., 1951. Hardbound. 153pp. Juvenile.

Small boy must battle his runt complex and the sneers of a larger rival on his junior high team. AGM

_____. *A Uniform for Harry.* Chicago: Follett Publishing Co., 1962. Hardbound. 29pp. Juvenile.

Watching a game on TV, Harry spots a flaw in slugger Hank Sharp's swing. His reward is a uniform, and he also gets a chance to make the local team. AGM

_____. *Midget League Catcher.* Chicago: Follett Publishing Co., 1966. Hardbound. 139pp. Juvenile.

Beezie wants to be a catcher, but his mom wants a golfer. AGM

(Written as COLIN LOCHLONS.) *Squeeze Play.* New York: Thomas Y. Crowell Co., 1950. Hardbound. 207pp. Juvenile.

Boys mature playing junior high baseball. AGM

_____. *Three-and-Two Pitcher.* New York: Thomas Y. Crowell Co., 1951. Hardbound. 206pp. Juvenile.

In American Legion junior baseball, boy must learn poise and persistence. AGM

_____. *Triple Play.* New York: Thomas Y. Crowell Co., 1952. Hardbound. 193pp. Juvenile.

Teenage immigrant from Germany tries to fit in, mostly through baseball. AGM

_____. *Barney of the Babe Ruth League.* New York: Thomas Y. Crowell Co., 1954. Hardbound. 148pp. Juvenile.

Boy is too old for Little League and too stubborn to play anything but shortstop. AGM

(Written with O. B. JACKSON.) *Hillbilly Pitcher.* New York: McGraw-Hill Book Co., 1956. Hardbound. 168pp. Juvenile.

Wilson makes believers of the big city boys. AGM

_____. *High School Backstop.* New York: McGraw-Hill Book Co., 1963. Hardbound. 160pp. Juvenile.

High school boy moves to catcher from 1B, but still must deal with the first baseman's resentment. An alumnus now in the bigs helps turn things around. AGM

JACKSON, O. B. *Southpaw in the Mighty Mite League.* New York: McGraw-Hill Book Co., 1965. Hardbound. 128pp. Juvenile.

JENKINS, JERRY B. *The Secret Baseball Challenge.* Chicago: Moody Press, 1986. Paper. 85pp. Juvenile.

A Christian book about a group of boys who put together a team, create a field from a vacant lot, and play a Little League all-star team from a league they weren't allowed into. AGM

_____. *Mystery at Raider Stadium.* Cincinnati: Standard Publications, 1986. Paper. 112pp. Juvenile mystery. nuc

Daniel sees his friend Chad kidnapped at Raider Stadium, where the distraction of a baseball game makes him the only witness. No. 10 in a series of Bradford family adventures. NUC

JENKINS, MacGREGOR. *Shiner Watson.* Indianapolis: The Bobbs-Merrill Co., 1929. Hardbound. 288pp. Young adult.

Book of boys' adventures with one long chapter on a baseball game. (They lose.) Nice color illustration on the cover of Our Hero swinging and missing. AGM

JENKS, GEORGE C. *Double Curve Dan, The Pitcher Detective.* New York: Beadle's Half-Dime Library No. 581, Sept. 11, 1888. Magazine. 16pp. Young adult mystery.

Dirty work at a game, then murder. The main character was Dan Manly, really a detective for the New York Secret Service. It's made clear that detecting is his real work and that professional baseball isn't really something a man can be proud of doing, although of course, Dan does it well. First known instance of a pitch that breaks twice on its way to the plate. Other improbabilities. AGM

_____. *The Pitcher Detective's Foil.* New York: Beadle's Half-Dime Library No. 608, March 19, 1889. Magazine. 16pp. Young adult mystery. djdej

_____. *The Pitcher Detective's Toughest Tussle.* New York: Beadle's Half-Dime Library No. 681, Aug. 12, 1890. Magazine. 16pp. Young adult mystery.

JOHNSON, LOIS W. *You're Worth More Than You Think.* Colorado Springs, Co: Navpress, 1988. Paper. 180pp. Juvenile.

Only two of the twenty-six stories in this book, plus the cover illustration, are about baseball. AGM

JOHNSON, NEIL. *Batter Up!* New York: Scholastic, Inc., 1990. Hardbound. 28pp. Juvenile.

Story and photographs follow Nick through his first year of Little League. AGM

JOHNSON, OWEN. *The Humming Bird.* New York: The Baker & Taylor Co., 1910. Hardbound. 86pp. Juvenile.

Boarding school baseball story with a wonderful, early (the first?) satire of Sportsuguese, the language where a ball is never called by so mundane an appellation. Rather, a sphere, a horsehide, a pellet. . . . AGM

_____. *The Varmint.* Boston: Little, Brown and Co., 1910. Hardbound. 396pp. Juvenile.

Another of Johnson's Lawrenceville (a prep school) stories. This one has one baseball scene. Also, Dink Stover, Johnson's usual hero, is set on his career as a football player for later Lawrenceville and Princeton books. AGM

JORDAN, PAT. *The Cheat.* New York: Villard Books, 1984. Hardbound. 259pp. Adult mystery.

The acclaimed magazine writer turns to fiction with this tale of a cheating reporter following on the death of a Steve Dalkowski soundalike and finding a Cy Young award winner with a faultless image may be a cheat, too. AGM

JORGENSEN, NELS L. *Dave Palmer's Diamond Mystery.* New York: Cupples & Leon Co., 1954. Hardbound. 221pp. Juvenile mystery.

Little League (and McCarthyism) come to Wayne. The Incas win their league, and Dave solves the mystery of the erratic play of their first baseman from Puerto Rico, whose father's past involvement in a vaguely communistic party is causing uncertainty. AGM

JOYCE, WILLIAM. *Dinosaur Bob and His Adventures with the Family Lazardo.* New York: Harper & Row, 1988. Hardbound. 32pp. Juvenile.

An African dinosaur becomes the star of the local ball team in this quirky book with wonderful illustrations by the author. AGM

KAHANER, ELLEN. *What's So Great About Fourth Grade?* Mahwah, NJ: Troll Associates, 1990. Hardbound. 92pp. Juvenile.

A lie from his brainy best friend threatens to bar Mark from playing baseball for his fourth grade team. NUC

KAHN, PEGGY. *The Care Bears: "Try, Try Again."* New York: Random House, Inc., 1985. Hardbound. 32pp. Juvenile.

Tommy must persevere to learn to catch, throw, and run, and the Care Bears help. AGM

KAHN, ROGER. *The Seventh Game.* New York: New American Library, 1982. Hardbound. 321pp. Adult.

The *Boys of Summer* boy's only baseball novel. Through flashback, a veteran pitching the seventh game of the World Series relives his career on and off the field. AGM

KALB, JONAH. *The Goof That Won the Pennant.* Boston: Houghton Mifflin Co., 1976. Hardbound. 103pp. Juvenile.

Team of Little League misfits begins to play well and eventually wins the pennant on a replay of the Merkle boner. Historical note explaining same is included. AGM

KARLINS, MARVIN. *The Last Man Is Out.* Englewood Cliffs, NJ: Prentice-Hall, Inc., 1969. Hardbound. 217pp. Adult science fiction.
College professor suddenly inherits the hapless Chicago AToms and turns to a former professor who plans to remake the team through the wonders of computers and positive reinforcement; also rewritten as *The AToms Bombshell* under the name Robert Browne. AGM

KATZ, STEVE. *Florry of Washington Heights.* Los Angeles: Sun & Moon Press, 1987. Hardbound. 206pp. Adult.
A novel of growing up in the 1950s in New York City. Follows a group of boys who are sort of a gang. Small amount of talk about baseball and a game at the end. AGM

KAY, HELEN. (Pseudonym: *See* Helen C. Goldfrank.)

KAYE, MARILYN. *Will You Cross Me?* New York: Harper & Row, 1985. Hardbound. 32pp. Juvenile.
Two boys have a difficult time trying to cross a busy street to play baseball. At times, they play catch across the street. AGM

KEATING, LAWRENCE. *Kid Brother.* Philadelphia: Westminster Press, 1956. Hardbound. 185pp. Juvenile.
Tom Bentley must come to terms with the reputation of his older brother, a BMOC at their high school and now playing in the American Association. He becomes team captain and leads the team to a league championship. AGM

_____. *Freshman Backstop.* Philadelphia: Westminster Press, 1957. Hardbound. 182pp. Juvenile.

_____. *Senior Challenge.* Philadelphia: Westminster Press, 1959. Hardbound. 208pp. Juvenile. agmonuc

KEIFETZ, NORMAN. *The Sensation.* New York: Atheneum, 1975. Hardbound. 304pp. Adult.
A young center fielder jeopardizes his career through a sexual obsession for young girls. JO

KEITH, HAROLD. *Shotgun Shaw: A Baseball Story.* New York: Thomas Y. Crowell Co., 1949. Hardbound. 163pp. Juvenile.

High school pitcher is lazy in class and on the field. He learns he has to study and to pick up a pitch to complement his overpowering fastball. AGM

KELLY, JEFFREY. *The Basement Baseball Club.* Boston: Houghton Mifflin Co., 1987. Hardbound. 175pp. Juvenile.
Bunch of boys with a losing neighborhood team try to recruit the big new kid in town. His little sister's a good player, but he had beaned a boy and is afraid of the ball himself. AGM

KENNEDY, LUCY. *The Sunlit Field.* New York: Crown Publishers, 1950. Hardbound. 333pp. Adult romance.
Baseball in Brooklyn circa 1860 is the backdrop of this romantic tale about an Irish colleen and her strapping ball player. Walt Whitman is also a character in what may be the first baseball novel written by a woman for an adult audience. JO

KENNEDY, WILLIAM. *Ironweed.* New York: Viking Press, 1983. Hardbound. 227pp. Adult
One in a fine cycle of books set in Albany. Francis Phelan, a drunk struggling to survive an Albany winter, tries to make peace with his past in the city. Phelan has a few flashbacks to his career as a big leaguer. AGM

KENT, JUSTIN. (A pseudonym.) *Fast Curve.* New York: The Vixen Press, 1953. Hardbound. 253pp. Adult pornography.
About half this book is game description as two teams fight for a major league pennant. The rest is pornographic. AGM

KESSLER, LEONARD P. *Here Comes the Strikeout.* New York: Harper & Row, 1965. Hardbound. 64pp. Juvenile.
Bobby learns the value of practice and stops being an easy out. AGM

_____. *Old Turtle's Baseball Stories.* New York: Greenwillow Books, 1982. Hardbound. 55pp. Juvenile.
There really is a hot stove here as Old Turtle tells his friends unbelievable baseball stories. AGM

_____. *The Worst Team Ever.* New York: Greenwillow Books, 1985. Hardbound. 48pp. Juvenile.
Old Turtle helps the worst team in the swamp. AGM

KEY, TED. *Phyllis*. New York: E. P. Dutton & Co., 1957. Hardbound. 60pp. Juvenile.

Whimsical tale of a sparrow who builds a nest in short left field in the Philadelphia Phillies ballpark. Special ground rules protect the nest, create cheap home runs, and help the Phils to the pennant. AGM

KIDD, RONALD. *Who Is Felix the Great?* New York: E. P. Dutton & Co., 1983. Hardbound. 135pp. Juvenile.

One of the better recent juveniles. Boy digs up his father's boyhood hero for a "where are they now" paper for school. He winds up driving the cranky, embittered man from Los Angeles to Chicago for an old-timer's game he hadn't been invited to. No game action. AGM

KING, FRANK. *Southpaw*. New York: Lynx Books, 1988. Paper. 229pp. Adult horror.

The ghost (and not too figuratively) of the minor league Oaktown Wolves' last great season returns. AGM

KINSELLA, W. P. *Shoeless Joe*. Boston: Houghton Mifflin Co., 1982. Hardbound. 265pp. Adult.

An engrossing fantasy of a farmer who constructs a diamond and bleachers in one of his fields so his father, Shoeless Joe Jackson, the other Black Sox, and J. D. Salinger can fulfill his and their dreams. Made into a 1989 movie, *Field of Dreams,* directed by Phil Alden Robinson and starring Kevin Costner. AGM

———. *The Thrill of the Grass*. New York: Penguin, 1985. Paper. 196pp. Adult collection.

A magical collection of short stories, most of which touch on baseball. Several serve as pieces of later work. The title story is the fantasy of every true baseball fan. AGM

———. *The Iowa Baseball Confederacy*. Boston: Houghton Mifflin Co., 1986. Hardbound. 310pp. Adult.

An eerily fantastic tale of a group of all-stars from the forgotten (if it ever existed) Iowa Baseball Confederacy and a game against the 1908 Chicago Cubs. AGM

W. P. Kinsella, author of four baseball fiction works, two novels and two books of short stories. His Shoeless Joe *was turned into the movie "Field of Dreams," somewhat ironic in that Kinsella's original title for the book was* Dream Field. *Photo by Robert Morfey.*
writer's agent

———. *The Further Adventures of Slugger McBatt*. Boston: Houghton Mifflin Co., 1988. Hardbound. 179pp. Adult collection.

Ten more wonderful baseball stories, including veteran coach "Comic Book" Demarco rambling to a rookie about today's lack of nicknames. AGM

KINSEY, ELIZABETH. *Donny and Company*. New York: Franklin Watts, Inc., 1953. Hardbound. 189pp. Juvenile.

Group of small town kids work together to create a diamond for their teams. AGM

KIRALY, SHERWOOD. *California Rush*. New York: Macmillan Publishing Co., 1990. Hardbound. 242pp. Adult.

Expansion team makes a run for the pennant as three old minor league teammates manage and coach. Very improbable action. AGM

KLASS, DAVID. *The Atami Dragons.* New York: Charles Scribner's Sons, 1984. Hardbound. 134pp. Young adult.
A recently widowed father takes his kids to Japan for a summer, and his son hooks up with the local high school team. AGM

_____. *A Different Season.* New York: E. P. Dutton & Co., 1988. Hardbound. 199pp. Young adult.
Ace high school pitcher Jim Roark struggles with his interest in Jennifer Douglas and his strong feelings she shouldn't be on the team. Also lessons on alcohol. AGM

KLEIN, DAVE. *Hit and Run.* New York: Ace Charter, 1982. Paper. 305pp. Adult mystery.
Star Yankee CF is blackmailed by a drug kingpin. New York sportswriter tries to help out. AGM

KLINE, SUZY. *Herbie Jones and the Monster Ball.* New York: G. P. Putnam's Sons, 1988. Hardbound. 126pp. Juvenile.
One of a number of Herbie Jones books. Herbie is upset when his college ballplayer-uncle returns to run the local park league team and he realizes he must play despite being terrible. His uncle proves a good coach. AGM

KLINKOWITZ, JERRY. *Short Season and Other Stories.* Baltimore: Johns Hopkins University Press, 1988. Hardbound. 187pp. Adult collection.
A nicely done collection of 28 short stories set on a minor league team. The characters carry over from story to story. Klinkowitz has worked as a Midwest League executive. AGM

KLISE, THOMAS S. *The Last Western.* Niles, Il: Argus Communications, 1974. Hardbound. 559pp. Adult.
A novel about the rise of an international religious leader in a world of the near future gone mad. As a young man, he achieves fame as a major league pitcher and some people respond to him later because of that, but his actual baseball career occupies only about 75 pages early. AGM

KLUGER, STEVE. *Changing Pitches.* New York: St. Martin's Press, 1984. Hardbound. 260pp. Adult.
A novel that answers the question, "What happens if a pitcher falls in love with his catcher's big blue eyes?" BP

KLUSMEYER, JOANN. *What About Me?* St. Louis: Concordia Publishing House, 1987. Paper. 119pp. Juvenile.
A young Christian is torn between his responsibilities toward his younger deaf sister and his desire to play baseball. Two games described. AGM

KNOPF, MEL. *The Batting Machine.* Great Neck, NY: Todd & Honeywell, Inc., 1981. Hardbound. 168pp. Adult.
Entrepreneur out of Ayn Rand builds a machine to teach poor hitters to hit, buys half the team, is named manager, and leads the previously hapless Portland Jacks to the World Series. AGM

KNOTT, BILL. *Junk Pitcher.* Chicago: Follett Publishing Co., 1963. Hardbound. 224pp. Juvenile.
Tom Faust makes the bigs on his fastball alone. Shoulder miseries force him back to the minors before he learns other pitches. AGM

(Written as BILL J. CAROL.) *Circus Catch.* Austin: The Steck Co., 1963. Hardbound. 156pp. Juvenile.
All of the Bill J. Carol books I have been able to read, a list that doesn't include this one, are set on the same Little League team, the Tigers, coached by Dan Farber. The main character changes every book or few books, but Farber and some of the subsidiary characters overlap. Very similar in many ways to the Curtis Bishop books, which Steck also published. AGM

_____. *Clutch Single.* Austin: The Steck Co., 1964. Hardbound. 132pp. Juvenile.
Jimmy alienates his teammates by bragging he's going to win the CF job and then has to live with being a backup. AGM

_____. *Hit Away!* Austin: Steck-Vaughn Co., 1965. Hardbound. 156pp. Juvenile.
Dave Ray learns to hit. See next listing. AGM

_____. *Hard Smash to Third.* Austin: Steck-Vaughn Co., 1966. Hardbound. 156pp. Juvenile.
Still bothered by an ankle he hurt in *Hit Away!,* Dave learns to play third base. AGM

_____. *Lefty's Long Throw*. Austin: Steck-Vaughn Co., 1967. Hardbound. 156pp. Juvenile.

Pete, a left-hander used to his own way, suddenly feels restricted by Little League rules and the return of his father, who's been in the Air Force. He learns self-discipline as a pitcher. AGM

_____. *Lefty Finds a Catcher*. Austin: Steck-Vaughn Co., 1968. Hardbound. 141pp. Juvenile.

His first catcher has moved on, and Lefty must help train a new catcher. He slows down his pitches and loses his control, then both he and the new catcher find the groove. AGM

_____. *Lefty Plays First*. Austin: Steck-Vaughn Co., 1969. Hardbound. 135pp. Juvenile.

Lefty hurts his arm and must find a new position. His father, now the temporary coach as Farber goes off to military duty, wants him at first, but Lefty thinks another boy should play because of his better bat. AGM

_____. *Sandy Plays Third*. Austin: Steck-Vaughn Co., 1970. Hardbound. 129pp. Juvenile.

Coach Farber is once again called away. Another temporary coach takes over, and he begins to move the players around to familiarize them with new positions. At first, it's a disaster, but the players learn. AGM

_____. *Squeeze Play*. Austin: Steck-Vaughn Co., 1971. Hardbound. 122pp. Juvenile.

Farber is back and the new central character is Mickey Ortega, who seeks to improve his play by consulting a major leaguer. AGM

_____. *High Fly to Center*. Austin: Steck-Vaughn Co., 1972. Hardbound. 141pp. Juvenile.

Mickey returns to his family vacation after running away to pursue his Little League (and future big-league) career. TS

_____. *Double-Play Ball*. Austin: Steck-Vaughn Co., 1973. Hardbound. 158pp. Juvenile.

A Little Leaguer reluctantly moves from 3B to SS for the good of his team. TS

_____. *Single to Center*. Austin: Steck-Vaughn Co., 1974. Hardbound. 152pp. Juvenile.

An eleven-year-old boy has to work out the problem of having his sister play while he sits on the bench. NUC

KNOX, JACKSON. (Pseudonym: *See* Anthony P. Morris.)

KNUDSON, R. R. *Zanboomer*. New York: Harper & Row, 1978. Hardbound. 183pp. Young adult.

One in a series of books in which Zan Hagen proves girls can compete with boys in all sports. Zan is leading the high school baseball team to victory when she hurts her arm and takes up cross-country. Baseball takes up about the first half of the book. AGM

KONIGSBURG, ELAINE L. *About the B'nai Bagels*. New York: Atheneum, 1969. Hardbound. 172pp. Juvenile.

One of the better recent juveniles. Mom, Little League, tolerance, and Jewishness are all wrapped together. Several games described. AGM

KOWETT, DON. *The 7th Game*. New York: Dell Publishing Co., 1977. Paper. 219pp. Adult mystery.

For plot, see Brady's *Seven Games in October,* but with one kidnappee. AGM

KRAMER, GEORGE. *The Left Hander*. New York: G. P. Putnam's Sons, 1964. Hardbound. 155pp. Juvenile.

Paul Reagan hurts his arm early in his pro career, is released, and must struggle to come back. He makes friends with catcher Bart Mackey and returns to the majors to strike out Willie Mays. AGM

_____. *Kid Battery*. New York: G. P. Putnam's Sons, 1968. Hardbound. 128pp. Juvenile.

The next spring, Paul and Bart fail to impress a new manager and are sent to AAA. There they find a kind manager being blackmailed by gamblers and must deal with this as well as build their chances of returning to the bigs. AGM

KRAUS, ROBERT. *How Spider Saved the Baseball Game.* New York: Scholastic, Inc., 1989. Paper. 30pp. Juvenile.

Spider wins a game v. a team composed of Babe Bedbug, Reggie Bedbug, Yogi Bedbug, Mookie Bedbug, and Rapid Robert Bedbug. AGM

LANDON, LUCINDA. *Meg Mackintosh and the Case of the Missing Babe Ruth Baseball*. Boston: Little, Brown and Co., 1986. Hardbound. 48pp. Juvenile mystery.

You and Meg follow the clues through the house to find the baseball autographed by Babe Ruth. AGM

LANE, BRADLEY. *The Big Time*. Belmont, Ca: Fearon Education, 1987. Paper. 59pp. Adult.

Aging catcher breaks his thumb and is made manager of his team's AAA club. In midseason, he is sent the major league club's prize rookie pitcher, who's trying to get over a beanball he threw. Written for an adult literacy program. AGM

LARDNER, RING. *You Know Me Al*. New York: George H. Doran Co., 1916. Hardbound. 218pp. Adult collection.

The first "serious" baseball fiction, actually a collection of humor pieces that appeared in *The Saturday Evening Post*. Each is a letter from busher Jack Keefe of the White Sox to his buddy, Al, back home. A classic. The Keefe character continues in the next two books. Lardner wrote a number of non-Keefe baseball stories which appear in collections such as *Round Up* (1929) and *How to Write Short Stories* (1924). AGM

_____. *Treat 'Em Rough*. Indianapolis: Bobbs-Merrill Co., 1918. Hardbound. 160pp. Adult.

Keefe joins the Army for World War I service. No games in this one although several discussions of the 1917 World Series and one letter comparing pitching to grenade throwing. AGM

_____. *The Real Dope*. Indianapolis: Bobbs-Merrill Co., 1919. Hardbound. 186pp. Adult. bpnuc

Follows Keefe to France where there is some baseball action. BP

_____. *Lose With a Smile*. New York: Charles Scribner's Sons, 1933. Hardbound. 174pp. Adult collection.

More letters from a ball player, this time Danny Warner, who is a bit more sophisticated than Jack Keefe. There are also letters back from his girlfriend. Casey Stengel, then a coach with the Dodgers, appears by name, and in character, as Warner's adviser. Other players of the era also appear and recognizable caricatures of Stengel, Max Carey, and Bill Terry appear in the book. AGM

_____. *Ring Lardner's You Know Me Al*. New York: Harcourt Brace Jovanovich Inc., 1979. Paper. 166pp. Adult cartoon.

This is a collection of 292 of some 700 cartoon strips for which Lardner wrote the text from 1922 to early 1925. The strip featured Jack Keefe, Lardner's character from *You Know Me Al*. While the strip starts, as the book did, with Keefe reporting to the White Sox, the plot soon digresses. The strip was set in the early 1920s and makes specific references to many of the teams and events of those years. Miller Huggins, Kid Gleason, and others appear as recognizable caricatures. AGM

LAURENCE, ALFRED D. *Homer Pickle, the Greatest*. New York: Platt & Munk, 1971. Hardbound. 138pp. Juvenile.

Homer plays more baseball than anything else but excels at everything in this campily written book that follows him from 12 to adult. AGM

LAWTON, CHARLES. (Pseudonym: *See* Noel Sainsbury.)

LEAVY, JANE. *Squeeze Play*. New York: Doubleday & Co., 1990. Hardbound. 373pp. Adult.

Follows an expansion Washington Senators through the 1989 season. Much locker room high jinks a la *Semi-Tough*. White Sox immortal Sammy Esposito appears as kind of a Greek chorus. AGM

LECKIE, ROBERT. (Written as Mark Porter.) *Winning Pitcher*. New York: Simon and Schuster, Inc., 1960. Hardbound. 190pp. Young adult.

Win Hadley pitches well, reforms teammates, does good. First of six Win Hadley books. AGM

LEE, ROBERT C. *The Iron Arm of Michael Glenn*. Boston: Little, Brown and Co., 1965. Hardbound. 153pp. Juvenile.

Right-handed boy accidentally puts his left arm into the middle of an experiment and it becomes phenomenally strong. He jumps from Little League to the San Francisco Giants. The experiment wears off on the mound at Candlestick. His regular right arm gets two more Dodger hitters. AGM

LEE, S. C. *Little League Leader.* Tomball, Tx: The Strode Publishers, 1974. Hardbound. 143pp. Juvenile.
When his father's work takes the family to Huntsville, Paul looks forward to playing with the Little League team and finding out more about the scary man next door. NUC

LEE, WAYNE C. *Slugging Backstop.* New York: Dodd, Mead & Co., 1958. Hardbound. 212pp. Juvenile.
Boy from small town high school must move to a higher level of play in American Legion ball. AGM

LE GRAND. (Pseudonym: *See* Legrand Henderson.)

LELCHUK, ALAN. *On Home Ground.* San Diego: Harcourt Brace Jovanovich, Inc., 1987. Hardbound. 72pp. Juvenile.
Tale of growing up Jewish in Brooklyn right after World War II. The Dodgers, and Jackie Robinson, are a big part of this, and several games are described. AGM

_____. *Brooklyn Boy.* New York: McGraw-Hill Publishing Co., 1990. Hardbound. 298pp. Adult.
While adult in theme and content, most of *On Home Ground* is incorporated into this book. Some punchball action along with much talk of Dodgers, portraits of various Boys of Summer, and descriptions of Ebbets Field and games there. AGM

LEONARD, BURGESS. *Rookie Southpaw.* Philadelphia: J. B. Lippincott Co., 1951. Hardbound. 218pp. Young adult.
Clem Gompers goes from Piedmont High to the bigs in a year, wins pennant with no-hitter in major league debut. AGM

_____. *Second-Season Jinx.* Philadelphia: J. B. Lippincott Co., 1953. Hardbound. 216pp. Young adult.
Clem struggles in his first full year, but they win it all. AGM

_____. *The Rookie Fights Back.* Philadelphia: J. B. Lippincott Co., 1954. Hardbound. 192pp. Young adult.
Small scrappy outfielder returns to the major league team for which he was a batboy. He overcomes skepticism and leads the Lancers to a pennant. AGM

_____. *Stretch Bolton Comes Back.* Philadelphia: J. B. Lippincott Co., 1958. Hardbound. 192pp. Young adult.
First of three books about a manager who is also a clutch shortstop when his perennially troubled back allows. Disabled as a player, and fired as a manager, baseball's boy wonder is given a second chance as a manager. But he must win the pennant and the World Series. AGM

_____. *Stretch Bolton's Rookies.* Philadelphia: J. B. Lippincott Co., 1961. Hardbound. 190pp. Young adult.
Now, Stretch must rebuild the veteran team and encourage some younger players. He barely plays in this one. AGM

_____. *Stretch Bolton: Mr. Shortstop.* Philadelphia: J. B. Lippincott Co., 1963. Hardbound. 192pp. Young adult.
Fired once again, he's signed just as a shortstop by another team. He still manages to manage the team to World Series victory. AGM

LEVINSON, MARILYN. *And Don't Bring Jeremy.* New York: Holt, Rinehart and Winston, 1985. Hardbound. 122pp. Juvenile.
Little League star must deal with the problems of an older brother so awkward the younger brother and his friends don't want anything to do with him. AGM

LEVY, ELIZABETH. *Something Queer at the Ball Park.* New York: Delacorte Press, 1975. Hardbound. 44pp. Juvenile mystery
Gwen solves the mystery of the bat stolen from her friend, Jill, the star of a Little League team. AGM

LEWINSTEIN, STEPHEN R. *Double Play.* Philadelphia: Westminster Press, 1970. Hardbound. 185pp. Juvenile.

Rick Jason's minor league pitching career is cut short by an arm injury. He's released but is picked up by his old high school coach, who's conveniently managing another team in the league. He prospers as a first baseman. AGM

_____. *Computer Coach.* Philadelphia: Westminster Press, 1971. Hardbound. 136pp. Juvenile.
Hubert is too uncoordinated to make the college baseball team, but he's a genius with computers. He programs the school's computer, replaces a coach who's lost 60 straight, and leads the team into the College World Series. AGM

LEWIS, JERRY D., ed. *Great Baseball Stories.* New York: Grosset & Dunlap, Inc., 1979. Paper. 309pp. Adult collection.
Contains pieces by Heywood Broun, James T. Farrell, Paul Gallico, John O'Hara, Frank O'Rourke (from *Flashing Spikes*), Zane Grey, Damon Runyon, Irwin Shaw, James Thurber, Edna Ferber, Mark Twain, P. G. Wodehouse, and Thomas Wolfe. AGM

LEWIS, MARJORIE. *Wrongway Applebaum.* New York: Coward-McCann, Inc., 1984. Hardbound. 63pp. Juvenile.
Stanley Applebaum is a dyslexic fifth grader with severe problems learning to play baseball. He's a real klutz but dreams of playing with the other kids. Much practice and eventually a big game. He hits a last-at-bat homer to win it but, true to his dyslexia, runs the bases backwards. AGM

LEXAU, JOAN M. *I'll Tell on You.* New York: E. P. Dutton & Co., 1976. Hardbound. 25pp. Juvenile.
After his dog bites the coach's daughter, a young boy doesn't tell anyone because he fears that it will keep him off the team. NUC

LINTHURST, RANDOLPH. *Journal of Leo Smith: Story of a Nineteenth Century Shortstop.* Chicago: Adams Press, 1976. Paper. 55pp. Adult.
Smith was an actual professional player, and many of the characters in this book are real. Diary entries are drawn from actual happenings of the era. Like a real diary, the book meanders. AGM

LIPSYTE, ROBERT. *Jock and Jill.* New York: Harper & Row, 1982. Hardbound. 153pp. Juvenile.

A tongue-in-cheek takeoff on the traditional sports juvenile. A teenage problem novel about a high school baseball player. There is a large concern with drugs, and instead of winning the big game, Our Hero seizes Yankee Stadium to protest a friend's arrest. TS

LITTLE, C. *The All Star Nine.* New York: Happy Days Nos. 1035–38, August 15 to Sept. 5, 1914. Magazine. Young adult. el

LITTLEFIELD, BILL. *Prospect.* Boston: Houghton Mifflin Co., 1989. Hardbound. 227pp. Adult.
Retired scout is inspired to a last try to find The Prospect. AGM

LOCHLONS, COLIN. (Pseudonym: *See* C. Paul Jackson.)

LONGMAN, HAROLD S. *The Fox in the Ball Park.* New York: McGraw-Hill Book Co., 1980. Hardbound. 164pp. Juvenile.
A fox takes up residence in Yankee Stadium during the winter. No baseball connection except the stadium. AGM

LONGSTRETH, T. MORRIS. *The Comeback Catcher.* New York: Dodd, Mead & Co., 1965. Hardbound. 186pp. Young adult.
Jim McNail tries to get into a fancy prep school through baseball, but wins by another method. AGM

LORD, BEMAN. *The Trouble with Francis.* New York: Henry Z. Walck, Inc., 1958. Hardbound. 54pp. Juvenile.
Francis Ward hates his name because he's teased that it's a girl's name. He earns a "real" nickname during a sandlot game. AGM

_____. *Bats and Balls.* New York: Henry Z. Walck, Inc., 1962. Hardbound. 60pp. Juvenile.
Bob gets hit by a pitch in the season's first game and breaks his finger. When he comes back, he must overcome his fear of the ball. AGM

_____. *The Perfect Pitch.* New York: Henry Z. Walck, Inc., 1965. Hardbound. 55pp. Juvenile.
Boy wants to be a pitcher and has his wishes granted by a man in the woods. Unfortunately, the man knows nothing about baseball. AGM

LORD, BETTY BAO. *In the Year of the Boar and Jackie Robinson.* New York: Harper & Row, 1984. Hardbound. 169pp. Juvenile.

Traces a young Chinese girl's first year in America. She learns about the country, plays right field, and eventually meets Jackie Robinson, her hero from a summer (1947) of listening to the Dodgers on the radio. AGM

LORD, SUZANNE. *Kissyfur of Paddlecab County.* New York: Scholastic, Inc., 1986. Paper. 32pp. Juvenile.

With drawings by Phil Mendez, who created the characters for a TV show. Kissyfur, a bear, makes friends by, among other things, teaching the forest animal children to play baseball. AGM

LORENZ, TOM. *Guys Like Us.* New York: Viking Press, 1980. Hardbound. 255pp. Adult.

A demon Chicago softball player pursues his disappearing youth and a city championship as his marriage, and life, disintegrate. AGM

LOVELACE, DELOS W. *That Dodger Horse.* New York: Thomas Y. Crowell Co., 1956. Hardbound. 177pp. Juvenile.

City boy worries he won't be able to find good baseball competition in a summer on a Minnesota farm. Fair amount of baseball but basically this is a horse story. AGM

LOWRY, LOIS. *Switcharound.* Boston: Houghton Mifflin Co., 1985. Hardbound. 118pp. Juvenile.

Two New York City children are mismatched with tasks when they go to spend the summer with their divorced father in Iowa. One of the tasks is coaching a baseball team of six-year-olds. AGM

LUNEMANN, EVELYN. *Pitcher's Choice.* Westchester, Il: Benefic Press, 1972. Hardbound. 71pp. Juvenile mystery.

Fatherless Bill Weeks is ridden by a mysterious man in the stands during his high school games. It's a scout trying to learn what he's made of. AGM

LYLE, SPARKY, with DAVID FISHER. *The Year I Owned the Yankees.* New York: Bantam, 1990. Hardbound. 313pp. Adult.

Sparky takes over the Yankees from George Steinbrenner (without help from Howie Spira). He brings back many of his old teammates (Reggie Jackson is the ego coach), and wins. Every tale of the 1970s and 1980s Yankees twisted and retold. AGM

MacKELLAR, WILLIAM. *Mound Menace.* Chicago: Follett Publishing Co., 1969. Hardbound. 187pp. Juvenile.

Traditionally losing high school team is cheered when a hot pitcher transfers in. They have to overcome his fear of hitting another batter. AGM

MacKENZIE, CHRISTINE B. *Out at Home.* St. Louis: Bethany Press, 1967. Hardbound. 176pp. Juvenile.

A high school junior develops and coaches thirteen- to fifteen-year-olds to an excellent season and earns a job as a camp counselor. AGM

MacNELLY, JEFF. *Shoe Goes to Wrigley Field.* Chicago: Bonus Books, 1988. Paper. 62pp. Adult cartoon.

Shoe cartoon strip characters suffer as only Cub fans love to. AGM

MAGNUSON, JAMES. *The Rundown.* New York: Dial Press. 1977. Hardbound. 207pp. Adult mystery.

An owner's daughter is kidnapped, and he is forced to turn to a scout who he done wrong years before. AGM

MAHER, RICHARD AUMERLE. (Written as Richard Aumerle.) *Between Friends.* New York: Benziger Brothers., 1909. Hardbound. 194pp. Young adult. bpnuc

_____. *Brownie and I.* New York: Benziger Brothers, 1910. Hardbound. 170pp. Juvenile.

This is a book of grade school sports and pranks, ending with a couple of baseball chapters. Also, there's a baseball illustration on the cover. AGM

MALAMUD, BERNARD. *The Natural.* New York: Harcourt, Brace & Co., 1952. Hardbound. 237pp. Adult.

Roy Hobbs, struck down on the edge of stardom by a bullet (*see* Eddie Waitkus) comes back dramatically. A fine novel made into an overdone

1984 movie directed by Barry Levinson and starring Robert Redford, Robert Duvall, Glenn Close, and Kim Basinger. AGM

MALCOLMSON, DAVID. *London: The Dog Who Made the Team.* New York: Duell, Sloan and Pearce, 1963. Hardbound. 100pp. Juvenile.

Major league pitcher is released and finds solace in training a dog while he tries to rehabilitate his arm. When he returns to the minors, the dog begins to perform on the field, and eventually his talents lead both away from baseball. Couple of games described. AGM

MANFRED, FREDERICK. *No Fun on Sunday.* Norman, Ok: University of Oklahoma Press, 1990. Hardbound. 287pp. Adult.

A teenager of immigrant German stock aspires to be a shortstop for the Chicago Cubs while growing up during the 1920s in the upper Midwest. His religious upbringing conflicts with his love for baseball. JO

MANN, ARTHUR. *Bob White: Bonus Player.* New York: David McKay Co., 1952. Hardbound. 207pp. Young adult.

High school hero signs, goes to minors. BRD

_____. *Bob White: Farm Club Player.* New York: David McKay Co., 1952. Hardbound. 186pp. Young adult.

_____. *Bob White: Spring Terror.* New York: David McKay Co., 1953. Hardbound. 179pp. Young adult.

(Written as A. R. THURMAN.) *Money Pitcher.* New York: David McKay Co., 1952. Hardbound. 185pp. Young adult.

A small inheritance, his surname, and an overzealous publicity man get Whitey "J. P." Morgan tagged as a moneyed pitcher. He has to prove he's a money pitcher, too. AGM

MANN, TED. *Making the Team.* Los Angeles: Sutton, 1978. Paper. Adult pornography. jtp

MARGULIES, LEO. *Baseball Roundup.* New York: Cupples & Leon Co., 1948. Hardbound. 248pp. Young adult collection

MARIS, ROGER, and JACK OGLE. *Slugger in Right.* Larchmont, NY: Argonaut Books, Inc., 1963. Hardbound. 190pp. Juvenile.

See the Berra/Ferdenzi book.

MARLOWE, DAN J. *The Comeback.* Belmont, Ca: Fearon Education, 1985. Paper. 28pp. Adult.

Veteran major league lefty's arm comes back after a fall. All the books listed for Marlowe were written for adult literacy programs. AGM

_____. *Double the Glory.* Belmont, Ca: Fearon Education, 1987. Paper. 30pp. Adult.

Teenager helping a Cincinnati sportswriter is in the press box for both of Johnny Vander Meer's back-to-back no-hitters. The framework is fiction, but Vander Meer's feat and the circumstances of it are very accurately reported. AGM

_____. *The Hitter.* Belmont, Ca: Fearon Education, 1987. Paper. 61pp. Adult.

Natural hitter has to work on his catching to make it to the Cubs. AGM

MARTIN, ANN M. *The Baby-Sitters Club: Kristy and the Walking Disaster.* New York: Scholastic Inc., 1989. Paper. 144pp. Juvenile.

Kristy, president of the Baby-Sitters Club, puts together a softball team from some of the klutzes and kids too young for organized baseball. One of a series about the members of the Club. AGM

MARZOLLO, JEAN. *The Pizza Pie Slugger.* New York: Random House, Inc., 1989. Paper. 64pp. Juvenile.

Billy must learn to shut out his baby half-sister's cheering to regain his slugging form. AGM

MATHEWSON, CHRISTY. (Ghost written by John Wheeler.) *Won in the Ninth.* New York: R. J. Bodmer Co., 1910. Hardbound. 298pp. Young adult.

First of "The Matty Books," six volumes ghosted by John Wheeler and trading on the name of a superstar with an excellent reputation, including recognition as a college man. This was probably the first book to extensively use characters clearly drawn from professional players. There is, for example, Hans "Honus" Hagner, a large, awkward-looking shortstop with enormous hands—clearly Honus Wagner. A sketch of second baseman Johnny Everson features Johnny Evers's prominent jaw. The central character is Hal Case, an innovatively slick-fielding first baseman from California who is accused of

WON IN THE NINTH

BY

CHRISTOPHER MATHEWSON
THE FAMOUS PITCHER OF THE NEW YORK GIANTS

THE FIRST OF A SERIES
OF STORIES FOR BOYS ON
SPORTS TO BE KNOWN AS
THE MATTY BOOKS

EDITED BY W. W. AULICK
THE WELL-KNOWN WRITER ON SPORTS

ILLUSTRATIONS BY
FELIX MAHONY

NEW YORK
R. J. BODMER COMPANY
1910

Christy Mathewson's Won in the Ninth *and Frank Chance's* The Bride and the Pennant, *both of which appeared in 1910, were the first baseball fiction to have players as their purported authors.*
Frontispiece and title page from Christy Mathewson's *Won in the Ninth,* 1910.

theft—interesting considering the speckled career of Hal Chase. Case, however, is innocent. The plot follows the college team and manager, all clearly recognizable from professional baseball, through a successful season. There are fourteen plates in the back showing Mathewson's grip for his pitches, including the famous fadeaway. AGM

_____. *Pitcher Pollock.* New York: Dodd, Mead and Co., 1914. Hardbound. 335pp. Young adult.
First of the alliterative Matty books. Nos. 2 through 4 also carried Matty's name but after Mathewson's injury during World War I, the series was switched to using the name of Everett "Deacon" Scott. For the first 100 pages this is an Alger-esque boy-makes-good story, but as Tom Pollock achieves financial success, he also begins to play baseball. This is a pattern repeated throughout the series. Tom becomes a successful pitcher on the Amesville high school and town teams despite no experience when the book begins. AGM

_____. *Catcher Craig.* New York: Dodd, Mead and Co., 1915. Hardbound. 347pp. Young adult.
Sam Craig, the catcher in the first book of the series, becomes the main character. He goes off to coach a summer camp team, then returns for a big game for the Amesville town team. He and Tom win that and then stage a dramatic rescue when Tom pegs a ball to Sam to set up a rescue of several people from a burning building. Sam also begins to make a success in his financial life, too. AGM

_____. *First Base Faulkner*. New York: Dodd, Mead and Co., 1916. Hardbound. 328pp. Young adult.

Joe Faulkner moves to Amesville, befriends Jack Strobe, goes into the newsstand business with him, and joins Pollock and Craig on the high school team. He's a success at them all, winding up the book by tracking down an absconding clerk and then beating Amesville's arch rival with an unassisted double play. AGM

_____. *Second Base Sloan*. New York: Dodd, Mead and Co., 1917. Hardbound. 302pp. Young adult.

This book doesn't follow the Amesville story. Instead Wayne Sloan and his black friend Junius Tasker run away from Georgia and wind up in Pennsylvania. Sloan eventually makes his way to a professional baseball career while Junius, a racist's delight, becomes a highly successful bellboy. AGM

MAULE, HAMILTON "TEX." *The Shortstop*. New York: David McKay Co., 1962. Hardbound. 180pp. Young adult.

First of three novels about Jim Beatty, a fictional Yankee shortstop, not the real Yankee pitcher. (He was Beattie.) The book is studded with players appearing under their own names (Stan Musial, Ralph Houk) and lightly disguised (Dick Smith for Mickey Mantle). Beatty himself is described as looking like Tony Kubek, and all the books have Kubek action pictures on their covers or dust jackets. Maule, a longtime *Sports Illustrated* writer, also has Beatty reading one of Mark Harris's baseball novels in one scene. Beatty moves from the University of Texas to the Yankees, to the minors, and back to the bigs in his rookie year. AGM

_____. *Beatty of the Yankees*. New York: David McKay Co., 1963. Hardbound. 209pp. Young adult.

Beatty's second season. He pursues Maris's single-season home run record and ties it. He leads the Yankees to a World Series win over the Giants and blows out his knee on the last play. AGM

_____. *The Last Out*. New York: David McKay Co., 1964. Hardbound. 209pp. Young adult.

Beatty tries to come back but his bad knee won't let him. He returns to Texas to practice law and coach kids. AGM

MAYER, ROBERT. *The Grace of Shortstops*. Garden City, NY: Doubleday & Co., 1984. Hardbound. 256pp. Adult.

A young boy's infant cousin is kidnapped, and he learns much about himself and his family while finding her. Throughout, in moments of trouble, he tries to conduct himself with the grace of his hero, Pee Wee Reese. A little stickball and much listening to the Dodgers on the radio (1947) dot the book. AGM

MAYS, WILLIE, and JEFF HARRIS. *Danger in Center Field*. Larchmont, NY: Argonaut Books, Inc., 1963. Hardbound. 192pp. Juvenile mystery.

Young black center fielder comes to the majors. He's a big success on the field, but he's receiving death threats from a teammate and must figure out who it is. Tips from Willie on CF play in back. See also the Berra/Ferdenzi book. AGM

McALPINE, GORDON. *Joy in Mudville*. New York: E. P. Dutton & Co., 1989. Hardbound. 212pp. Adult.

A comic book for adults with Babe Ruth, Al Capone, Clark Kent, and Woody Guthrie as characters. JO

McCALL, EDITH. *The Buttons and the Little League*. Chicago: Benefic Press, 1961. Hardbound. 95pp. Juvenile.

One of at least a dozen books on the Button family. Bucky goes out for Little League and learns how to hit and about lucky #13. AGM

McCORMACK, TOM. *Strictly Amateur*. New York: Pinnacle, 1982. Paper. 294pp. Adult mystery.

Caper novel about a kidnapping. The victim is a star major leaguer. His manager and other team officials get involved. Very small amount of game description. AGM

McCORMICK, WILFRED. *The Three-Two Pitch*. New York: G. P. Putnam's Sons, 1948. Hardbound. 186pp. Young adult.

McCormick was a prolific writer of sports stories covering all kinds of sports. His main characters were Bronc Burnett (twenty-seven books) and

Rocky McCune (sixteen). In this, sixteen-year-old Bronc must conquer rabbit ears and find his place as a pitcher on the Sonora High team, leading it to a league championship. AGM

_____. *Legion Tourney.* New York: G. P. Putnam's Sons, 1948. Hardbound. 180pp. Young adult.
Bronc and the boys move over to American Legion ball. They win the New Mexico state championship after overcoming too much concern with portents. AGM

_____. *Fielder's Choice.* New York: G. P. Putnam's Sons, 1949. Hardbound. 180pp. Young adult.
Then, the regional play-offs, which they win with a tricky pickoff play (McCormick loves tricky pickoff plays, which occur in both series). Bronc is much concerned with how much publicity he's getting. AGM

_____. *Bases Loaded.* New York: G. P. Putnam's Sons, 1950. Hardbound. 182pp. Young adult.
Bronc and the boys run into some strange umpiring calls at the Western sectional play-offs, but Bronc toughs it out and the Sonorans pull the same pickoff as in the previous book. The Bronc books are full of stories from baseball history, but this seems to have more, from Fred Merkle to Larry Doby, than the others. AGM

_____. *Grand-Slam Homer.* New York: G. P. Putnam's Sons, 1951. Hardbound. 183pp. Young adult.
McCormick seems to be getting confused. Bronc had pitched the last inning of the sectionals with a broken finger. But in this book, supposedly just a few days later, no mention of the finger is made. The theme in this one is hunches versus calculations (much discussion of Connie Mack starting Howard Ehmke in first game of 1929 World Series). Bronc wins American Legion national championship with grand slam in Yankee Stadium. AGM

_____. *The Man on the Bench.* New York: David McKay Co., 1955. Hardbound. 181pp. Young adult.
The first Rocky McCune story; ace athlete Rocky returns to Koulee High School as a coach. He overcomes school board interference and returns

Koulee to its past glories by winning their league. AGM

_____. *The Hot Corner.* New York: David McKay Co., 1958. Hardbound. 175pp. Young adult.
A year later, Rocky leads Koulee to another championship season and reforms Red Bostic, an urban kid who's too slick for his own good. Bostic will be the main playing character for the rest of the McCune series. AGM

_____. *The Big Ninth.* New York: G. P. Putnam's Sons, 1958. Hardbound. 188pp. Young adult.
Overconfidence haunts Bronc and the boys on their way home from winning the nationals. They must win a tough series against a team from a neighboring town coached by an ex-big leaguer. AGM

_____. *The Proud Champions.* New York: David McKay Co., 1959. Hardbound. 176pp. Young adult.
Rocky's team begins a series of double elimination tourneys that cover the rest of the series and the rest of the summer. In this, Koulee wins despite the boys getting carried away with promoting Rocky. AGM

_____. *The Automatic Strike.* New York: David McKay Co., 1960. Hardbound. 173pp. Young adult.
Another double elimination tourney won by another pickoff play. Rocky must battle the boys over their belief that there are lucky and unlucky days. Very reminiscent of *Legion Tourney*. AGM

_____. *The Last Put-Out.* New York: G. P. Putnam's Sons, 1960. Hardbound. 192pp. Young adult.
Bronc and the guys go to Chicago to beat the Mexican junior champions led by "Chico" Moya. Bronc wins the duel at Wrigley. AGM

_____. *One O'Clock Hitter.* New York: David McKay Co., 1960. Hardbound. 182pp. Young adult.
To Mexico for a rematch with Chico Moya. Bronc is having trouble hitting during games, and a fight between his dad and the shortstop's dad involves the two boys. AGM

_____. *The Bluffer.* New York: David McKay Co., 1961. Hardbound. 151pp. Young adult.

Bronc's buddy, catcher Fat Crompton, is charmed into indiscretions by a player for the French national junior champion team the boys are in Montreal to play. AGM

_____. *The Double Steal.* New York: David McKay Co., 1961. Hardbound. 180pp. Young adult.

Rocky's boys "borrow" a few too many souvenirs from their hotel at the next tournament and get themselves a reputation for larceny on and off the field. AGM

_____. *Home-Run Harvest.* New York: David McKay Co., 1962. Hardbound. 179pp. Young adult.

Another tournament for Rocky, this one against a team with a bully of a coach and a penchant for stretching the rules. Guess who wins. AGM

_____. *Rebel with a Glove.* New York: David McKay Co., 1962. Hardbound. 148pp. Young adult.

Bronc gets labelled a poor sport when the Sonorans go to Vancouver to play a champion team formed at a boys home. AGM

_____. *Once a Slugger.* New York: David McKay Co., 1963. Hardbound. 177pp. Young adult.

Bronc and his friends are in Alaska for a tournament, and Bronc's attempts to shield his friend and catcher, Fat Crompton, whose parents have separated, cause misunderstanding with his hosts. Some ads on earlier volumes said this book would be titled *The Fence Busters.* AGM

_____. *The Phantom Shortstop.* New York: David McKay Co., 1963. Hardbound. 178pp. Young adult.

The opposing team in the tournament uses a big computer to chart tendencies. Rocky points out the computer does no more than reflect conventional wisdom, but both he and the opposing coach realize what a psychological effect it has on their teenagers. AGM

_____. *The Starmaker.* New York: Robert Speller & Sons, 1963. Hardbound. 160pp. Young adult.

Second of short-lived series about Dyke Redman. His college team is pretty deep except at pitcher, and the coach wants catcher Dyke to

make the hurler a star even though he's selfish and obnoxious. AGM

_____. *The Throwing Catcher.* New York: David McKay Co., 1964. Hardbound. 179pp. Young adult.

In a rematch with the team from *The Bluffer,* minus the bluffer himself, Bronc hits the Canadian pitcher. He has a tough time convincing them it was an accident. AGM

_____. *The Long Pitcher.* New York: Duell, Sloan and Pearce, 1964. Hardbound. 172pp. Young adult.

The only instance of girl trouble in a Wilfred McCormick baseball book. But one winds up helping Rocky, Red, and Koulee win yet another tournament. AGM

_____. *The Go-Ahead Runner.* New York: David McKay Co., 1965. Hardbound. 181pp. Young adult.

At a tournament in Los Angeles, which has financial problems, a publicity decision is made to portray Bronc as a heavy. The publicity gets too close to reality for Bronc and his teammates who are playing the Canadian team from *Rebel With a Glove* at Dodger Stadium. AGM

_____. *Wild on the Bases.* New York: Duell, Sloan and Pearce, 1965. Hardbound. 152pp. Young adult.

Rocky's tournament rivals this time are an all American-Indian team. Red Bostic makes an unfortunate remark about an Indian maiden that alienates opponents and hosts. But they win. AGM

_____. *Tall at the Plate.* Indianapolis: Bobbs-Merrill Co., 1966. Hardbound. 188pp. Young adult.

Bronc and the guys are rematched with a souped up version of their opponents from *Once a Slugger.* They win on yet another tricky pickoff play. AGM

_____. *The Incomplete Pitcher.* Indianapolis: Bobbs-Merrill Co., 1967. Hardbound. 180pp. Young adult.

Bronc goes to Angor college to play for Rocky on the frosh team. He must deal with a duel between his own Fat Crompton and Rocky's Ralph

Piers to be the team's catcher. The key incident echoes that in *The Man on the Bench* and involves Piers in a very similar way. AGM

_____. *Rookie on First.* New York: G. P. Putnam's Sons, 1967. Hardbound. 218pp. Young adult.
Yankee farmhand Roy Rolfe must convince a skeptical manager that he can perform in the clutch, and he finally does so in an exhibition game against the big club. AGM

McGOVERN, ANN. *Scram, Kid!* New York: Viking Press, 1974 Hardbound. 39pp. Juvenile.
Joey wants into a neighborhood game. When he keeps being told to scram, he imagines numerous suitable fates for his tormentors. He eventually settles for sailing on a boat. AGM

McGRAW, FRANK E. "TUG," Jr. *Lumpy.* Philadelphia: Running Press, Inc., 1981. Paper. 40pp. Juvenile cartoon.
Cartoons of a baseball character by the flaky reliever. The ball dreams of making the Hall of Fame. The book also contained a record. AGM

_____. (with MIKE WITTE.) *Scroogie.* New York: New American Library, 1976. Paper. 180pp. Juvenile cartoon.
A collection from McGraw's short-lived comic strip of the same name. The strip is set on a major league team, and real ball players of that era, including McGraw himself, appear by name or as recognizable caricatures. AGM

_____. *Hello There, Ball!* New York: New American Library, 1977. Paper. 180pp. Juvenile cartoon.
More adventures for Scroogie. AGM

McMAHON, WILLIAM R. *A Doodletown Dodger.* Philadelphia: Dorrance & Co., 1973. Hardbound. 51pp. Juvenile. nucbip
Jimmy had the batting and pitching skills to be an all-time star for the Doodletown Dodgers, but his skin was the wrong color. NUC

McMANUS, JAMES. *Chin Music.* New York: Crown Publishers, 1985. Hardbound. 199pp. Adult.
The first nuclear holocaust baseball novel. White Sox pitcher leaves the cancelled third game of the World Series to make his way home as World War III begins. BP

McSHERRY, FRANK D., Jr., CHARLES WAUGH, and M. H. GREENBERG, eds. *Baseball 3000.* New York: Elsevier/Nelson Books, 1981. Hardbound. 210pp. Adult science fiction collection.
Eleven science fiction stories from as far back as 1938. Includes Frank O'Rourke (from *The Heavenly World Series),* Rod Serling, and Paul Gallico, who contributes a story about the Babe as a saint. AGM

McVEY, R. PARKER. *Mystery at the Ball Game.* Mahwah, NJ: Troll Associates, 1985. Hardbound. 120pp. Juvenile mystery.
Another of those make-a-decision-and-go-to-different-pages books. A Little Leaguer thwarts the kidnapping of another player in his league. AGM

MENDELSOHN, FELIX, Jr. *Superbaby.* Los Angeles: Nash Publishing, 1969. Hardbound. 211pp. Adult.
Gene research creates a superman, and he goes for pro baseball. Most of this is concentrated in the latter half of the book. AGM

MICHAEL, D. J. (Pseudonym: *See* Charles Einstein.)

MICHAELS, RALPH. *The Girl on First Base.* New York: Nordon Publications, Inc. 1981. Paper. 256pp. Young adult romance.
She was good enough to be the first woman pro but threw it over for love. Her school and minor league career take up a good bit of the book. AGM

MICHAELS, SKI. (Pseudonym: *See* Michael Pellowski.)

MIERS, EARL SCHENCK. *Monkey Shines.* Cleveland: World Publishing Co., 1952. Hardbound. 207pp. Young adult.
Sleepy Jones forms a Little League team, gets ex-big leaguer as coach, learns team play, has monkey mascot. AGM

_____. *The Kid Who Beat the Dodgers and Other Sports Stories.* Cleveland: World Publishing Co., 1954. Hardbound. 190pp. Young adult collection.
Only the title story of this twelve-story collection is about baseball. An enthusiastic rookie catcher rekindles a veteran's competitiveness. AGM

_____. *Ball of Fire*. Cleveland: World Publishing Co., 1956. Hardbound. 220pp. Young adult.

Monkey Shines characters reappear at the Pony League level. Ends with homer to win regional championship. AGM

MILLAR, JEFF, and BILL HINDS. *If I Quit Baseball, Will You Still Love Me?* Mission, Ks: Sheed and Ward, Inc., 1976. Paper. 87pp. Juvenile cartoon.

From the Tank McNamara comic strip. Tank coaches some Little Leaguers to have fun despite parental pressure on him and the kids. AGM

MOFFAT, WILLIAM. *The Crimson Banner*. New York: Chatterton-Peck Company, 1907. Hardbound. 287pp. Juvenile.

Reissued as *Belmont College*. Also appeared as a serial in one of Frank Munsey's publications in 1890. Follows the Belmont College nine in pursuit of the Crimson Banner, the championship of their New England college league. AGM

_____. *Belmont College*. (Undated.)

See *The Crimson Banner*.

MOLARSKY, OSMOND. *Robbery in Right Field*. New York: Henry Z. Walck, Inc., 1978. Hardbound. 55pp. Juvenile.

Cynthia Rose, Bagley's star gymnast, surprises the town by quitting gymnastics to go out for Little League. Her success while "throwing just like a girl" throws the league into turmoil. AGM

MOLLOY, PAUL. *A Pennant for the Kremlin*. Garden City, NY: Doubleday & Co., 1964. Hardbound. 185pp. Adult.

The Supreme Soviet inherits the Chicago White Sox from an eccentric millionaire and tries to run them with a commissar. AGM

MONTGOMERY, ROBERT. *Rabbit Ears*. New York: New American Library, 1985. Paper. 159pp. Juvenile.

Catcher must help the team's only pitcher overcome rabbit ears, but he then develops a case of his own. They recover to win a national high school championship in the Astrodome. AGM

_____. *Home Run!* Mahwah, NJ: Troll Associates, 1990. Hardbound. 176pp. Juvenile. nucpub

First in the six-book Iron Mask of Gary Carter series. pub

_____. *Grand Slam*. Mahwah, NJ: Troll Associates, 1990. Hardbound. 176pp. Juvenile. nucpub

Second in the Iron Mask of Gary Carter series. pub

_____. *Triple Play*. Mahwah, NJ: Troll Associates, 1990. Hardbound. 176pp. Juvenile. nucpub

Third in the Iron Mask of Gary Carter series. pub

_____. *MVP*. Mahwah, NJ: Troll Associates, 1990. Hardbound. 176pp. Juvenile. nucpub

Fourth in the Iron Mask of Gary Carter series. pub

_____. *Hitting Streak*. Mahwah, NJ: Troll Associates, 1990. Hardbound. 176pp. Juvenile. nucpub

Fifth in the Iron Mask of Gary Carter series. pub

_____. *The Show!* Mahwah, NJ: Troll Associates, 1990. Hardbound. 176pp. Juvenile. nucpub

Sixth in the Iron Mask of Gary Carter series. pub

MOORE, HARRY. (Pseudonym: *See* S. A. D. Cox.)

MOORE, JOSEPH A. *Two Strikes on Lefty*. Boston: W. A. Wilde Co., 1954. Hardbound. 224pp. Juvenile. fp

_____. *Hot Shot at Third*. New York: Duell, Sloan and Pearce, 1958. Hardbound. 184pp. Juvenile.

MOOSER, STEPHEN. *Monsters in the Outfield*. New York: Dell Publishing, 1989. Paper. 70pp. Juvenile.

The Creepy Creatures Club challenges the Sharks to a grudge baseball match AGM

MORGENSTEIN, GARY. *Take Me Out to the Ballgame*. New York: St. Martin's Press, 1980. Hardbound. 296pp. Adult.

A baseball season degenerates into violence when a new owner tries to promote his team among frenzied fans. JO

_____. *The Man Who Wanted to Play Centerfield for the New York Yankees*. New York: Atheneum, 1983. Hardbound. 272pp. Adult.

A thirty-three-year-old businessman fulfills a fantasy by becoming the New York Yankees center fielder. JO

MORRIS, ANTHONY P. (Written as Jackson Knox.) *Short Stop Maje*. New York: Beadle's Dime

Library No. 515, Sept. 5, 1888. Magazine. 16pp. Young adult mystery. moaj

A medical college baseball team, with the shortstop as detective and a house with secret doors, etc. AJ

MULLER, CHARLES G. *The Baseball Detective.* New York: Harper & Bros., 1928. Hardbound. 333pp. Juvenile mystery.

MULLINS, RICHARD. *Most Valuable Player.* New York: Funk & Wagnalls Co., 1962. Hardbound. 179pp. Young adult.

Two high school boys duel to win a state championship, a girl, the team MVP award, and the college scholarship that goes with it. AGM

MUNN, VELLA. *Summer Season.* New York: Harlequin Books, 1983. Paper. 255pp. Adult romance.

Little in the way of ball games, but Our Heroine is the trainer for an A's minor league team in Oregon (also a former softball player). The man of her dreams is the GM of the team, and the team's manager and some of the players figure in the plot. AGM

MURPHY, ELSPETH CAMPBELL. *God Cares When I Don't Like Myself.* Elgin, Il: David C. Cook Publishing Co., 1983. Paper. 23pp. Juvenile.

Boy fails to catch a ball during a Little League game, among other problems. But prayer revives his self-confidence. AGM

MYERS, WALTER D. *Me, Mop, and the Moondance Kid.* New York: Delacorte Press, 1988. Hardbound. 154pp. Juvenile.

Three Little Leaguers, two recently adopted and one trying desperately, play through a season. AGM

NAPJUS, JAMES. *Trouble On The Infield.* Princeton, NJ: D. Van Nostrand Co., 1967. Hardbound. 170pp. Juvenile.

Young shortstop learns lessons from his father and a troubled teammate. AGM

NEEDHAM, HENRY B. *The Double Squeeze.* Garden City, NY: Doubleday, Page & Co., 1915. Hardbound. 249pp. Young adult collection.

Introduction by Connie Mack who was a friend of Needham's and says while most of the book is great he doesn't like one of the stories, "Releasing the Film Princess," quite as much. Mack is clearly the model for Tris Ford, the manager of the "Giant-Killers" and the unifying character in the book's four stories. AGM

NEIGOFF, MIKE. *Nine Make a Team.* Chicago: Albert Whitman & Co., 1963. Hardbound. 128pp. Juvenile.

In junior high, Ronnie must learn to be a team player, with lessons also drawn from major league baseball and sports broadcasting. AGM

_____. *Two on First.* Chicago: Albert Whitman & Co., 1967. Hardbound. 127pp. Juvenile.

Captain and first baseman is divided when a talented new player transfers to his junior high. He plays 1B, too, and the competition divides the team. Our Hero moves to right. AGM

NEUGEBOREN, JAY. *Sam's Legacy.* New York: Holt, Rinehart and Winston, 1973. Hardbound. 370pp. Adult.

Novel that in part centers around an ex-Negro League player and his mysterious manuscript, "My life and death in the Negro American Baseball League. A slave narrative." BP

NEWLIN, PAUL. *It Had to be a Woman.* New York: Stein and Day, 1979. Hardbound. 222pp. Adult.

Darrell Morgan drives through the old Midwest trying to decide whether to commit suicide, as his boyhood idol Cincinnati Reds' catcher Willard Hershberger did during the 1940 season. No live baseball action, but Darrell is continually fantasizing himself as a star reliever coming in to save a Reds' game with Hershberger behind the plate. AGM

NICHOLS. *Baseball, A Fairy Story.* 1890. Paper. Juvenile. ag

A short story with cartoon sketches published as a booklet. AG. There is no listing of this as a book in major library data bases or the Library of Congress catalogue. AGM

NIGHBERT, DAVID F. *Strikezone.* New York: St. Martin's Press, 1989. Hardbound. 180pp. Adult mystery.

Two former minor league buddies (one of them had a cup of coffee) are victim and hero of this book. No game action, but some use of the well-thrown baseball. AGM

NIXON, JOAN LOWERY. *Danger in Dinosaur Valley.* New York: G. P. Putnam's Sons, 1978. Hardbound. 47pp. Juvenile.

A young dinosaur learns how to deal with the terrible Tyrannosaurus Rex after encountering the tiny Giants and a thing called the World Series. NUC

NYE, BUD. *Stay Loose.* Garden City, NY: Doubleday & Co., 1959. Hardbound. 261pp. Adult.

Social researchers try to create the perfect baseball team by bringing in athletic South Pacific Islanders who won't get choked up by the pressures of the game. AGM

O'CONNOR, PHILIP F. *Stealing Home.* New York: Alfred A. Knopf, Inc., 1979. Hardbound. 308pp. Adult.

Father in the midst of a family crisis volunteers to manage his son's Little League team. BP

OECHSLI, KELLY. *Mice at Bat.* New York: Harper & Row, 1986. Hardbound. 64pp. Juvenile.

A team of mice who live in a baseball stadium take over the park to play their rivals after the human game is over. AGM

OFFIT, SIDNEY. *The Boy Who Won the World Series.* New York: Lothrop, Lee & Shepard Co., 1960. Hardbound. 160pp. Juvenile.

Batboy joins his heroes as the youngest player ever to sign a major league contract. AGM

_____. *Soupbone.* New York: St. Martin's Press, 1963. Hardbound. 125pp. Juvenile.

Boys invent invisible formula to help their hero, fading major leaguer Soupbone McDexter, win the big game. He rejects their help and wins anyway. AGM

OLEKSY, WALTER. *Quacky and the Crazy Curve Ball.* New York: McGraw-Hill Book Co., 1981. Hardbound. 172pp. Juvenile.

Second book about 12-year-old detective Walter Quackenbush. He solves a mystery and makes a Little League team with the help of a big leaguer who's run away from his team. AGM

OLGIN, JOSEPH. *Little League Champions.* New York: E. P. Dutton & Co., 1954. Hardbound. 189pp. Juvenile.

Boys from both sides of the tracks unite to win the Little League World Series and ease the differences in their town. Foreword by Phil Rizzuto and a cameo in the story by Joe Dimaggio, who tells Our Hero he's made "the greatest play I've ever seen." AGM

_____. *Battery Feud.* Boston: Houghton Mifflin Co., 1959. Hardbound. 179pp. Juvenile.

A sequel to *Little League Champs,* Babe Ruth League pitcher and catcher duel all the way to the national finals in Griffith Stadium. AGM

OLSON, GENE. *Bonus Boy.* New York: Dodd, Mead & Co., 1963. Hardbound. 184pp. Juvenile.

Follows a star high school left-hander through his senior year as he deals with scouts, coaches, and relatives, all of them pushing him in different directions. AGM

_____. *Three Men on Third.* Philadelphia: Westminster Press, 1965. Hardbound. 174pp. Juvenile.

Star shortstop and captain's senior year of high school is about to begin when the coach leaves. The replacement knows nothing about baseball, and Our Hero also must coach this team of oddballs. AGM

O'ROURKE, FRANK. *Flashing Spikes.* New York: A. S. Barnes and Co., 1948. Hardbound. 245pp. Adult.

One of the earliest in a notable attempt by A. S. Barnes to produce serious baseball novels in a field that had previously been almost completely juvenile. In this, a rookie shortstop must prove himself in the heat of a pennant race. One character in the story echoes the Black Sox' Swede Risberg. AGM

_____. *The Team.* New York: A. S. Barnes and Co., 1949. Hardbound. 237pp. Adult.

The 1949 Phillies (a year from being the Whiz Kids) rendered in a very thin disguise—Robbie Ashton for Richie Ashburn, for example. Follows the team through the year told through the eyes of coach Benny (Bengough). Players on other teams are called by their real names, a device that held true through most of O'Rourke's books. AGM

_____. *Bonus Rookie.* New York: A. S. Barnes and Co., 1950. Hardbound. 179pp. Adult.

A sequel to *The Team,* a bonus player who should be in the minors must learn to pitch. The Phillies are still recognizable (and the similarity is acknowledged on the dust jacket), although this book isn't told by the Bengough character. Our Hero strikes out Gil Hodges to win the pennant. AGM

_____. *The Greatest Victory and Other Baseball Stories.* New York: A. S. Barnes and Co., 1950. Hardbound. 206pp. Adult collection.

A collection of a dozen of O'Rourke's baseball short stories. One story is titled "Flashing Spikes" and served as part of O'Rourke's book of the same name. AGM

_____. *Never Come Back.* New York: A. S. Barnes and Co., 1952. Hardbound. 182pp. Adult.

Player drinks himself out of the majors and then comes back with the Quakers/Phillies of *The Team* and *Bonus Rookie.* AGM

_____. *Nine Good Men.* New York: A. S. Barnes and Co., 1952. Hardbound. 215pp. Adult.

A manager searches for the title of the book. DJ

_____. *The Heavenly World Series.* New York: A. S. Barnes and Co., 1952. Hardbound. 192pp. Adult collection.

Nine short stories, from a match in heaven between National League and American League allstar teams managed by John McGraw and Miller Huggins to the last days of Joe Dimaggio. Also several stories involving his players from the Quakers/ Phillies of earlier books. AGM

_____. *The Catcher and the Manager.* New York: A. S. Barnes and Co., 1953. Hardbound. 144pp. Adult.

Two novellas, one the story of a catcher with marginal skills while the other traces the career of a hired-to-be-fired manager. AGM

OVERTON, MARK. *Jack Winters' Baseball Team.* New York: M. A. Donohue & Co., 1919. Hardbound. 183pp. Juvenile.

Jack's baseball team wins a series with a rival town despite gamblers and various other alarums. First of four books in the Jack Winters series. AGM

OWEN, FRANK, ed. *Teen-age Baseball Stories.* New York: Lantern Press, Inc., 1948. Hardbound. 255pp. Juvenile collection.

A collection of magazine stories. A paperback version was published as *Baseball Stories.* AGM

PAINE, HORACE. *Jack Standfast's Keen Batting.* Cleveland: Boys Best Weekly No. 17, 1909. Magazine. 64pp. Young adult. el

For the first year or so of its life, *Boys Best Weekly* was not dated. It endured about a year and half, ending with the last listed here. EL

_____. *Jack Standfast's Sacrifice Hit.* Cleveland: Boys Best Weekly No. 18, 1909. Magazine. 64pp. Young adult. el

_____. *Jack Standfast's Great Pitching.* Cleveland: Boys Best Weekly No. 20, 1909. Magazine. 64pp. Young adult. el

_____. *Jack Standfast's Hard Luck.* Cleveland: Boys Best Weekly No. 46, April 1, 1910. Magazine. 32pp. Young adult.

_____. *Jack Standfast's Fidelity.* Cleveland: Boys Best Weekly No. 49, April 22, 1910. Magazine. 32pp. Young adult. el

_____. *Jack Standfast's First Game.* Cleveland: Boys Best Weekly No. 50, April 29, 1910. Magazine. 32pp. Young adult. el

_____. *Jack Standfast's Infield Stars.* Cleveland: Boys Best Weekly No. 51, May 6, 1910. Magazine. 32pp. Young adult. el

_____. *Jack Standfast to the Rescue.* Cleveland: Boys Best Weekly No. 53, May 20, 1910. Magazine. 32pp. Young adult.

_____. *Jack Standfast's Clever Catch.* Cleveland: Boys Best Weekly No. 54, May 27, 1910. Magazine. 32pp. Young adult. el

_____. *Jack Standfast in the Box Again.* Cleveland: Boys Best Weekly No. 55, June 3, 1910. Magazine. 32pp. Young adult. el

_____. *Jack Standfast's Baseball Signals.* Cleveland: Boys Best Weekly No. 58, June 24, 1910. Magazine. 32pp. Young adult. el

PAINE, RALPH D. *The Fugitive Freshman.* New York: Charles Scribner's Sons, 1910. Hardbound. 304pp. Juvenile.

Pitcher and son of a rich man is deep in debt and fearful he is about to flunk his freshman year at college for the second time. He flees, winds up building a railroad across the Florida Keys, pitches for the team there, becomes a man, and reconciles with pater. He then returns to college baseball triumphs. Several baseball chapters. AGM

PALLAS, NORVIN. *The Baseball Mystery.* New York: Ives Washburn, Inc., 1963. Hardbound. 147pp. Juvenile mystery.

Eleventh of fifteen Ted Wilford mysteries. The young reporter exposes gambling at a state-wide amateur tournament. AGM

PALMER, BERNARD. *Danny Orlis and Jim Morgan's Scholarship.* Chicago: Moody Press, 1968. Paper. 125pp. Juvenile. jo

PARISH, PEGGY. *Play Ball, Amelia Bedelia.* New York: Harper & Row, 1972. Hardbound. 64pp. Juvenile.

One in a series of books about an all-too-literal maid. In this, she gets involved in a neighborhood ball game. AGM

PARK, BARBARA. *Skinnybones.* New York: Alfred A. Knopf, Inc., 1982. Hardbound. 112pp. Juvenile.

Alex Frankovitch is a very small smart mouth who has managed to antagonize Little League star T. J. Stoner and then must face him in The Big Game. AGM

PARKER, ROBERT B. *Mortal Stakes.* Boston: Houghton Mifflin Co., 1975. Hardbound. 172pp. Adult mystery.

One of the early Spenser detective novels. Hired by the Boston Red Sox, he must determine if the team's star pitcher is throwing games. No baseball action but interesting as a meditation on the nature of the professional ethic. TS

PARKINSON, ETHELYN M. *Good Old Archibald.* New York: Abingdon Press, 1960. Hardbound. 160pp. Juvenile.

Boarding school boys have various adventures leading up to The Big Game. AGM

PARKS, EDD WINFIELD. *Safe on Second.* Indianapolis: Bobbs-Merrill Co., 1953. Hardbound. 199pp. Juvenile.

Practice, practice, practice earns reward for Little League second baseman. AGM

PATTEN, GILBERT. *The Rockspur Nine.* New York: Street & Smith Publications, Inc., 1900. Hardbound. 287pp. Young adult.

Gilbert Patten, actually George William Patten, is most famous as the creator of Frank and Dick Merriwell, which he wrote under the Burt L. Standish pseudonym. A boy fascinated with dime novels, he grew into one of their most famous writers. He did a number of other series and wrote for most of the popular publishers of his day, although he developed an antipathy for Stratemeyer. He later became the editor of *Top Notch,* a popular weekly, and many of his books first appeared as serials in it. This is the first of three books in the Rockspur Athletic series and Patten's first full-length book. Its main character shares some of Patten's own history—an enthusiastic ball player on a Maine town team hampered by a tall and gawky frame and a mother who insists on not fighting back. But John Smith wins respect from his teammates and a place pitching for the town team. AGM

_____. *Bill Bruce of Harvard.* New York: Dodd, Mead and Co., 1910. Hardbound. 371pp. Young adult.

Probably the most interesting of Patten's books. It contains many incidents with echoes from Patten's own life. Our Hero's father, a large, strong, working man with strict religious views, is felled by an illness. Our Hero also gets involved in a three-team summer league in Maine full of college players risking their amateur status for the summer money. Patten managed in such a league for a couple of seasons. One of his players was future Red Sox catcher and manager Bill "Rough" Carrigan. Also, though not an echo of Patten's life, there is a seduction and eventual death at an abortion clinic between the lines, highly unusual for American popular fiction of this time. Our Hero preserves his amateur status and returns to Harvard. Appeared as a serial in *The Popular Magazine* in 1909. AGM

_____. *Clif Stirling, Captain of the Nine*. Philadelphia: David McKay Co., 1910. Hardbound. 322pp. Young adult.

First of five Clif Stirling books. It originally appeared as a serial in *Top Notch* magazine in 1910. For some reason, Patten signed them J(ulian). G. St. Dare in *Top Notch* and then used his own name when they came out as books. AGM

_____. *The College Rebel*. New York: Barse & Hopkins, 1914. Hardbound. 313pp. Young adult.

Second of the six-book College Life series, which was also serialized in *Top Notch*. Only one game is described, but it's the culmination of the book. Overly impressed with the independence won from his father in the first book of the series, *Boltwood of Yale*, Roger Boltwood rejects an offer from the captain of the Yale nine. He slowly comes to an understanding of real independence and joins the varsity barely in time to pitch them over Harvard. AGM

_____. *Clif Stirling, Sophomore at Stormbridge*. Philadelphia: David McKay Co., 1916. Hardbound. 333pp. Young adult. nuc

Last of the Clif Stirling series. DJ

_____. *The Call of the Varsity*. New York: Barse & Hopkins, 1920. Hardbound. 203pp. Young adult.

Fourth of the College Life series. Early in the season, Boltwood hurts his arm. He then recruits an unworthy to take his place but recovers later in the season. AGM

_____. *Sons of Old Eli*. New York: Barse & Hopkins, 1923. Hardbound. 248pp. Young adult.

Fifth of the College Life series and following immediately on the heels of the previous. Boltwood beats Harvard twice and then turns pro. He helps a college friend turn around a struggling minor league club. AGM

(Written as GORDON BRADDOCK.) *Rex Kingdon of Ridgewood High*. New York: Hurst & Co., 1914. Hardbound. 310pp. Young adult.

First of the five-volume Rex Kingdon series. Rex shows up in Ridgewood with a mysterious set of skills, makes the high school baseball team as a catcher, wins the Big Game, and breaks up a smuggling ring. AGM

_____. *Rex Kingdon Behind the Bat*. New York: Hurst & Co., 1916. Hardbound. 321pp. Young adult.

Fourth in the series. Rex is now at Walcott Hall, a prep school where he is captain of the nine. He reforms several obstreperous characters and makes them talented contributors to the team. AGM

_____. *Rex Kingdon on Storm Island*. New York: Hurst & Co., 1917. Hardbound. 305pp. Young adult.

Rex and some chums take up summer residence on what is supposedly a deserted island off the Maine coast only to find another group of boys has gained residence by claiming to be Rex's crowd. A sometimes bitter rivalry ensues, but Rex's team wins the baseball games. Our Hero even turns the other team's sneering star into a recruit for Walcott Hall when the summer's over. Last in the series. AGM

(Written as MORGAN SCOTT.) *Rival Pitchers of Oakdale*. New York: Hurst & Co., 1911. Hardbound. 311pp. Young adult.

Third in the six-book Oakdale series. Jealousy disrupts a prep school team until two disgruntled pitchers come to the light. AGM

_____. *The New Boys at Oakdale*. New York: Hurst & Co., 1913. Hardbound. 311pp. Young adult.

Last of the Oakdale series. The captain of the Oakdale team struggles and succeeds in getting a potential star to be a team player. Most of the characters carry over from the earlier book, but the two protagonists are new. AGM

(Written as BURT L. STANDISH.) *Frank Merriwell's School Days*. New York: Street & Smith Publications, Inc., 1901. Hardbound. 302pp. Young adult.

Under this pseudonym, Patten created Frank Merriwell and, when Frank grew too old for college, his brother Dick. Frank was the apotheosis of the truth-telling, handsome, athletic, modest, fun-loving, etc., boys' hero, and Dick was more of the same. The brothers had adventures all over the world, but chiefly at Fardale Academy, a military school, and Yale. The Merriwell stories were originally published in *Tip Top Weekly* as dime novels. Patten wrote virtually all from April 18, 1896 until 1911, when he burned out on the weekly grind. For about five months in 1900, the series was turned over to John H. Whitson (who did his own Jack Lightfoot series a few years later), but Patten plotted the episodes and edited Whitson's work. This was while Patten wrote the Rockspur series. When Patten finally quit the Merriwells for good, it began to deteriorate even more quickly as it passed among Street & Smith stable writers Whitson, William Wallace Cook, and William A. Wolf. The dime novels were rechristened *The New Tip Top Weekly* soon after, and Frank's son, Frank Merriwell, Jr., appeared as a reincarnation of father and uncle. The Merriwell family saga ran for 823 episodes under Patten and another 145 before *New Tip Top* died in 1915. Beginning in 1898, Street & Smith began to turn the dime novels into paperback books, each usually containing three to five of the dime novels, pared and rewritten to make them flow. There were eventually 245 Merriwell books, in which all but 36 of the dime novels were collected. Street & Smith, and later other publishers, began to issue the books in cloth covers. These never sold well, presumably because the cheaper paperbacks were so widely available, and only 28 Merriwells were published in hardbound. The Merriwell books were reprinted into the 1930s, and some were even reissued in the 1980s. Also in the 1930s, the saga was converted into a comic strip and radio show. There is some baseball in many of the books, and Street & Smith did love to put a baseball cover on anything with the slightest bit of the sport inside. With reprints, Street & Smith updated the covers, and it is possible to see uniforms and playing fields change over the years in the illustrations. Listed here are the Merriwell books that contain baseball and the three dime novels that contained baseball material but were never bound into books. Finding all the Merriwell

books is difficult. I have, however, seen all the Merriwell dime novels and using Guinon (see Sources) determined which books should have baseball content. These are noted as dn in the source space of each entry. The books are listed in the order in which the Merriwell stories they contain originally appeared as dime novels. Many of the early paperback books were released in cloth covers several years later. The publishing information is thus about the cloth edition, but it is placed chronologically where the paperback edition appeared. AGM. In this first book, Frank shows up at Fardale and helps the plebes beat the upperclassmen at baseball, the game taking up part of the book's final third. FP

_____. *Frank Merriwell at Yale.* Philadelphia: David McKay Co., 1903. Hardbound. 383pp. Young adult. dnfp
Frank's freshman year at Yale. Concerns mostly incidents of freshmen v. sophomores, with much fond description of Yale student customs and traditions and some sports competition, including a baseball game against Harvard. FP

_____. *Frank Merriwell's Races.* Philadelphia: David McKay Co., 1903. Hardbound. 288pp. Young adult. nucfp
A little baseball in a book dominated by horse racing, wrestling, crew, and running the mile. FP

_____. *Frank Merriwell's Skill.* Philadelphia: David McKay Co., 1903. Hardbound. 315pp. Young adult.
Returning from a trip Out West, Frank's party of nine, called the "Yale Combine," plays an exhibition game against Fort Worth of the Southern League, compete in a horse race at Churchill Downs, and elsewhere in other sports. FP

_____. *Frank Merriwell's Danger.* New York: Street & Smith Publications, Inc., 1897. Paper. 256pp. Young adult. dnnuc
The first mention of Frank's famous "double shoot," a pitch that broke in two directions on its way to the plate. Includes Yale v. Princeton and Harvard after Frank is named captain. AGM

_____. *Frank Merriwell's Cruise.* Philadelphia: David McKay Co., 1898. Hardbound. 246pp. Young adult. dnnuc

Includes one brief ball game as Frank gets off the boat to join a town team. AGM

_____. *Frank Merriwell's Struggle.* New York: Street & Smith Publications, Inc., 1898. Paper. 213pp. Young adult. fp

Mostly concerned with various adventures sailing Frank's yacht along the Maine coast. In one chapter, Frank amazes local players at a practice by throwing his double shoot. FP

_____. *Frank Merriwell's Duel.* New York: Street & Smith Publications, Inc., 1899. Paper. 244pp. Young adult. fp

Frank and Yale friends adventure in France and England, then return to New England where Frank manages the Maplewood team seeking entry as the fourth team in the (summer) Trolley League. Baseball occupies most of last third. FP

_____. *Frank Merriwell's Double Shot.* New York: Street & Smith Publications, Inc., 1899. Paper. 272pp. Young adult.

This book picks up in the middle of the tournament that Frank's team must sweep to get into the Trolley League. The book then follows the summer league season. Frank refuses to sell the secret of his secret pitch, now called the "double shot." Mostly baseball. AGM

_____. *Frank Merriwell's Baseball Victories.* New York: Street & Smith Publications, Inc., 1899. Paper. 251pp. Young adult.

Maplewood begins to climb in the standings helped by, among other things, a one-armed shortstop. AGM

_____. *Frank Merriwell's Confidence.* New York: Street & Smith Publications, Inc., 1899. Paper. 254pp. Young adult. dnnuc

Finishes the Trolley League season in a blaze of glory. Mostly baseball. FP

_____. *Frank Merriwell's Luck, or, A Pinch Hit.* New York: Street & Smith Publications, Inc., 1900. Paper. 286pp. Young adult. nucdn

Two games described, a chapter apiece. One is a game deliberately played by silly rules. AGM

_____. *Frank Merriwell's Phantom.* New York: Street & Smith Publications, Inc., 1900. Paper. 319pp. Young adult. fp

The spring of Frank's junior year, much baseball, culminating in Yale v. Princeton. FP

_____. *Frank Merriwell's Faith.* Philadelphia: David McKay Co., 1900. Hardbound. 320pp. Young adult.

Frank and "Merriwell's Yale Athletic Team" summer in the Adirondacks, play baseball v. the "University Nine," as well as other sports. Seven of 26 chapters have baseball. FP

_____. *Frank Merriwell's Victories.* Philadelphia: David McKay Co., 1900. Hardbound. 319pp. Young adult.

Frank continues a summer tour with his chums. Between kidnappings, etc., the Merriwells defeat a minor league team from Toronto and what is identified as the Chicago National League club. Frank makes one of his patented sudden reappearances to beat the "Colts," as the Cubs were known then. AGM

_____. *Frank Merriwell's Iron Nerve.* New York: Street & Smith Publications, Inc., 1900. Paper. 306pp. Young adult. dnnuc

Includes rodeo, archery, and baseball games in Denver and somewhere else Out West. AGM

_____. *Frank Merriwell in Kentucky.* New York: Street & Smith Publications, Inc., 1900. Paper. 320pp. Young adult. fp

Frank and the Yalies are still on summer vacation and playing teams in Indiana and Kentucky. A fair amount of baseball. FP

_____. *Frank Merriwell's Club.* New York: Street & Smith Publications, Inc., 1901. Paper. 316pp. Young adult.

Includes an indoor baseball game in Baltimore, less than a quarter of the book. AGM

_____. *Frank Merriwell's False Friend.* Philadelphia: David McKay Co., 1901. Hardbound. 315pp. Young adult.

The book is built around spring practice and a Southern trip for the Yale nine. But there are only three innings of baseball action as Frank returns from being lured away and wins the game against the University of Virginia. AGM

_____. *Frank Merriwell's Strong Arm*. New York: Street & Smith Publications, Inc., 1901. Paper. 319pp. Young adult. dnnuc

One drunken game at night after selections are made for Yale's secret societies. Also, two games against Princeton. AGM

_____. *Frank Merriwell as Coach*. New York: Street & Smith Publications, Inc., 1901. Paper. 309pp. Young adult. dnnuc

Track, crew, and another defeat of the Harvard nine. AGM

_____. *Frank Merriwell's Brother*. Philadelphia: David McKay Co., 1901. Hardbound. 314pp. Young adult. dnnuc

Frank finds he has a brother. Dick proves a baseball wonder. AGM

_____. *Frank Merriwell's Marvel*. New York: Street & Smith Publications, Inc., 1901. Paper. 319pp. Young adult.

Frank and his touring baseball team, including 13-year-old Dick, play teams in the Rocky Mountains, going West. FP

_____. *Frank Merriwell's Support*. New York: Street & Smith Publications, Inc., 1901. Paper. 322pp. Young adult. dnnuc

Merriwell's traveling team v. the Philadelphia Athletics plus town all-stars of Omaha, St. Paul, and Minneapolis. Winds up with game in New York against team of Frank's old chums. Lots of baseball. AGM

_____. *Dick Merriwell's Revenge*. New York: Street & Smith Publications, Inc., 1902. Paper. 314pp. Young adult. dnnuc

A freshman at Fardale, Dick makes the varsity as a pitcher. AGM

_____. *Dick Merriwell's Ruse*. New York: Street & Smith Publications, Inc., 1902. Paper. 313pp. Young adult. dnnuc

Several games, more adventures, including a suspension and an enemy blowing up the mound with Dick on it. He finishes the game. AGM

_____. *Dick Merriwell's Delivery*. New York: Street & Smith Publications, Inc., 1902. Paper. 316pp. Young adult. nucdn

Dick moves up to captain. Includes an alumni game as Frank and his alumni chums return to win in 14 innings. AGM

_____. *Dick Merriwell's Wonders*. New York: Street & Smith Publications, Inc., 1902. Paper. 318pp. Young adult.

With Fardale's season over, Dick works up a couple of games against the seasoned Uniontown Athletic Association team. AGM

_____. *Frank Merriwell's Honor*. New York: Street & Smith Publications, Inc., 1902. Paper. 320pp. Young adult. nucdn

With school over, Frank recruits Dick to join him out in mining country for a season in the Mad River Baseball League. AGM

_____. *Dick Merriwell's Diamond*. New York: Street & Smith Publications, Inc., 1902. Paper. 313pp. Young adult.

Frank's Tip Top team stays ahead despite a devious league president who tries to put Dick on another team. Diamond of the title is an actual gem. AGM

_____. *Frank Merriwell's Winners*. New York: Street & Smith Publications, Inc., 1902. Paper. 317pp. Young adult. dnnuc

Triumph in the Mad River Baseball League, both on the field and off. AGM

_____. *Dick Merriwell's Backstop*. New York: Street & Smith Publications, Inc., 1903. Paper. 309pp. Young adult. nucdn

Winter baseball practice indoors as Dick gets ready for his second season at Fardale. Season begins, several baseball chapters. AGM

_____. *Dick Merriwell's Western Mission*. New York: Street & Smith Publications, Inc., 1903. Paper. 316pp. Young adult. dnnuc

Fardale wins its league despite the machinations of Chester Arlington—a villain for many episodes and brother of the beauteous June. AGM

_____. *Frank Merriwell's Rescue.* New York: Street & Smith Publications, Inc., 1903. Paper. 320pp. Young adult. dnjrc

Most of this book is Frank dealing with various scoundrels around his mine. At the end, Dick arrives from Fardale for summer baseball, and Chester Arlington turns up managing a rival team. One game. AGM

_____. *Frank Merriwell's Encounter.* New York: Street & Smith Publications, Inc., 1903. Paper. 308pp. Young adult. dnjrc

Dick and Frank duel various Chester Arlington teams Out West. AGM

_____. *Dick Merriwell's Marked Money.* New York: Street & Smith Publications, Inc., 1903. Paper. 304pp. Young adult. dnnuc

The summer tour continues. Chester conspires to take away the Merriwell mine. A new and long-running character, Cap'n Wiley, appears with his Wind Jammers baseball team. The Wind Jammers actually beat Dick in one game. AGM

_____. *Frank Merriwell's Nomads.* New York: Street & Smith Publications, Inc., 1903. Paper. 320pp. Young adult. fpnuc

Frank's team plays baseball in the Rockies, in Illinois, and in Boston v. the American League team. FP

_____. *Dick Merriwell's Grit.* New York: Street & Smith Publications, Inc., 1904. Paper. 320pp. Young adult. dnnuc

Dick begins his third season at Fardale, winning despite a sore arm. AGM

_____. *Dick Merriwell's Assurance.* New York: Street & Smith Publications, Inc., 1904. Paper. 320pp. Young adult. dnnuc

Fardale continues to triumph. AGM

_____. *Dick Merriwell's Long Slide.* New York: Street & Smith Publications, Inc., 1904. Paper. 316pp. Young adult. dnnuc

Fardale concludes a winning season, then Dick joins Frank's summer team, which defeats Manhattan College. AGM

_____. *Frank Merriwell's Rough Deal.* New York: Street & Smith Publications, Inc., 1904. Paper. 320pp. Young adult. dnnuc

Frank's team defeats Harvard and Yale, then Frank gets an offer to return to Maplewood of the 1899 books. He can't, so he sends Dick to manage a team in the Trolley League. Maplewood rejects Dick as too young, so he and his chums join the Fairhaven team in the league. AGM

_____. *Dick Merriwell's Threat.* New York: Street & Smith Publications, Inc., 1904. Paper. 320pp. Young adult. nucdn

Fairhaven fights its way into contention. AGM

_____. *Dick Merriwell's Persistence.* New York: Street & Smith Publications, Inc., 1904. Paper. 317pp. Young adult. dnnuc

Fairhaven stays near the top despite the machinations of Maplewood big shots trying to cover up for spurning Dick. AGM

_____. *Dick Merriwell's Day.* New York: Street & Smith Publications, Inc., 1904. Paper. 310pp. Young adult. dnnuc

Fairhaven wins the Trolley League. AGM

_____. *Frank Merriwell's Pride.* New York: Street & Smith Publications, Inc., 1905. Paper. 315pp. Young adult. dnnuc

Includes a spring-training game v. the Cubs in Los Angeles. AGM

_____. *Frank Merriwell's Challengers.* New York: Street & Smith Publications, Inc., 1905. Paper. 318pp. Young adult. dnjrc

Includes a game against Stanford University. AGM

_____. *Frank Merriwell's Endurance.* New York: Street & Smith Publications, Inc., 1905. Paper. 320pp. Young adult. dnnuc

Frank's barnstormers play town teams in Iowa and Wisconsin. AGM

_____. *Dick Merriwell's Cleverness.* New York: Street & Smith Publications, Inc., 1905. Paper. 320pp. Young adult. dnnuc

On a tour of Asia, Dick's team defeats Japanese teams. AGM

_____. *Frank Merriwell's Marriage.* New York: Street & Smith Publications, Inc., 1905. Paper. 320pp. Young adult. dnnuc

One interesting baseball section in which Frank's boys defeat a team formed from last-minute cuts by major league teams. References are made to several real players and managers. Also, Frank marries. AGM

_____. *Dick Merriwell, the Wizard*. New York: Street & Smith Publications, Inc., 1905. Paper. 319pp. Young adult. djnuc
After adventures recrossing the Pacific, Dick's team plays in San Francisco and Out West. AGM

_____. *Dick Merriwell's Stroke*. New York: Street & Smith Publications, Inc., 1905. Paper. 304pp. Young adult. dnnuc
More barnstorming. Dick is saved from using a bat packed with nitroglycerine. AGM

_____. *Dick Merriwell's Polo Team*. New York: Street & Smith Publications, Inc., 1906. Paper. 311pp. Young adult. nucdn
One game of indoor baseball, played in February. AGM

_____. *Frank Merriwell's New Boy*. New York: Street & Smith Publications, Inc., 1906. Paper. 309pp. Young adult. dnnuc
Frank is now a master at Farnham Hall, a rival of his own Fardale, and he puts together a county championship team. AGM

_____. *Dick Merriwell's Home Run*. New York: Street & Smith Publications, Inc., 1906. Paper. 320pp. Young adult. dnnuc
Dick, at Fardale, beats Frank's Farnham team. AGM

_____. *Dick Merriwell's Dare*. New York: Street & Smith Publications, Inc., 1906. Paper. 311pp. Young adult. nucdn
Much prep school baseball with Fardale, Farnham, and rivals. AGM

_____. *Frank Merriwell's Son*. New York: Street & Smith Publications, Inc., 1906. Paper. 317pp. Young adult. nucdn
Frank Merriwell, Jr., born. Frank and some of his old athletic mates get in some games against the school boys. AGM

_____. *Dick Merriwell's Team Mate*. New York: Street & Smith Publications, Inc., 1906. Paper. 315pp. Young adult. dnnuc
Beginning of a summer season in the Catskill-like Blue Hills. Several games. AGM

_____. *Frank Merriwell's Leaguers*. New York: Street & Smith Publications, Inc., 1906. Paper. 310pp. Young adult. dnnuc
Frank goes about setting up a summer league in the Blue Hills. AGM

_____. *Frank Merriwell's Happy Camp*. New York: Street & Smith Publications, Inc., 1906. Paper. 309pp. Young adult. dnnuc
Frank's Happy Camp team struggles in the league. Dick stars. AGM

_____. *Dick Merriwell's Influence*. New York: Street & Smith Publications, Inc., 1906. Paper. 305pp. Young adult. dnnuc
The league is won despite blackguard tricks. Then a trip to New York for a game against the New York college all-stars. AGM

_____. *Dick Merriwell, Freshman*. New York: Street & Smith Publications, Inc., 1906. Paper. 305pp. Young adult. nucdn
Dick begins his Yale career. A small amount of fall baseball at the beginning. Mostly hazing and other Yale customs. AGM

_____. *Dick Merriwell's Regret*. New York: Street & Smith Publications, Inc., 1907. Paper. 311pp. Young adult. dnnuc
Part of one chapter is a description of spring practice. AGM

_____. *Dick Merriwell's Magnetism*. New York: Street & Smith Publications, Inc., 1907. Paper. 317pp. Young adult. dnnuc
Dick's signals are sold to rivals. The culprit must be found. AGM

_____. *Dick Merriwell's Backers*. New York: Street & Smith Publications, Inc., 1907. Paper. 314pp. Young adult. dnnuc
Freshman baseball v. Tufts and Williams. Dick also coaches varsity pitchers to success. AGM

_____. *Dick Merriwell's Best Work*. New York: Street & Smith Publications, Inc., 1907. Paper. 320pp. Young adult. nucdn
Skulduggery and the defeat of the Columbia and Harvard frosh. AGM

_____. *Dick Merriwell's Distrust*. New York: Street & Smith Publications, Inc., 1907. Paper. 320pp. Young adult. nucdn

In one section, Dick beats the Harvard freshmen again. AGM

———. *Dick Merriwell's Debt.* New York: Street & Smith Publications, Inc., 1907. Paper. 309pp. Young adult. nucdn
Off to summer baseball in Maine. Dick and the chums are caught in a business dispute over the field they play on. Several games. AGM

———. *Dick Merriwell's Mastery.* New York: Street & Smith Publications, Inc., 1907. Paper. 309pp. Young adult. dnnuc
The summer league rivalry continues amidst a labor dispute. AGM

———. *Dick Merriwell Adrift.* New York: Street & Smith Publications, Inc., 1907. Paper. 311pp. Young adult. nucdn
One baseball game, Pineville v. Smoketown, wrapping up the summer league season. AGM

———. *Frank Merriwell's Hard Case.* New York: Street & Smith Publications, Inc., 1908. Paper. 318pp. Young adult. dnnuc
Back to Frank at Farnham, where he's training some promising but inexperienced youngsters. AGM

———. *Dick Merriwell's Stand.* New York: Street & Smith Publications, Inc., 1908. Paper. 320pp. Young adult. nucdn
Dick fights anti-Semitism in his first year on the Yale varsity, sticking up for team member Joe Cohen—interesting, as earlier Merriwell works had referred to a character's ''Sheeny-like voice'' and used a number of Jewish stereotypes. AGM

———. *Dick Merriwell Doubted.* New York: Street & Smith Publications, Inc., 1908. Paper. 322pp. Young adult. dnnuc
Dick's shoulder is hurt, but coaching and pinch-hitting, he leads Yale over Princeton, Brown, and Syracuse. AGM

———. *Frank Merriwell's Steadying Hand.* New York: Street & Smith Publications, Inc., 1908. Paper. 319pp. Young adult. dnnuc
Frank's Farnham boys beat a pro barnstorming team. AGM

———. *Dick Merriwell's Example.* New York: Street & Smith Publications, Inc., 1908. Paper. 318pp. Young adult. dnnuc
Dick wins two games v. Harvard, evades death, leads crew, etc. AGM

———. *Dick Merriwell's Rally.* New York: Tip Top Weekly No. 672, February 27, 1909. Magazine. 32pp. Young adult.
Indoor baseball, as Dick leads Yale to victory and silences those who question his leadership. This and the next are the only two baseball Merriwell dime novels that were not collected into books. AGM

———. *Dick Merriwell's Eye.* New York: Tip Top Weekly No. 679, April 17, 1909. Magazine. 32pp. Young adult.
Early baseball practice with much emphasis on how to become a 300 (no decimal point) hitter. Also, see previous entry. AGM

———. *Dick Merriwell's Honors.* New York: Street & Smith Publications, Inc., 1909. Paper. 307pp. Young adult. dnnuc
Yale plays and defeats Holy Cross and one of its dirty players. Dick then rescues the bad sport from drowning. AGM

———. *Frank Merriwell's Wizard.* New York: Street & Smith Publications, Inc., 1909. Paper. 299pp. Young adult. dnnuc
Frank trains a new star pitcher over the course of Farnham's season. AGM

———. *Dick Merriwell's Race.* New York: Street & Smith Publications, Inc., 1909. Paper. 303pp. Young adult. dnnuc
Dick has various adventures camping, then returns to find and win a challenge from a cowboy team in Nebraska. AGM

———. *Frank Merriwell at Phantom Lake.* New York: Street & Smith Publications, Inc., 1909. Paper. 313pp. Young adult. dnjrc
Frank starts a summer camp and coaches his boys to wins over a neighboring town. AGM

———. *Dick Merriwell a Winner.* New York: Street & Smith Publications, Inc., 1909. Paper. 315pp. Young adult. dnnuc

Dick forms a ranch team to play the local town. Includes a tall tale of an armless pitcher. AGM

———. *Frank Merriwell's Old Form.* New York: Street & Smith Publications, Inc., 1910. Paper. 313pp. Young adult. dnnuc
Back from a winter in Latin America, Frank and his chums put together a team in Texas to play some of the local talent. AGM

———. *Dick Merriwell, Game to the Last.* New York: Street & Smith Publications, Inc., 1910. Paper. 316pp. Young adult. dnjrc
Ivy League baseball. Dick collapses on the mound. There are rumors he's an opium addict, but it turns out to be merely typhoid. Yale beats Harvard yet again. AGM

———. *Dick Merriwell, Motor King.* New York: Street & Smith Publications, Inc., 1910. Paper. 316pp. Young adult. dnnuc
Mostly about cars and racing, but one game described at length. AGM

———. *Dick Merriwell's Tussle.* New York: Street & Smith Publications, Inc., 1910. Paper. 307pp. Young adult. dnnuc
Various adventures. A game takes up a couple of chapters. AGM

———. *Dick Merriwell's Aero Dash.* New York: Street & Smith Publications, Inc., 1910. Paper. 306pp. Young adult. dnnuc
Two baseball sections. In one, Dick's trusty right arm is hurt, so he pitches and wins with his left. The other appears to be a crib from *Frank Merriwell's Marriage* (1905). AGM

———. *Dick Merriwell's Perception.* New York: Street & Smith Publications, Inc., 1911. Paper. 320pp. Young adult. djnuc
Dick can't be reelected captain but he's still the leader. Yale v. Cornell and Williams early in the season. AGM

———. *Dick Merriwell's Detective Work.* New York: Street & Smith Publications, Inc., 1911. Paper. 320pp. Young adult. dnnuc
Dick is knocked out of the box! Fordham manages it as Dick puzzles over who the familiar face on the Fordham team is. He's a ringer. AGM

———. *Dick Merriwell's Commencement.* New York: Street & Smith Publications, Inc., 1911. Paper. 320pp. Young adult. dnjrc
Dick retains his amateur status despite a plot and defeats Harvard. Frank returns for Dick's commencement, is recognized and cheered during the Harvard game. AGM

———. *Dick Merriwell's Coolness.* New York: Street & Smith Publications, Inc., 1911. Paper. 315pp. Young adult. nucdn
Off to summer baseball where Dick and his mates are beaten by a rube pitcher who doffs his disguise to reveal—Frank. Baseball in opening chapters only. AGM

———. *Dick Merriwell's Reliance.* New York: Street & Smith Publications, Inc., 1911. Paper. 320pp. Young adult. djnuc
Over a couple of chapters, Dick admires a young pitcher and wants to send him to Yale. But the young man, Jim Phillips, disappears. AGM

———. *Dick Merriwell's Counsel.* New York: Street & Smith Publications, Inc., 1912. Paper. 314pp. Young adult. nucdn
Since *Dick Merriwell's Reliance,* Patten had quit writing the stories. Dick has been named coach for all Yale teams in all sports and has found the Jim Phillips lost in *Reliance.* This contains hares and hounds, hockey, trapshooting and, finally in the last few chapters, spring baseball. AGM

———. *Dick Merriwell, Universal Coach.* New York: Street & Smith Publications, Inc., 1912. Paper. 320pp. Young adult. nucdn
On Southern training swing, Yale nine plays Georgetown, University of Virginia, West Point, survives bomb plot, etc. AGM

———. *Dick Merriwell's Varsity Nine.* New York: Street & Smith Publications, Inc., 1912. Paper. 312pp. Young adult. agnuc
Yale nine v. Penn, Cornell, Princeton and Michigan, winning one when Dick's star pitcher injures one arm and must use the other. AGM

———. *Dick Merriwell's Heroic Players.* New York: Street & Smith Publications, Inc., 1912. Paper. 307pp. Young adult. nucdn
Series against Harvard for championship. AGM

_____. *Frank Merriwell, Jr., Tested.* New York: Street & Smith Publications, Inc., 1912. Paper. 320pp. Young adult.

The first of the Frank Merriwell, Jr. books. He's often called Chip as in "Chip off the old. . . ." Out West, he deals with a dastard and plays a couple of games against town teams. AGM

_____. *Frank Merriwell, Jr.'s Conquests.* New York: Street & Smith Publications, Inc., 1912. Paper. 316pp. Young adult.

More of same. Bad guys and two ball games. AGM

_____. *Frank Merriwell, Jr.'s Rivals.* New York: Street & Smith Publications, Inc., 1912. Paper. 311pp. Young adult. nucdn

More wild West mining adventures. One ball game. AGM

_____. *Frank Merriwell, Jr. in Arizona.* New York: Street & Smith Publications, Inc., 1912. Paper. 313pp. Young adult. dnjrc

Though it's December, Chip's where a game is playable. Ophir beats Gold Hill on a last-inning home run by Our Hero. AGM

_____. *Frank Merriwell, Jr. in the Desert.* New York: Street & Smith Publications, Inc., 1913. Paper. 311pp. Young adult. nucdn

Includes another game between mining camp teams. AGM

_____. *Frank Merriwell, Jr.'s Fight for Right.* New York: Street & Smith Publications, Inc., 1913. Paper. 313pp. Young adult.

Boxing, track, and rowing all figure in this book, still set in the West. It winds up with a seven-chapter baseball game. AGM

_____. *Frank Merriwell, Jr.'s Athletic Team.* New York: Street & Smith Publications, Inc., 1913. Paper. 315pp. Young adult. djnuc

Preparatory to a summer athletic swing, Chip and the gang have adventures. Couple of games described. AGM

_____. *Frank Merriwell, Jr.'s Peck of Trouble.* New York: Street & Smith Publications, Inc., 1913. Paper. 314pp. Young adult. djnuc

Many scheduled games delayed for mysterious reasons, but finally the series against the Mavericks is finished. AGM

_____. *Frank Merriwell, Jr.'s Ordeal.* New York: Street & Smith Publications, Inc., 1913. Paper. 311pp. Young adult. djnuc

One extra-inning game takes up several chapters. AGM

_____. *Frank Merriwell, Jr., Birdman.* New York: Street & Smith Publications, Inc., 1913. Paper. 320pp. Young adult. djnuc

Among other daring deeds, Chip hits a bad guy with a pitch to help solve a mystery. Also features a boxing kangaroo who is not named Matilda. AGM

_____. *Frank Merriwell, Jr. on the Border.* New York: Street & Smith Publications, Inc., 1914. Paper. 308pp. Young adult. nucdn

One Christmas Day ball game described. AGM

_____. *Owen Clancy's Diamond Deal.* New York: The New Tip Top Weekly No. 91, April 25, 1914. Magazine. 32pp. Young adult.

For 18 weeks, Street & Smith tried to pick up the sagging fortunes of the Merriwell family saga by promoting Frank, Jr.'s boon companion Owen Clancy to lead player status. The Owen Clancy stories were never put out in book form. This is the only Owen Clancy dime novel with baseball content. Owen helps a friend win a diamond mine on the diamond. Get it? AGM

_____. *Frank Merriwell's Diamond Foes.* New York: Street & Smith Publications, Inc., 1914. Paper. 314pp. Young adult. dnnuc

Back at the Fardale of his forefathers, Frank, Jr. wins several games. AGM

_____. *Dick Merriwell and June Arlington.* New York: Street & Smith Publications, Inc., 1914. Paper. 316pp. Young adult. nucdn

Mostly about a turquoise mine Out West, but begins with a game against an Army team in Santa Fe. AGM

_____. *Merriwell, or, Blood Will Tell.* New York: Street & Smith Publications, Inc., 1914. Paper. 311pp. Young adult. nucdn

Winds up with a game of Frank pitching v. Dick, with Frank, Jr. on Dick's team. Final, Frank 3, youngsters 2. AGM

_____. *Dick Merriwell and the Burglar.* New York: Street & Smith Publications, Inc., 1914. Paper. 320pp. Young adult. nucdn

Three games chronicled. Only Dick and Chip are here. AGM

_____. *Frank Merriwell at the Cowboy Carnival.* New York: Street & Smith Publications, Inc., 1914. Paper. 312pp. Young adult. dnjrc

A patented Frank returns from captivity to win a game. Actually, he's early, arriving in the eighth. AGM

_____. *Lefty O' the Bush.* New York: Barse & Hopkins, 1914. Hardbound. 305pp. Young adult.

The first of the sixteen-book Big League series, which Patten began work on soon after quitting the Merriwell books. Many of these appeared first as serials in *Top Notch.* In this, Tom "Lefty" Locke begins his pro career in a Maine professional league. As in most of the books in the series, there's a mystery about the character that is not explained until late in the book. Lefty, it appears, is really Philip Hazleton, lawyer and onetime Princeton pitcher. AGM

_____. *Lefty O' the Big League.* New York: Barse & Hopkins, 1914. Hardbound. 311pp. Young adult.

Lefty shows up at the camp of the Hornets of the Big League of the series title. An old rival, Bert Elgin, does him dirty. Lefty's released but surfaces with the rival Blue Stockings to beat the Hornets in the season's opening game. A second book was published under this title but containing the full first four books of the series. FP

_____. *Lefty O' the Blue Stockings.* New York: Barse & Hopkins, 1914. Hardbound. 299pp. Young adult.

The manager, Kennedy, who uncovered Lefty is fired. The new manager hates him. Lefty is suspended and loses his memory in a train wreck near his old manager's farm. Both return trium-

'WITH A LAST DESPERATE LEAP HE FLUNG HIMSELF FORWARD, GLOVED HANDS THRUST UPWARD'

The angle and the pancake glove make it unlikely even someone as phenomenally skilled as Brick King could make the catch, although artist C. H. Lawrence apparently thought so. The Big League series, of which the Brick King book was volume five, was the second great success by Gilbert Patten under the Burt L. Standish pseudonym.
Frontispiece from Gilbert Patten's *Brick King, Backstop,* 1914.

phantly to the Blue Stockings at the end of the season. AGM

_____. *Lefty O' the Training Camp.* New York: Barse & Hopkins, 1914. Hardbound. 295pp. Young adult.

At spring training the next season, Lefty helps Kennedy straighten out rookie pitcher Nels Savage, who suffers Jekyll-and-Hyde transformations on and off the field. FP

_____. *Brick King, Backstop.* New York: Barse & Hopkins, 1914. Hardbound. 317pp. Young adult.

This is the first of the Big League series that doesn't focus on Lefty. Brick King advances from bench warmer to outstanding catcher and handler of pitchers. In an echo of the first Lefty Locke book, King is not his real last name (the mystery) and it's Kingdon, the name of the hero in another of Patten's series. Brick plays with the Wolves, another of the Big League teams, and makes friends with Pebble Stone, who appears in a number of other books in the series. Lefty makes a cameo appearance near the end. AGMFP

_____. *The Making of a Big Leaguer.* New York: Barse & Hopkins, 1915. Hardbound. 307pp. Young adult.

This volume returns to an earlier period of Pebble Stone's career. He hates professional ball but is determined to show his former big-leaguer father that he can succeed. He rises through the minors to the Wolves. FP

_____. *Courtney of the Center Garden.* New York: Barse & Hopkins, 1915. Hardbound. 320pp. Young adult.

Bob Courtney, the Wolves's center fielder in his 14th Big League season, strives to overcome personal and physical problems to make his final year a success. FP

_____. *Covering the Look-In Corner.* New York: Barse & Hopkins, 1915. Hardbound. 316pp. Young adult.

Baseball saves Jack Keeper from vagrancy as he stars at third base for the Hillsboro Buccaneers of the bush Middle River League. In later books, he plays for Big League Wolves. FP

_____. *Lefty Locke, Pitcher-Manager.* New York: Barse & Hopkins, 1916. Hardbound. 317pp. Young adult.

Back to Lefty, appointed manager. He struggles through an off-season to overcome an arm injury and thwart parties who would oust Blue Stockings owner Charles Collier. Lefty eventually becomes part owner. Patten reveals a strong anti-Federal League bias and preaches the impossibility of fixing World Series games. FP

_____. *Guarding the Keystone Sack.* New York: Barse & Hopkins, 1917. Hardbound. 254pp. Young adult.

Blue Stockings rookies Matt Schuyler, 2B, and Rick Armstrong, SS, make good, but the team is in the cellar at midseason and must struggle upward. FP

_____. *The Man on First.* New York: Barse & Hopkins, 1920. Hardbound. 235pp. Young adult.

Untested rookie pitcher Ken Tapland becomes the Blue Stockings emergency first baseman for the World Series. FP

_____. *Lego Lamb, Southpaw.* New York: Barse & Hopkins, 1923. Hardbound. 250pp. Young adult.

Truly one of the great names of baseball fiction. Spotted by a scout at a sandlot game, Bob Allen, alias Lego Lamb, makes the Big League Specters while enduring possible exposure as an ex-convict, imprisoned for a theft he did not commit. FP

_____. *The Grip of the Game.* New York: Barse & Co., 1924. Hardbound. 245pp. Young adult.

Lego Lamb's brilliant pitching spurs the Specters' pennant fight in spite of the machinations of disgruntled teammate Dorsey. FP

_____. *Lefty Locke, Owner.* New York: Barse & Co., 1925. Hardbound. 242pp. Young adult.

Lefty and reporter-friend Jack Stillman (who's been a character since book two) battle against Universal Consolidated's master plan to control U.S. industry, including big-league baseball. More murder and evil doing than baseball in this improbable plot. FP

_____. *Lefty Locke Wins Out.* New York: Barse & Co., 1926. Hardbound. 240pp. Young adult.

During a World War I spring, the Blue Stockings work through spring training and the season's opening weeks. The plot centers more on rookie pitchers Chesty Blake and Hobe Bolt, the hero, and veterans Pop Doyle and Tighe Rawson than it does Lefty. FP

_____. *Crossed Signals.* New York: Barse & Co., 1928. Hardbound. 220pp. Young adult. agmonuc

A rivalry between Tideport and Rockshore, town semipro teams, involves catcher Jack Ladd, who arrives in Tideport a stranger. In this last book of the Big League series, the only reference to its teams and characters is one mention of Lefty Locke. FP

PAULOS, SHEILA. *Wild Roses*. New York: Dell Publishing Co., 1983. Paper. 185pp. Adult romance.

Sports broadcaster and softball player finds true love with ace pitcher. A couple of games described and some other action at the ballpark. No. 108 of the Candlelight Ecstasy Romances. AGM

PECK, ROBERT NEWTON. *Last Sunday*. Garden City, NY: Doubleday & Co., 1977. Hardbound. 142pp. Young adult.

Bat girl helps town team and her friend the drunk/pitcher through a big Sunday game. AGM

PECK, WALLACE. *A Stitch in Time Saves the Nine*. New York: Publisher unknown, 1888. Paper. 24pp. Juvenile. agnuc

Humorous illustrated descriptions of players of each position. Circular book made to look like a baseball with seams. AG

PELLOWSKI, MICHAEL. *Baseball Bear*. Worthington, Oh: Willowisp Press, 1987. Paper. 24pp. Juvenile. bippub

(Written as SKI MICHAELS.) *The Baseball Bat*. Mahwah, NJ: Troll Associates, 1986. Hardbound. 48pp. Juvenile.

Bart Bat wants to play baseball but has to find a way to play at night, when he can stay awake. AGM

PERKINS, AL. *Don and Donna Go to Bat*. New York: Random House, Inc., 1966. Hardbound. 64pp. Juvenile.

Twins go out for the team. He's the star. She becomes the equipment manager despite proving she can play. AGM

PERRY, LAWRENCE. *The Big Game*. New York: Charles Scribner's Sons, 1918. Hardbound. 259pp. Young adult. jofp

PETERSEN, P. J., and BETSY JAMES. *The Fireplug is First Base*. New York: Dutton's Children's Books, 1990. Hardbound. 60pp. Juvenile.

Urban street baseball; a younger brother works his way into the game. AGM

PHILBROOK, CLEM. *The Magic Bat*. New York: The Macmillan Co., 1954. Hardbound. 167pp. Juvenile. jomo

Boy gets a bat from his hero, Yogi Berra. AGM

_____. *Ollie's Team and the Baseball Computer*. New York: Hastings House, 1967. Hardbound. 122pp. Juvenile.

The first of an eight-book series about Ollie and his friends, four of which have some baseball. Philbrook has some problems keeping ages, coaches, teammates, and other details consistent from book to book. In this, sixth-grader Ollie and his team are all unhappy with the positions their coach has assigned them. Then Ollie's father has a computer assign their positions and they start winning. AGM

_____. *Ollie's Team Plays Biddy Baseball*. New York: Hastings House, 1970. Hardbound. 123pp. Juvenile.

Ollie is studying bees and decides he wants to be a drone rather than a worker. But, he finds, drones don't win games for their baseball teams. This book is set in fifth grade. AGM

_____. *Ollie's Team and the 200 Pound Problem*. New York: Hastings House, 1972. Hardbound. 125pp. Juvenile.

Back in sixth grade, Ollie and his teammates try to help Jumbo, last season's star player, lose 25 pounds in six weeks. AGM

_____. *Ollie's Team and the Million Dollar Mistake*. New York: Hastings House, 1973. Hardbound. 125pp. Juvenile.

A series of problems at the local bank wind up helping Ollie's class save the money for a trip and help Ollie become a better baseball player. AGM

PHYSICAL DIRECTOR. (Pseudonym: *See* H. Irving Hancock.)

PIER, ARTHUR STANWOOD. *The Crashaw Brothers*. Boston: Houghton Mifflin Co., 1910. Hardbound. 222pp. Young adult.

Older brother Charles is captain of the eleven at school. Younger brother Edward, a baseball player, wants to distinguish himself from his brother and goes to a rival school. Three of eleven chapters in this year-at-school book contain baseball. Fourth of the eleven-book St. Timothy's series. AGM

_____. *The Rigor of the Game.* Boston: Houghton Mifflin Co., 1929. Hardbound. 203pp. Young adult collection.

This is included in Grobani, but only three of ten short stories include baseball. AGM

_____. *The Captain.* Philadelphia: Penn Publishing Co., 1929. Hardbound. 244pp. Young adult.

A tale of social class and high school baseball. Poor boy makes good as catcher, team captain, and exemplar to rich and poor alike. AGM

_____. *The Cheerleader.* Philadelphia: Penn Publishing Co., 1930. Hardbound. 267pp. Young adult.

A boy matures over a summer of work. Tone is set in an early chapter when he acts as a cheerleader while his high school defeats their main rival in baseball. No other baseball material. AGM

PLATT, KIN. *The Screwball King Murder.* New York: Random House, Inc., 1978. Hardbound. 184pp. Adult mystery.

Young Dodgers lefty Hondo Kenyon turns up dead. Ace L.A. private investigator Max Roper is called in. Good mystery by a good mystery writer. BP

PLAYFAIR, ROBERT SMITH. *Colonel of the Crimson.* Boston: Houghton Mifflin Co., 1940. Hardbound. 233pp. Juvenile.

PLIMPTON, GEORGE. *The Curious Case of Sidd Finch.* New York: Macmillan Publishing Co., 1987. Hardbound. 275pp. Adult.

An expansion of Plimpton's April 1, 1985, Sports Illustrated put-on about the Buddhist pitcher for the Mets. AGM

POMERANZ, GARY. *Out at Home.* Boston: Houghton Mifflin Co., 1985. Hardbound. 231pp. Adult.

Suspense, the fixing of games, and eventually murders spice this tale of Cub fans in the 1950s. Much of the action occurs off the field; consequently, Cub fans will enjoy this one. TS

PORTER, MARK. (Pseudonym: *See* Robert Leckie.)

POTOK, CHAIM. *The Chosen.* New York: Simon and Schuster, Inc., 1967. Hardbound. 284pp. Adult.

A novel of Hasidic Judaism and a boy's coming to terms with his heritage. In an early chapter, two of the main characters meet during a ferocious school baseball game, the only baseball in the book. AGM

POWELL, TALMAGE. *Cellar Team.* Racine, Wi: Western Publishing Co., 1972. Hardbound. 210pp. Young adult.

Promising pro career cut short by an injury, Jim Ferrell turns to coaching a high school team with a losing tradition. AGM

POWERS, RON. *Toot-Toot-Tootsie, Good-bye.* New York: Delacorte Press, 1981. Hardbound. 304pp. Adult.

A beauty queen is introduced into a team's radio booth to boost ratings, and both she and the veteran announcer are forced to examine their lives. Some interesting reflections on the changes in baseball broadcasting over the years. Powers is a radio/TV writer. AGM

PROBOZ, KATHILYN SOLOMON with LEAH JEROME. (*See* Lucy Ellis.)

PUECHNER, RAY. *A Grand Slam.* New York: Warner Books, 1973. Paper. 176pp. Adult.

This first woman in the majors is a second baseman who's a parody of early 1970s counterculture. Much sex along the way to a division championship. AGM

QUARRINGTON, PAUL. *Home Game.* Toronto: Doubleday Canada Ltd., 1983. Hardbound. 412pp. Adult.

A territorial dispute leads to a baseball game between a sideshow troupe and a religious sect. JO

QUIGLEY, MARTIN. *Today's Game.* New York: Viking Press, 1965. Hardbound. 176pp. Adult.

One game, in June, between the Warriors and the Blue Jays that could determine the future of the Jays' manager and the whole season. An inside look at the game from the manager's point of view. BP

_____. *The Original Colored House of David.* Boston: Houghton Mifflin Co., 1981. Hardbound. 215pp. Adult.

A young white boy spends a summer with a barnstorming black team in the 1920s. Marvelous book. AGM

QUIRK, LESLIE. *"Midget" Blake, Pitcher.* New York: McLoughlin Bros., 1906. Hardbound. 92pp. Young adult. agmonuc

Some of Quirk's other books (*Baby Elton, Quarterback,* 1904) also contain baseball material. AGM

_____. *Freshman Dorn, Pitcher.* New York: Century Co., 1911. Hardbound. 335pp. Young adult. monuc

Compiled from earlier magazine stories. Dorn does little but play sports in his freshman year at college. About a third baseball. AGM

_____. *The Third Strike.* Boston: Little, Brown and Co., 1914. Hardbound. 349pp. Young adult. monuc

Third of the four-book Wellworth College series. DJ

_____. *Playing the Game.* Chicago: M. A. Donohue & Co., 1915. Hardbound. 312pp. Young adult. mojonuc

RAND, ADDISON. (Pseudonym: *See* Adolph C. Regli.)

RATHBORNE, ST. GEORGE. (Written as John Warden.) *Phenomenal Paul, the Wizard Pitcher.* New York: Log Cabin Library No. 23, August 22, 1889. Magazine. 32pp. Young adult. el

Rathborne wrote a great many dime novels and books over the years as well as the standard detectives, westerns, histories, etc. AGM

_____. *The Brotherhood Detective, or, Short-Stop Sam.* New York: Nugget Library No. 35, April 24, 1890. Magazine. 16pp. Young adult. el

Reissued as *Short Stop Sam, or, The Baseball Detective* in New York Five Cent Library, No. 136, June 8, 1895.

_____. *Brotherhood Buck, or, The Players League in the South.* New York: Log Cabin Library No. 59, May 1, 1890. Magazine. 32pp. Young adult. el

_____. *Play Ball, or, Brotherhood Boys in Florida.* New York: Log Cabin Library No. 65, June 12, 1890. Magazine. 32pp. Young adult. el

_____. *A Home Run, or, How the Game Was Won.* New York: Log Cabin Library No. 68, July 3, 1890. Magazine. 32pp. Young adult. el

_____. *Short Stop Sam, or, The Baseball Detective.* (June 6, 1895). See *The Brotherhood Detective,* April 24, 1890.

RAYMOND, P. T. *The Nine Wonders.* New York: Happy Days Nos. 206–12, Sept. 24 to Nov. 5, 1898. Magazine. Young adult. el

_____. *Young King Kelly.* New York: Happy Days Nos. 447–50, May 9 to May 30, 1903. Magazine. Young adult. el

_____. *Base-ball Hal.* New York: Happy Days Nos. 503–6, June 4 to June 25, 1904. Magazine. Young adult. el

_____. *Winning the Pennant.* New York: Happy Days Nos. 551–54, May 6 to May 27, 1905. Magazine. Young adult. el

_____. *Prince of the Diamond.* New York: Happy Days Nos. 559–62, July 1 to July 22, 1905. Magazine. Young adult. el

_____. *Right off the Bat.* New York: Happy Days Nos. 602–5, April 28 to May 19, 1906. Magazine. Young adult. el

_____. *Little Star, the Boy Baseball Wonder.* New York: Happy Days Nos. 660–63, June 8 to June 29, 1907. Magazine. Young adult. el

_____. *The Boss Boy Battery.* New York: Happy Days Nos. 668–71, August 3 to August 24, 1907. Magazine. Young adult. el

_____. *Little South Paw.* New York: Happy Days Nos. 707–10, May 2 to May 23, 1908. Magazine. Young adult. el

_____. *The Champion Nine.* New York: Happy Days Nos. 716–19, July 4 to July 25, 1908. Magazine. Young adult. el

_____. *The Red Pennant.* New York: Happy Days Nos. 721–24, August 8 to August 29, 1908. Magazine. Young adult. el

_____. *The Boy Pitcher.* New York: Happy Days Nos. 759–62, May 1 to May 22, 1909. Magazine. Young adult. el

_____. *At the Head of the League.* New York: Happy Days Nos. 764–67, June 5 to June 26, 1909. Magazine. Young adult. el

_____. *Captain Hal's Champion Nine.* New York: Happy Days Nos. 780–83, Sept. 25 to Oct. 16, 1909. Magazine. Young adult. el

_____. *The Fastest Nine in the League.* New York: Happy Days Nos. 811–14, April 30 to May 21, 1910. Magazine. Young adult. el

_____. *Racing for the Pennant.* New York: Happy Days Nos. 820–23, July 2 to July 23, 1910. Magazine. Young adult. el

_____. *Baseball Billy, the King of the Diamond.* New York: Happy Days Nos. 863–66, April 29 to May 20, 1911. Magazine. Young adult. el

_____. *The Prince of Pitchers.* New York: Happy Days Nos. 880–83, August 26 to Sept. 16, 1911. Magazine. Young adult. el

_____. *Little Iron-Arm, the Boy King of the Diamond.* New York: Happy Days Nos. 890–93, Nov. 4 to Nov. 25, 1911. Magazine. Young adult. el

_____. *Charley, the Champion.* New York: Happy Days Nos. 916–19, May 4 to May 25, 1912. Magazine. Young adult. el

_____. *The Nine of Norton.* New York: Happy Days Nos. 922–25, June 15 to July 6, 1912. Magazine. Young adult. el

_____. *King of the Box.* New York: Happy Days Nos. 926–29, July 13 to August 3, 1912. Magazine. Young adult. el

_____. *Phil, the Pitcher.* New York: Happy Days Nos. 937–40, Sept. 28 to Oct. 19, 1912. Magazine. Young adult. el

_____. *Batting to Win.* New York: Happy Days Nos. 972–75, May 31 to June 21, 1913. Magazine. Young adult. el

_____. *The Boy Battery.* New York: Happy Days Nos. 980–83, July 26 to August 16, 1913. Magazine. Young adult. el

_____. *Following the Game.* New York: Happy Days Nos. 990–93, Oct. 4 to Oct. 25, 1913. Magazine. Young adult. el

_____. *The Boy Backstop.* New York: Happy Days Nos. 1020–23, May 2 to May 23, 1914. Magazine. Young adult. el

REAL, RORY, and BOB PELKOWSKI. *A Baseball Dream.* Hauppauge, NY: Barron's Educational Series, Inc., 1990. Paper. 32pp. Juvenile.

One of eight books on different sports featuring the Sport Mite Kids. They play baseball and attend a major league game in this one. AGM

RECK, FRANKLIN. *Varsity Letter.* New York: Thomas Y. Crowell Co., 1942. Hardbound. 238pp. Young adult collection. agmobrd

REGAN, JACK, and WILL E. STAHL. *Around the World with the Baseball Bugs.* Chicago: J. Regan & Co., 1910. Paper. 93pp. Young adult. jtpnuc
A collection of poems, songs, anecdotes, and other material. EM

REGLI, ADOLPH C. (Written as Addison Rand.) *Southpaw Fly Hawk.* New York: Longmans, Green and Co., 1952. Hardbound. 183pp. Juvenile.
The only book I've found set on a real-life minor league team and its ballpark, the Minneapolis Millers and old Nicollet Park. Eighteen-year-old Eddie Hadley goes from sandlot ball to a victory in the Little World Series in a year. AGM

RENICK, MARION. *The Dooleys Play Ball.* New York: Charles Scribner's Sons, 1949. Hardbound. 165pp. Juvenile.
Family of boys are all ball players. Then a girl cousin comes to join them and proves an adept softball player. AGM

_____. *Pete's Home Run.* New York: Charles Scribner's Sons, 1952. Hardbound. 117pp. Juvenile.
Pete keeps trying to make an impression on his older brother and his brother's Little League teammates. Eventually he does, by learning to hit. AGM

_____. *The Heart for Baseball.* New York: Charles Scribner's Sons, 1953. Hardbound. 234pp. Juvenile.
Little League comes to Allenville. The boys learn to play. They also devise a way to use baseball signals to pass a classical music test devised by the town bluenose before she'll build a clubhouse for them. AGM

_____. *Bats & Gloves of Glory.* New York: Charles Scribner's Sons, 1956. Hardbound. 215pp. Juvenile.
Bruce Edwards needs to make a good showing for the school hobby show. His hobby is baseball, and after learning about making an extra effort,

he puts together a collection of autographs, pictures, baseball cards, uniforms, and other material he helped collect with the aid of a minor league player and a scout. AGM

_____. *Boy at Bat.* New York: Charles Scribner's Sons, 1961. Hardbound. 32pp. Juvenile.

New glove, old dreams get boy into neighborhood game. AGM

RENICK, MARION, and JAMES L. *Steady.* New York: Charles Scribner's Sons, 1942. Hardbound. 137pp. Juvenile.

George earns his nickname with his steady catching as his youth league team wins the town championship. Heavily interlarded with material on how baseball is played and structured. AGM

RESCINITI, ANGELO. *The Baseball from Outer Space.* Mississauga. Ont: School Book Fairs, Inc., 1980. Hardbound. 92pp. Juvenile science fiction.

A stranded Betelgeusean spaceship turns itself into a baseball to help itself escape earth and a boy get through some baseball and family problems. AGM

REYS, MARGRET and H. A. *Curious George Plays Baseball.* Boston: Houghton Mifflin Co., 1986. Hardbound. 30pp. Juvenile.

The famous monkey gets into trouble at the ballpark. AGM

RHOADES, JONATHAN. *Over the Fence is Out.* New York: Holt, Rinehart and Winston, 1961. Hardbound. 128pp. Adult collection.

Whimsical tales of growing up. Cover illustration, title, and one story are about baseball. AGM

RICE, DAMON. (A pseudonym.) *Seasons Past.* New York: Praeger Publishers, Inc., 1976. Hardbound. 435pp. Adult.

An intertwined history of a Brooklyn family and New York baseball over a century. The baseball content is mostly nonfiction although this family sure knows a lot of players. Research by Peter Bjarkman indicates this book was written by Harold Rosenthal, Svein Arber, and Ford Hovis. AGM

RICHARD, JAMES R. (Pseudonym: *See* Robert Sidney Bowen.)

RITZ, DAVID. *The Man Who Brought the Dodgers Back to Brooklyn.* New York: Simon and Schuster, Inc., 1981. Hardbound. 288pp. Adult.

A fantasy of the rebuilding of Ebbets Field, the discovery of a female Koufax, and the return of the Dodgers. AGM

ROBBINS, KEN. *At the Ballpark.* New York: Viking Press, 1988. Hardbound. 32pp. Juvenile.

Hand-tinted photographs from both major and minor league games and parks plus a simple text describing what goes on at a ball game. AGM

ROSEN, RICHARD D. *Strike Three You're Dead.* New York: Walter and Co., 1984. Hardbound. 234pp. Adult mystery.

The first novel featuring Harvey Blissberg, who gives up a journeyman career as an outfielder to become a detective after his roommate is murdered. AGM

_____. *Saturday Night Dead.* New York: Viking Press, 1988. Hardbound. 274pp. Adult mystery.

After a basketball novel (*Fadeaway,* Harper & Row, 1986), Harvey Blissberg returns to keep the American League MVP sober for the week he's scheduled to host a "Saturday Night Live" clone. When the show's producer is murdered, Bliss handles that, too. No game action. Rosen spent some time writing for the real SNL. AGM

ROTH, PHILIP. *The Great American Novel.* New York: Holt, Rinehart and Winston, 1973. Hardbound. 382pp. Adult.

You knew the Great American Novel had to be about baseball. Actually, it's wartime baseball and a strange team of misfits and classical allusions. AGM

ROTHWEILER, PAUL R. *The Sensuous Southpaw.* New York: G. P. Putnam's Sons, 1976. Hardbound. 253pp. Adult.

The first major league female revisited. AGM

RUBIN, JEFF, and RICK RAEL. *Baseball Brothers.* New York: Lothrop, Lee & Shepard Co., 1976. Hardbound. 47pp. Juvenile.

Two boys who are big Hank Aaron fans set out to see him play. They eventually meet him, and he gets them into the stadium (apparently County). Some discussion of Hank's career. AGM

RUBIN, LOUIS D., Jr. *Surfaces of a Diamond.* Baton Rouge, La: Louisiana State University Press, 1981. Hardbound. 209pp. Adult.

A coming-of-age story in the South just before World War II. The main character plays in a neighborhood league for teenagers and also has some other involvement with the game, but baseball is just one theme in the book. AGM

RUSSELL, PATRICK. *Going, Going, Gone.* Garden City, NY: Doubleday & Co., 1967. Hardbound. 144pp. Juvenile.

High school hitter has to learn to field his position before he can attract scouts. AGM

RUTH, BABE. *The Home-Run King.* New York: H. K. Fly Co., 1920. Hardbound. 240pp. Young adult.

I assume the Babe himself didn't write this, if for no other reason than he has Our Hero bat seventh. Pep Pindar is a prep school boy with a big bat. (He seemingly never has to make a play in the field.) One chapter finds the team hosted at the Polo Grounds by manager McGilraw (McGraw) and watching Chris Meaker and Joe Good (Tris Speaker and Joe Wood) play. There is a biography of Babe, emphasizing his boyhood, in the front and written in the third person. The book appeared just after Babe had smashed the one-season homer record by hitting 54. AGM

SACHS, MARILYN. *Matt's Mitt.* Garden City, NY: Doubleday & Co., 1975. Hardbound. 29pp. Juvenile.

Matt has a glove with supernatural qualities, and both of them wind up in Cooperstown. Very nice two-page drawing of a Yankee Stadium-like park by illustrator Hilary Knight. A book combining *Matts Mitt* and *Fleet-Footed Florence* but with different illustrations was published by E. P. Dutton in 1988. AGM

_____. *Fleet-footed Florence.* Garden City, NY: Doubleday & Co., 1981. Hardbound. 50pp. Juvenile. A sequel to *Matt's Mitt.* Matt has an exceptionally fast daughter who plays in the big leagues. AGM

SAINSBURY, NOEL, Jr. *Stirring Baseball Stories.* New York: Cupples & Leon Co., 1934. Hardbound. 615pp. Young adult collection.

Collects the three following books. AGM

_____. *Cracker Stanton.* New York: Cupples & Leon Co., 1934. Hardbound. 202pp. Young adult. First of eight books in the Champion Sports Stories series set at Clarkville, a Connecticut prep school. Boy whose father's death left the family in straitened circumstances rescues a girl and wins a scholarship to Clarkville where he must grind at the books to prepare for a West Point entrance exam. He is eventually persuaded to go out for baseball and proves a star. Baseball games only in last third. AGM

(Written as CHARLES LAWTON.) *Clarkville's Battery.* New York: Cupples & Leon Co., 1937. Hardbound. 203pp. Young adult.

Fourth in the series. With the pseudonym, comes a change of themes as well. No longer Algeresque poor boy makes good, subplots have Our Heroes rescuing people during a flood and outwitting gangsters trying to break up the team. The main plot involves four boys struggling to be the team's pitcher and catcher. Much game action. The main characters are new, but the coach and secondary characters carry over from the first book. AGM

_____. *Home Run Hennessey.* New York: Cupples & Leon Co., 1941. Hardbound. 210pp. Young adult. Clarkville's greatest home run hitter is sidetracked by a beating, recovers his courage, leads Clarkville to league title and then league all-star team to victory in a game in Cuba. Adventures on the boat on way to Cuba. Seventh in the series. New hero, but the battery from the previous book as well as coach and other players carry over. AGM

ST. SAUVER, DENNIS. *Pro Fever.* St. Paul, Mn: EMC Corp., 1974. Hardbound. 32pp. Juvenile. nucbip

Rick's concern with offers from professional baseball scouts overshadows his concern for the success of his high school team until an injury to his pitching hand changes the picture. NUC

SANDBERG, HAROLD W. *Dunk O'Malley Sports Stories.* New York: Lantern Press, Inc., 1949. Hardbound. 256pp. Young adult collection.

Five baseball, two football, and one basketball stories make up this volume on the scintillating Dunk at prep school. AGM

SANDMEL, FRANCES FOX. *All on the Team.* New York: Abingdon Press, 1959. Hardbound. 126pp. Juvenile.

Jewish boy moves to a new town and slowly works his way on to the grade school team with much explanation of Judaism. Then the Big Game falls on Yom Kippur, and he must decide whether to play. He doesn't, and the team elects him captain anyway. AGM

SANGREE, ALLEN. *The Jinx.* New York: G. W. Dillingham Co., 1911. Hardbound. 311pp. Young adult collection.

Humorous collection of magazine stories. A young woman decides she is a jinx for her true love's team. Two drunken stars get on the wrong boat to start a road trip and wake up part way to Rio. AGM

SAWYER, WALTER L. (Written as Winn Standish.) *Jack Lorimer's Champions.* Boston: L. C. Page & Co., 1907. Hardbound. 300pp. Young adult.

Second of five Jack Lorimer books. All the books contain many sports. Baseball predominates in this one as the boys play in both a high school and a town league. AGM

SAYLES, JOHN. *Pride of the Bimbos.* Boston: Little, Brown and Co., 1975. Hardbound. 258pp. Adult.

An early work by the man who later directed the movie "Eight Men Out." A five-man softball team and a young boy tour the deep South, the men playing in drag and the boy learning about manhood. JO

SCHIFFER, MICHAEL. *Ballpark.* New York: Simon and Schuster, Inc., 1982. Hardbound. 267pp. Adult.

Raneer is the owner who's created a giant amusement park complete with its own major league team. Pardee is his all-star third baseman. Reese is the sportswriter, emotionally and physically involved with Pardee, professionally involved in exposing Raneer. BP

SCHOLEFIELD, EDMUND O. (Pseudonym: *See* William Butterworth.)

SCHOLZ, JACKSON. *Soldiers at Bat.* New York: William Morrow & Co., 1942. Hardbound. 271pp. Young adult.

The first of a long line of baseball novels by the 1924 Olympic medal winner, who also wrote on other sports. In this one, Kip Dane is drafted and a newspaper story makes the minor league star look like a braggart. He shows 'em. AGM

_____. *Batter Up.* New York: William Morrow & Co., 1946. Hardbound. 212pp. Young adult.

Marty Baron's brother owns a baseball team, but Marty wants to make it on his own. AGM

_____. *Fielder from Nowhere.* New York: William Morrow & Co., 1948. Hardbound. 222pp. Young adult.

Man with a criminal past tries to hide it while making the big leagues. Of course, he'd been jailed unjustly. AGM

_____. *Keystone Kelly.* New York: William Morrow & Co., 1950. Hardbound. 250pp. Young adult.

Second baseman cruises quickly to the majors but then gets spike-shy at the thought of losing his sizable bonus. The bonus would be paid only after he's spent a year in the majors. AGM

_____. *Deep Short.* New York: William Morrow & Co., 1952. Hardbound. 249pp. Young adult.

_____. *Base Burglar.* New York: William Morrow & Co., 1955. Hardbound. 221pp. Young adult.

Cliff Connor can't impress scouts because he has only one asset, his speed. But he pulls a trick at a tryout camp, gets a contract, and begins to learn to hit and catch as well as run. AGM

_____. *Man in a Cage.* New York: William Morrow & Co., 1957. Hardbound. 255pp. Young adult.

Born to the circus life, Ted Kirby moves to catching. AGM

_____. *Bench Boss.* New York: William Morrow & Co., 1958. Hardbound. 255pp. Young adult.

Major leaguer with a reputation for on-the-field pranks, both for fun and to win, finds he has to mend his ways as a minor league manager. AGM

_____. *The Perfect Game.* New York: William Morrow & Co., 1959. Hardbound. 253pp. Young adult.

Probably the best of Scholz's books. A struggling young pitcher throws a perfect game in the seventh game of the World Series and then must deal with the fact he still has to learn how to pitch. AGM

_____. *Little League Town.*
Grobani listed this title for Scholz as being published by Morrow in 1959. Morrow said it has no record of ever having published such a book. AGM

_____. *Center-Field Jinx.* New York: William Morrow & Co., 1961. Hardbound. 220pp. Young adult.
Jerry Connor goes back to minors to learn how to not just put up good numbers but carry his team. AGM

_____. *Dugout Tycoon.* New York: William Morrow & Co., 1963. Hardbound. 254pp. Young adult.
Bored major league bench warmer makes a mint in stocks, befriends a con man, and becomes part owner of a boxer. Also tries to play regularly at second base. AGM

_____. *Spark Plug at Short.* New York: William Morrow & Co., 1966. Hardbound. 191pp. Young adult.
Traded to the cellar team, Jimmy Teal shoots off his mouth to a sportswriter, and his words come back to haunt him when he's happily settled in. AGM

_____. *The Big Mitt.* New York: William Morrow & Co., 1968. Hardbound. 190pp. Young adult.
He's a pinch hitter without a position until he tries catcher. He then straightens out the team's ace and leads them to the World Series. AGM

_____. *Hot-Corner Hank.* New York: William Morrow & Co., 1970. Hardbound. 189pp. Young adult.
The entire baseball world is shocked when the major league Quakers give a recently graduated college baseball star eight weeks to prove he is justified in demanding a major league contract. And this is years before Bob Horner. AGM

SCHULZ, CHARLES M. *Charlie Brown's All-Stars.* Cleveland: World Publishing Co., 1966. Hardbound. 44pp. Juvenile cartoon.

Charlie Brown and other characters from the "Peanuts" cartoon strip attempt to find a sponsor for their baseball team. AGM

_____. *Charlie Brown's Yearbook.* New York: World Publishing Co., 1969. Hardbound. 182pp. Juvenile cartoon. nuc
Includes *Charlie Brown's All-Stars* and three other nonbaseball stories. NUC

_____. *Winning May Not be Everything, But Losing Isn't Anything.* San Francisco: Determined Publications, Inc., 1970. Hardbound. 40pp. Juvenile cartoon.
Over the years, Schulz used baseball scenes a great deal in the "Peanuts" strips. The strips have been collected, published, reshuffled, and republished many times. Most of the rest of the books listed here are collections of those strips, unlike *Charlie Brown's All-Stars,* which is a separate story. Baseball strips are in many of the books. The only ones listed here are those where titles or summaries in the Library of Congress catalogue indicate baseball content. This one is nineteen four-panel baseball strips, few related to each other. AGM

_____. *Win a Few, Lose a Few, Charlie Brown.* New York: Holt, Rinehart and Winston, 1973. Hardbound. 128pp. Juvenile cartoon. djnuc

_____. *Play Ball, Snoopy.* New York: Fawcett Crest, 1974. Paper. 126pp. Juvenile cartoon.
The first half of *Win a Few, Lose a Few, Charlie Brown.* It contains 13 strips of Snoopy trying to break Babe Ruth's career home run record before Hank Aaron does. AGM.

_____. *Sandlot Peanuts.* New York: Holt, Rinehart and Winston, 1977. Hardbound. 184pp. Juvenile cartoon.
The best of the "Peanuts" baseball collections. This one is all baseball. Many of the strips are reproduced in color. Introduction by Joe Garagiola. AGM

_____. *It's Hard Work Being Bitter.* New York: Holt, Rinehart and Winston, 1977. Hardbound. 200pp. Juvenile cartoon. nuc

A selection including Lucy's removal from the baseball team by Charlie Brown. NUC

_____. *There Goes the Shutout*. New York: Henry Holt & Co., 1977. Paper. 200pp. Juvenile cartoon. bipnuc

A selection of cartoons featuring Charlie Brown's baseball team. Introduction by Joe Garagiola. NUC

_____. *It's Great to be a Superstar*. New York: Holt, Rinehart and Winston, 1977. Hardbound. 190pp. Juvenile cartoon. nuc

A selection of cartoons including panels where Snoopy is voted Rookie of the Year for Charlie Brown's baseball team. NUC

_____. *It's Arbor Day, Charlie Brown*. New York: Random House, Inc., 1977. Hardbound. 39pp. Juvenile cartoon.

This book is also a separate story, rather than a collection of strips. A misdirected Arbor Day project winds up with Charlie Brown's ball field replanted. But the first game of the season starts anyway. AGM

_____. *Slide, Charlie Brown! Slide!* New York: Fawcett Crest, 1982. Paper. 124pp. Juvenile cartoon.

About a quarter of the strips are baseball. AGM

_____. *Big League Peanuts*. New York: Holt, Rinehart and Winston, 1985. Paper. 156pp. Juvenile cartoon.

All the strips in this collection are baseball. AGM

_____. *Strike Three, Charlie Brown*. New York: Fawcett Crest, 1987. Paper. 124pp. Juvenile cartoon.

Selected strips from *Big League Peanuts*. AGM

_____. *Good Catch, Snoopy!* New York: Fawcett Crest, 1987. Paper. 124pp. Juvenile cartoon.

More selected strips from *Big League Peanuts*. AGM

SCOTT, EVERETT "DEACON." *Third Base Thatcher*. New York: Dodd, Mead and Co., 1923. Hardbound. 284pp. Young adult.

This is a continuation of the series started under the Christy Mathewson name, and therefore this one, too, was presumably written by John Wheeler. Scott was a star shortstop for the Red Sox and Yankees and held the record for consecutive games played, which was broken by Lou Gehrig. Jeff Thatcher is kicked out of college after a fight. He becomes a hero as a cub reporter and returns to duel his (unworthy) boxing rival for the 3B job on the varsity. To make everything clear, the last chapter is titled "The Big Game." AGM

SCOTT, MORGAN. (Pseudonym: *See* Gilbert Patten.)

SEAVER, TOM, with HERB RESNICOW. *Beanball: Murder at the World Series*. New York: William Morrow & Co., 1989. Hardbound. 228pp. Adult mystery.

Mundane murder mystery involving characters with resemblances to George Steinbrenner, Billy Martin, and other New York baseball figures. Solved by Our Hero, the sportwriter-detective. The mystery is played out over the course of a World Series, and the games and unrealistic lineup concoctions play a big role. AGM

SHACKLEFORD, HARVEY K. *King of the Bat*. New York: Happy Days Nos. 32–39, May 25 to July 13, 1895. Magazine. Young adult. moel

Shackleford was one of the most prolific of the dime novel writers. Many of the titles he produced for Happy Days were later reprinted in Frank Tousey's other serials, especially Pluck and Luck. AGM

_____. *King of the Diamond*. New York: Happy Days Nos. 84–90, May 23 to July 4, 1896. Magazine. Young adult. el

_____. *The "Red Boys," or, The Youngest Champion of the Diamond*. New York: Happy Days Nos. 100–105, Sept. 12 to Oct. 17, 1896. Magazine. Young adult. el

_____. *The Winning Nine*. New York: Happy Days Nos. 134–41, May 8 to June 26, 1897. Magazine. Young adult. el

_____. *The Nine of Ninevah*. New York: Happy Days Nos. 142–49, July 3 to August 21, 1897. Magazine. Young adult. el

_____. *The Busy Bats*. New York: Happy Days Nos. 186–93, May 7 to June 25, 1898. Magazine. Young adult. el

_____. *The Nine in Blue.* New York: Happy Days Nos. 196–203, July 16 to Sept. 3, 1898. Magazine. Young adult. el

(Written as COL. RALPH FENTON.) *The Rival Baseball Clubs.* New York: Golden Weekly Nos. 31–38, June 12 to July 31, 1890. Magazine. Young adult. el

This story was published with authorship attributed to Fenton and Allyn Draper *(Pluck and Luck,* 1903 and 1918). Both of these were names used by the writing stable of publisher Frank Tousey. Shackleford, Edward S. Ten Eyck, and Francis W. Doughty are known to have written using the Draper pseudonym. Exact authorship remains unclear. AGM

(Written with GEORGE W. GOODE.) (Written as HAL STANDISH.) *Fred Fearnot's B.B. Club.* New York: Work and Win Weekly No. 24, May 19, 1899. Magazine. 32pp. Young adult.

The Fred Fearnot series was begun to compete with Frank Merriwell, published by Tousey's rival Street & Smith. Several early titles were signed by "The author of Fred Fearnot" and only with later titles did "Hal Standish" appear as the author. The Fearnot stories were almost all reprinted as Work and Win issues in the 1920s. The series ran to 732 numbers, plus reprints, only some of them involving baseball for Fred's talents were legion. AGM

_____. *Fred Fearnot's Home Run.* New York: Work and Win Weekly No. 29, June 23, 1899. Magazine. 32pp. Young adult.

_____. *Fred Fearnot's Challenge.* New York: Work and Win Weekly No. 132, June 14, 1901. Magazine. 32pp. Young adult. el

_____. *Fred Fearnot's Great Game.* New York: Work and Win Weekly No. 133, June 21, 1901. Magazine. 32pp. Young adult. el

_____. *Fred Fearnot on the Diamond.* New York: Work and Win Weekly No. 393, June 15, 1906. Magazine. 32pp. Young adult.

_____. *Fred Fearnot's Baseball Boys.* New York: Work and Win Weekly No. 397, July 13, 1906. Magazine. 32pp. Young adult.

_____. *Fred Fearnot and His No Hit Game.* New York: Work and Win Weekly No. 399, July 27, 1906. Magazine. 32pp. Young adult. dj

_____. *Fred Fearnot and His Puzzling Curves.* New York: Work and Win Weekly No. 401, August 10, 1906. Magazine. 32pp. Young adult. dj

_____. *Fred Fearnot's Triple Play.* New York: Work and Win Weekly No. 402, August 17, 1906. Magazine. 32pp. Young adult. dj

_____. *Fred Fearnot's Opening Game.* New York: Work and Win Weekly No. 441, May 17, 1907. Magazine. 32pp. Young adult. dj

_____. *Fred Fearnot's Only Assist.* New York: Work and Win Weekly No. 442, May 24, 1907. Magazine. 32pp. Young adult. dj

_____. *Fred Fearnot and the Swifton Sports.* New York: Work and Win Weekly No. 443, May 31, 1907. Magazine. 32pp. Young adult. dj

_____. *Fred Fearnot at Second Base.* New York: Work and Win Weekly No. 444, June 7, 1907. Magazine. 32pp. Young adult.

_____. *Fred Fearnot's Great Challenge.* New York: Work and Win Weekly No. 445, June 14, 1907. Magazine. 32pp. Young adult. dj

_____. *Fred Fearnot's Loyal Rooters.* New York: Work and Win Weekly No. 446, June 21, 1907. Magazine. 32pp. Young adult. dj

_____. *Fred Fearnot and the Boy Wonders.* New York: Work and Win Weekly No. 447, June 28, 1907. Magazine. 32pp. Young adult. dj

_____. *Fred Fearnot's Double Header.* New York: Work and Win Weekly No. 448, July 5, 1907. Magazine. 32pp. Young adult. dj

_____. *Fred Fearnot and the Rube Pitcher.* New York: Work and Win Weekly No. 449, July 12, 1907. Magazine. 32pp. Young adult.

_____. *Fred Fearnot's Best Ball.* New York: Work and Win Weekly No. 450, July 19, 1907. Magazine. 32pp. Young adult. dj

_____. *Fred Fearnot and the Tricky Umpire.* New York: Work and Win Weekly No. 451, July 26, 1907. Magazine. 32pp. Young adult. dj

_____. *Fred Fearnot's Boy Twirler.* New York: Work and Win Weekly No. 452, August 2, 1907. Magazine. 32pp. Young adult.

_____. *Fred Fearnot on the Coaching Line.* New York: Work and Win Weekly No. 453, August 9, 1907. Magazine. 32pp. Young adult.

_____. *Fred Fearnot and Old "Well! Well!"* New York: Work and Win Weekly No. 454, August 16, 1907. Magazine. 32pp. Young adult.
Old "Well! Well!" was the nickname of Frank H. Wood, a die-hard New York Giants fan. Wood had a foghorn voice to broadcast the phrase that gave him his nickname. The cover illustration appears to match with the written descriptions I have seen of Wood, who was also the subject of a short story in Zane Grey's *The Redheaded Outfield*. AGM

_____. *Fred Fearnot and the Scrappy Nine.* New York: Work and Win Weekly No. 455, August 23, 1907. Magazine. 32pp. Young adult. dj

_____. *Fred Fearnot's Final Game.* New York: Work and Win Weekly No. 456, August 30, 1907. Magazine. 32pp. Young adult. dj

_____. *Fred Fearnot as a Backstop.* New York: Work and Win Weekly No. 489, April 17, 1908. Magazine. 32pp. Young adult. dj

_____. *Fred Fearnot and the One-Armed Wonder.* New York: Work and Win Weekly No. 491, May 1, 1908. Magazine. 32pp. Young adult. dj

_____. *Fred Fearnot's Lucky Hit.* New York: Work and Win Weekly No. 493, May 15, 1908. Magazine. 32pp. Young adult.

_____. *Fred Fearnot's Steal to Second.* New York: Work and Win Weekly No. 495, May 29, 1908. Magazine. 32pp. Young adult. dj

_____. *Fred Fearnot's School Boy Stars.* New York: Work and Win Weekly No. 498, June 19, 1908. Magazine. 32pp. Young adult.

_____. *Fred Fearnot and the Rival Players.* New York: Work and Win Weekly No. 500, July 3, 1908. Magazine. 32pp. Young adult.

_____. *Fred Fearnot and the Boy Puzzle.* New York: Work and Win Weekly No. 502, July 17, 1908. Magazine. 32pp. Young adult. dj

_____. *Fred Fearnot Playing Inside Ball.* New York: Work and Win Weekly No. 504, July 31, 1908. Magazine. 32pp. Young adult. dj

_____. *Fred Fearnot's Pinch Hit.* New York: Work and Win Weekly No. 506, August 14, 1908. Magazine. 32pp. Young adult. dj

_____. *Fred Fearnot's Steal Home.* New York: Work and Win Weekly No. 508, August 28, 1908. Magazine. 32pp. Young adult. dj

_____. *Fred Fearnot's "Hit-and-Run Boys."* New York: Work and Win Weekly No. 510, Sept. 11, 1908. Magazine. 32pp. Young adult. dj

_____. *Fred Fearnot's Base-Ball Stars.* New York: Work and Win Weekly No. 541, April 16, 1909. Magazine. 32pp. Young adult. dj

_____. *Fred Fearnot and "Little Iron-Arm."* New York: Work and Win Weekly No. 543, April 30, 1909. Magazine. 32pp. Young adult. eldj

_____. *Fred Fearnot's New Delivery.* New York: Work and Win Weekly No. 545, May 14, 1909. Magazine. 32pp. Young adult. eldj

_____. *Fred Fearnot's Inside Game.* New York: Work and Win Weekly No. 547, May 28, 1909. Magazine. 32pp. Young adult. eldj

_____. *Fred Fearnot and the Errorless Wonder.* New York: Work and Win Weekly No. 595, April 29, 1910. Magazine. 32pp. Young adult. dj

_____. *Fred Fearnot's Ninth Inning Finish.* New York: Work and Win Weekly No. 599, May 27, 1910. Magazine. 32pp. Young adult. dj

_____. *Fred Fearnot's Champion Colts.* New York: Work and Win Weekly No. 601, June 10, 1910. Magazine. 32pp. Young adult. dj

_____. *Fred Fearnot's Clever Play.* New York: Work and Win Weekly No. 605, July 8, 1910. Magazine. 32pp. Young adult. dj

_____. *Fred Fearnot at the Plate.* New York: Work and Win Weekly No. 607, July 22, 1910. Magazine. 32pp. Young adult. dj

_____. *Fred Fearnot's Twenty-Inning Game.* New York: Work and Win Weekly No. 609, August 5, 1910. Magazine. 32pp. Young adult. dj

_____. *Fred Fearnot's Training Trip.* New York: Work and Win Weekly No. 644, April 7, 1911. Magazine. 32pp. Young adult. dj

_____. *Fred Fearnot's Baseball Giants.* New York: Work and Win Weekly No. 646, April 21, 1911. Magazine. 32pp. Young adult. dj

_____. *Fred Fearnot Playing the Game.* New York: Work and Win Weekly No. 649, May 12, 1911. Magazine. 32pp. Young adult. eldj

_____. *Fred Fearnot's Clever Curves.* New York: Work and Win Weekly No. 652, June 2, 1911. Magazine. 32pp. Young adult. dj

_____. *Fred Fearnot's Boy Marvel.* New York: Work and Win Weekly No. 654, June 16, 1911. Magazine. 32pp. Young adult. eldj

_____. *Fred Fearnot's Three-Bagger.* New York: Work and Win Weekly No. 657, July 7, 1911. Magazine. 32pp. Young adult. eldj

_____. *Fred Fearnot's Best Pitching.* New York: Work and Win Weekly No. 659, July 21, 1911. Magazine. 32pp. Young adult. eldj

_____. *Fred Fearnot's Ninth Inning Rally.* New York: Work and Win Weekly No. 661, August 4, 1911. Magazine. 32pp. Young adult. eldj

_____. *Fred Fearnot's Hardest Game.* New York: Work and Win Weekly No. 667, Sept. 15, 1911. Magazine. 32pp. Young adult. djdej

_____. *Fred Fearnot's Baseball Victory.* New York: Work and Win Weekly No. 670, Oct. 6, 1911. Magazine. 32pp. Young adult. eldj

_____. *Fred Fearnot's Young Nine.* New York: Work and Win Weekly No. 697, April 12, 1912. Magazine. 32pp. Young adult. eldj

_____. *Fred Fearnot in the Box.* New York: Work and Win Weekly No. 699, April 26, 1912. Magazine. 32pp. Young adult. eldj

_____. *Fred Fearnot Behind the Bat.* New York: Work and Win Weekly No. 701, May 10, 1912. Magazine. 32pp. Young adult. eldj

_____. *Fred Fearnot's Curious Curve.* New York: Work and Win Weekly No. 705, June 7, 1912. Magazine. 32pp. Young adult. eldj

_____. *Fred Fearnot's Hard Hitting.* New York: Work and Win Weekly No. 707, June 21, 1912. Magazine. 32pp. Young adult. eldj

_____. *Fred Fearnot's Base Running.* New York: Work and Win Weekly No. 710, July 12, 1912. Magazine. 32pp. Young adult. eldj

_____. *Fred Fearnot and the Rowdy Players.* New York: Work and Win Weekly No. 713, August 2, 1912. Magazine. 32pp. Young adult. eldj

_____. *Fred Fearnot's Young Backstop.* New York: Work and Win Weekly No. 716, August 23, 1912. Magazine. 32pp. Young adult. eldj

_____. *Fred Fearnot's Post Season Games.* New York: Work and Win Weekly No. 719, Sept. 13, 1912. Magazine. 32pp. Young adult. eldj

SHAPIRO, IRWIN. *Casey Jones and Locomotive No. 638.* New York: Julian Messner, Inc., 1944. Hardbound. 51pp. Juvenile.
Casey's boss tries to get the famous engineer to give up pitching, luring him with the offer of a new locomotive in which to set records and be heroic. AGM

SHARP, PAUL. *Paul the Pitcher.* Chicago: Childrens Press, 1984. Hardbound. 29pp. Juvenile.
Rhymed text on how Paul likes to pitch. AGM

SHAW, IRWIN. *Voices of a Summer Day.* New York: Delacorte Press, 1965. Hardbound. 223pp. Adult.
Benjamin Federov relives his life while watching his teenage son play baseball on a warm summer day. The novel switches back and forth between game descriptions and recollection. BP

SHEA, CORNELIUS. *Three Strikes and Out.* New York: Happy Days Nos. 342–45, May 4 to May 25, 1901. Magazine. Young adult. el

_____. *Home Run Harry.* New York: Happy Days Nos. 397–400, May 24 to June 14, 1902. Magazine. Young adult. el

_____. *Shortstop Sam.* New York: Happy Days Nos. 563–66, July 29 to August 19, 1905. Magazine. Young adult. el

_____. *Charlie Cooper's Curves.* New York: Happy Days Nos. 608–11, June 9 to June 30, 1906. Magazine. Young adult. el

_____. *The Never-Heard-Of Nine.* New York: Happy Days Nos. 620–23, Sept. 1 to Sept. 22, 1906. Magazine. Young adult. el

_____. *Behind the Bat.* New York: Happy Days Nos. 817–20, June 11 to July 2, 1910. Magazine. Young adult. el

_____. *Lining Them Out.* New York: Happy Days Nos. 831–34, Sept. 17 to Oct. 8, 1910. Magazine. Young adult. el

_____. *The Little Giants.* New York: Happy Days Nos. 871–74, June 24 to July 15, 1911. Magazine. Young adult. el

_____. *Ben and His Baseball Boys.* New York: Happy Days Nos. 1027–30, June 20 to July 11, 1914. Magazine. Young adult. el

SHEA, GEORGE. *Big Bad Ernie.* Mankato, Mn: Creative Education, Inc., 1978. Hardbound. 56pp. Juvenile.

No one denies that Ernie is a skilled hitter, but can he control his temper and learn to work within the team? AGM

_____. *Strike Two.* Belmont, Ca: Fearon Education, 1981. Paper. 60pp. Adult.

Designed for an adult literacy program. Al Sanchez must overcome his past while playing for a Cardinals' farm club. AGM

_____. *Make the Play-offs!* New York: Simon & Schuster, Inc., 1983. Paper. 117pp. Juvenile.

One of those books where the reader's decision on what to do in a given situation sends him to alternative pages of the book. Object—see the title. AGM

SHEED, WILFRID. *The Boys of Winter.* New York: Alfred A. Knopf, Inc., 1987. Hardbound. 280pp. Adult.

A novel of the literary set in the Hamptons whose title is a play on Roger Kahn's book about the 1950s Dodgers. The plot moves along on the organization of a team to play a climactic softball game v. a visiting movie crew. TS

SHELDON, CHARLES M. *The Captain of the Orient Baseball Nine.* 1882. Paper. Juvenile. agmo

Grobani describes this as "a short story by the future author of the religious best seller *In His Steps.*" I have been able to find no evidence of publication as a separate item, only as a four-page short story in the October, 1882, issue of *St. Nicholas,* the premier children's magazine of the era. A prep school team wins the Big Game but the captain feels compelled to admit he trapped the ball for the final out. Sheldon's later writings are foreshadowed clearly in the moral struggles. AGM

SHEPPARD, W. CRISPIN. *The Rambler Club's Ball Nine.* Philadelphia: Penn Publishing Co., 1913. Hardbound. 316pp. Juvenile. jomo

One of 15 Rambler Club books. DJ

SHERIDAN, FRANK. (Pseudonym: *See* John De-Morgan.)

SHERMAN, HAROLD M. *Fight 'em, Big Three.* New York: D. Appleton and Co., 1926. Hardbound. 263pp. Young adult.

Three boys and their freshman year in high school. They engage in bicycling, camping, law enforcement, football, and for the last third of the book, baseball. AGM

_____. *Bases Full.* New York: Grosset & Dunlap, Inc., 1928. Hardbound. 250pp. Young adult.

First of five in the Home Run series. Ernie Powers is a sophomore at State (evidently the same school later attended by Chip Hilton). In the first known intrusion of Sigmund Freud into children's baseball fiction, a cheerleader identifies Ernie as having an "inferiority complex." She encourages Ernie to go out for baseball and improve his confidence. He does. AGM

_____. *Hit by Pitcher.* New York: Grosset & Dunlap, Inc., 1928. Hardbound. 241pp. Young adult.

Second of Home Run series. Wally Coburn pouts when he isn't elected his high school team captain, then reforms when he realizes the other fellow deserved it more. The next year, Wally is elected captain but then must overcome fear after a bad beaning. AGM

_____. *Safe!* New York: Grosset & Dunlap, Inc., 1928. Hardbound. 308pp. Young adult.

Dolf Redding must learn the perils of debt before he can steal bases. Third of Home Run series. AGM

_____. *Flashing Steel.* New York: Grosset & Dunlap, Inc., 1929. Hardbound. 264pp. Young adult.

This is, to all appearances, a high school hockey novel. But about halfway through, it turns to baseball and stays that way. AGM

_____. *Hit and Run!* New York: Grosset & Dunlap, Inc., 1929. Hardbound. 248pp. Young adult.

Fourth of Home Run series. Rivalry between East Siders and West Siders extends to the high school baseball team. Sandy Sanderson, 3B, wins new respect for the East Siders and brings the team together. AGM

_____. *Batter Up!* New York: Grosset & Dunlap, Inc., 1930. Hardbound. 304pp. Young adult.
An American Legion coach must reconcile factions from both sides of the tracks. He does so and Traverse City, Michigan, wins the American Legion national title in Yankee Stadium. AGM

_____. *Strike Him Out!* Chicago: Goldsmith Publishing Co., 1931. Hardbound. 240pp. Young adult.
Our Hero strikes out his bench-jockey rival in the Big Game. Second of eight-book All American Sports series. AGM

_____. *Double Play and Other Baseball Stories.* New York: Grosset & Dunlap, Inc., 1932. Hardbound. 244pp. Young adult collection.
Last of Home Run series. A novella about a boy who must overcome fears from an old knee injury to slide. Also five short stories. AGM

_____. *Last Man Out.* Akron, Oh: Saalfield Publishing Co., 1937. Hardbound. 156pp. Young adult.
Young player is given the second base job, breaking up a veteran combination at his prep school. This and Heyliger's *Three-Finger Joe* are the two baseball books in the four-book Saalfield Sports Books series. AGM

SILVERS, EARL REED. *Dick Arnold of the Varsity.* New York: D. Appleton and Co., 1923. Hardbound. 258pp. Young adult. joagmo
Third of three Dick Arnold stories. AGM

_____. *Jackson of Hillsdale High.* New York. D. Appleton and Co., 1923. Hardbound. 251pp. Young adult.
Second of three Hillsdale High books. One summer-camp game described. AGM

_____. *Team First.* New York: D. Appleton and Co., 1929. Hardbound. 247pp. Young adult. agmonuc

SIMON, TONY, ed. *Crooked Arm and Other Baseball Stories.* New York: Scholastic Book Service, 1968. Paper. 144pp. Juvenile collection.

Includes stories by Jackson Scholz, Charles Van Loan (from *Score by Innings),* and Stephen Meader. AGM

SKOWRON, BILL, and JACK LANG. *New Blood at First. See* Berra and Ferdenzi's *Behind the Plate.*

SLATTERY, MARTY. *Diamonds Are Trumps.* Memphis, Tn: St. Luke's Press, 1990. Hardbound. 264pp. Adult.
Forty-year-old minor league pitcher reviews his life as the Lodi Dodgers struggle for a California League title. AGM

SLOTE, ALFRED. *Stranger on the Ball Club.* Philadelphia: J. B. Lippincott Co., 1970. Hardbound. 172pp. Juvenile.
New boy in town, 11-year-old Tim Foster, learns about honor, truthfulness, and teamwork the hard way in a junior league. Good and credible on baseball detail and moral points. Told in first person. FP. All of Slote's juveniles that I have seen, including this one, are set in Arborville, Michigan, clearly borrowed from Ann Arbor. AGM

_____. *Jake.* Philadelphia: J. B. Lippincott Co., 1971. Hardbound. 155pp. Juvenile.
Boys' team tries to operate without a coach as Our Hero lives with an uncle who is rarely around. Uncle becomes more of a parent and also the coach as the kids find him a place to practice with his band. AGM

_____. *The Biggest Victory.* Philadelphia: J. B. Lippincott Co., 1972. Hardbound. 154pp. Juvenile.
Randy would rather go fishing than be on a Little League team, but he plays because his father wants him to continue the tradition of a very baseball family. He gets hurt and learns to appreciate baseball and his teammates. Dad goes fishing. AGM

_____. *My Father, the Coach.* Philadelphia: J. B. Lippincott Co., 1972. Hardbound. 157pp. Juvenile.
The only way Ezell Corkins and his friends can form a team is to have his father as coach—and dad knows zilch about baseball. AGM

_____. *Hang Tough, Paul Mather.* Philadelphia: J. B. Lippincott Co., 1973. Hardbound. 156pp. Juvenile.

Paul has leukemia. He's moved to a new town and a new doctor but can't play Little League. He fakes his way on to a team, but his disease catches up to him and he can only root for his teammates. AGM

_____. *Tony and Me.* Philadelphia: J. B. Lippincott Co., 1974. Hardbound. 156pp. Juvenile.
Our Hero, the Little League shortstop, is the only decent player on his team. Then they get another. At first, he's jealous, then they become fast friends until Tony's dad sends him back to Kentucky for various crimes. AGM

_____. *Matt Gargan's Boy.* Philadelphia: J. B. Lippincott Co., 1975. Hardbound. 158pp. Juvenile.
His dad's a big-league catcher and he's the star of his local team, but Danny Gargan still has problems, especially a girl playing on his team. AGM

_____. *Rabbit Ears.* New York: J. B. Lippincott Co., 1982. Hardbound. 110pp. Juvenile.
A star at 13, Tip O'Hara moves to a 14-year-old league and must learn to ignore catcalls. AGM

_____. *Make-Believe Ballplayer.* New York: J. B. Lippincott Co., 1989. Hardbound. 104pp. Juvenile.
Henry's imaginary baseball games are hindering his development as a Little Leaguer. Then one of his whimsies helps win a game. AGM

_____. *The Trading Game.* New York: J. B. Lippincott Co., 1990. Hardbound. 200pp. Juvenile.
Family relationships between a Little Leaguer and his former-major-leaguer grandfather. Grandpa coaches and the boy tries to trade for a card of his grandfather. AGM

SMALL, DAVID. *Almost Famous.* New York: W. W. Norton & Co., 1982. Hardbound. 416pp. Adult.
A young man's baseball career is ended by a car accident, leaving him with the challenge of overcoming the loss of fame. JO

SMITH, CAROLE. *The Hit-and-Run Connection.* Chicago: Albert Whitman & Co., 1982. Hardbound. 126pp. Juvenile mystery.
A boy is hit while riding his bike, and his two friends set out to solve the crime. The suspects are all members of the Chicago White Sox whom the boys have befriended. Minimal game descrip-tion and some detecting at Comiskey Park. Illustrations show the Sox tunic uniforms of the period. AGM

SMITH, DORIS BUCHANAN. *Last Was Lloyd.* New York: Viking Press, 1981. Hardbound. 124pp. Juvenile.
Fat boy, scorned by all, is always chosen last for school-yard games. He actually can hit but refuses to show it to his tormentors. Eventually, he comes out of his shell. AGM

SMITH, H. ALLEN. *Rhubarb.* Garden City, NY: Doubleday & Co., 1946. Hardbound. 301pp. Adult.
Novel about a cat that ends up owning a major league team. BP

SMITH, ROBERT. *Little League Catcher.* New York: A. S. Barnes and Co., 1953. Hardbound. 156pp. Juvenile.
A primer on baseball, especially catching, and long division. This is the same Robert Smith who has written many non-fiction baseball books. AGM

SMITH, ROBERT KIMMEL. *Bobby Baseball.* New York: Delacorte Press, 1989. Hardbound. 165pp. Juvenile.
Ten-year-old Bobby is passionate about baseball and convinced that he is a great player. His father, a former minor leaguer and his coach, tries to introduce a sense of reality. It takes a season. AGM

SNYDER, DON J. *Veterans Park.* New York: Franklin Watts, Inc., 1987. Hardbound. 257pp. Adult.
During the summer of 1969, a young woman in a Maine town falls in love with a minor league pitcher whose brother is serving in Vietnam. Class differences complicate the romance. JO

SOBOL, DONALD J. *Encyclopedia Brown and the Case of the Secret Pitch.* New York: Elsevier/Nelson Books, 1965. Hardbound. 96pp. Juvenile mystery.
Only the first story in this book of juvenile mysteries is about baseball, but there is a baseball illustration on the cover. Encyclopedia exposes a fraud when a boy claims to have won a bet by

selling his trick pitch to a big leaguer. First of many Encyclopedia Brown books. AGM

SORRENTINO, GILBERT. *Flawless Play Restored: The Masque of Fungo.* Los Angeles: Black Sparrow Press, 1974. Hardbound. 83pp. Adult.

A strange metafiction, which makes use of the conventions of baseball and some of its famous names. Also published as part of Sorrentino's *Mulligan Stew,* (Grove Press, 1979). TS

SOTO, GARY. *Baseball in April and Other Stories.* San Diego: Harcourt Brace Jovanovich, 1990. Hardbound. 111pp. Juvenile collection.

Only one of 11 stories is about baseball. AGM

SPENCER, ROSS H. *The Stranger City Caper.* New York: Avon Books, 1980. Paper. 160pp. Adult mystery.

A spoof of the hard-boiled detective novel, this mystery relates in single-sentence paragraphs the investigation into strange doings on a minor league baseball team. One practice session and part of a game are the only baseball action described. JOBP. In addition to this and the following book, Spencer also wrote *The Fifth Script* and *The Devereaux File,* with chief detective Lacey Lockington, who spouts a lot of baseball trivia and clues based on same. AGM

———. *Kirby's Last Circus.* New York: Donald I. Fine, Inc., 1987. Hardbound. 253pp. Adult mystery. Birch Kirby, the world's most incompetent, but luckiest, detective, goes underground for the CIA as the bull-pen catcher of the Grizzly Gulch No Sox. The baseball is basically irrelevant to the story, though there is some game action. BP

SPRINGSTUBB, TRICIA. *With a Name like Lulu, Who Needs More Trouble?* New York: Delacorte Press, 1989. Hardbound. 167pp. Juvenile.

Lulu is a Cleveland Indians fan who lacks confidence. Modest amount of baseball. No game action. AGM

STADLER, JOHN. *Hooray for Snail.* New York: Thomas Y. Crowell Co., 1984. Hardbound. 32pp. Juvenile.

Snail hits the ball to the moon, but he's so slow there's a question if he'll be able to score. AGM

STANDISH, BURT L. (Pseudonym: *See* Gilbert Patten.)

STANDISH, HAL. (Pseudonym: *See* H. K. Shackleton and George W. Goode.)

STANDISH, WINN. (Pseudonym: *See* Walter L. Sawyer.)

STANSBERRY, DOMENIC. *The Spoiler.* New York: Atlantic Monthly Press, 1987. Hardbound. 278pp. Adult mystery.

Disappointing mystery about a down-and-out reporter who lands in a corrupt small town with a lousy minor league team. Hanging around the ballpark soon involves him in a web of corruption that reaches from the diamond to the state capitol, involving drugs, murder, and arson. BP

STAPP, ARTHUR. *Too Steep for Baseball.* New York: Harper & Row, 1964. Hardbound. 153pp. Juvenile.

Despite title, very little baseball. Boy's family spends lots of time at a cabin so far out in the woods they can't even get the games of his favorite Yankees on the radio. He gains other interests. AGM

STARRETT, VINCENT. *The Great All-Star Animal League Ball Game.* New York: Dodd, Mead & Co., 1957. Hardbound. 53pp. Juvenile.

A game of barnyard v. forest animals won when a donkey kicks a grand-slam homer. AGM

STEIN, HARRY. *Hoopla.* New York: Alfred A. Knopf, Inc., 1983. Hardbound. 366pp. Adult.

A fictional account of the Black Sox scandal "told," in part, by Buck Weaver. Ty Cobb also figures as a major character. JO

STEVENS, MAURICE. (Pseudonym: *See* John H. Whitson.)

STINE, MEGAN, and H. WILLIAM. *Baseball Card Fever.* New York: Ballantine Books, 1989. Paper. 74pp. Juvenile mystery.

Jeffrey's father loans him some old baseball cards, but they disappear. Second in the Jeffrey and the Fourth Grade Ghost series. AGM

STOCKER, FERN NEAL. *Billy Sunday, Baseball Preacher.* Chicago: Moody Press, 1985. Paper. 141pp. Juvenile.

Another biography so hoked up with conversations nobody could have recorded that it's fiction. Most of the book is his boyhood, including baseball. Only a couple of chapters on his pro years. AGM

STONE, DAVID. *Yank Brown, Pitcher*. New York: Barse & Hopkins, 1924. Hardbound. 224pp. Juvenile. A multitalented hero of six books, Yank takes up pitching. It's the end of Yank's freshman year in college, and he leads the frosh team over the varsity. Baseball takes up most of book. AGM

STONE, NATALIE. (Pseudonym: *See* Sally Goldenbaum.)

STONE, RAYMOND. (Pseudonym: *See* Edward Stratemeyer.)

STRATEMEYER, EDWARD. *Dave Porter at Oak Hall*. Boston: Lothrop, Lee & Shepard Co., 1905. Hardbound. 312pp. Young adult.

Edward Stratemeyer, who started his career writing dime novels for Street & Smith, was the founder of a syndicate that has produced thousands of children's books since it was started in 1906. The vast majority were not written by Stratemeyer himself, but since his authors signed agreements not to reveal that they'd written for the syndicate, tracing actual authorship is difficult. In general, Stratemeyer and the writer agreed on an outline, and the writer then produced the book. Sports books were actually a small part of the Stratemeyer empire, with the Hardy Boys, Nancy Drew, the Bobbsey Twins, the Rover Boys, Bomba the Jungle Boy, and Tom Swift (Sr. and Jr.) all in the stable. Where something is known, I've tried to indicate possible authorship of a series. This was the first of 15 Dave Porter books, many having a baseball chapter or so. This one includes many sports but winds up with the big baseball game. AGM

_____. *The Baseball Boys of Lakeport*. (1908). See Bonehill's *The Winning Run*.
Second of six in the Lakeport series. AGM

(Written as CAPTAIN RALPH BONEHILL.) *Camp and Diamond*. New York: Bright Days, July to Sept. 19, 1896. Magazine. Young adult. dej

Edward Stratemeyer, probably the most important force ever in children's fiction—not for his writing, for Baseball Joe was a tad unbelievable, but for the organization of his syndicate and the series it spun out. Some of those series, such as the Hardy Boys and Nancy Drew, are going full blast sixty years after his death.
Simon and Schuster

Bonehill was a pseudonym Stratemeyer generally reserved for himself. AGM

_____. *The Winning Run*. New York: A. S. Barnes and Co., 1905. Hardbound. 315pp. Young adult.
Reissued as *The Baseball Boys of Lakeport* under Stratemeyer's own name. The boys form a baseball club and play a successful round of

games against other town teams. Also, a mystery is solved. AGM

(Written as LESTER CHADWICK.) *The Rival Pitchers*. New York: Cupples & Leon Co., 1910. Hardbound. 303pp. Young adult.

In baseball terms, this was the most prolific of the Stratemeyer pseudonyms, and fittingly it was chosen to echo that of Henry Chadwick, inventor of the box score, and one of the important early figures in popularizing and codifying the game. Tom Parsons, a "hayseed," and his friends Phil and Sid make good on the scrub team of Randall College. First of six in the College Sports series. AGM

_____. *Batting to Win*. New York: Cupples & Leon Co., 1911. Hardbound. 308pp. Young adult.

Sid is falsely accused of gambling and kicked off the team. He is cleared just in time for the Big Game. DEJ

_____. *Baseball Joe of the Silver Stars*. New York: Cupples & Leon Co., 1912. Hardbound. 246pp. Young adult.

The first of the major series books devoted almost exclusively to baseball and to a single hero whose principal role is as a baseball player—the fabulous "Baseball Joe" Matson. The major earlier series hero—Frank Merriwell—didn't play baseball in many of his books. And Joe was the first series hero who was a professional baseball player, rather than a school hero. In this first of 14 books, 15-year-old Joe begins his career on the Riverside town team. In case you didn't guess, he's very good. He wins his place on the team and then helps his father protect his machinery inventions (a continuing subplot of the series) so Joe can fulfill his dream of going to a boarding school. Howard Garis worked on many of the Baseball Joe series, but Garis's son relates in a biography of his father that Stratemeyer died while thinking he was holding a conversation with Joe, so perhaps Stratemeyer wrote a number of these himself. However, a similar story is attributed to his family in his obituary, but that story has him dreaming of the characters in the Buck and Larry series (Elmer Dawson), which was being produced at the time of Stratemeyer's death. Whoever did the writing, especially of the first ten books or so, was clearly a baseball fan. Names—Mornsby for a Cardinal infielder, Zach Treat and Dizzy Rance, Dodger outfielder and fireballer—are clearly borrowed from real life, as are situations. Many of the early books contain long bits of baseball history. AGM

_____. *Baseball Joe on the School Nine*. New York: Cupples & Leon Co., 1912. Hardbound. 244pp. Young adult.

Joe overcomes the bad guys and makes the prep school team a success. AGM

_____. *Baseball Joe at Yale*. New York: Cupples & Leon Co., 1913. Hardbound. 248pp. Young adult.

Joe pitches for the varsity in his second year, beats Princeton, shows up the snobs, and then departs for his real career. Apparently, he was sent to Yale as a matter of boys' book formula, for Joe makes it clear even before he goes to New Haven that he wants to be a pro and isn't cut out to be a college man. AGM

_____. *Baseball Joe in the Central League*. New York: Cupples & Leon Co., 1914. Hardbound. 246pp. Young adult.

Joe tears up the minors, reforms a former big leaguer who's turned into a drunken hobo, and meets the love of his life, Mabel Varley. AGM

_____. *Baseball Joe in the Big League*. New York: Cupples & Leon Co., 1915. Hardbound. 250pp. Young adult.

Joe makes it to the bigs with the Cardinals, where he plays for manager "Muggins" Watson (Miller Huggins). AGM

_____. *Baseball Joe on the Giants*. New York: Cupples & Leon Co., 1916. Hardbound. 244pp. Young adult.

But then John McRae (McGraw), manager of the Giants, trades for him. He wins 20. One chapter has Joe run into a member of the 1869 Cincinnati Red Stockings, the first professional baseball team. An interesting glimpse of how 1916 viewed the origins of the game. AGM

(a)
HE WAS A GLORIOUS FIGURE OF YOUNG MANHOOD.
Baseball Joe in the World Series.   Page 214

(b)
IT WAS A HAMMER-AND-TONGS CONFLICT FROM START TO FINISH.
Baseball Joe Around the World   Page 221

(c)
IT WAS THE LONGEST HIT THAT EVER HAD BEEN MADE ON THE POLO GROUNDS.
"Baseball Joe, Home Run King."   Page 133

(d)
MR. WATSON'S ARM MUST HAVE ABSOLUTE REST.
"Baseball Joe Club Owner."   Page 53

Four illustrations from the incredible career of Baseball Joe. Above left, *the hero as hero by R. Emmett Owen;* right, *Owen's vision of Joe pitching in front of the pyramids in* Baseball Joe Around the World; below left, *Thelma Gooch portrays Joe's newfound mastery at bat in* Baseball Joe, Home Run King; right, *an unknown artist captures the key moment of* Baseball Joe, Club Owner *while an ignorant captioneer errs on Joe's last name (Matson).*

a: Frontispiece from *Baseball Joe in the World Series,* 1917; b: Illustration on page 221 of *Baseball Joe Around the World,* 1918; c: Frontispiece from *Baseball Joe, Home Run King,* 1922; and d: Illustration on page 53 of *Baseball Joe, Club Owner,* 1926.

_____. *Baseball Joe in the World Series.* New York: Cupples & Leon Co., 1917. Hardbound. 242pp. Young adult.

This book follows immediately on the heels of the previous. Joe foils an attempt to kidnap him and fix the Series. He also beats a Boston Red Sox left-hander named Roth (Ruth) and wins three games. Oh, yes, he proposes to Mabel and is accepted. AGM

_____. *Baseball Joe Around the World.* New York: Cupples & Leon Co., 1918. Hardbound. 246pp. Young adult.

This book picks up immediately after the last, with a tour of the world by the Giants and an all-star team. The basic plot is a book-long screed against any player who'd be a traitor to his team by joining the Federal League, a third major league that had actually folded three years earlier. The foreign climes also allow Joe some new twists on scenes familiar from earlier books. The rescue-by-throwing scene in which Joe uses his pitching skills is performed on a shark, and he also uses a hook slide to stop a Malay run amok. AGM

_____. *Baseball Joe, Home Run King.* New York: Cupples & Leon Co., 1922. Hardbound. 244pp. Young adult.

After a hiatus, which was probably due to World War I, Joe returns not as a pitcher but as a slugger. Interestingly, while this mirrors a major change in baseball at the time, the books don't deal with the fact that Joe has been described consistently as a weak hitter in earlier volumes. Ruth, who was Roth in earlier books, has become Kid Rose. The Giants and the Yanks win their leagues and meet in the World Series. While Joe has been playing the outfield some, he pitches the ninth game, hits three homers (nine for the Series), and strikes out Rose twice. In another effort to clean up the leftovers of previous books, Joe finally marries Mabel. AGM

_____. *Baseball Joe, Saving the League.* New York: Cupples & Leon Co., 1923. Hardbound. 248pp. Young adult.

Only Joe could do it, and a dastardly conspiracy it was, too. He exposes two teammates who are trying to throw the pennant. AGM

_____. *Baseball Joe, Captain of the Team.* New York: Cupples & Leon Co., 1924. Hardbound. 248pp. Young adult.

Joe is elevated to captain and produces another pennant. AGM

_____. *Baseball Joe, Champion of the League.* New York: Cupples & Leon Co., 1925. Hardbound. 246pp. Young adult.

Before the season, Joe promises to lead the league in batting average, home runs, stolen bases, strikeouts (as a pitcher), earned run average, consecutive wins and also to lead the Giants to their greatest number of wins in a season. He does so. AGM

_____. *Baseball Joe, Club Owner.* New York: Cupples & Leon Co., 1926. Hardbound. 244pp. Young adult.

Arm injured, Joe goes home to Riverside and turns the town team into a powerhouse. First edition contains an early Jello advertisement (featuring Robinson Crusoe) in the book. Also features the first appearance of Moe Russnak, a "low, greasy" Jew who figures as a villain in the next two books. Levy, the Riverside team's shortstop, is condescendingly mentioned in an attempt to assure us Russnak isn't typical. AGM

_____. *Baseball Joe, Pitching Wizard.* New York: Cupples & Leon Co., 1928. Hardbound. 210pp. Young adult.

Cured by rest, Joe returns. Late in the season, he escapes from a weeks-long kidnapping by Russnak to find the Giants in the second division and two regulars hurt. The team rallies in a magnificent final charge, but the rookie replacements are making errors at key points. In the final game against the Cubs to decide the pennant race, Joe realizes he cannot count on them and thus must strike out every Cub batter. He does, 27 straight. Presumably unable to top this, the Baseball Joe series was not revived. AGM

(Written as ALLEN CHAPMAN.) *The Darewell Chums*. New York: Cupples & Leon Co., 1908. Hardbound. 224pp. Young adult.

First of five Darewell Chums books. Various schoolboy adventures. One baseball game described. Reissued as *The Heroes of the School.* AGM

_____. *Fred Fenton the Pitcher.* New York: Cupples & Leon Co., 1913. Hardbound. 206pp. Young adult mystery.

First of five in the Fred Fenton series where Fred mixes athletic prowess with detective work. In this, Fred takes over as pitcher for the high school team while foiling the attempt of the father of his pitching rival to take over a claim the Fenton family should have on some vaguely defined riches in Alaska. AGM

_____. *The Heroes of the School.* (1917). See *The Darewell Chums.*

(Written as JOHN R. COOPER.) *The Mystery at the Ball Park.* New York: Cupples & Leon Co., 1947. Hardbound. 208pp. Young adult mystery.

The first of a series of mysteries featuring star pitcher Mel Martin. A high school junior, Mel must beat out a senior, discover what's fishy about the new coach, solve a string of robberies, and save the ballpark. The first four books were reissued by Simon and Schuster in 1982. AGM

_____. *The Southpaw's Secret.* New York: Cupples & Leon Co., 1947. Hardbound. 212pp. Young adult mystery.

Many strands of mystery come together at the end as Mel and the gang win a summer camp league championship. One key mystery involves a man who has developed a formula to make bats more resilient. AGM

_____. *The Phantom Homer.* Garden City, NY: Garden City Books, 1952. Hardbound. 189pp. Young adult mystery.

Mel, now a senior, and the boys win their high school league and foil a counterfeiting operation. AGM

_____. *First Base Jinx.* Garden City, NY: Garden City Books, 1952. Hardbound. 191pp. Young adult mystery.

The main mystery here is who stole the prototype for a revolutionary type of first baseman's mitt. The chums win an amateur league title. AGM

_____. *The College League Mystery.* Garden City, NY: Garden City Books, 1953. Hardbound. 191pp. Young adult mystery.

Now at Starbuck College, Mel and the boys must deal with the jealousy of a varsity pitcher and win a freshmen league. Also features the introduction of the immortal shortstop Chico Gomez, who the dust jacket describes as a "droll" Cuban with "the zest of chile con carne." AGM

_____. *The Fighting Shortstop.* Garden City, NY: Garden City Books, 1953. Hardbound. 192pp. Young adult mystery.

Chico takes the boys to work on his uncle's sugar plantation and they play in a summer league. They save the Gomez business from rivals and win the league. AGM

(Written as SPENCER DAVENPORT.) *The Rushton Boys at Rally Hall.* New York: Hearst's International Library Co., 1916. Hardbound. 244pp. Young adult.

The book follows the boys through a full year at school. Much of the space is devoted to football, but three chapters at the end cover the big year-end baseball game against Mt. Vernon. There were two later books in the series, neither containing baseball. AGM

(Written as ELMER DAWSON.) *The Pick-up Nine.* New York: Grosset & Dunlap, Inc., 1930. Hardbound. 262pp. Young adult.

First of the five-book Buck and Larry series. Stratemeyer was plotting the series when he died in May, 1930. His family told the Newark Evening News that he had envisioned a series that would take the boys from the sandlots to the majors. His planning included box scores for some of the important games. In this book, two brothers organize a sandlot team and then defeat the town team run by snob and rival Roy Spencer. AGM

_____. *Buck's Winning Hit.* New York: Grosset & Dunlap, Inc., 1930. Hardbound. 216pp. Young adult.

Buck and Larry organize a summer league and then meet a new team organized by Spencer. Various subplots. Second of series. TS

_____. *Larry's Fadeaway*. New York: Grosset & Dunlap, Inc., 1930. Hardbound. 244pp. Young adult.

Third of Buck and Larry series. The boys go off to prep school and Larry learns the fadeaway from an old friend of Christy Mathewson's. AGM

_____. *Buck's Home Run Drive*. New York: Grosset & Dunlap, Inc., 1931. Hardbound. 246pp. Young adult.

Fourth of Buck and Larry series. The boys play sandlot games and solve crimes. AGM

_____. *Larry's Speedball*. New York: Grosset & Dunlap, Inc., 1932. Hardbound. 246pp. Young adult. joagmo

Fifth of Buck and Larry series. DJ

(Written as FRANKLIN W. DIXON.) *The Hardy Boys: Danger on the Diamond*. New York: Simon and Schuster, Inc., 1988. Paper. 148pp. Juvenile mystery.

Frank, Joe, and their Bayport High teammates are attending a baseball camp run by an ex-big leaguer when strange and threatening things begin to happen. Only a small amount of baseball action. The Hardy Boys series began in 1927 and has run to almost 100 books, of which this is the 90th. AGM

(Written as GRAHAM FORBES.) *The Boys of Columbia High on the Diamond*. New York: Grosset & Dunlap, Inc., 1911. Hardbound. 227pp. Young adult.

Frank Allen and his chums win a high school league in a three-game series spread around various adventures. St. George Rathborne often was assigned the Graham Forbes pseudonym. Second of an eight-book series. Reissued as *Frank Allen—Pitcher*. AGM

_____. *The Boys of Columbia High in Camp*. New York: Grosset & Dunlap, Inc., 1920. Hardbound. 214pp. Young adult.

The boys have gone off to college but return for old home week. Soon, they're off on a camping trip and accepting challenges from similar groups of their old rivals. A couple of big games and a mystery solved. Remarkably, although generations and generations of old grads have returned, seven of the nine starters were on the team in the earlier book. Last of the Boys of Columbia High series. Reissued as *Frank Allen in Camp*. AGM

_____. *Frank Allen — Pitcher*. (1926). See *The Boys of Columbia High on the Diamond*.

Fifth of the 14-book Frank Allen series. AGM

_____. *Frank Allen in Camp*. (1926). See *The Boys of Columbia High in Camp*.

Seventh in the Frank Allen series. Book covers for the series mentioned another title, *Frank Allen Pitching His Best*, but this was apparently never issued. DEJ

(Written as RAYMOND STONE.) *Tommy Tiptop and His Baseball Nine*. New York: Graham & Matlack, 1912. Hardbound. 126pp. Juvenile.

First of six Tommy Tiptop books. Although the Stratemeyer syndicate produced a number of series for younger readers, this, *Donald Dare*, and *Bobby Blake* are the only baseball stories in the bunch. Ten-year-old Tommy moves to a new town, organizes a team, has adventures, and eventually defeats a team of chums from his old town. AGM

_____. *Donald Dare: The Champion Boy Pitcher*. New York: Charles E. Graham & Co., 1914. Paper. 33pp. Juvenile.

First of a two-book series on Donald. Two boys' teams prepare for and play a game. AGM

(Written as FRANK WARNER.) *Bobby Blake on the School Nine*. New York: Barse & Co., 1917. Hardbound. 250pp. Juvenile.

Sixth of 12 Bobby Blake books. Baseball doesn't appear until halfway through this tale of junior high boys' adventures. Bobby leads the team to triumph in the Monatook Lake League. AGM

(Written as FRANK V. WEBSTER.) *The High School Rivals*. New York: Cupples & Leon Co., 1911. Hardbound. 206pp. Young adult.

Several baseball chapters in this tale of rivalry between two boys and their fathers. AGM

(Written as ARTHUR M. WINFIELD.) *The Rover Boys at School*. New York: The Mershon Co., 1899. Hardbound. 250pp. Young adult.

The Rover Boys series, which Stratemeyer generally wrote himself, extended to 30 books and a couple of generations of Rovers. Many contain some baseball, although usually not much. This is the first in the series. It covers a year at boarding school and contains a chapter covering a baseball game. AGM

_____. *The Rover Boys Down East.* New York: Grosset & Dunlap, 1911. Hardbound. 288pp. Young adult.

This is the 15th in the series. The opening chapter is a game between the teams at Brill College, where the boys are now. That's it for baseball as the rest of the book finds the boys struggling once again to save the inheritances of their lady loves. AGM

_____. *The Rover Boys in Business.* New York: Grosset & Dunlap, 1915. Hardbound. 290pp. Young adult.

This book, 19th in the series, covers the boys' adventures recovering some stolen bonds and Tom Rover's marriage. Three chapters are also spent on the boys' Brill College baseball team against their arch rival. AGM

_____. *The Rover Boys on a Tour.* New York: Grosset & Dunlap, 1916. Hardbound. 326pp. Young adult.

Three chapters covering one college game in the middle. 20th in the series. AGM

_____. *The Rover Boys in the Land of Luck.* New York: Grosset & Dunlap, 1921. Hardbound. 310pp. Young adult.

Now featuring the original Rovers' sons. This recounts several prep school games before the boys head off to strike it rich in the oil fields. 25th in the series. AGM

_____. *The Rover Boys at Big Horn Ranch.* New York: Grosset & Dunlap, 1922. Hardbound. 312pp. Young adult.

One baseball chapter before they head Out West. 26th in series. AGM

_____. *The Rover Boys at Big Bear Lake.* New York: Grosset & Dunlap, 1923. Hardbound. 310pp. Young adult.

This is the 27th in the series. The book covers a series of summer adventures including a chapter on a baseball game between boys from the Rovers' prep school and their rivals. AGM

(Written as CLARENCE YOUNG.) *Jack Ranger's School Victories.* New York: Cupples & Leon Co., 1908. Hardbound. 286pp. Young adult.

Third of six Jack Ranger books. The *Dictionary of Literary Biography* lists Howard Garis as the author of the Jack Ranger series. This one follows Jack through a school year. Many adventures on and off playing fields and even some academic competition. The year ends with practice for, and the playing of, the big baseball game. This section occupies three of 35 chapters. AGM

STRONG, ROD. *The Lady Umpire's Hot Hands.* Canoga Park, Ca: Brandon Books, 1977. Paper. Adult pornography. jtp

SULLIVAN, SILKY. *Henry and Melinda.* Chicago: Childrens Press, 1982. Hardbound. 31pp. Juvenile.

Older brother, younger sister learning to play ball together. AGM

SUMMERS, RICHARD. *Ball-Shy Pitcher.* Austin: Steck-Vaughn Co., 1970. Hardbound. 152pp. Juvenile.

Boy is afraid of the ball, but a Little League manager solves the problem. Much emphasis on racial/ethnic understanding. AGM

SUZANNE, JAMIE. *Sweet Valley Twins: Standing Out.* New York: Bantam Books, 1989. Paper. 101pp. Juvenile romance.

Ace Little League pitcher Belinda "Billie" Layton must face the end of her days as a tomboy and learn to like being a girl. One of a series of books about a group of junior high-age girls, with the twins of the title counseling Billie. One game described. AGM

SWED, TREBOR. (Pseudonym: *See* Robert Dews.)

TAGGARD, EDWARD T. *Baseball Bob, or, The King of the Third Base.* New York: Nugget Library No. 10, Oct. 31, 1889. Magazine. 16pp. Young adult. el

TAPPLY, WILLIAM G. *Follow the Sharks.* New York: Charles Scribner's Sons, 1985. Hardbound. 228pp. Adult mystery.

Former pitching phenom is selling sneakers in a mall when his little boy is kidnapped. The first third of the book is a flashback to his career, which proves important to the solution of the mystery. BP

TAVES, ISABELLA. *Not Bad for a Girl.* New York: M. Evans & Co., 1972. Hardbound. 95pp. Juvenile.

An 11-year-old girl playing for a Little League team experiences hatred and abuse from adults whose traditional thinking reserves baseball for boys. NUC

TAYLOR, FLORANCE W. *Ball Two!* Minneapolis: Lerner Publications Co., 1971. Hardbound. 26pp. Juvenile.

The boys from a migrant labor camp break a window in town playing baseball and must get it fixed. AGM

TEASER, TOM. (*See* Cecil B. Burleigh.)

TEMPLE, WILLARD H. *Pitching for Pawling.* New York: Farrar & Rinehart, Inc., 1940. Hardbound. 267pp. Juvenile.

A year-at-school book with the major subplot being Our Hero's efforts to be successful as the prep school's pitcher. Some of the better schoolboy pranks and maneuvers in this class of book. Second in a two-book series about Ren Wilcox at Pawling. AGM

TENNENBAUM, SILVIA. *Rachel, the Rabbi's Wife.* New York: William Morrow & Co., 1978. Hardbound. 395pp. Adult.

A woman finds some relief from a disappointing marriage by sharing her teenage son's passion for the New York Mets. Baseball is a minor narrative thread here. JO

TESTER, SYLVIA. *Rover, Jr.'s Baseball Career.* Elgin, Il: The Child's World, 1976. Hardbound. 32pp. Juvenile.

Instructional for beginners disguised as a dog's attempt to learn baseball. Rover, Jr. decides there isn't much fun to baseball except for the running. AGM

THOMAS, DAVID, ed. *Teen-Age Stories of the Diamond.* New York: Lantern Press, Inc., 1950. Hardbound. 253pp. Juvenile collection.

Includes stories by Jackson Scholz, Harold Sherman, Adolph Regli, William Heyliger, and Charles Coombs. AGM

THURMAN, A. R. (Pseudonym: *See* Arthur Mann.)

TOLLE, JEAN B. *The Great Pete Penney.* New York: Atheneum, 1979. Hardbound. 90pp. Juvenile.

Pete is actually Priscilla, a tomboy with pitching ambitions. She meets a leprechaun who endows her with a wonderful curve, and her Little League team winds up playing at Wrigley Field. AGM

TOMLINSON, EVERETT. *Ward Hill at Weston.* Philadelphia: A. J. Rowland, 1897. Hardbound. 336pp. Young adult.

The first of four Ward Hill books, it features one baseball chapter as Ward goes through a tough year at prep school. AGM

———. *Ward Hill, the Senior.* Philadelphia: A. J. Rowland, 1898. Hardbound. 360pp. Young adult.

Ward redeems himself academically and socially during a school year. Two baseball games (three chapters) in the middle help. Second in the series. AGM

———. *Ward Hill at College.* Philadelphia: A. J. Rowland, 1899. Hardbound. 258pp. Young adult.

Ward's freshman year at college finds him making a general success in both studies and good works. Three chapters describe a victory of the freshman baseball team, led by Ward, over the sophomores. In the course of that game, it's noted that Ward is the only freshman on the varsity nine, but no other mention of that is made. Third in the series. AGM

———. *The Pennant.* Philadelphia: Griffith and Rowland Press, 1912. Hardbound. 319pp. Young adult.

First of a four-book series about Tait school. Dan Richards strikes out 15 in a town game, and his rich friend persuades his father to sponsor Dan at Tait. Dan leads the school team. AGM

TOTH, PAMELA. *Fever Pitch*. New York: Dell Publishing Co., 1986. Paper. 188pp. Adult romance.

Star softball pitcher strikes him out and then hits it big with former major league slugger. She pitches several games, including some in a national tournament, and whether she should quit softball is a constant subplot. No. 442 of Candlelight Ecstasy Romances. AGM

TRACY, JAMES P. (Written as A Self-Made Man.) *The Boy Magnate, or, Making Baseball Pay.* New York: Fame and Fortune Weekly No. 89, June 14, 1907. Magazine. 32pp. Young adult. djel

_____. *Bound to Be a Manager.* New York: Fame and Fortune Weekly No. 355, July 19, 1912. Magazine. 32pp. Young adult.

TUNIS, JOHN R. *The Kid from Tomkinsville.* New York: Harcourt, Brace & Co., 1940. Hardbound. 355pp. Young adult.

The first baseball book by the finest boys' book writer of his day. Tunis was so popular with his readers that all of his baseball books were reissued in the late 1980s and early 1990s, several in hard covers, so the first generation of readers could buy them for their children. Most of his books are set on the Dodgers, and many characters reappear from book to book. In this, Roy Tucker comes from a small town to success as a pitcher. An injury cuts his pitching short, so he makes it as an outfielder. While Tucker himself is a composite, many characters in these books are drawn from life. A copy of Tunis's notes matching characters and real players for this book appears in Allen's "The Kid from Rowayton." AGM

_____. *World Series.* New York: Harcourt, Brace & Co., 1941. Hardbound. 318pp. Young adult.

Game by game through Tucker's first World Series. AGM

_____. *Keystone Kids.* New York: Harcourt, Brace & Co., 1943. Hardbound. 209pp. Young adult.

A shortstop-second base brother combination battle to the big leagues. When the SS/older brother becomes manager, he must battle his brother over a Jewish catcher whose courage is questioned. AGM

John R. Tunis, author of books that set the target for other juvenile fiction writers from just before World War II to the late 1950s. His books are still being reissued in the 1990s. Photo by Lotte Jacoby.
publisher

_____. *Rookie of the Year.* New York: Harcourt, Brace & Co., 1944. Hardbound. 199pp. Young adult.

A rookie pitcher in the heat of a pennant race. AGM

_____. *The Kid Comes Back.* New York: William Morrow & Co., 1946. Hardbound. 245pp. Young adult.

Roy Tucker, injured when shot down over France during World War II, returns to the Dodgers. AGM

_____. *Highpockets.* New York: William Morrow & Co., 1948. Hardbound. 189pp. Young adult.

A selfish ballplayer is changed when he inadvertently injures a young boy who isn't a baseball fan. AGM

_____. *Young Razzle.* New York: William Morrow & Co., 1949. Hardbound. 192pp. Young adult.

A young player on the way up meets the father who abandoned him years before—the Raz Nugent (Van Lingle Mungo) of earlier books. The father is on the way down, but an encounter with his sneering son reinvigorates him. AGM

_____. *Buddy and the Old Pro.* New York: William Morrow & Co., 1955. Hardbound. 189pp. Young adult.

Buddy looks up to a Stankyish former major leaguer until he becomes the boy's coach and begins to teach him how to cheat. AGM

_____. *Schoolboy Johnson.* New York: William Morrow & Co., 1958. Hardbound. 192pp. Young adult.

Schoolboy (who bears many resemblances to Don Drysdale) must learn to control his temper. Roy Tucker and a veteran who resembles Sal Maglie show him how. AGM

TURNER, MORRIE. *Nipper.* Philadelphia: Westminster Press, 1970. Hardbound. 32pp. Juvenile cartoon.

Cartoons with a definite Peanuts flavor trace Nipper and his baseball team. AGM

URMSTON, MARY. *Larry's Luck.* Garden City, NY: Doubleday & Co., 1952. Hardbound. 189pp. Juvenile.

Baseball illustration on the dust jacket and a chapter or so of games inside. AGM

VALENTINE, VICTOR. *The Oakdale B.B. Club and the Great Game They Played.* New York: Golden Hours, April 28 to June 16, 1888. Magazine. Young adult. el

VAN LOAN, CHARLES. *The Big League.* Boston: Small, Maynard & Co., 1911. Hardbound. 252pp. Young adult collection.

Van Loan was a prolific writer of magazine stories, and the books listed here are collections of them. However, undoubtedly his greatest contribution to baseball literature was to persuade the editor of the Saturday Evening Post to print Ring Lardner's Jack Keefe stories, which the editor had rejected previously. AGM

_____. *The $10,000 Arm and Other Tales of the Big League.* Boston: Small, Maynard & Co., 1912. Hardbound. 336pp. Young adult collection.

_____. *The Lucky Seventh.* Boston: Small, Maynard & Co., 1913. Hardbound. 337pp. Young adult collection.

_____. *Score by Innings.* New York: George H. Doran Co., 1919. Hardbound. 349pp. Young adult collection.

Ten stories, several set in California, and a picture of Ty Cobb on the cover. AGM

VAN RIPER, GUERNSEY, Jr. *Lou Gehrig, Boy of the Sand Lots.* Indianapolis: Bobbs-Merrill Co., 1949. Hardbound. 194pp. Juvenile.

A biography so manufactured and embroidered it's considered fiction. AGM

_____. *Babe Ruth, Baseball Boy.* Indianapolis: Bobbs-Merrill Co., 1954. Hardbound. 200pp. Juvenile.

See the previous entry. AGM

VAN STEENWYK, ELIZABETH. *The Southpaw from Sonora Mystery.* Chicago: Childrens Press, 1983. Hardbound. 63pp. Juvenile mystery.

Boys become friends despite competing for a position on a Little League team and suspicions of theft by one. They solve the mystery of the stolen balls and the stolen gold. AGM

VERRAL, CHARLES SPAIN. *The King of the Diamond.* New York: Thomas Y. Crowell Co., 1955. Hardbound. 179pp. Juvenile. monuc

Third of five sports books about Frenchy Beaumont. AGM

_____. *Mighty Men of Baseball.* New York: American Book Co., 1955. Hardbound. 140pp. Juvenile.

This is actually Verral's choices for the greatest team of all time: Cobb, Ruth, Mathewson, etc. However, a fictional former major leaguer does the selecting with some reflecting on his own career. And, each selection is made while (after time travel) viewing a game of the player in question. Several of these vignettes are dressed up with touches of fiction. AGM

_____. *The Wonderful World Series.* New York: Thomas Y. Crowell Co., 1956. Hardbound. 154pp. Juvenile.

Fourth in the Frenchy Beaumont series. A boys' baseball team is given tickets to the World Series but then must overcome a series of hurdles to earn expense money and get there. No game action. AGM

_____. *Play Ball!* New York: Simon and Schuster, Inc., 1958. Hardbound. 22pp. Juvenile.

A Little Golden Book in which Tommy is introduced to baseball on a neighborhood team. About half simple instructional material. AGM

VOGAN, SARA. *In Shelly's Leg.* New York: Alfred A. Knopf, Inc., 1981. Hardbound. 248pp. Adult.

Fine novel of live, love, and softball, set in Montana and centering on the tavern—Shelly's Leg. BP

WADE, ROBERT. *Knave of Eagles.* New York: Random House, Inc., 1969. Hardbound. 211pp. Adult mystery.

A spy thriller set mostly in Castro's Cuba. The plot involves an attempt to spirit away star pitcher Chombo Herrera, who's returned to Havana to marry and is now stuck. A couple of Chombo's innings are described, and he does bop a bad guy with a pitched baseball at a crucial moment, but that's it. AGM

WALDEN, AMELIA ELIZABETH. *Three Loves Has Sandy.* New York: McGraw-Hill Book Co., 1955. Hardbound. 160pp. Young adult romance.

The three loves are softball (she's a pitcher), horses, and Bill. About a third of the book is descriptions of games or practices. AGM

_____. *Play Ball, McGill.* Philadelphia: Westminster Press, 1972. Hardbound. 191pp. Young adult romance.

Story of a high school softball pitcher's senior year. Ginger McGill's older brother Karl is a minor league baseball player. TS

WALDMAN, FRANK. *Bonus Pitcher.* Boston: Houghton Mifflin Co., 1951. Hardbound. 156pp. Young adult.

He gets $40,000 to sign but then must learn to pitch. He helps the Boston Red Sox to a pennant over the Yankees and then a series win over the Dodgers. Several Yankee and Dodger players of the era appear under their real names. AGM

_____. *Delayed Steal.* Boston: Houghton Mifflin Co., 1952. Hardbound. 150pp. Young adult.

His father's the N.Y. Yankees' manager but doesn't want him to play pro ball. He does anyway and leads the Tigers over the Yanks in a pennant race. AGM

_____. *Lucky Bat Boy.* Cleveland: World Publishing Co., 1956. Hardbound. 216pp. Young adult.

Boy runs away to see his hero play, is hurt by a foul ball. Hero visits him in hospital, and boy helps rejuvenate hero's career. AGM

(Written as JOE WEBSTER.) *The Rookie from Junction Flats.* New York: Ariel Books, 1952. Hardbound. 151pp. Young adult.

Classic hick uncovered in a publicity stunt leads the St. Louis Browns to respectability. AGM

_____. *Dodger Doubleheader.* New York: Ariel Books, 1952. Hardbound. 160pp. Young adult.

Twins play for the Bums. AGM

WALDMAN, JERI and NEIL. *Pitcher in Left Field.* Englewood, NJ: Prentice-Hall Inc., 1979. Hardbound. 63pp. Juvenile.

A frustrated pitcher's resentment at playing left field causes him to make so many errors he brings down the whole Little League team. AGM

WALKER, DAVID G. *Rick Goes to Little League.* Aurora, Il: Caroline House Publishers, 1981. Hardbound. 70pp. Juvenile.

An instructional disguised as a boy talking about his team's season. AGM

WALLACE, FRANCIS. *Big League Rookie.* Philadelphia: Westminster Press, 1950. Hardbound. 186pp. Juvenile. joagmo

WALLOP, DOUGLAS. *The Year the Yankees Lost the Pennant.* New York: W. W. Norton & Co., 1954. Hardbound. 250pp. Adult.

The book from which the musical ''Damn Yankees'' was developed. A Washington Senators fan trades his soul to the devil for the chance to be a young player who can lead his team over the Yankees. AGM

_____. (Adapted by Warren Halliburton.) *The Year the Yankees Lost the Pennant.* New York:

McGraw-Hill Book Co., 1968. Paper. 85pp. Young adult.

A severe condensation of the original done to encourage teen reading. AGM

WALPOLE, JOSEPH A. *The Diamond Pinheads*. Brooklyn: Theo. Gaus' Sons, Inc., 1966. Paper. 38pp. Juvenile. agnuc

"A tale about a baseball player extraordinary." AG

WARDEN, JOHN. (Pseudonym: *See* St. George Rathborne.)

WARNER, FRANK. (Pseudonym: *See* Edward Stratemeyer.)

WASSERMAN, SELMA. *Sailor Jack and the Ball Game*. Westchester, Il: Benefic Press, 1962. Hardbound. 64pp. Juvenile.

WAYNE, RICHARD. (Pseudonym: *See* Duane Decker.)

WEAVER, GORDON. *The Eight Corners of the World*. Chelsea, Vt: Chelsea Green Publishing Co., 1988. Hardbound. 382pp. Adult.

Fascinating novel of a Japanese moviemaker's life told in a collection of fifty years of American slang. The first quarter of the book follows him as interpreter for the American all-star barnstorming team of 1935 in Japan, including Babe Ruth and catcher/spy Moe Berg. AGM

WEAVER, ROBERT. *Nice Guy, Go Home*. New York: Harper & Row, 1968. Hardbound. 180pp. Young adult.

Amish boy is rejected by his family because of his desire to play professional baseball. He then feels he must reject some of his Amish values to be an effective competitor. Set against the backdrop of the civil rights struggle in the South. AGM

WEBB, VAUGHAN. *Hot Streak and Other Sports Stories*. Mahwah, NJ: Watermill Press, 1983. Paper. 96pp. Juvenile collection.

Only one of the eight stories in this extremely simplistic book is about baseball — a boy learning to conquer his fear of being hit by the pitch. However, the cover, which shows a left-handed catcher and a batter finishing his swing in an unlikely position, might trap you. AGM

WEBSTER, FRANK V. (Pseudonym: *See* Edward Stratemeyer.)

WEBSTER, JOE. (Pseudonym: *See* Frank Waldman.)

WEEKS, JACK. *The Hard Way*. New York: A. S. Barnes and Co., 1953. Hardbound. 192pp. Adult.

Mario Canto fights his way onto a big league roster. He comes from a tough neighborhood and must struggle through the minors and injury. AGM

_____. *The Take-Charge Guy*. New York. A. S. Barnes and Co., 1955. Hardbound. 192pp. Adult.

Mario establishes himself as a star and then must risk his career to control a player in cahoots with Mario's gambler-brother during the World Series. AGM

WELLS, BOB. *Five-Yard Fuller of the N.Y. Gnats*. New York: G. P. Putnam's Sons, 1967. Hardbound. 191pp. Juvenile.

A hulking football player is drafted out of the stands to pitch for the hapless Gnats. The book is in the tall tales tradition and breaks the bounds of baseball credulity. Second of four Five-Yard Fuller books. AGM

WENK, RICHARD. *The Great Baseball Championship*. New York: Scholastic Book Service, 1983. Paper. 59pp. Juvenile.

A book where the reader is asked to make decisions about a game. Different decisions send the reader to alternative pages and affect the outcome of the game. AGM

WHEELER, EDWARD L. *High Hat Harry, the Baseball Detective*. New York: Beadle's Half-Dime Library No. 416, July 14, 1885. Magazine. 16pp. Young adult mystery. agmoaj

A detective story set at an East Coast summer resort. Harry always wears a top hat, even when pitching, and has a neck that he can extend until his chin is a foot and a half above his shoulders. Wheeler is more famous as the author of the *Deadwood Dick* series, also published in Beadle's Half-Dime Library. AJRC

WHITEHEAD, PATRICIA. *Arnold Plays Baseball*. Mahwah, NJ: Troll Associates, 1985. Hardbound. 28pp. Juvenile.

ABCs book following Arnold who can't play ball on a rainy day. AGM

WHITING, ROBERT RUDD. *The Fat Mascot.* New York: J. S. Ogilvie Publishing Co., 1902. Paper. 123pp. Adult collection. nucrutgers
Nineteen tall baseball tales in the Paul Bunyan tradition, including a one-armed outfielder. Paper reprint issued by Lincoln-Herndon Press in 1987. The reprint also contains the text of Whiting's *A Ball of Yarn: Its Unwinding* (Paul Elder & Co., 1907), which contains another dozen tall tales from the New York Sun, three of them with baseball themes. AGM

_____. *Crazy Baseball Stories.* New York: J. S. Ogilvie Publishing Co., 1902. Paper. Adult collection. ag
There is a possibility that this is an alternative title for *The Fat Mascot.* I have been unable to locate a copy of this book, and the Rutgers copy of *Mascot* lists that title on the cover and *Baseball Stories, or, How We Won the Game* on the title page. Neither of the major library data bases in the country, nor the Library of Congress, has any record of this title. The only historical reference to it I have seen, besides Grobani, is in a copy of *The American Catalog: 1900–1905,* put out by Publishers' Weekly in 1905, which purports to list all books published in the U. S. in those years. It shows a *Baseball Stories,* minus the *Crazy,* published in paper by Ogilvie in 1902 while listing *The Fat Mascot* as a separate book. AGM

WHITSON, JOHN H. (Written as MAURICE STEVENS.) *Jack Lightfoot's Trump Curve.* New York: All-Sports Library No. 6, March 18, 1905. Magazine. 32pp. Young adult. modj
Jack Lightfoot was yet another Frank Merriwell imitation, who concentrated more on sports. Proving his reputation in the genre, Whitson was one of the writers who was brought in to take over the Merriwell saga when Patten quit. AGM

_____. *Jack Lightfoot's Crack Nine.* New York: All-Sports Library No. 7, March 25, 1905. Magazine. 32pp. Young adult. dj

_____. *Jack Lightfoot's Teamwork.* New York: All-Sports Library No. 10, April 15, 1905. Magazine. 32pp. Young adult. djdej

_____. *Jack Lightfoot's Home Run.* New York: All-Sports Library No. 11, April 22, 1905. Magazine. 32pp. Young adult. dj

_____. *Jack Lightfoot, Magician.* New York: All-Sports Library No. 14, May 13, 1905. Magazine. 32pp. Young adult. dj

_____. *Jack Lightfoot's Lightning Battery.* New York: All-Sports Library No. 15, May 20, 1905. Magazine. 32pp. Young adult. dj

_____. *Jack Lightfoot's Dilemma.* New York: All-Sports Library No. 18, June 10, 1905. Magazine. 32pp. Young adult. dj

_____. *Jack Lightfoot's Cyclone Finish.* New York: All-Sports Library No. 19, June 17, 1905. Magazine. 32pp. Young adult. djdej

_____. *Jack Lightfoot's "Stone Wall" Infield.* New York: All-Sports Library No. 22, July 8, 1905. Magazine. 32pp. Young adult. dj

_____. *Jack Lightfoot's Talisman.* New York: All-Sports Library No. 23, July 15, 1905. Magazine. 32pp. Young adult. dj

_____. *Jack Lightfoot's Hard Luck.* New York: All-Sports Library No. 26, August 5, 1905. Magazine. 32pp. Young adult. dj

_____. *Jack Lightfoot's Iron Arm.* New York: All-Sports Library No. 27, August 12, 1905. Magazine. 32pp. Young adult.

_____. *Jack Lightfoot in the Box.* New York: All-Sports Library No. 30, Sept. 2, 1905. Magazine. 32pp. Young adult.

_____. *Jack Lightfoot's Lucky Find.* New York: All-Sports Library No. 31, Sept. 9, 1905. Magazine. 32pp. Young adult.

_____. *Jack Lightfoot's Decision.* New York: All-Sports Library No. 34, Sept. 30, 1905. Magazine. 32pp. Young adult. dj

_____. *Jack Lightfoot, Pennant Winner.* New York: All-Sports Library No. 35, Oct. 7, 1905. Magazine. 32pp. Young adult. el

WIBBERLEY, LEONARD P. O. *Little League Family.* Garden City, NY: Doubleday & Co., 1978. Hardbound. 189pp. Juvenile.

A father is drawn into running the local Little League. He winds up losing one job but gaining another because of it as his boys make the all stars and have some tournament success. AGM

WIER, ESTER. *Easy Does It.* New York: Vanguard Press, 1965. Hardbound. 126pp. Juvenile.

Little baseball action in this book, but it permeates the story. An 11-year-old boy is in a new neighborhood and just fitting in with a local sandlot ball club when a black boy moves in next door. He befriends the new kid and is ostracized. Eventually the other boys, and the town, come round, aided by the black boy's cousin, a famous big-league pitcher. AGM

WILLARD, NANCY. *The Highest Hit.* New York: Harcourt Brace Jovanovich, Inc., 1978. Hardbound. 117pp. Juvenile.

The title refers to a hit Kate's mom makes in a neighborhood game after Kate gives her baseball lessons for her birthday. Not much other baseball. AGM

_____. *Things Invisible to See.* New York: Alfred A. Knopf, Inc., 1984. Hardbound. 263pp. Adult.

Fantasy in which a young girl is paralyzed after being hit on the head with a baseball and is cured. It ends with a ball game played between former major leaguers managed by Death and the mothers of a former neighborhood team. TS

WILLIAMS, HAWLEY. (Pseudonym: *See* William Heyliger.)

WILLIAMS, KAREN LYNN. *Baseball and Butterflies.* New York: Lothrop, Lee & Shepard, 1990. Hardbound. 79pp. Juvenile.

Boy interested in butterflies has a little brother interested in baseball. AGM

WINSTON, PETER. *Luke.* New York: Manor Books, 1976. Paper. 318pp. Adult.

Another bad *Semi-Tough* imitation. Luke is a baseball player. Most of the action is off the field, but several games. AGM

WISE, FRANCIS H. *Play Ball.* Thousand Oaks, Ca: Wise Publishing Co., 1975. Paper. 21pp. Juvenile.

A book from the ''See Jane Run'' level of reading. The first half covers baseball. AGM

WITWER, H. C. *From Baseball to Boches.* Boston: Small, Maynard & Co., 1918. Hardbound. 366pp. Adult.

This is an imitation Jack Keefe written by a lesser Ring Lardner. Witwer was a well-known magazine humorist of the day. This book has baseball in the title, is divided into nine sections that are called innings, has a big leaguer for the hero, and contains sort of a game in the last chapter. But there's not much baseball. It's structured as letters home to a friend about Ed Harmon's (the famous southpaw) experiences as he enlists and goes to France to fight in World War I. AGM

_____. *There's No Base Like Home.* Garden City, NY: Doubleday, Page & Co., 1920. Hardbound. 284pp. Adult.

More of the same, but back in the U.S. of A. in the majors. There's quite a bit more baseball as Our Hero returns to his prewar profession. The ''innings'' in this book had previously appeared in Collier's magazine. AGM

WOLFF, MILES, Jr. *Season of the Owl.* New York: Stein and Day, 1980. Hardbound. 181pp. Adult.

A murder near a minor league ballpark brings changes for Tom and his uncle, who runs the team. Wolff is the owner of the Durham Bulls of the Carolina League and publisher of Baseball America. AGM

WOODLEY, RICHARD. *The Bad News Bears.* New York: Dell Publishing Co., 1976. Paper. 203pp. Juvenile.

A 1976 movie that was made into a book. The movie was directed by Michael Ritchie and starred Walter Matthau and Tatum O'Neal. Former big leaguer makes over team of Little League rejects. Bill Lancaster, son of Burt, did the screenplay for this and the *Go to Japan* movies. AGM

_____. *The Bad News Bears in Breaking Training.* New York: Dell Publishing Co., 1977. Paper. 221pp. Juvenile.

A sequel. They go to play in the Astrodome. The 1977 epic was directed by Michael Pressman and starred William Devane. AGM

_____. *The Bad News Bears Go to Japan.* New York: Dell Publishing Co., 1978. Paper. 160pp. Juvenile.

The Bears go to Japan for a game against the Asian champs, and both teams outwit various cardboard adults. From the screenplay of the 1978 blockbuster starring Tony Curtis and directed by John Berry. AGM

WOOLLEY, CATHERINE. *David's Campaign Buttons.* New York: William Morrow and Co., 1959. Hardbound. 191pp. Juvenile.

Neighborhood ball club gets involved in politics while trying to get the city to build them a diamond. AGM

WRIGHT, EDWARD NEEDLES. *Chestnut Bur Lions.* Rose Valley, Pa: Whimsie Press, 1977. Hardbound. 26pp. Adult.

Tale of a mythical team and league in the early years of the century. Highly idiosyncratic, with drawings and statistics. AGM

YOUNG, ERNEST A. *Boats, Bats and Bicycles.* New York: Street & Smith, Publishers, 1902. Hardbound. 257pp. Juvenile.

Despite the title, baseball appears in only one chapter as the boys beat their rivals who've imported a ringer as pitcher. Many adventures in boating and bicycling, however. AGM

YOUNG, ISADOR S. *A Hit and a Miss.* Chicago: Wilcox and Follett, 1952. Hardbound. 240pp. Juvenile.

Two high school boys compete on the baseball team and for the affections of a girl. AGM

_____. *Carson at Second.* Chicago: Follett Publishing Co., 1966. Hardbound. 191pp. Juvenile.

ZACHARIA, IRWIN. *Grandstand Rookie.* Canoga Park, Ca: Major Books, 1977. Paper. 191pp. Adult.

An amazingly banal novel of a player who learns the meaning of love. AGM

ZANGER, JACK. *Baseball Spark Plug.* Garden City, NY: Doubleday & Co., 1963. Hardbound. 143pp. Juvenile.

Immodest boy learns teamwork on the high school team. AGM

ZIEFERT, HARRIET. *Strike Four!* New York: Penguin, 1988. Paper. 29pp. Juvenile.

Debbie practices baseball in her backyard and causes some of the trouble predicted when she was throwing her ball inside the house. AGM

ZIRPOLI, JANE. *Roots in the Outfield.* Boston: Houghton Mifflin Co., 1988. Hardbound. 149pp. Young adult.

A boy learns to field, and to trust himself, with a big leaguer's help. AGM

ZUBRO, MARK RICHARD. *A Simple Suburban Murder.* New York: St. Martin's Press, 1989. Hardbound. 215pp. Adult mystery.

Two gay lovers search for the murderer of a teacher in the high school where one of them teaches. The other is a pitcher on an unnamed Chicago major league team. No game action. AGM

_____. *Why Isn't Becky Twitchell Dead?* New York: St. Martin's Press, 1990. Hardbound. 189pp. Adult mystery.

The characters from the previous book solve the murder of the girlfriend of one of the teacher's students. In this one, we meet a couple of the pitcher's teammates. AGM

OTHER FICTION WITH SOME BASEBALL CONTENT

Many books by recognized authors contain some baseball material, but not enough to warrant inclusion in the bibliography. Here is a short list of some of those books.

ALGREN, NELSON. *Never Come Morning.*
ANDERSON, SHERWOOD. *Beyond Desire.*
ARDIZZONE, TONY. *In the Name of the Father.*
DOCTOROW, E. L. *Ragtime.*
EARLY, ROBERT. *The Jealous Ear.*
FARRELL, JAMES T. *Studs Lonigan.*
FARRELL, JAMES T. *A World I Never Made.*
FARRELL, JAMES T. *No Star is Lost.*
FARRELL, JAMES T. *Father and Son.*
FAULKNER, WILLIAM. *Sanctuary.*
FITZGERALD, F. SCOTT. *The Great Gatsby.*
HEMINGWAY, ERNEST. *The Old Man and the Sea.*
JACKSON, SHIRLEY. *Raising Demons.*
LEHRER, JIM. *Crown Oklahoma.*
LEWIS, SINCLAIR. *Babbit.*
MOSHER, HOWARD FRANK. *A Stranger in the Kingdom.*
RICHLER, MORDECAI. *St. Urbain's Horseman.*
ROTH, PHILIP. *Portnoy's Complaint.*
SALINGER, J. D. *Catcher in the Rye.*
SHEPARD, JIM. *Flights.*
SHULMAN, MAX. *Rally Round the Flag, Boys.*
THOMPSON, KENT. *Shacking Up.*
TWAIN, MARK. *A Connecticut Yankee in King Arthur's Court.*
WODEHOUSE, P. G. *Piccadilly Jim.*
WOLFE, THOMAS. *The Web and the Rock.*
WOLFE, THOMAS. *You Can't Go Home Again.*
WOLFE, THOMAS. *Of Time and the River.*
ZIELINSKI, DAVID. *A Genuine Monster.*
ZUCKERMAN, GEORGE. *Farewell, Frank Merriwell.*

SOURCES

The sources list is divided into two parts. First is a traditional bibliography, composed of the books, articles, and other written material I used in preparing the baseball fiction bibliography.

The second part is a list of the people and/or written sources who contributed to the individual listings and the annotations in the bibliography. These are alphabetical by the initials used to identify the source in the listings.

SOURCES BIBLIOGRAPHY

Extensive use was made of *Book Review Digest, Book Review Index, Books in Print, Dime Novel Round-Up, Yellowback Library, The New York Times Book Review,* and the *National Union Catalogue,* sometimes known as the Library of Congress catalogue. Use was also made of catalogues by book dealers, especially Bobby Plapinger, Bernard Titowsky, and the proprietors of Joseph the Provider.

ADIMARI, RALPH, ed. "The Library of Congress Pseudonyms." *Dime Novel Round-Up* 27, no. 6, issue 321 (15 June 1959): 5–51.

_____. "The Ralph Adimari Pseudonyms." *Dime Novel Round-Up* 27, no. 9, issue 324 (15 September 1959): 74–79.

_____. "The J. Edward Leithead Pseudonyms." *Dime Novel Round-Up* 28, no. 2, issue 329 (15 February 1960): 10–11.

_____. "Miscellaneous Pseudonyms." *Dime Novel Round-Up* 29, no. 2, issue 341 (15 February 1961): 10–13.

ALLEN, MEL R. "The Kid From Rowayton." *Yankee* 53, no. 12 (December 1989): 76–81, 116–19.

American Book Trade Directory. New York: R. R. Bowker. Published annually.

Author unknown. "A Quick Synopsis of the Merriwell Saga." *Dime Novel Round-Up* 48, no. 3, issue 537, (June 1979): 48–49.

BAUER, ANDREW, ed. *The Hawthorn Dictionary of Pseudonyms.* New York: Hawthorn Books, 1971.

BERGEN, PHILIP. "The Books of John R. Tunis." *The SABR Review of Books,* Premiere Issue, 1986.

BILLMAN, CAROL. *The Secret of the Stratemeyer Syndicate.* New York: The Unger Publishing Co., 1986.

BJARKMAN, PETER C. "Diamonds Are A Gal's Worst Friend: Women in Baseball History and Fiction." *The SABR Review of Books.* Volume IV. (Summer 1989): 79–95.

_____. "Introduction." In *Baseball & The Game of Life,* edited by Peter C. Bjarkman. Otisville, NY: Birch Brook Press, 1990.

BRAGIN, CHARLES. *Dime Novels Bibliography: 1860–1928.* Brooklyn, NY: Self-published, 1938.

BURNS, GRANT. *The Sports Pages.* Metuchen, NJ: The Scarecrow Press, 1987.

CANTWELL, ROBERT. "A Sneering Laugh with the Bases Loaded." *Sports Illustrated* 23 (23 April 1962): 67–76.

CECH, JOHN, ed. *Dictionary of Literary Biography, Vol. 22, American Writers for Children, 1900–1960.* Detroit: Gale Research, 1983.

COOK, MICHAEL. *Dime Novel Round-Up Annotated Index, 1931–1981.* Bowling Green, Oh: Bowling Green University Popular Press, 1983.

CURTI, MERLE. "Dime Novels in the American Tradition." *Yale Review* 26 (Summer 1937): 761–78.

CUTLER, JOHN LEVI. *Gilbert Patten and his Frank Merriwell Saga.* Orono, Me: University of Maine Studies, Second Series, no. 31 (1934).

DURHAM, PHILIP. "A General Classification of 1,531 Dime Novels." *Huntington Library Quarterly* 17 (May 1954).

_____. "Dime Novels: An American Heritage." *Western Humanities Review* IX, no. 1 (Winter 1954–55): 33–43.

EAMES, JOHN DOUGLAS. *The Paramount Story.* New York: Crown Publishers, 1985.

ELDER, DONALD. *Ring Lardner.* Garden City, NY: Doubleday & Co., 1956.

ERISMAN, FRED. "The Strenuous Life in Practice: The School and Sports Stories of Ralph Henry Barbour." *Rocky Mountain Social Science Review* VII, no. 1 (April 1970): 29–37.

ESTES, GLENN E. *Dictionary of Literary Biography, Vol. 42, American Writers for Children, Before 1900.* Detroit: Gale Research, 1985.

_____. *Dictionary of Literary Biography, American Writers for Children, Since 1960.* Detroit: Gale Research, 1986.

EVANS, WALTER. "All-American Boys, A Study of Boys Sports Fiction." *Journal of Popular Culture* VI, no. 1 (1972): 104–21.

GARDNER, MARTIN. *The Annotated Casey at the Bat.* New York: Clarkson N. Potter, 1967.

GARIS, ROGER. *My Father was Uncle Wiggly.* New York: McGraw-Hill Book Co., 1966.

GOODSTONE, TONY, ed. *The Pulps.* New York: Chelsea House, 1970.

GRABER, RALPH S. "Baseball in American Fiction." *English Journal* 56, no. 8 (November 1967).

GROBANI, ANTON, ed. *Guide to Baseball Literature.* Detroit: Gale Research, 1975.

GUINON, J. P. "Reprints of the Merriwell Stories." *Dime Novel Round-Up* 23, no. 4 (April 1955): 26–33.

HARRIS, MARK. "Bring Back That Old Sandlot Novel." *The New York Times Book Review* (16 October 1988).

JOHANNSEN, ALBERT. *The House of Beadle and Adams.* 3 vols. Norman, Ok: University of Oklahoma Press, 1950.

JOHNSON, DEIDRE. *Stratemeyer Pseudonyms and Series Books: An Annotated Checklist of Stratemeyer and Stratemeyer Syndicate Publications.* Westport, Ct: Greenwood Press, 1982.

JONES, LYNDS E., comp. *The American Catalogue.* New York: A. C. Armstrong & Son, 1880.

KAVANAGH, JACK. "Baseball Joe Matson." *The SABR Review of Books,* Premiere Issue, 1986.

KILGOUR, RAYMOND L. *Lee and Shepard, Publishers for the People.* Hamden, Ct: The Shoe String Press, 1965.

KURIAN, GEORGE THOMAS. *The Directory of American Book Publishing.* New York: Simon and Schuster, 1975.

LAUTERBACH, ED and KAREN. "Before Brains Benton." *Yellowback Library* no. 62 (August 1989).

LEBLANC, EDWARD T., ed. *Street & Smith Dime Novel Bibliography, Part I, Black and White Era, 1889–1897.* Fall River, Ma: Self-published, 1987.

_____. "Dime Novels." *Antiques & Collecting* (December 1987).

LEITHEAD, J. EDWARD. "The Anatomy of Dime Novels." *Dime Novel Round-Up* 39, nos. 7–8 (15 July and 15 August 1970).

LOWENFISH, LEE, and TONY LUPIEN. *The Imperfect Diamond.* New York: Stein and Day, 1980.

MACGOWAN, KENNETH. *Behind the Screen: The History and Techniques of the Motion Picture.* New York: Dell Publishing, 1965.

MESSENGER, CHRISTIAN KARL. *Sport and the Spirit of Play in American Fiction: Hawthorne to Faulkner.* New York: Columbia University Press, 1981.

MILLER, W. C. *Dime Novel Authors.* Grafton, Ma: Ralph Cummings, 1933.

MURDOCK, EUGENE C. *Mighty Casey: All American.* Westport, Ct: Greenwood Press, 1984.

NEWARK EVENING NEWS. "Services at Home Tonight For Edward Stratemeyer." *Newark Evening News,* section 1 (12 May 1930): 15.

O'DONNELL, JIM. "A Short History of Literary Baseball." *Crosscurrents* (published by the Washington Community College Humanities Association) 7, no. 1 (Fall/Winter 1988).

O'DONNELL, JIM, and RALPH S. GRABER. "Baseball Fiction for Adults, 1973–1985" in

Douglas A. Noverr and Lawrence E. Ziewacz, eds., *Sport History, Selected Reading Lists and Course Outlines from American Colleges and Universities* 15 (New York: Marcus Weiner Publishing, 1987).

ORIARD, MICHAEL. *Dreaming of Heroes: American Sports Fiction, 1868–1980*. Chicago: Nelson-Hall Inc., 1982.

_____. "On the Current Status of Sports Fiction." *Arete* 1, no. 1, (Fall 1983).

PATRICK, WALTON R. *Ring Lardner*. New York: Twayne Publishing, 1963.

PATTEN, GILBERT. *Frank Merriwell's Father: An Autobiography of Gilbert Patten*. Edited by Harriet Hinsdale. Norman, Ok: University of Oklahoma Press, 1964.

PEARSON, EDMUND L. *Dime Novels*. Boston: Little Brown, 1929.

PRAGER, ARTHUR. *Rascals at Large, or, The Clue in the Old Nostalgia*. Garden City, NY: Doubleday & Co., 1971.

The Publishers Trade List Annual. New York: F. Leypoldt, 1882, 1883, 1890, 1891.

REYNOLDS, QUENTIN. *The Fiction Factory*. New York: Random House, 1955.

SALISBURY, LUKE. "Why is Baseball Fiction so Hard to Write?" *The SABR Review of Books*, Volume II, 1987.

SMITH, LEVERETT T. "The Diameter of Frank Chance's Diamond: Ring Lardner and Professional Sports." *Journal of Popular Culture* VI, no. 1 (Summer 1972): 133–56.

_____. "Baseball Juvenile Literature." *The SABR Review of Books*, Premiere Issue, 1986.

SMITH, MYRON J., Jr., ed. *Baseball: A Comprehensive Bibliography*. Jefferson, NC: McFarland & Co., 1986.

SOJKA, GREGORY S. "Going from Rags to Riches with Baseball Joe." *Journal of American Culture* 2, no. 1 (Spring 1979): 48–49.

STERN, MADELEINE B. *Publishers of Mass Entertainment in Nineteenth Century America*. Boston: G. K. Hall & Co., 1980.

TEBBEL, JOHN. *A History of Book Publishing in the United States*. 3 vols. New York: R. R. Bowker, 1975–1977.

TUNIS, JOHN R. *A Measure of Independence: The Autobiography of John R. Tunis*. New York: Atheneum, 1964.

UNIVERSITY OF SOUTH FLORIDA LIBRARY ASSOCIATES. *American Boys Series Books, 1900–1980*. Tampa: University of South Florida Library Associates, 1987. Barbara A. Bishop, compiler and project coordinator. Often referred to as *The Hudson Bibliography*.

WISE, SUZANNE. *Sports Fiction for Adults*. New York: Garland Publishing Co., 1986.

SPECIFIC ENTRY SOURCES
AND ANNOTATORS

Individuals listed here provided the information from books in their possession or in publications they wrote, which are listed in full in the Sources Bibliography.

ag	Anton Grobani's *Guide to Baseball Literature.*
agm	Andy McCue is co-chairman of SABR's bibliography committee and a newspaper editor.
aj	Albert Johannsen's *The House of Beadle and Adams.*
bip	Books in Print.
bp	Bobby Plapinger is a baseball book dealer in Ashland, Oregon.
brd	Book Review Digest.
dej	Deidre Johnson is an author and a librarian at the Research Center for Children's Books at the University of Minnesota.
dj	Material taken from the dust jacket of a book or from the cover listing of back issues on a dime novel.
dn	See the annotation under the first of the Frank Merriwell books, written by Gilbert Patten under the Burt L. Standish pseudonym.
el	Edward LeBlanc is editor of *Dime Novel Round-Up,* a bimonthly for dime novel collectors.
em	Eugene Murdock, author of *Mighty Casey: All American.*
fp	Frank Phelps is cochairman of SABR's bibliography committee.
go	Gil O'Gara is publisher of *Yellowback Library,* a monthly for juvenile series book collectors.
jel	J. Edward Leithead's articles in *Dime Novel Round-Up.*
jo	Jim O'Donnell is a professor of English at Edmonds Community College and a bibliographer and collector of baseball books.
jrc	J. Randolph Cox is a collector of dime novels and series books.
jtp	Catalogues of Joseph the Provider, Santa Barbara, Ca. bookstore.
mo	Michael Oriard's *Dreaming of Heroes.*
nuc	The National Union Catalogue, the Library of Congress's published card catalogue.
pb	Phil Bergen is a member of SABR and a writer on several boys' baseball authors.
pub	The book's publisher.
rc	Robert Cantwell's *Sports Illustrated* article.
rutgers	Rutgers University Library.
tps	John Eames's *The Paramount Story.*
ts	Leverett T. Smith is a professor of English at North Carolina Wesleyan and a writer on children's literature.

OTHER WAYS TO FIND LISTINGS

The bibliography can be looked at many different ways. The following few pages are ways of breaking down either all the works listed by some common categories or a few of them by some common characteristic. Dime novels and serials have been eliminated from these lists. The books are listed by the author's name on the cover, whether it's a pseudonym or not.

The first two lists contain virtually all the books in the bibliography, broken down chronologically and alphabetically by title. The later lists break the books down by type and then by common narrative themes, such as integration or books that are set on a real major league team. These latter lists are probably not complete as I have not been able to find every book listed in the bibliography.

CHRONOLOGICALLY—1868 – 1990

The first reference to the game of "base ball" in literature is actually in Jane Austen's *Northanger Abbey*, finished in 1803 but not published until almost fifteen years later. The reference included other childhood games, such as cricket. Clearly the "base ball" reference was to one of those vaguely known games that preceded the American game. Nevertheless, there it is. The next fictional reference was in America in 1868, when a couple of chapters in a book of boys' adventures were taken up by the game. From there, it grew. A few books where the publication date isn't known have been removed from this list.

1868

Everett, William. *Changing Base.*

1869

Davis, Caroline E. Kelly. *The Yachtville Boys.*

1871

Everett, William. *Double Play.*

1880

Brooks, Noah. *The Fairport Nine.*

1884

Brooks, Noah. *Our Base Ball Club and How It Won the Championship.*

1887

Grant, Robert. *Jack Hall, or, The School Days of an American Boy.*

1888

Peck, Wallace. *A Stitch in Time Saves the Nine.*

1891

Everett, William. *Thine Not Mine.*

1897

Standish, Burt L. *Frank Merriwell's Danger.*
Tomlinson, Everett. *Ward Hill at Weston.*

1898

Brooks, Noah. *The Boys of Fairport.*
Standish, Burt L. *Frank Merriwell's Cruise.*
Standish, Burt L. *Frank Merriwell's Struggle.*
Tomlinson, Everett. *Ward Hill, the Senior.*

1899

Standish, Burt L. *Frank Merriwell's Duel.*
Standish, Burt L. *Frank Merriwell's Double Shot.*
Standish, Burt L. *Frank Merriwell's Baseball Victories.*
Standish, Burt L. *Frank Merriwell's Confidence.*

Tomlinson, Everett. *Ward Hill at College.*
Winfield, Arthur M. *The Rover Boys at School.*

1900

Patten, Gilbert. *The Rockspur Nine.*
Standish, Burt L. *Frank Merriwell's Luck, or, A Pinch Hit.*
Standish, Burt L. *Frank Merriwell's Phantom.*
Standish, Burt L. *Frank Merriwell's Faith.*
Standish, Burt L. *Frank Merriwell's Victories.*
Standish, Burt L. *Frank Merriwell's Iron Nerve.*
Standish, Burt L. *Frank Merriwell in Kentucky.*

1901

Ellis, Edward S. *Our Jim.*
French, Allen. *The Junior Cup.*
Standish, Burt L. *Frank Merriwell's School Days.*
Standish, Burt L. *Frank Merriwell's Club.*
Standish, Burt L. *Frank Merriwell's False Friend.*
Standish, Burt L. *Frank Merriwell's Strong Arm.*
Standish, Burt L. *Frank Merriwell as Coach.*
Standish, Burt L. *Frank Merriwell's Brother.*
Standish, Burt L. *Frank Merriwell's Marvel.*
Standish, Burt L. *Frank Merriwell's Support.*

1902

Standish, Burt L. *Dick Merriwell's Delivery.*
Standish, Burt L. *Dick Merriwell's Revenge.*
Standish, Burt L. *Dick Merriwell's Ruse.*
Standish, Burt L. *Dick Merriwell's Wonders.*
Standish, Burt L. *Frank Merriwell's Honor.*
Standish, Burt L. *Dick Merriwell's Diamond.*
Standish, Burt L. *Frank Merriwell's Winners.*
Whiting, Robert Rudd. *The Fat Mascot.*
Whiting, Robert Rudd. *Crazy Baseball Stories.*
Young, Ernest A. *Boats, Bats and Bicycles.*

1903

Barbour, Ralph Henry. *Weatherby's Inning.*
Standish, Burt L. *Frank Merriwell at Yale.*
Standish, Burt L. *Frank Merriwell's Races.*
Standish, Burt L. *Frank Merriwell's Skill.*
Standish, Burt L. *Dick Merriwell's Backstop.*
Standish, Burt L. *Dick Merriwell's Western Mission.*
Standish, Burt L. *Frank Merriwell's Rescue.*

Standish, Burt L. *Frank Merriwell's Encounter.*
Standish, Burt L. *Dick Merriwell's Marked Money.*
Standish, Burt L. *Frank Merriwell's Nomads.*

1904

Dudley, Albertus True. *Making the Nine.*
Standish, Burt L. *Dick Merriwell's Assurance.*
Standish, Burt L. *Dick Merriwell's Grit.*
Standish, Burt L. *Dick Merriwell's Long Slide.*
Standish, Burt L. *Frank Merriwell's Rough Deal.*
Standish, Burt L. *Dick Merriwell's Threat.*
Standish, Burt L. *Dick Merriwell's Persistence.*
Standish, Burt L. *Dick Merriwell's Day.*

1905

Bonehill, Captain Ralph. *The Winning Run, or, The Baseball Boys of Lakeport.*
Standish, Burt L. *Dick Merriwell's Cleverness.*
Standish, Burt L. *Frank Merriwell's Pride.*
Standish, Burt L. *Frank Merriwell's Challengers.*
Standish, Burt L. *Frank Merriwell's Endurance.*
Standish, Burt L. *Dick Merriwell's Cleverness.*
Standish, Burt L. *Frank Merriwell's Marriage.*
Standish, Burt L. *Dick Merriwell, the Wizard.*
Standish, Burt L. *Dick Merriwell's Stroke.*
Stratemeyer, Edward. *Dave Porter at Oak Hall.*

1906

Barbour, Ralph Henry. *The Crimson Sweater.*
Dudley, Albertus True. *With Mask and Mitt.*
Quirk, Leslie. *"Midget" Blake, Pitcher.*
Standish, Burt L. *Dick Merriwell's Polo Team.*
Standish, Burt L. *Frank Merriwell's New Boy.*
Standish, Burt L. *Dick Merriwell's Home Run.*
Standish, Burt L. *Dick Merriwell's Dare.*
Standish, Burt L. *Frank Merriwell's Son.*
Standish, Burt L. *Dick Merriwell's Team Mate.*
Standish, Burt L. *Frank Merriwell's Leaguers.*
Standish, Burt L. *Frank Merriwell's Happy Camp.*
Standish, Burt L. *Dick Merriwell's Influence.*
Standish, Burt L. *Dick Merriwell, Freshman.*

1907

Burleigh, C. B. *Raymond Benson at Krampton.*
Burleigh, C. B. *The Kenton Pines.*

Dudley, Albertus True. *The Great Year.*
Moffat, William. *The Crimson Banner.*
Standish, Burt L. *Dick Merriwell's Regret.*
Standish, Burt L. *Dick Merriwell's Magnetism.*
Standish, Burt L. *Dick Merriwell's Backers.*
Standish, Burt L. *Dick Merriwell's Best Work.*
Standish, Burt L. *Dick Merriwell's Distrust.*
Standish, Burt L. *Dick Merriwell's Debt.*
Standish, Burt L. *Dick Merriwell's Mastery.*
Standish, Burt L. *Dick Merriwell Adrift.*
Standish, Winn. *Jack Lorimer's Champions.*

1908

Chapman, Allen. *The Darewell Chums, or,
The Heroes of the School.*
Standish, Burt L. *Frank Merriwell's Hard Case.*
Standish, Burt L. *Dick Merriwell's Stand.*
Standish, Burt L. *Dick Merriwell Doubted.*
Standish, Burt L. *Frank Merriwell's Steadying Hand.*
Standish, Burt L. *Dick Merriwell's Example.*
Stratemeyer, Edward. *The Baseball Boys of Lakeport.*
Young, Clarence. *Jack Ranger's School Victories.*

1909

Aumerle, Richard. *Between Friends.*
Barbour, Ralph Henry. *Double Play.*
Earl, John P. *The School Team in Camp.*
Grey, Zane. *The Short-stop.*
Standish, Burt L. *Dick Merriwell's Honors.*
Standish, Burt L. *Frank Merriwell's Wizard.*
Standish, Burt L. *Dick Merriwell's Race.*
Standish, Burt L. *Frank Merriwell at Phantom Lake.*
Standish, Burt L. *Dick Merriwell a Winner.*

1910

Aumerle, Richard. *Brownie and I.*
Chadwick, Lester. *The Rival Pitchers.*
Chance, Frank. *The Bride and the Pennant.*
Dudley, Albertus True. *At the Home Plate.*
Earl, John P. *Captain of the School Team.*
Hancock, Harrie Irving. *The High School Pitcher.*
Johnson, Owen. *The Humming Bird.*
Johnson, Owen. *The Varmint.*
Mathewson, Christy. *Won in the Ninth.*
Paine, Ralph D. *The Fugitive Freshman.*

Patten, Gilbert. *Clif Stirling, Captain of the Nine.*
Patten, Gilbert. *Bill Bruce of Harvard.*
Pier, Arthur. *The Crashaw Brothers.*
Regan, Jack, and Will E. Stahl. *Around the World
with the Baseball Bugs.*
Standish, Burt L. *Frank Merriwell's Old Form.*
Standish, Burt L. *Dick Merriwell, Game to the Last.*
Standish, Burt L. *Dick Merriwell, Motor King.*
Standish, Burt L. *Dick Merriwell's Tussle.*
Standish, Burt L. *Dick Merriwell's Aero Dash.*

1911

Baker, Etta Anthony. *The Captain of the S.I.G.'s.*
Barbour, Ralph Henry. *Finkler's Field.*
Brainerd, Norman. *Winning the Junior Cup.*
Chadwick, Lester. *Batting to Win.*
Colton, Matthew. *Frank Armstrong's Second Term.*
Earl, John P. *The School Team on the Diamond.*
Forbes, Graham. *The Boys of Columbia High on the
Diamond.*
Grey, Zane. *The Young Pitcher.*
Hancock, Harrie Irving. *The Grammar School Boys in
Summer Athletics.*
Heyliger, William. *Bartley, Freshman Pitcher.*
Quirk, Leslie. *Freshman Dorn, Pitcher.*
Sangree, Allen. *The Jinx: Stories of the Diamond.*
Scott, Morgan. *Rival Pitchers of Oakdale.*
Standish, Burt L. *Dick Merriwell's Perception.*
Standish, Burt L. *Dick Merriwell's Detective Work.*
Standish, Burt L. *Dick Merriwell's Commencement.*
Standish, Burt L. *Dick Merriwell's Coolness.*
Standish, Burt L. *Dick Merriwell's Reliance.*
Van Loan, Charles. *The Big League.*
Webster, Frank V. *The High School Rivals.*
Winfield, Arthur M. *The Rover Boys Down East.*

1912

Chadwick, Lester. *Baseball Joe on the School Nine.*
Chadwick, Lester. *Baseball Joe of the Silver Stars.*
Garis, Howard Roger. *Those Smith Boys on the
Diamond.*
Heyliger, William. *The Captain of the Nine.*
Standish, Burt L. *Dick Merriwell's Counsel.*
Standish, Burt L. *Dick Merriwell, Universal Coach.*
Standish, Burt L. *Dick Merriwell's Varsity Nine.*

Standish, Burt L. *Dick Merriwell's Heroic Players.*

Standish, Burt L. *Frank Merriwell, Jr., Tested.*

Standish, Burt L. *Frank Merriwell, Jr.'s Conquests.*

Standish, Burt L. *Frank Merriwell, Jr.'s Rivals.*

Standish, Burt L. *Frank Merriwell, Jr. in Arizona.*

Stone, Raymond. *Tommy Tiptop and His Baseball Nine.*

Tomlinson, Everett. *The Pennant.*

Van Loan, Charles. *The $10,000 Arm and Other Tales of the Big League.*

Williams, Hawley. *Batter Up!*

1913

Chadwick, Lester. *Baseball Joe at Yale.*

Chapman, Allen. *Fred Fenton the Pitcher.*

Colton, Matthew. *Frank Armstrong, Captain of the Nine.*

Douglas, Captain Alan. *Fast Nine, or, A Challenge from Fairfield.*

Duffield, J. W. *Bert Wilson's Fadeaway Ball.*

Heyliger, William. *Strike Three!*

Scott, Morgan. *The New Boys at Oakdale.*

Sheppard, W. Crispin. *The Rambler Club's Ball Nine.*

Standish, Burt L. *Frank Merriwell, Jr. in the Desert.*

Standish, Burt L. *Frank Merriwell, Jr.'s Fight for Right.*

Standish, Burt L. *Frank Merriwell, Jr.'s Athletic Team.*

Standish, Burt L. *Frank Merriwell, Jr.'s Peck of Trouble.*

Standish, Burt L. *Frank Merriwell, Jr.'s Ordeal.*

Standish, Burt L. *Frank Merriwell, Jr., Birdman.*

Van Loan, Charles. *The Lucky Seventh.*

1914

Barton, George. *The Bell Haven Nine.*

Braddock, Gordon. *Rex Kingdon of Ridgewood High.*

Camp, Walter. *Captain Danny.*

Chadwick, Lester. *Baseball Joe in the Central League.*

Hopper, James. *Coming Back With the Spitball: A Pitcher's Romance.*

Mathewson, Christy. *Pitcher Pollock.*

Patten, Gilbert. *The College Rebel.*

Quirk, Leslie. *The Third Strike.*

Standish, Burt L. *Frank Merriwell, Jr. on the Border.*

Standish, Burt L. *Frank Merriwell's Diamond Foes.*

Standish, Burt L. *Dick Merriwell and June Arlington.*

Standish, Burt L. *Merriwell, or, Blood Will Tell.*

Standish, Burt L. *Dick Merriwell and the Burglar.*

Standish, Burt L. *Frank Merriwell at the Cowboy Carnival.*

Standish, Burt L. *Lefty O' the Bush.*

Standish, Burt L. *Lefty O' the Big League.*

Standish, Burt L. *Lefty O' the Blue Stockings.*

Standish, Burt L. *Lefty O' the Training Camp.*

Standish, Burt L. *Brick King, Backstop.*

Stone, Raymond. *Donald Dare: The Champion Boy Pitcher.*

Williams, Hawley. *The Winning Hit.*

Williams, Hawley. *Johnson of Lansing.*

1915

Barbour, Ralph Henry. *The Lucky Seventh.*

Chadwick, Lester. *Baseball Joe in the Big League.*

Curtiss, Philip. *The Ladder: The Story of a Casual Man.*

Ferguson, William Blair Morton. *A Man's Code.*

Fullerton, Hugh. *Jimmy Kirkland of the Shasta Boys' Team.*

Fullerton, Hugh. *Jimmy Kirkland of the Cascade College Team.*

Fullerton, Hugh. *Jimmy Kirkland and the Plot for a Pennant.*

Grey, Zane. *The Redheaded Outfield and Other Baseball Stories.*

Hale, Harry. *Jack Race's Baseball Nine.*

Heyliger, William. *Against Odds.*

Mathewson, Christy. *Catcher Craig.*

Needham, Henry B. *The Double Squeeze.*

Quirk, Leslie. *Playing the Game.*

Standish, Burt L. *The Making of a Big Leaguer.*

Standish, Burt L. *Courtney of the Center Garden.*

Standish, Burt L. *Covering the Look-In Corner.*

Winfield, Arthur M. *The Rover Boys in Business.*

1916

Barbour, Ralph Henry. *The Purple Pennant.*

Braddock, Gordon. *Rex Kingdon Behind the Bat.*

Chadwick, Lester. *Baseball Joe on the Giants.*

Davenport, Spencer. *The Rushton Boys at Rally Hall.*
Heyliger, William. *Captain Fair-and-Square.*
Lardner, Ring. *You Know Me Al.*
Mathewson, Christy. *First Base Faulkner.*
Patten, Gilbert. *Clif Stirling, Sophomore at Storm-bridge.*
Standish, Burt L. *Lefty Locke, Pitcher-Manager.*
Winfield, Arthur M. *The Rover Boys on a Tour.*

1917

Barbour, Ralph Henry. *Winning His Game.*
Braddock, Gordon. *Rex Kingdon on Storm Island.*
Chadwick, Lester. *Baseball Joe in the World Series.*
Chapman, Allen. *The Heroes of the School.*
Corcoran, Brewer. *The Barbarian.*
Heyliger, William. *The County Pennant.*
Mathewson, Christy. *Second Base Sloan.*
Standish, Burt L. *Guarding the Keystone Sack.*
Warner, Frank. *Bobby Blake on the School Nine.*

1918

Chadwick, Lester. *Baseball Joe Around the World.*
Gollomb, Joseph. *That Year at Lincoln High.*
Heyliger, William. *Fighting for Fairview.*
Lardner, Ring. *Treat 'Em Rough.*
Perry, Lawrence. *The Big Game.*
Witwer, H. C. *From Baseball to Boches.*

1919

Ferguson, Donald. *Chums of Scranton High Out for the Pennant.*
Lardner, Ring. *The Real Dope.*
Overton, Mark. *Jack Winters' Baseball Team.*
Van Loan, Charles. *Score by Innings.*

1920

Forbes, Graham. *The Boys of Columbia High in Camp.*
Heyliger, William. *Bean-Ball Bill and Other Stories.*
Patten, Gilbert. *The Call of the Varsity.*
Ruth, Babe. *The Home-Run King.*
Standish, Burt L. *The Man on First.*
Witwer, H. C. *There's No Base Like Home.*

1921

Barbour, Ralph Henry. *Tod Hale on the Nine.*

Barbour, Ralph Henry. *Three-Base Benson.*
Beaumont, Gerald. *Hearts and the Diamond.*
Winfield, Arthur M. *The Rover Boys in the Land of Luck.*

1922

Chadwick, Lester. *Baseball Joe, Home Run King.*
Winfield, Arthur M. *The Rover Boys at Big Horn Ranch.*

1923

Barbour, Ralph Henry. *Nid and Nod.*
Broun, Heywood. *The Sun Field.*
Chadwick, Lester. *Baseball Joe, Saving the League.*
Heyliger, William. *The Spirit of the Leader.*
Patten, Gilbert. *Sons of Old Eli.*
Scott, Everett "Deacon." *Third Base Thatcher.*
Silvers, Earl Reed. *Dick Arnold of the Varsity.*
Silvers, Earl Reed. *Jackson of Hillsdale High.*
Standish, Burt L. *Lego Lamb, Southpaw.*
Winfield, Arthur M. *The Rover Boys at Big Bear Lake.*

1924

Barbour, Ralph Henry. *Infield Rivals.*
Chadwick, Lester. *Baseball Joe, Captain of the Team.*
Standish, Burt L. *The Grip of the Game.*
Stone, David. *Yank Brown, Pitcher.*

1925

Barbour, Ralph Henry. *Bases Full.*
Chadwick, Lester. *Baseball Joe, Champion of the League.*
Standish, Burt L. *Lefty Locke, Owner.*

1926

Chadwick, Lester. *Baseball Joe, Club Owner.*
Forbes, Graham. *Frank Allen in Camp.*
Forbes, Graham. *Frank Allen—Pitcher.*
Griffith, Peggy. *The New Klondike.*
Heyliger, William. *Dorset's Twister.*
Sherman, Harold M. *Fight 'em, Big Three.*
Standish, Burt L. *Lefty Locke Wins Out.*

1927

Barbour, Ralph Henry. *The Relief Pitcher.*
Barbour, Ralph Henry. *Tod Hale at Camp.*
Chadwick, George B. *Chuck Blue of Sterling.*

1928

Barbour, Ralph Henry. *Lovell Leads Off.*
Chadwick, Lester. *Baseball Joe, Pitching Wizard.*
Heyliger, William. *The Macklin Brothers.*
Muller, Charles G. *The Baseball Detective.*
Sherman, Harold M. *Hit by Pitcher.*
Sherman, Harold M. *Bases Full.*
Sherman, Harold M. *Safe!*
Standish, Burt L. *Crossed Signals.*

1929

Barbour, Ralph Henry. *Grantham Gets On.*
Berndt, Walter. *Smitty at the Ball Game.*
Jenkins, MacGregor. *Shiner Watson.*
Pier, Arthur. *The Rigor of the Game.*
Pier, Arthur. *The Captain.*
Sherman, Harold M. *Flashing Steel.*
Sherman, Harold M. *Hit and Run!*
Silvers, Earl Reed. *Team First.*

1930

Allen, Merritt Parmalee. *Tied in the Ninth.*
Dawson, Elmer. *The Pick-up Nine.*
Dawson, Elmer. *Buck's Winning Hit.*
Dawson, Elmer. *Larry's Fadeaway.*
Pier, Arthur. *The Cheerleader.*
Sherman, Harold M. *Batter Up!*

1931

Barbour, Ralph Henry. *Danby's Error.*
Barbour, Ralph Henry. *Squeeze Play.*
Dawson, Elmer. *Buck's Home Run Drive.*
Haines, Donal Hamilton. *The Southpaw.*
Sherman, Harold M. *Strike Him Out!*

1932

Barbour, Ralph Henry. *Cub Battery.*
Dawson, Elmer. *Larry's Speedball.*
Sherman, Harold M. *Double Play and Other Baseball Stories.*

1933

Burrough, Ruth J. *Mystery House.*
Heyliger, William. *The Gallant Crosby.*
Lardner, Ring. *Lose With a Smile.*

1934

Barbour, Ralph Henry. *Southworth Scores.*
Fitzsimmons, Cortland. *Death on the Diamond.*
Sainsbury, Noel, Jr. *Stirring Baseball Stories.*
Sainsbury, Noel, Jr. *Cracker Stanton.*

1936

Barbour, Ralph Henry. *Merritt Leads the Nine.*
Heyliger, William. *The Big Leaguer.*

1937

Barbour, Ralph Henry. *The Score is Tied.*
Heyliger, William. *The Loser's End.*
Heyliger, William. *Three-Finger Joe.*
Lawton, Charles. *Clarksville's Battery.*
Sherman, Harold. *Last Man Out.*

1938

Barbour, Ralph Henry. *Rivals on the Mound.*
Davis, Clyde Brion. *Northend Wildcats.*
Hart, Frank J. *The Speed Boy.*

1940

Alexander, Holmes M. *Dust in the Afternoon.*
Barbour, Ralph Henry. *Ninth Inning Rally.*
Corbert, Mack. *Play the Game.*
DeVries, Julian. *The Strike-Out King.*
Playfair, Robert Smith. *Colonel of the Crimson.*
Temple, Willard H. *Pitching for Pawling.*
Tunis, John R. *The Kid from Tomkinsville.*

1941

Barbour, Ralph Henry. *Infield Twins.*
Lawton, Charles. *Home Run Hennessey.*
Tunis, John R. *World Series.*

1942

Reck, Franklin. *Varsity Letter.*
Renick, James and Marion. *Steady.*
Scholz, Jackson. *Soldiers at Bat.*

1943

Tunis, John R. *Keystone Kids.*

1944

Shapiro, Irwin. *Casey Jones and Locomotive No. 638.*
Tunis, John R. *Rookie of the Year.*

1946

Scholz, Jackson. *Batter Up.*
Smith, H. Allen. *Rhubarb.*
Tunis, John R. *The Kid Comes Back.*

1947

Anderson, Ken. *Tom Huntner, Sophomore Pitcher.*
Bagby, George. *The Twin Killing.*
Bonner, Mary G. *Out to Win.*
Cooper, John R. *The Mystery at the Ball Park.*
Cooper, John R. *The Southpaw's Secret.*
Decker, Duane. *Good Field, No Hit.*
Fishel, Dick, and Clair Hare. *Terry and Bunky Play Baseball.*

1948

Amarant, Jiggs. *Tall Baseball Stories.*
Bowen, Robert Sidney. *The Winning Pitch.*
Decker, Duane. *Starting Pitcher.*
Emery, Russell G. *High, Inside!*
Felsen, Henry Gregor. *Bertie Takes Care.*
Fitzgerald, Ed. *The Turning Point.*
Harkins, Philip. *Southpaw from San Francisco.*
Hayes, Florence. *Skid.*
Margulies, Leo. *Baseball Round-Up.*
McCormick, Wilfred. *Legion Tourney.*
McCormick, Wilfred. *The Three-Two Pitch.*
O'Rourke, Frank. *Flashing Spikes.*
Owen, Frank, ed. *Teen-age Baseball Stories.*
Scholz, Jackson. *Fielder from Nowhere.*
Tunis, John R. *Highpockets.*

1949

Bee, Clair. *Strike Three!*
Bee, Clair. *Clutch Hitter!*
Bowen, Robert Sidney. *Player-Manager.*
Davies, Valentine. *It Happens Every Spring.*
Decker, Duane. *Hit and Run.*

Flood, Richard T. *The Fighting Southpaw.*
Keith, Harold. *Shotgun Shaw: A Baseball Story.*
McCormick, Wilfred. *Fielder's Choice.*
O'Rourke, Frank. *The Team.*
Renick, Marion. *The Dooleys Play Ball.*
Sandberg, Harold W. *Dunk O'Malley Sports Stories.*
Tunis, John R. *Young Razzle.*
Van Riper, Guernsey, Jr. *Lou Gehrig, Boy of the Sand Lots.*

1950

Bee, Clair. *Pitchers' Duel.*
Bowen, Robert Sidney. *Ball Hawk.*
Brier, Howard M. *Shortstop Shadow.*
Clymer, Eleanor. *Treasure at First Base.*
Coombs, Charles. *Young Readers' Baseball Stories.*
Decker, Duane. *The Catcher from Double-A.*
Edmunds, Murrell. *Behold, Thy Brother.*
Fitzgerald, Ed. *College Slugger.*
Jackson, C. Paul. *Rookie First Baseman.*
Kennedy, Lucy. *The Sunlit Field.*
Lochlons, Colin. *Squeeze Play.*
McCormick, Wilfred. *Bases Loaded.*
O'Rourke, Frank. *Bonus Rookie.*
O'Rourke, Frank. *The Greatest Victory and Other Baseball Stories.*
Richard, James R. *The Club Team.*
Scholz, Jackson. *Keystone Kelly.*
Thomas, David, ed. *Teen-Age Stories of the Diamond.*
Wallace, Francis. *Big League Rookie.*

1951

Allison, Bob, and Frank E. Hill. *The Kid Who Batted 1.000.*
Bishop, Curtis K. *Banjo Hitter.*
Bonner, Mary G. *The Base-Stealer.*
Bowen, Robert Sidney. *Hot Corner.*
Coombs, Charles. *Young Readers' Stories of the Diamond.*
Decker, Duane. *Fast Man on a Pivot.*
Graber, Ralph S., ed. *The Baseball Reader.*
Hano, Arnold. *The Big Out.*
Harkins, Philip. *Double Play.*
Heuman, William. *Wonder Boy.*
Jackson, C. Paul. *Shorty at Shortstop.*

Leonard, Burgess. *Rookie Southpaw.*
Lochlons, Colin. *Three-and-Two Pitcher.*
McCormick, Wilfred. *Grand-Slam Homer.*
Waldman, Frank. *Bonus Pitcher.*
Wayne, Richard. *Clutch Hitter.*

1952

Bee, Clair. *Dugout Jinx.*
Bowen, Robert Sidney. *Pitcher of the Year.*
Cooper, John R. *The Phantom Homer.*
Cooper, John R. *First Base Jinx.*
Decker, Duane. *The Big Stretch.*
Fenner, Phyllis R., ed. *Crack of the Bat.*
Fitzgerald, Ed. *Yankee Rookie.*
Jackson, C. Paul. *Clown at Second Base.*
Jackson, C. Paul. *Little Leaguer's First Uniform.*
Lochlons, Colin. *Triple Play.*
Malamud, Bernard. *The Natural.*
Mann, Arthur. *Bob White: Bonus Player.*
Mann, Arthur. *Bob White: Farm Club Player.*
Miers, Earl Schenck. *Monkey Shines.*
O'Rourke, Frank. *The Heavenly World Series.*
O'Rourke, Frank. *Never Come Back.*
O'Rourke, Frank. *Nine Good Men.*
Rand, Addison. *Southpaw Fly Hawk.*
Renick, Marion. *Pete's Home Run.*
Scholz, Jackson. *Deep Short.*
Thurman, A. R. *Money Pitcher.*
Urmston, Mary. *Larry's Luck.*
Waldman, Frank. *Delayed Steal.*
Wayne, Richard. *Wrong-Way Rookie.*
Webster, Joe. *The Rookie from Junction Flats.*
Webster, Joe. *Dodger Doubleheader.*
Young, Isador S. *A Hit and a Miss.*

1953

Bee, Clair. *Fence Busters.*
Bishop, Curtis K. *Larry of Little League.*
Bonner, Mary G. *Dugout Mystery.*
Bowen, Robert Sidney. *Behind the Bat.*
Cooper, John R. *The College League Mystery.*
Cooper, John R. *The Fighting Shortstop.*
Decker, Duane. *Switch Hitter.*
Emery, Russell G. *Relief Pitcher.*
Gartner, John. *Ace Pitcher.*

Harris, Mark. *The Southpaw.*
Heuman, William. *Little League Champs.*
Jackson, C. Paul. *Giant in the Midget League.*
Kent, Justin. *Fast Curve.*
Kinsey, Elizabeth. *Donny and Company.*
Leonard, Burgess. *Second-Season Jinx.*
Mann, Arthur. *Bob White: Spring Terror.*
O'Rourke, Frank. *The Catcher and the Manager.*
Parks, Edd Winfield. *Safe on Second.*
Renick, Marion. *The Heart for Baseball.*
Smith, Robert. *Little League Catcher.*
Weeks, Jack. *The Hard Way.*

1954

Bishop, Curtis K. *Larry Leads Off.*
Bowen, Robert Sidney. *Infield Spark.*
Carlin, Steve. *Rootie Kazootie, Baseball Star.*
Christopher, Matthew F. *The Lucky Baseball Bat.*
Coombs, Charles. *Young Infield Rookie.*
Decker, Duane. *Mister Shortstop.*
Friendlich, Dick. *Baron of the Bullpen.*
Jorgensen, Nels L. *Dave Palmer's Diamond Mystery.*
Leonard, Burgess. *The Rookie Fights Back.*
Lochlons, Colin. *Barney of the Babe Ruth League.*
Michael, D. J. *Win–or Else!*
Miers, Earl Schenck. *The Kid Who Beat the Dodgers and Other Sports Stories.*
Moore, Joseph A. *Two Strikes on Lefty.*
Olgin, Joseph. *Little League Champions.*
Philbrook, Clem. *The Magic Bat.*
Van Riper, Guernsey, Jr. *Babe Ruth, Baseball Boy.*
Wallop, Douglas. *The Year the Yankees Lost the Pennant.*

1955

Archibald, Joe. *Double Play Rookie.*
Asinof, Eliot. *Man on Spikes.*
Bishop, Curtis K. *Larry Comes Home.*
Bowen, Robert Sidney. *The Big Inning.*
Brooks, Walter R. *Freddy and the Baseball Team from Mars.*
Chandler, Edna W. *The Missing Mitt.*
Coombs, Charles. *Sleuth at Shortstop.*
Einstein, Charles. *The Only Game in Town.*
Emery, Russell G. *Hyland of the Hawks.*

Fulton, Reed. *Rookie Coach.*
Gardner, Lillian. *Somebody Called Booie.*
Hirshberg, Al. *Battery for Madison High.*
Holland, Marion. *Billy's Clubhouse.*
McCormick, Wilfred. *The Man on the Bench.*
Scholz, Jackson. *Base Burglar.*
Tunis, John R. *Buddy and the Old Pro.*
Verral, Charles Spain. *The King of the Diamond.*
Verral, Charles Spain. *Mighty Men of Baseball.*
Walden, Amelia Elizabeth. *Three Loves Has Sandy.*
Weeks, Jack. *The Take-Charge Guy.*

1956

Archibald, Joe. *Full Count.*
Bishop, Curtis K. *Little Leaguer.*
Bowen, Robert Sidney. *The Fourth Out.*
Breslin, Howard. *Autumn Comes Early.*
Christopher, Matthew F. *Baseball Pals.*
Friendlich, Dick. *Clean Up Hitter.*
Harris, Mark. *Ticket for a Seamstitch.*
Harris, Mark. *Bang the Drum Slowly.*
Heuman, William. *Strictly from Brooklyn.*
Hirshberg, Al. *Varsity Double Play.*
Jackson, C. P. and O. B. *Hillbilly Pitcher.*
Keating, Lawrence. *Kid Brother.*
Lovelace, Delos W. *That Dodger Horse.*
Miers, Earl Schenck. *Ball of Fire.*
Renick, Marion. *Bats & Gloves of Glory.*
Verral, Charles Spain. *The Wonderful World Series.*
Waldman, Frank. *Lucky Bat Boy.*

1957

Archibald, Joe. *Circus Catch.*
Bishop, Curtis K. *The Little League Way.*
Bowen, Robert Sidney. *No Hitter.*
Emery, Russell G. *Action at Third.*
Fitzgerald, Ed. *The Ballplayer.*
Keating, Lawrence. *Freshman Backstop.*
Key, Ted. *Phyllis.*
Scholz, Jackson. *Man in a Cage.*
Starrett, Vincent. *The Great All-Star Animal League Ball Game.*

1958

Anderson, Catherine Corley. *Sister Beatrice Goes to Bat.*

Archibald, Joe. *Catcher's Choice.*
Bee, Clair. *Pay-Off Pitch.*
Bishop, Curtis K. *Lank of the Little League.*
Bonner, Mary G. *Two-Way Pitcher.*
Bowen, Robert Sidney. *The Big Hit.*
Christopher, Matthew F. *Slide, Danny, Slide.*
Christopher, Matthew F. *Two Strikes on Johnny.*
Decker, Duane. *Long Ball to Left Field.*
Fitzpatrick, Burgess. *Casey's Redemption.*
Lee, Wayne C. *Slugging Backstop.*
Le Grand. *How Baseball Began in Brooklyn.*
Leonard, Burgess. *Stretch Bolton Comes Back.*
Lord, Beman. *The Trouble with Francis.*
McCormick, Wilfred. *The Hot Corner.*
McCormick, Wilfred. *The Big Ninth.*
Moore, Joseph A. *Hot Shot at Third.*
Scholz, Jackson. *Bench Boss.*
Tunis, John R. *Schoolboy Johnson.*
Verral, Charles Spain. *Play Ball!*

1959

Archibald, Joe. *Bonus Kid.*
Bee, Clair. *No-Hitter.*
Bonner, Mary G. *Spray Hitter.*
Bowen, Robert Sidney. *Triple Play.*
Christopher, Matthew F. *Little Lefty.*
Coombs, Charles. *Young Readers Baseball Mystery.*
Cummings, Parke, ed. *Baseball Stories.*
Decker, Duane. *Third-Base Rookie.*
Friendlich, Dick. *Lead-Off Man.*
Jackson, C. Paul. *Little League Tournament.*
Kay, Helen. *The Magic Mitt.*
Keating, Lawrence. *Senior Challenge.*
McCormick, Wilfred. *The Proud Champions.*
Nye, Bud. *Stay Loose.*
Olgin, Joseph. *Battery Feud.*
Sandmel, Frances Fox. *All on the Team.*
Scholz, Jackson. *The Perfect Game.*
Woolley, Catherine. *David's Campaign Buttons.*

1960

Archibald, Joe. *First Base Hustler.*
Bishop, Curtis K. *Little League Heroes.*
Bowen, Robert Sidney. *Pennant Fever.*
Christopher, Matthew F. *Long Stretch at First Base.*

Decker, Duane. *Showboat Southpaw.*
Hoff, Syd. *Who Will Be My Friends?*
Jackson, C. Paul. *World Series Rookie.*
McCormick, Wilfred. *The Automatic Strike.*
McCormick, Wilfred. *The Last Put-Out.*
McCormick, Wilfred. *One O'Clock Hitter.*
Offit, Sidney. *The Boy Who Won the World Series.*
Parkinson, Ethelyn. *Good Old Archibald.*
Porter, Mark. *Winning Pitcher.*

1961

Archibald, Joe. *Outfield Orphan.*
Bowen, Robert Sidney. *Million-Dollar Rookie.*
Decker, Duane. *Rebel in Right Field.*
Doliner, Roy. *The Orange Air.*
Feldspar, Walter. *Squeeze Play.*
Friendlich, Dick. *Backstop Ace.*
Gelman, Steve. *Baseball Bonus Kid.*
Greene, Carla. *I Want to be a Baseball Player.*
Jackson, C. Paul. *Bullpen Bargain.*
Leonard, Burgess. *Stretch Bolton's Rookies.*
McCall, Edith. *The Buttons and the Little League.*
McCormick, Wilfred. *The Bluffer.*
McCormick, Wilfred. *The Double Steal.*
Renick, Marion. *Boy at Bat.*
Rhoades, Jonathan. *Over the Fence is Out.*
Scholz, Jackson. *Center-Field Jinx.*

1962

Archibald, Joe. *Shortstop on Wheels.*
Berra, Yogi, and Til Ferdenzi. *Behind the Plate.*
Bishop, Curtis K. *Little League Double Play.*
Bowen, Robert Sidney. *Bat Boy.*
Christopher, Matthew F. *Challenge at Second Base.*
Ford, Whitey, and Jack Lang. *The Fighting Southpaw.*
Heuman, William. *Rookie Backstop.*
Jackson, Caary. *A Uniform for Harry.*
Lord, Beman. *Bats and Balls.*
Maule, Hamilton "Tex." *The Shortstop.*
McCormick, Wilfred. *Rebel with a Glove.*
McCormick, Wilfred. *Home-Run Harvest.*
Mullins, Richard. *Most Valuable Player.*
Wasserman, Selma. *Sailor Jack and the Ball Game.*

1963

Archibald, Joe. *Big League Busher.*
Bethell, Jean. *Barney Beagle Plays Baseball.*
Bishop, Curtis K. *The Big Game.*
Bowen, Robert Sidney. *Perfect Game.*
Carol, Bill J. *Circus Catch.*
Christopher, Matthew F. *Baseball Flyhawk.*
Cox, William R. *The Wild Pitch.*
Jackson, C. Paul. *Little Major Leaguer.*
Jackson, C. P. and O. B. *High School Backstop.*
Knott, Bill. *Junk Pitcher.*
Leonard, Burgess. *Stretch Bolton: Mr. Shortstop.*
Malcolmson, David. *London: The Dog Who Made the Team.*
Maris, Roger, and Jack Ogle. *Slugger in Right.*
Maule, Hamilton "Tex." *Beatty of the Yankees.*
Mays, Willie, and Jeff Harris. *Danger in Center Field.*
McCormick, Wilfred. *The Starmaker.*
McCormick, Wilfred. *Once a Slugger.*
McCormick, Wilfred. *The Phantom Shortstop.*
Neigoff, Mike. *Nine Make a Team.*
Offit, Sidney. *Soupbone.*
Olson, Gene. *Bonus Boy.*
Pallas, Norvin. *The Baseball Mystery.*
Scholz, Jackson. *Dugout Tycoon.*
Zanger, Jack. *Baseball Spark Plug.*

1964

Archibald, Joe. *Old Iron Glove.*
Bee, Clair. *Home Run Feud.*
Bishop, Curtis K. *Little League Amigo.*
Bowen, Robert Sidney. *Hot Corner Blues.*
Boys Life, Editors of. *The Boys Life Book of Baseball Stories.*
Carol, Bill J. *Clutch Single.*
Christopher, Matthew F. *Catcher with a Glass Arm.*
Decker, Duane. *The Grand-Slam Kid.*
Drury, Maxine. *Glory for Gil.*
Friendlich, Dick. *Relief Pitcher.*
Heuman, William. *The Horse that Played the Outfield.*

Jackson, C. Paul. *Pee Wee Cook of the Midget League.*
Kramer, George. *The Left Hander.*
Maule, Hamilton "Tex." *The Last Out.*
McCormick, Wilfred. *The Long Pitcher.*
McCormick, Wilfred. *The Throwing Catcher.*
Molloy, Paul. *A Pennant for the Kremlin.*
Stapp, Arthur. *Too Steep for Baseball.*

1965

Archibald, Joe. *The Easy Out.*
Archibald, Joe. *Southpaw Speed.*
Bishop, Curtis K. *Little League Stepson.*
Bowen, Robert Sidney. *Rebel Rookie.*
Carol, Bill J. *Hit Away!*
Christopher, Matthew F. *Too Hot to Handle.*
Corbett, Scott. *The Baseball Trick.*
Cox, William R. *Big League Rookie.*
Creighton, Don. *Little League Giant.*
Dunham, Montrew. *Abner Doubleday, Young Baseball Pioneer.*
Frederic, Mike. *Frank Merriwell Returns.*
Friendlich, Dick. *Pinch Hitter.*
Grantham, Kenneth L. *Baseball's Darkest Days.*
Heavilin, Jay. *Fast Ball Pitcher.*
Jackson, C. Paul. *Minor League Shortstop.*
Jackson, O. B. *Southpaw in the Mighty Mite League.*
Kessler, Leonard P. *Here Comes the Strikeout.*
Lee, Robert C. *The Iron Arm of Michael Glenn.*
Longstreth, T. Morris. *The Comeback Catcher.*
Lord, Beman. *The Perfect Pitch.*
McCormick, Wilfred. *Wild on the Bases.*
McCormick, Wilfred. *The Go-Ahead Runner.*
Olson, Gene. *Three Men on Third.*
Quigley, Martin. *Today's Game.*
Shaw, Irwin. *Voices of a Summer Day.*
Sobol, Donald J. *Encyclopedia Brown and the Case of the Secret Pitch.*
Wier, Ester. *Easy Does It.*

1966

Bee, Clair. *Hungry Hurler.*
Bishop, Curtis K. *Little League Visitor.*
Bowen, Robert Sidney. *Man on First.*
Carol, Bill J. *Hard Smash to Third.*

Christopher, Matthew F. *The Reluctant Pitcher.*
Cox, William R. *Trouble at Second Base.*
Creighton, Don. *The Secret Little Leaguer.*
Cretan, Gladys Yessayan. *All Except Sammy.*
Etter, Les. *Bull Pen Hero.*
Herskowitz, Mickey. *Letters from Lefty.*
Heuman, William. *Hillbilly Hurler.*
Jackson, C. Paul. *Rookie Catcher with the Atlanta Braves.*
Jackson, Caary. *Midget League Catcher.*
McCormick, Wilfred. *Tall at the Plate.*
Perkins, Al. *Don and Donna Go to Bat.*
Scholefield, Edmund. *Tiger Rookie.*
Scholz, Jackson. *Spark Plug at Short.*
Schulz, Charles M. *Charlie Brown's All-Stars.*
Walpole, Joseph A. *The Diamond Pinheads.*
Young, Isador S. *Carson at Second.*

1967

Archibald, Joe. *Right Field Rookie.*
Asinof, Eliot. *The Bedfellow.*
Bishop, Curtis K. *Little League Victory.*
Bowen, Robert Sidney. *Lightning Southpaw.*
Carol, Bill J. *Lefty's Long Throw.*
Christopher, Matthew F. *Miracle at the Plate.*
Creighton, Don. *Little League Old-Timers.*
Gault, William C. *The Lonely Mound.*
Gold, R. C. *Memoirs of a Pussycad.*
Green, Gerald. *To Brooklyn With Love.*
Jackson, C. Paul. *Bud Baker, High School Pitcher.*
MacKenzie, Christine B. *Out at Home.*
McCormick, Wilfred. *The Incomplete Pitcher.*
McCormick, Wilfred. *Rookie on First.*
Napjus, James. *Trouble on the Infield.*
Neigoff, Mike. *Two on First.*
Philbrook, Clem. *Ollie's Team and the Baseball Computer.*
Potok, Chaim. *The Chosen.*
Russell, Patrick. *Going, Going, Gone.*
Scholefield, Edmund. *L'il Wildcat.*
Wells, Bob. *Five-Yard Fuller of the N.Y. Gnats*

1968

Archibald, Joe. *Mitt Maverick.*
Bishop, Curtis K. *Little League Little Brother.*

Carol, Bill J. *Lefty Finds a Catcher.*

Christopher, Matthew F. *The Year Mom Won the Pennant.*

Coover, Robert. *The Universal Baseball Association, Inc., J. Henry Waugh, Prop.*

Creighton, Don. *Little League Ball Hawk.*

Friendlich, Dick. *The Sweet Swing.*

Heuman, William. *Horace Higby and the Scientific Pitch.*

Hoff, Syd. *The Witch, the Cat and the Baseball Bat.*

Jackson, C. Paul. *Second Time Around Rookie.*

Jackson, C. Paul. *Big Play in the Small League.*

Kramer, George. *Kid Battery.*

Palmer, Bernard. *Danny Orlis and Jim Morgan's Scholarship.*

Scholefield, Edmund. *Maverick on the Mound.*

Scholz, Jackson. *The Big Mitt.*

Simon, Tony, ed. *Crooked Arm and Other Baseball Stories.*

Weaver, Robert. *Nice Guy, Go Home.*

1969

Archibald, Joe. *Two Time Rookie.*

Ball, John. *Johnny Get Your Gun.*

Bowen, Robert Sidney. *Infield Flash.*

Bradbury, Bianca. *Andy's Mountain.*

Carol, Bill J. *Lefty Plays First.*

Christopher, Matthew F. *Hard Drive to Short.*

Drdek, Richard. *Lefty's Boy.*

Gault, William C. *Stubborn Sam.*

Heuman, William. *The Goofer Pitch.*

Higdon, Hal. *The Horse that Played Center Field.*

Hoff, Syd. *Baseball Mouse.*

Jackson, C. Paul. *Pennant Stretch Drive.*

Karlins, Marvin. *The Last Man Is Out.*

Kongisburg, E. L. *About the B'nai Bagels.*

MacKellar, William. *Mound Menace.*

Mendelsohn, Felix, Jr. *Superbaby.*

Schulz, Charles M. *Charlie Brown's Yearbook.*

Wade, Robert. *Knave of Eagles.*

1970

Carol, Bill J. *Sandy Plays Third.*

Christopher, Matthew F. *Shortstop from Toyko.*

Christopher, Matthew F. *Lucky Seven.*

Corbett, Scott. *The Baseball Bargain.*

Foreman, Harvey. *Awk.*

Harmon, A. W. *Base Hit.*

Heuman, William. *Home Run Henri.*

Jackson, C. Paul. *Bud Baker, College Pitcher.*

Lewinstein, Stephen R. *Double Play.*

Philbrook, Clem. *Ollie's Team Plays Biddy Baseball.*

Scholz, Jackson. *Hot-Corner Hank.*

Schulz, Charles M. *Winning May Not be Everything, But Losing Isn't Anything.*

Slote, Alfred. *Stranger on the Ball Club.*

Summers, Richard. *Ball-Shy Pitcher.*

Turner, Morrie. *Nipper.*

1971

Archibald, Joe. *Payoff Pitch.*

Blassingame, Wade. *John Henry and Paul Bunyan Play Baseball.*

Carley, Wayne. *Percy the Parrot Strikes Out.*

Carol, Bill J. *Squeeze Play.*

Christopher, Matthew F. *Look Who's Playing First Base.*

Cox, William R. *Big League Sandlotters.*

Honig, Donald. *Johnny Lee.*

Jackson, C. Paul. *Tom Mosely—Midget Leaguer.*

Laurence, Alfred D. *Homer Pickle, the Greatest.*

Lewinstein, Stephen R. *Computer Coach.*

Slote, Alfred. *Jake.*

Taylor, Florance W. *Ball Two!*

1972

Archibald, Joe. *Right Field Runt.*

Ball, John. *Death for a Playmate.*

Beckham, Barry. *Runner Mack.*

Carol, Bill J. *High Fly to Center.*

Christian Science Publishing Society. *Bats, Bullies and Buddies.*

Christopher, Matthew F. *The Kid Who Only Hit Homers.*

Cox, William R. *Chicano Cruz.*

Foley, Louise M. *Somebody Stole Second.*

Green, Phyllis. *The Fastest Quitter in Town.*

Heuman, William. *Little League Hotshots.*

Jackson, C. Paul. *Fifth Inning Fade-Out.*

Lunemann, Evelyn. *Pitcher's Choice.*

Parish, Peggy. *Play Ball, Amelia Bedelia.*
Philbrook, Clem. *Ollie's Team and the 200 Pound Problem.*
Powell, Talmage. *Cellar Team.*
Slote, Alfred. *The Biggest Victory.*
Slote, Alfred. *My Father, the Coach.*
Taves, Isabella. *Not Bad for a Girl.*
Walden, Amelia Elizabeth. *Play Ball, McGill.*

1973

Allen, Alex B. *No Place for Baseball.*
Archibald, Joe. *The Fifth Base.*
Brashler, William. *The Bingo Long Traveling All-Stars and Motor Kings.*
Carol, Bill J. *Double-Play Ball.*
Christopher, Matthew F. *Mystery Coach.*
Corbett, Scott. *The Home Run Trick.*
Dawson, Fielding. *A Great Day for a Ballgame.*
Fish, Robert L., and Henry Rothblatt. *A Handy Death.*
Foster, Alan S. *Goodbye, Bobby Thompson! Goodbye, John Wayne!*
Gault, Clare and Frank. *Norman Plays Second Base.*
Gault, William C. *Trouble at Second.*
Graham, John Alexander. *Babe Ruth Caught in a Snowstorm.*
Gray, Genevieve. *Stand-Off.*
Guthrie, A. B., Jr. *Wild Pitch.*
Hegner, William. *The Idolaters.*
Honig, Donald. *Way to Go, Teddy.*
Hood, Robert. *Let's Go to a Baseball Game.*
McMahon, William R. *A Doodletown Dodger.*
Neugeboren, Jay. *Sam's Legacy.*
Philbrook, Clem. *Ollie's Team and the Million Dollar Mistake.*
Puechner, Ray. *A Grand Slam.*
Roth, Philip. *The Great American Novel.*
Schulz, Charles M. *Win a Few, Lose a Few, Charlie Brown.*
Slote, Alfred. *Hang Tough, Paul Mather.*

1974

Archibald, Joe. *Centerfield Rival.*
Bachman, Fred. *Hang In At the Plate.*
Bliss, Ronald G. *Indian Softball Summer.*
Bunting, A. E. *Pitcher to Center Field.*

Carol, Bill J. *Single to Center.*
Christopher, Matthew F. *No Arm in Left Field.*
Christopher, Matthew F. *Jinx Glove.*
Cohen, Barbara. *Thank You, Jackie Robinson.*
Dubrovin, Vivian. *Baseball Just for Fun.*
Higdon, Hal. *The Last Series.*
Holton, Leonard. *The Devil to Play.*
Honig, Donald. *The Professional.*
Klise, Thomas S. *The Last Western.*
Lee, S. C. *Little League Leader.*
McGovern, Ann. *Scram, Kid!*
St. Sauver, Dennis. *Pro Fever.*
Schulz, Charles M. *Play Ball, Snoopy.*
Slote, Alfred. *Tony and Me.*
Sorrentino, Gilbert. *Flawless Play Restored: The Masque of Fungo.*
Walt Disney Productions. *Mickey Mouse and the Great Lot Plot.*

1975

Burchard, Marshall and Sue. *I Know a Baseball Player.*
Christopher, Matthew F. *The Team that Stopped Moving.*
Craig, John. *All G.O.D.'s Children.*
Curtis, Richard. *The Pro #3: Strike Zone.*
Gault, William C. *The Underground Skipper.*
Keifetz, Norman. *The Sensation.*
Levy, Elizabeth. *Something Queer at the Ball Park.*
Parker, Robert B. *Mortal Stakes.*
Sachs, Marilyn. *Matt's Mitt.*
Sayles, John. *Pride of the Bimbos.*
Slote, Alfred. *Matt Gargan's Boy.*
Wise, Francis H. *Play Ball.*

1976

Christopher, Matthew F. *The Submarine Pitch.*
Delaney, Ned. *Two Strikes, Four Eyes.*
Hoff, Syd. *The Littlest Leaguer.*
Honig, Donald. *Hurry Home.*
Isadora, Rachel. *Max.*
Kalb, Jonah. *The Goof That Won the Pennant.*
Lexau, Joan M. *I'll Tell on You.*
Linthurst, Randolph. *Journal of Leo Smith: Story of a Nineteenth Century Shortstop.*

McGraw, Tug, with Mike Witte. *Scroogie.*
Millar, Jeff, and Bill Hinds. *If I Quit Baseball, Will You Still Love Me?*
Rice, Damon. *Seasons Past.*
Rothweiler, Paul R. *The Sensuous Southpaw.*
Rubin, Jeff, and Rick Rael. *Baseball Brothers.*
Tester, Sylvia. *Rover, Jr.'s Baseball Career.*
Winston, Peter. *Luke.*
Woodley, Richard. *The Bad News Bears.*

1977

Christopher, Matthew F. *The Diamond Champs.*
Christopher, Matthew F. *Johnny No Hit.*
Donohue, James F. *Spitballs and Holy Water.*
Hemmings, T. J. *Fish Strikes Out.*
Herrin, Lamar. *The Rio Loja Ringmaster.*
Honig, Donald. *Winter Always Comes.*
Kowett, Don. *The 7th Game.*
McGraw, Tug, with Mike Witte. *Hello There, Ball!*
Magnuson, James. *The Rundown.*
Peck, Robert Newton. *Last Sunday.*
Schulz, Charles M. *Sandlot Peanuts.*
Schulz, Charles M. *It's Great to be a Superstar.*
Schulz, Charles M. *It's Hard Work Being Bitter.*
Schulz, Charles M. *It's Arbor Day, Charlie Brown.*
Schulz, Charles M. *There Goes the Shutout.*
Strong, Rod. *The Lady Umpire's Hot Hands.*
Swed, Trebor. *Whichaway?*
Woodley, Richard. *The Bad News Bears in Breaking Training.*
Wright, Edward Needles. *Chestnut Bur Lions.*
Zacharia, Irwin. *Grandstand Rookie.*

1978

Christian, Mary Blount. *The Sand Lot.*
Christopher, Matthew F. *The Fox Steals Home.*
Clifton, Merritt. *A Baseball Classic.*
Cooney, Nancy Evans. *The Wobbly Tooth.*
Cox, William R. *Battery Mates.*
Dickmeyer, Lowell. *Baseball is for Me.*
Fisher, Leonard Everett. *Noonan: A Novel About Baseball, ESP, and Time Warps.*
Grant, J. Jason. *Dugout Brother.*
Knudson, R. R. *Zanboomer.*
Mann, Ted. *Making the Team.*

Molarsky, Osmond. *Robbery in Right Field.*
Nixon, Joan Lowery. *Danger in Dinosaur Valley.*
Platt, Kin. *The Screwball King Murder.*
Shea, George. *Big Bad Ernie.*
Tennenbaum, Silvia. *Rachel, the Rabbi's Wife.*
Wibberley, Leonard P. O. *Little League Family.*
Willard, Nancy. *The Highest Hit.*
Woodley, Richard. *The Bad News Bears Go to Japan.*

1979

Bell, Marty. *Breaking Balls.*
Brady, Charles. *Seven Games in October.*
Caroselli, Remus F. *The Mystery Cottage in Left Field.*
Charyn, Jerome. *The Seventh Babe.*
Cohen, Dan. *The Case of the Battling Ball Clubs.*
Corcoran, Barbara. *"Me and You and a Dog Named Blue."*
Craig, John. *Chappie and Me.*
Harris, Mark. *It Looked Like For Ever.*
Hemphill, Paul. *Long Gone.*
Hoff, Syd. *Slugger Sal's Slump.*
Holtzman, Jerome, ed. *Fielder's Choice.*
Honig, Donald. *The Last Great Season.*
Lardner, Ring. *Ring Lardner's You Know Me Al.*
Lewis, Jerry D., ed. *Great Baseball Stories.*
Newlin, Paul. *It Had to be a Woman.*
O'Connor, Philip F. *Stealing Home.*
Tolle, Jean B. *The Great Pete Penney.*
Waldman, Jeri and Neil. *Pitcher in Left Field.*

1980

Andersen, Richard. *Muckaluck.*
Broekel, Ray. *The Mystery of the Stolen Base.*
Browne, Robert. *The New AToms Bombshell.*
Burksaze, Phil F. *A Special Season.*
Christopher, Matthew F. *Wild Pitch.*
Cohler, David Keith. *Gamemaker.*
Corbett, Scott. *The Great McGonigle Switches Pitches.*
Cronley, Jay. *Screwballs.*
Due, Linnea A. *High and Outside.*
Gantos, Jack, and Nicole Rubel. *Willy's Raiders.*
Giff, Patricia. *Left-Handed Shortstop.*
Greene, Laura. *I Am Somebody.*

Harris, Robie H. *Rosie's Double Dare.*
Longman, Harold S. *The Fox in the Ball Park.*
Lorenz, Tom. *Guys Like Us.*
Morgenstein, Gary. *Take Me Out to the Ballgame.*
Resciniti, Angelo. *The Baseball from Outer Space.*
Spencer, Ross H. *The Stranger City Caper.*
Wolff, Miles, Jr. *Season of the Owl.*

1981

Gordon, Sharon. *Play Ball, Kate!*
Hughes, Dean. *Hooper Haller.*
Hurwitz, Johanna. *Baseball Fever.*
Knopf, Mel. *The Batting Machine.*
McGraw, Frank E. "Tug," Jr. *Lumpy.*
McSherry, Frank D., Jr., Charles Waugh, and M. H. Greenberg, eds. *Baseball 3000.*
Michaels, Ralph. *The Girl on First Base.*
Oleksy, Walter. *Quacky and the Crazy Curve Ball.*
Powers, Ron. *Toot-Toot-Tootsie, Good-bye.*
Quigley, Martin. *The Original Colored House of David.*
Ritz, David. *The Man Who Brought the Dodgers Back to Brooklyn.*
Rubin, Louis D., Jr. *Surfaces of a Diamond.*
Sachs, Marilyn. *Fleet-footed Florence.*
Shea, George. *Strike Two.*
Smith, Doris Buchanan. *Last Was Lloyd.*
Vogan, Sara. *In Shelly's Leg.*
Walker, David G. *Rick Goes to Little League.*

1982

Aaseng, Nate. *Batting Ninth for the Braves.*
Adams, Phyllis, Eleanore Hartson, and Mark Taylor. *Time Out!*
Adler, David A. *Cam Jansen and the Mystery of the Babe Ruth Baseball.*
Anderson, Margaret Jean. *The Brain on Quartz Mountain.*
Batting, Joan. *Katie and the Very Little League.*
Brandt, Keith. *The Case of the Missing Dinosaurs.*
Carmona, Al. *Andy: The First Switch-Pitcher.*
Clifton, Merritt. *Baseball Stories for Girls and Boys (Past Puberty).*
DeAndrea, William L. *Five O'Clock Lightning.*
Dessent, Michael. *Baseball Becky.*
Kahn, Roger. *The Seventh Game.*

Kessler, Leonard P. *Old Turtle's Baseball Stories.*
Kinsella, W. P. *Shoeless Joe.*
Klein, Dave. *Hit and Run.*
Lipsyte, Robert. *Jock and Jill.*
McCormack, Tom. *Strictly Amateur.*
Park, Barbara. *Skinnybones.*
Schiffer, Michael. *Ballpark.*
Schulz, Charles M. *Slide, Charlie Brown! Slide!*
Slote, Alfred. *Rabbit Ears.*
Small, David. *Almost Famous.*
Smith, Carole. *The Hit-and-Run Connection.*
Sullivan, Silky. *Henry and Melinda.*

1983

Broun, Hob. *Odditorium.*
Cebulash, Mel. *Ruth Marini of the Dodgers.*
Cebulash, Mel. *Ruth Marini, Dodger Ace.*
Engleman, Paul. *Dead in Centerfield.*
Everett, Percival L. *Suder.*
Gelman, Mitch. *Can You Win the Pennant?*
Greenberg, Eric Rolfe. *The Celebrant.*
Harper, Elaine. *Short Stop for Romance.*
Kennedy, William. *Ironweed.*
Kidd, Ronald. *Who Is Felix the Great?*
Morgenstein, Gary. *The Man Who Wanted to Play Centerfield for the New York Yankees.*
Munn, Vella. *Summer Season.*
Murphy, Elspeth Campbell. *God Cares When I Don't Like Myself.*
Paulos, Sheila. *Wild Roses.*
Quarrington, Paul. *Home Game.*
Shea, George. *Make the Play-Offs!*
Stein, Harry. *Hoopla.*
Stone, Natalie. *Double Play.*
Van Steenwyk, Elizabeth. *The Southpaw from Sonora Mystery.*
Webb, Vaughan. *Hot Streak and Other Sports Stories.*
Wenk, Richard. *The Great Baseball Championship.*

1984

Adler, David A. *Jeffrey's Ghost and the Leftover Baseball Team.*
Baron, Nancy. *Tuesday's Child.*
Benjamin, Paul. *Squeeze Play.*
Carkeet, David. *The Greatest Slump of All Time.*

Cooney, Ellen. *All the Way Home.*
Dixon, Michael B., and Valerie Smith. *Striking Out!*
Frank, Morry. *Every Young Man's Dream: Confessions of a Southern League Shortstop.*
Hays, Donald. *The Dixie Association.*
Hopper, Nancy J. *Ape Ears and Beaky.*
Jordan, Pat. *The Cheat.*
Klass, David. *The Atami Dragons.*
Kluger, Steve. *Changing Pitches.*
Lewis, Marjorie. *Wrongway Applebaum.*
Lord, Betty Bao. *In the Year of the Boar and Jackie Robinson.*
Mayer, Robert. *The Grace of Shortstops.*
Rosen, Richard D. *Strike Three You're Dead.*
Sharp, Paul. *Paul the Pitcher.*
Stadler, John. *Hooray for Snail.*
Willard, Nancy. *Things Invisible to See.*

1985

Abels, Harriette. *A Good Sport.*
Beardslee, Ken. *Partners.*
Cebulash, Mel. *Ruth Marini, World Series Star.*
Christopher, Matthew F. *Supercharged Infield.*
DeMarco, Gordon. *Frisco Blues.*
Eller, Scott. *Short Season.*
Eyster, Richard H. *Barefoot Bear Plays Ball.*
Gelman, Mitch. *Opening Day.*
Guy, David. *Second Brother.*
Heller, Pete. *Peppy Learns to Play Baseball.*
Kahn, Peggy. *The Care Bears: "Try, Try Again!"*
Kaye, Marilyn. *Will You Cross Me?*
Kessler, Leonard P. *The Worst Team Ever.*
Kinsella, W. P. *The Thrill of the Grass.*
Levinson, Marilyn. *And Don't Bring Jeremy.*
Lowry, Lois. *Switcharound.*
Marlowe, Dan J. *The Comeback.*
McManus, James. *Chin Music.*
McVey, R. Parker. *Mystery at the Ball Game.*
Montgomery, Robert. *Rabbit Ears.*
Pomeranz, Gary. *Out at Home.*
Schulz, Charles M. *Big League Peanuts.*
Stocker, Fern Neal. *Billy Sunday, Baseball Preacher.*
Tapply, William G. *Follow the Sharks.*
Whitehead, Patricia. *Arnold Plays Baseball.*

1986

Ardizzone, Tony. *Heart of the Order.*
Author unknown. *Switch-Hitting Big-Leaguer.*
Berenstain, Stan and Jan. *The Berenstain Bears Go Out for the Team.*
Burch, Mark H. *Road Game: A Summer's Tale.*
Conte, Sal. *Child's Play.*
Coomer, Joe. *A Flatland Fable.*
Geller, Mark. *My Life in the 7th Grade.*
Hough, John, Jr. *The Conduct of the Game.*
Jenkins, Jerry B. *The Secret Baseball Challenge.*
Jenkins, Jerry B. *Mystery at Raider Stadium.*
Kinsella, W. P. *The Iowa Baseball Confederacy.*
Landon, Lucinda. *Meg Mackintosh and the Case of the Missing Babe Ruth Baseball.*
Lord, Suzanne. *Kissyfur of Paddlecab County.*
Michaels, Ski. *The Baseball Bat.*
Oechsli, Kelly. *Mice at Bat.*
Reys, Margret and H. A. *Curious George Plays Baseball.*
Toth, Pamela. *Fever Pitch.*

1987

Adler, David A. *Benny, Benny, Baseball Nut.*
Bowen, Michael. *Can't Miss.*
Cosgrove, Stephen. *Popp Fly.*
Crutcher, Chris. *The Crazy Horse Electric Game.*
Dolan, Ellen M. *Casey at the Bat.*
Franklin, Lance. *Double Play.*
Gethers, Peter. *Getting Blue.*
Gill, Charles. *The Boozer Challenge.*
Greenberg, Martin H., ed. *On the Diamond.*
Gregorich, Barbara. *She's On First.*
Hudson, Anna. *Fun and Games.*
Katz, Steve. *Florry of Washington Heights.*
Kelly, Jeffrey. *The Basement Baseball Club.*
Klusmeyer, Joann. *What About Me?*
Lane, Bradley. *The Big Time.*
Marlowe, Dan J. *Double the Glory.*
Marlowe, Dan J. *The Hitter.*
Pellowski, Michael. *Baseball Bear.*
Plimpton, George. *The Curious Case of Sidd Finch.*
Schulz, Charles M. *Good Catch, Snoopy.*
Schulz, Charles M. *Strike Three, Charlie Brown.*
Sheed, Wilfrid. *The Boys of Winter.*

Snyder, Don J. *Veterans Park.*
Spencer, Ross H. *Kirby's Last Circus.*
Stansberry, Domenic. *The Spoiler.*

1988

Aaseng, Nate. *A Winning Season for the Braves.*
Aiello, Barbara, and Jeffrey Shulman. *It's Your Turn at Bat.*
Bernstein, Joanne E., and Paul Cohen. *Grand Slam Riddles.*
Christopher, Matthew F. *The Dog That Pitched a No-Hitter.*
Christopher, Matthew F. *The Hit-Away Kid.*
Christopher, Matthew F. *The Spy on Third Base.*
Dixon, Franklin W. *The Hardy Boys: Danger on the Diamond.*
Dygard, Thomas. *The Rookie Arrives.*
Geller, Michael. *Major League Murder.*
Giff, Patricia. *Ronald Morgan Goes to Bat.*
Gilchrist, Guy. *Tiny Dinos Playing Together.*
Gordon, Alison. *The Dead Pull Hitter.*
Johnson, Lois W. *You're Worth More Than You Think.*
Joyce, William. *Dinosaur Bob and His Adventures with the Family Lazardo.*
King, Frank. *Southpaw.*
Kinsella, W. P. *The Further Adventures of Slugger McBatt.*
Klass, David. *A Different Season.*
Kline, Suzy. *Herbie Jones and the Monster Ball.*
Klinkowitz, Jerry. *Short Season and Other Stories.*
Lelchuk, Alan. *On Home Ground.*
MacNelly, Jeff. *Shoe Goes to Wrigley Field.*
Myers, Walter D. *Me, Mop, and the Moondance Kid.*
Robbins, Ken. *At the Ballpark.*
Rosen, Richard D. *Saturday Night Dead.*
Weaver, Gordon. *The Eight Corners of the World.*
Ziefert, Harriet. *Strike Four!*
Zirpoli, Jane. *Roots in the Outfield.*

1989

Cairns, Bob. *The Comeback Kids.*
Deford, Frank. *Casey on the Loose.*
Economos, Chris. *The New Kid.*
Ethridge, Kenneth. *Viola, Furgy, Bobbi, and Me.*

Freeman, Mark. *Play Ball!*
Freeman, Mark. *Squeeze Play.*
Freeman, Mark. *Spring Training.*
Freeman, Mark. *Big-League Break.*
Freeman, Mark. *Play-Off Pressure.*
Freeman, Mark. *Series Showdown.*
Gerberg, Mort. *Bear-ly Bear-able Baseball.*
Glenn, Mel. *Squeeze Play.*
Kraus, Robert. *How Spider Saved the Baseball Game.*
Littlefield, Bill. *Prospect.*
Martin, Ann M. *The Baby-Sitters Club: Kristy and the Walking Disaster.*
Marzollo, Jean. *The Pizza Pie Slugger.*
McAlpine, Gordon. *Joy in Mudville.*
Mooser, Stephen. *Monsters in the Outfield.*
Nighbert, David F. *Strikezone.*
Seaver, Tom, with Herb Resnicow. *Beanball: Murder at the World Series.*
Slote, Alfred. *Make-Believe Ballplayer.*
Smith, Robert Kimmel. *Bobby Baseball.*
Springstubb, Tricia. *With a Name like Lulu, Who Needs More Trouble?*
Stine, Megan, and H. William. *Baseball Card Fever.*
Suzanne, Jamie. *Sweet Valley Twins: Standing Out.*
Zubro, Mark Richard. *A Simple Suburban Murder.*

1990

Aaseng, Nate. *Batter Up!*
Bjarkman, Peter C., ed. *Baseball & The Game of Life.*
Bowering, George, ed. *Taking the Field.*
Brock, Darryl. *If I Never Get Back.*
Curtis, Gavin. *Grandma's Baseball.*
Dagavarian, Debra A., ed. *A Century of Children's Baseball Stories.*
Day, Alexandra. *Frank and Ernest Play Ball.*
Elish, Dan. *Jason and the Baseball Bear.*
Ellis, Lucy. *The Girls Strike Back: The Making of the Pink Parrots.*
Ellis, Lucy. *All That Jazz.*
Friend, David. *Baseball, Football, Daddy and Me.*
Grosser, Morton. *The Fabulous Fifty.*
Hallowell, Tommy. *Duel on the Diamond.*
Haynes, Mary. *The Great Pretender.*
Hughes, Dean. *Making the Team.*
Hughes, Dean. *Big Base Hit.*

Hughes, Dean. *Winning Streak.*
Hughes, Dean. *What a Catch!*
Hughes, Dean. *Rookie Star.*
Hughes, Dean. *Pressure Play.*
Hughes, Dean. *Line Drive.*
Hughes, Dean. *Championship Game.*
Irvine, Robert. *Gone to Glory.*
Johnson, Neil. *Batter Up!*
Kahaner, Ellen. *What's So Great About Fourth Grade?*
Kiraly, Sherwood. *California Rush.*
Leavy, Jane. *Squeeze Play.*
Lelchuk, Alan. *Brooklyn Boy.*
Lyle, Sparky, and David Fisher. *The Year I Owned the Yankees.*
Manfred, Frederick. *No Fun on Sunday.*

Montgomery, Robert. *Home Run!*
Montgomery, Robert. *Grand Slam.*
Montgomery, Robert. *Triple Play.*
Montgomery, Robert. *MVP.*
Montgomery, Robert. *Hitting Streak.*
Montgomery, Robert. *The Show!*
Petersen, P. J., and Betsy James. *The Fireplug is First Base.*
Real, Rory, and Bob Pelkowski. *A Baseball Dream.*
Slattery, Marty. *Diamonds Are Trumps.*
Slote, Alfred. *The Trading Game.*
Soto, Gary. *Baseball in April and Other Stories.*
Williams, Karen Lynn. *Baseball and Butterflies.*
Zubro, Mark Richard. *Why Isn't Becky Twitchell Dead?*

The most popular title is *Squeeze Play* by a narrow margin over *Double Play*. Honorable mention goes to Little League, which appears in the titles of over twenty books. The Merriwell books have been removed from this list.

Abner Doubleday, Young Baseball Pioneer. Dunham, Montrew.

About the B'nai Bagels. Kongisburg, E. L.

Ace Pitcher. Gartner, John.

Action at Third. Emery, Russell G.

Against Odds. Heyliger, William.

All Except Sammy. Cretan, Gladys Yessayan.

All G.O.D.'s Children. Craig, John.

All on the Team. Sandmel, Frances Fox.

All that Jazz. Ellis, Lucy.

All the Way Home. Cooney, Ellen.

Almost Famous. Small, David.

And Don't Bring Jeremy. Levinson, Marilyn.

Andy: The First Switch-Pitcher. Carmona, Al.

Andy's Mountain. Bradbury, Bianca.

Ape Ears and Beaky. Hopper, Nancy J.

Arnold Plays Baseball. Whitehead, Patricia.

Around the World with the Baseball Bugs. Regan, Jack, and Will E. Stahl.

At the Ballpark. Robbins, Ken.

At the Home Plate. Dudley, Albertus True.

Atami Dragons, The. Klass, David.

Automatic Strike, The. McCormick, Wilfred.

Autumn Comes Early. Breslin, Howard.

Awk. Foreman, Harvey.

Babe Ruth, Baseball Boy. Van Riper, Guernsey, Jr.

Babe Ruth Caught in a Snowstorm. Graham, John Alexander.

Baby-Sitters Club: Kristy and the Walking Disaster, The. Martin, Ann M.

Backstop Ace. Friendlich, Dick.

Bad News Bears, The. Woodley, Richard.

Bad News Bears Go to Japan, The. Woodley, Richard.

Bad News Bears in Breaking Training, The. Woodley, Richard.

Ball Hawk. Bowen, Robert Sidney.

Ball of Fire. Miers, Earl Schenck.

Ballpark. Schiffer, Michael.

Ballplayer, The. Fitzgerald, Ed.

Ball-Shy Pitcher. Summers, Richard.

Ball Two! Taylor, Florance W.

Bang the Drum Slowly. Harris, Mark.

Banjo Hitter. Bishop, Curtis K.

Barbarian, The. Corcoran, Brewer.

Barefoot Bear Plays Ball. Eyster, Richard H.

Barney Beagle Plays Baseball. Bethell, Jean.

Barney of the Babe Ruth League. Lochlons, Colin.

Baron of the Bullpen. Friendlich, Dick.

Bartley, Freshman Pitcher. Heyliger, William.

Base Burglar. Scholz, Jackson.

Base Hit. Harmon, A. W.

Baseball & the Game of Life. Bjarkman, Peter C., ed.

Baseball and Butterflies. Williams, Karen Lynn.

Baseball Bargain, The. Corbett, Scott.

Baseball Bat, The. Michaels, Ski.

Baseball Bear. Pellowski, Michael.

Baseball Becky. Dessent, Michael.

Baseball Bonus Kid. Gelman, Steve.

Baseball Boys of Lakeport, The. Stratemeyer, Edward.

Baseball Brothers. Rubin, Jeff, and Rick Rael.

Baseball Card Fever. Stine, Megan, and H. William.

Baseball Classic, A. Clifton, Merritt.

Baseball Detective, The. Muller, Charles G.

Baseball Dream, A. Real, Rory, and Bob Pelkowski.

Baseball Fever. Hurwitz, Johanna.

Baseball Flyhawk. Christopher, Matthew F.

Baseball, Football, Daddy and Me. Friend, David.

Baseball from Outer Space, The. Resciniti, Angelo.

Baseball in April and Other Stories. Soto, Gary.

Baseball is for Me. Dickmeyer, Lowell.

Baseball Joe Around the World. Chadwick, Lester.

Baseball Joe at Yale. Chadwick, Lester.

Baseball Joe, Captain of the Team. Chadwick, Lester.

Baseball Joe, Champion of the League. Chadwick, Lester.

Baseball Joe, Club Owner. Chadwick, Lester.

Baseball Joe, Home Run King. Chadwick, Lester.

Baseball Joe in the Big League. Chadwick, Lester.

Baseball Joe in the Central League. Chadwick, Lester.

Baseball Joe in the World Series. Chadwick, Lester.

Baseball Joe of the Silver Stars. Chadwick, Lester.

Baseball Joe on the Giants. Chadwick, Lester.

Baseball Joe on the School Nine. Chadwick, Lester.
Baseball Joe, Pitching Wizard. Chadwick, Lester.
Baseball Joe, Saving the League. Chadwick, Lester.
Baseball Just for Fun. Dubrovin, Vivian.
Baseball Mouse. Hoff, Syd.
Baseball Mystery, The. Pallas, Norvin.
Baseball Pals. Christopher, Matthew F.
Baseball Reader, The. Graber, Ralph S., ed.
Baseball Round-Up. Margulies, Leo.
Baseball Spark Plug. Zanger, Jack.
Baseball Stories. Cummings, Parke, ed.
Baseball Stories for Girls and Boys (Past Puberty). Clifton, Merritt.
Baseball 3000. McSherry, Frank D., Jr., Charles Waugh, and M. H. Greenberg, eds.
Baseball Trick, The. Corbett, Scott.
Baseball's Darkest Days. Grantham, Kenneth L.
Basement Baseball Club, The. Kelly, Jeffrey.
Bases Full. Barbour, Ralph Henry.
Bases Full. Sherman, Harold M.
Bases Loaded. McCormick, Wilfred.
Base-Stealer, The. Bonner, Mary G.
Bat Boy. Bowen, Robert Sidney.
Bats & Gloves of Glory. Renick, Marion.
Bats and Balls. Lord, Beman.
Bats, Bullies, and Buddies. Christian Science Publishing Society.
Batter Up! Aaseng, Nate.
Batter Up! Johnson, Neil.
Batter Up! Sherman, Harold M.
Batter Up! Williams, Hawley.
Batter Up. Scholz, Jackson.
Battery Feud. Olgin, Joseph.
Battery for Madison High. Hirshberg, Al.
Battery Mates. Cox, William R.
Batting Machine, The. Knopf, Mel.
Batting Ninth for the Braves. Aaseng, Nate.
Batting to Win. Chadwick, Lester.
Bean-Ball Bill and Other Stories. Heyliger, William.
Beanball: Murder at the World Series. Seaver, Tom, with Herb Resnicow.
Bear-ly Bear-able Baseball. Gerberg, Mort.
Beatty of the Yankees. Maule, Hamilton "Tex."
Bedfellow, The. Asinof, Eliot.
Behind the Bat. Bowen, Robert Sidney.

Behind the Plate. Berra, Yogi, and Til Ferdenzi.
Behold, Thy Brother. Edmunds, Murrell.
Bell Haven Nine, The. Barton, George.
Bench Boss. Scholz, Jackson.
Benny, Benny, Baseball Nut. Adler, David A.
Berenstain Bears Go Out for the Team, The. Berenstain, Stan and Jan.
Bert Wilson's Fadeaway Ball. Duffield, J. W.
Bertie Takes Care. Felsen, Henry Gregor.
Between Friends. Aumerle, Richard.
Big Bad Ernie. Shea, George.
Big Base Hit. Hughes, Dean.
Big Game, The. Bishop, Curtis K.
Big Game, The. Perry, Lawrence.
Big Hit, The. Bowen, Robert Sidney.
Big Inning, The. Bowen, Robert Sidney.
Big League, The. Van Loan, Charles.
Big-League Break. Freeman, Mark.
Big League Busher. Archibald, Joe.
Big League Peanuts. Schulz, Charles M.
Big League Rookie. Cox, William R.
Big League Rookie. Wallace, Francis.
Big League Sandlotters. Cox, William R.
Big Leaguer, The. Heyliger, William.
Big Mitt, The. Scholz, Jackson.
Big Ninth, The. McCormick, Wilfred.
Big Out, The. Hano, Arnold.
Big Play in the Small League. Jackson, C. Paul.
Big Stretch, The. Decker, Duane.
Big Time, The. Lane, Bradley.
Biggest Victory, The. Slote, Alfred.
Bill Bruce of Harvard. Patten, Gilbert.
Billy Sunday, Baseball Preacher. Stocker, Fern Neal.
Billy's Clubhouse. Holland, Marion.
Bingo Long Traveling All-Stars and Motor Kings, The. Brashler, William.
Bluffer, The. McCormick, Wilfred.
Boats, Bats and Bicycles. Young, Ernest A.
Bob White: Bonus Player. Mann, Arthur.
Bob White: Farm Club Player. Mann, Arthur.
Bob White: Spring Terror. Mann, Arthur.
Bobby Baseball. Smith, Robert Kimmel.
Bobby Blake on the School Nine. Warner, Frank.
Bonus Boy. Olson, Gene.
Bonus Kid. Archibald, Joe.

Bonus Pitcher. Waldman, Frank.

Bonus Rookie. O'Rourke, Frank.

Boozer Challenge, The. Gill, Charles.

Boy at Bat. Renick, Marion.

Boy Who Won the World Series, The. Offit, Sidney.

Boys Life Book of Baseball Stories, The. Boys Life, Editors of.

Boys of Columbia High in Camp, The. Forbes, Graham.

Boys of Columbia High on the Diamond, The. Forbes, Graham.

Boys of Fairport, The. Brooks, Noah.

Boys of Winter, The. Sheed, Wilfrid.

Brain on Quartz Mountain, The. Anderson, Margaret Jean.

Breaking Balls. Bell, Marty.

Brick King, Backstop. Standish, Burt L.

Bride and the Pennant, The. Chance, Frank.

Brooklyn Boy. Lelchuk, Alan.

Brownie and I. Aumerle, Richard.

Buck's Home Run Drive. Dawson, Elmer.

Buck's Winning Hit. Dawson, Elmer.

Bud Baker, College Pitcher. Jackson, C. Paul.

Bud Baker, High School Pitcher. Jackson, C. Paul.

Buddy and the Old Pro. Tunis, John R.

Bull Pen Hero. Etter, Les.

Bullpen Bargain. Jackson, C. Paul.

Buttons and the Little League, The. McCall, Edith.

California Rush. Kiraly, Sherwood.

Call of the Varsity, The. Patten, Gilbert.

Cam Jansen and the Mystery of the Babe Ruth Baseball. Adler, David A.

Can You Win the Pennant? Gelman, Mitch.

Can't Miss. Bowen, Michael.

Captain Danny. Camp, Walter.

Captain Fair-and-Square. Heyliger, William.

Captain of the Nine, The. Heyliger, William.

Captain of the S. I. G.'s, The. Baker, Etta Anthony.

Captain of the School Team. Earl, John P.

Captain, The. Pier, Arthur.

Care Bears: "Try, Try Again!", The. Kahn, Peggy.

Carson at Second. Young, Isador S.

Case of the Battling Ball Clubs, The. Cohen, Dan.

Case of the Missing Dinosaurs, The. Brandt, Keith.

Casey at the Bat. Dolan, Ellen M.

Casey Jones and Locomotive No. 638. Shapiro, Irwin.

Casey on the Loose. Deford, Frank.

Casey's Redemption. Fitzpatrick, Burgess.

Catcher and the Manager, The. O'Rourke, Frank.

Catcher Craig. Mathewson, Christy.

Catcher from Double-A, The. Decker, Duane.

Catcher with a Glass Arm. Christopher, Matthew F.

Catcher's Choice. Archibald, Joe.

Celebrant, The. Greenberg, Eric Rolfe.

Cellar Team. Powell, Talmage.

Center-Field Jinx. Scholz, Jackson.

Centerfield Rival. Archibald, Joe.

Century of Children's Baseball Stories, A. Dagavarian, Debra A., ed.

Challenge at Second Base. Christopher, Matthew F.

Championship Game. Hughes, Dean.

Changing Base. Everett, William.

Changing Pitches. Kluger, Steve.

Chappie and Me. Craig, John.

Charlie Brown's All-Stars. Schulz, Charles M.

Charlie Brown's Yearbook. Schulz, Charles M.

Cheat, The. Jordan, Pat.

Cheerleader, The. Pier, Arthur.

Chestnut Bur Lions. Wright, Edward Needles.

Chicano Cruz. Cox, William R.

Child's Play. Conte, Sal.

Chin Music. McManus, James.

Chosen, The. Potok, Chaim.

Chuck Blue of Sterling. Chadwick, George B.

Chums of Scranton High Out for the Pennant. Ferguson, Donald.

Circus Catch. Archibald, Joe.

Circus Catch. Carol, Bill J.

Clarkville's Battery. Lawton, Charles.

Clean Up Hitter. Friendlich, Dick.

Clif Stirling, Captain of the Nine. Patten, Gilbert.

Clif Stirling, Sophomore at Stormbridge. Patten, Gilbert.

Clown at Second Base. Jackson, C. Paul.

Club Team, The. Richard, James R.

Clutch Hitter! Bee, Clair.

Clutch Hitter. Wayne, Richard.

Clutch Single. Carol, Bill J.

College League Mystery, The. Cooper, John R.

College Rebel, The. Patten, Gilbert.

College Slugger. Fitzgerald, Ed.

Colonel of the Crimson. Playfair, Robert Smith.

Comeback, The. Marlowe, Dan J.

Comeback Catcher, The. Longstreth, T. Morris.

Comeback Kids, The. Cairns, Bob.

Coming Back with the Spitball: A Pitcher's Romance. Hopper, James.

Computer Coach. Lewinstein, Stephen R.

Conduct of the Game, The. Hough, John, Jr.

County Pennant, The. Heyliger, William.

Courtney of the Center Garden. Standish, Burt L.

Covering the Look-In Corner. Standish, Burt L.

Crack of the Bat. Fenner, Phyllis R., ed.

Cracker Stanton. Sainsbury, Noel, Jr.

Crashaw Brothers, The. Pier, Arthur.

Crazy Baseball Stories. Whiting, Robert Rudd.

Crazy Horse Electric Game, The. Crutcher, Chris.

Crimson Banner, The. Moffat, William.

Crimson Sweater, The. Barbour, Ralph Henry.

Crooked Arm and Other Baseball Stories. Simon, Tony, ed.

Crossed Signals. Standish, Burt L.

Cub Battery. Barbour, Ralph Henry.

Curious Case of Sidd Finch, The. Plimpton, George.

Curious George Plays Baseball. Reys, Margret and H. A.

Danby's Error. Barbour, Ralph Henry.

Danger in Center Field. Mays, Willie, and Jeff Harris.

Danger in Dinosaur Valley. Nixon, Joan Lowery.

Danny Orlis and Jim Morgan's Scholarship. Palmer, Bernard.

Darewell Chums, or, The Heroes of the School, The. Chapman, Allen.

Dave Palmer's Diamond Mystery. Jorgensen, Nels. L.

Dave Porter at Oak Hall. Stratemeyer, Edward.

David's Campaign Buttons. Woolley, Catherine.

Dead in Centerfield. Engleman, Paul.

Dead Pull Hitter, The. Gordon, Alison.

Death for a Playmate. Ball, John.

Death on the Diamond. Fitzsimmons, Cortland.

Deep Short. Scholz, Jackson.

Delayed Steal. Waldman, Frank.

Devil to Play, The. Holton, Leonard.

Diamond Champs, The. Christopher, Matthew F.

Diamond Pinheads, The. Walpole, Joseph A.

Diamonds are Trumps. Slattery, Marty.

Dick Arnold of the Varsity. Silvers, Earl Reed.

Different Season, A. Klass, David.

Dinosaur Bob and His Adventures with the Family Lazardo. Joyce, William.

Dixie Association, The. Hays, Donald.

Dodger Doubleheader. Webster, Joe.

Dog That Pitched a No-Hitter, The. Christopher, Matthew F.

Don and Donna Go to Bat. Perkins, Al.

Donald Dare: The Champion Boy Pitcher. Stone, Raymond.

Donny and Company. Kinsey, Elizabeth.

Doodletown Dodger, A. McMahon, William R.

Dooleys Play Ball, The. Renick, Marion.

Dorset's Twister. Heyliger, William.

Double Play. Barbour, Ralph Henry.

Double Play. Everett, William.

Double Play. Franklin, Lance.

Double Play. Harkins, Philip.

Double Play. Lewinstein, Stephen R.

Double Play. Stone, Natalie.

Double Play and Other Baseball Stories. Sherman, Harold M.

Double-Play Ball. Carol, Bill J.

Double Play Rookie. Archibald, Joe.

Double Squeeze, The. Needham, Henry B.

Double Steal, The. McCormick, Wilfred.

Double the Glory. Marlowe, Dan J.

Duel on the Diamond. Hallowell, Tommy.

Dugout Brother. Grant, J. Jason.

Dugout Jinx. Bee, Clair.

Dugout Mystery. Bonner, Mary G.

Dugout Tycoon. Scholz, Jackson.

Dunk O'Malley Sports Stories. Sandberg, Harold W.

Dust in the Afternoon. Alexander, Holmes M.

Easy Does It. Wier, Ester.

Easy Out, The. Archibald, Joe.

Eight Corners of the World, The. Weaver, Gordon.

Encyclopedia Brown and the Case of the Secret Pitch. Sobol, Donald J.

Every Young Man's Dream: Confessions of a Southern League Shortstop. Frank, Morry.

Fabulous Fifty, The. Grosser, Morton.

Fairport Nine, The. Brooks, Noah.

Fast Ball Pitcher. Heavilin, Jay.

Fast Curve. Kent, Justin.

Fast Man on a Pivot. Decker, Duane.

Fast Nine, or, A Challenge from Fairfield. Douglas, Captain Alan.

Fastest Quitter in Town, The. Green, Phyllis.

Fat Mascot, The. Whiting, Robert Rudd.

Fence Busters. Bee, Clair.

Fever Pitch. Toth, Pamela.

Fielder from Nowhere. Scholz, Jackson.

Fielder's Choice. Holtzman, Jerome, ed.

Fielder's Choice. McCormick, Wilfred.

Fifth Base, The. Archibald, Joe.

Fifth Inning Fade-out. Jackson, C. Paul.

Fight 'em, Big Three. Sherman, Harold M.

Fighting for Fairview. Heyliger, William.

Fighting Shortstop, The. Cooper, John R.

Fighting Southpaw, The. Flood, Richard T.

Fighting Southpaw, The. Ford, Whitey, and Jack Lang.

Finkler's Field. Barbour, Ralph Henry.

Fireplug Is First Base, The. Petersen, P. J., and Betsy James.

First Base Faulkner. Mathewson, Christy.

First Base Hustler. Archibald, Joe.

First Base Jinx. Cooper, John R.

Fish Strikes Out. Hemmings, T. J.

Five O'Clock Lightning. DeAndrea, William L.

Five-Yard Fuller of the N.Y. Gnats. Wells, Bob.

Flashing Spikes. O'Rourke, Frank.

Flashing Steel. Sherman, Harold.

Flatland Fable, A. Coomer, Joe.

Flawless Play Restored: The Masque of Fungo. Sorrentino, Gilbert.

Fleet-footed Florence. Sachs, Marilyn.

Florry of Washington Heights. Katz, Steve.

Follow the Sharks. Tapply, William G.

Fourth Out, The. Bowen, Robert Sidney.

Fox in the Ball Park, The. Longman, Harold S.

Fox Steals Home, The. Christopher, Matthew F.

Frank Allen in Camp. Forbes, Graham.

Frank Allen — Pitcher. Forbes, Graham.

Frank and Ernest Play Ball. Day, Alexandra.

Frank Armstrong, Captain of the Nine. Colton, Matthew.

Frank Armstrong's Second Term. Colton, Matthew.

Fred Fenton the Pitcher. Chapman, Allen.

Freddy and the Baseball Team from Mars. Brooks, Walter R.

Freshman Backstop. Keating, Lawrence.

Freshman Dorn, Pitcher. Quirk, Leslie.

Frisco Blues. DeMarco, Gordon.

From Baseball to Boches. Witwer, H. C.

Fugitive Freshman, The. Paine, Ralph D.

Full Count. Archibald, Joe.

Fun and Games. Hudson, Anna.

Further Adventures of Slugger McBatt, The. Kinsella, W. P.

Gallant Crosby, The. Heyliger, William.

Gamemaker. Cohler, David Keith.

Getting Blue. Gethers, Peter.

Giant in the Midget League. Jackson, C. Paul.

Girl on First Base, The. Michaels, Ralph.

Girls Strike Back, The. Ellis, Lucy.

Glory for Gil. Drury, Maxine.

Go-Ahead Runner, The. McCormick, Wilfred.

God Cares When I Don't Like Myself. Murphy, Elspeth Campbell.

Going, Going, Gone. Russell, Patrick.

Gone to Glory. Irvine, Robert.

Good Catch, Snoopy. Schulz, Charles M.

Good Field, No Hit. Decker, Duane.

Good Old Archibald. Parkinson, Ethelyn M.

Good Sport, A. Abels, Harriette.

Goodbye, Bobby Thompson! Goodbye, John Wayne! Foster, Alan S.

Goof That Won the Pennant, The. Kalb, Jonah.

Goofer Pitch, The. Heuman, William.

Grace of Shortstops, The. Mayer, Robert.

Grammar School Boys in Summer Athletics, The. Hancock, Harrie Irving.

Grand Slam. Montgomery, Robert.

Grand Slam, A. Puechner, Ray.

Grand-Slam Homer. McCormick, Wilfred.

Grand-Slam Kid, The. Decker, Duane.

Grand Slam Riddles. Bernstein, Joanne E., and Paul Cohen.

Grandma's Baseball. Curtis, Gavin.

Grandstand Rookie. Zacharia, Irwin.

Grantham Gets On. Barbour, Ralph Henry.

Great All-Star Animal League Ball Game, The. Starrett, Vincent.

Great American Novel, The. Roth, Philip.

Great Baseball Championship, The. Wenk, Richard.

Great Baseball Stories. Lewis, Jerry D., ed.

Great Day for a Ballgame, A. Dawson, Fielding.

Great McGonigle Switches Pitches, The. Corbett, Scott.

Great Pete Penney, The. Tolle, Jean B.

Great Pretender, The. Haynes, Mary.

Great Year, The. Dudley, Albertus True.

Greatest Slump of All Time, The. Carkeet, David.

Greatest Victory and Other Baseball Stories, The. O'-Rourke, Frank.

Grip of the Game, The. Standish, Burt L.

Guarding the Keystone Sack. Standish, Burt L.

Guys Like Us. Lorenz, Tom.

Handy Death, A. Fish, Robert L., and Henry Rothblatt.

Hang In At the Plate. Bachman, Fred.

Hang Tough, Paul Mather. Slote, Alfred.

Hard Drive to Short. Christopher, Matthew F.

Hard Smash to Third. Carol, Bill J.

Hard Way, The. Weeks, Jack.

Hardy Boys: Danger on the Diamond, The. Dixon, Franklin W.

Heart for Baseball, The. Renick, Marion.

Heart of the Order. Ardizzone, Tony.

Hearts and the Diamond. Beaumont, Gerald.

Heavenly World Series, The. O'Rourke, Frank.

Hello There, Ball! McGraw, Tug, with Mike Witte.

Henry and Melinda. Sullivan, Silky.

Herbie Jones and the Monster Ball. Kline, Suzy.

Here Comes the Strikeout. Kessler, Leonard P.

Heroes of the School, The. Chapman, Allen.

High and Outside. Due, Linnea A.

High Fly to Center. Carol, Bill J.

High, Inside! Emery, Russell G.

High School Backstop. Jackson, C. P. and O. B.

High School Pitcher, The. Hancock, Harrie Irving.

High School Rivals, The. Webster, Frank V.

Highest Hit, The. Willard, Nancy.

Highpockets. Tunis, John R.

Hillbilly Hurler. Heuman, William.

Hillbilly Pitcher. Jackson, C. P. and O. B.

Hit and a Miss, A. Young, Isador S.

Hit and Run! Sherman, Harold M.

Hit and Run. Decker, Duane.

Hit and Run. Klein, Dave.

Hit-and-Run Connection, The. Smith, Carole.

Hit Away! Carol, Bill J.

Hit-Away Kid, The. Christopher, Matthew F.

Hit by Pitcher. Sherman, Harold M.

Hitter, The. Marlowe, Dan J.

Hitting Streak. Montgomery, Robert.

Home Game. Quarrington, Paul.

Home Run! Montgomery, Robert.

Home Run Feud. Bee, Clair.

Home-Run Harvest. McCormick, Wilfred.

Home Run Hennessey. Lawton, Charles.

Home Run Henri. Heuman, William.

Home-Run King, The. Ruth, Babe.

Home Run Trick, The. Corbett, Scott.

Homer Pickle, the Greatest. Laurence, Alfred D.

Hooper Haller. Hughes, Dean.

Hoopla. Stein, Harry.

Hooray for Snail. Stadler, John.

Horace Higby and the Scientific Pitch. Heuman, William.

Horse that Played Center Field, The. Higdon, Hal.

Horse that Played the Outfield, The. Heuman, William.

Hot Corner. Bowen, Robert Sidney.

Hot Corner, The. McCormick, Wilfred.

Hot Corner Blues. Bowen, Robert Sidney.

Hot-Corner Hank. Scholz, Jackson.

Hot Shot at Third. Moore, Joseph A.

Hot Streak and Other Sports Stories. Webb, Vaughan.

How Baseball Began in Brooklyn. Le Grand.

How Spider Saved the Baseball Game. Kraus, Robert.

Humming Bird, The. Johnson, Owen.

Hungry Hurler. Bee, Clair.

Hurry Home. Honig, Donald.

Hyland of the Hawks. Emery, Russell G.

I Am Somebody. Greene, Laura.

I Know a Baseball Player. Burchard, Marshall and Sue.

I Want to be a Baseball Player. Greene, Carla.

Idolaters, The. Hegner, William.

If I Never Get Back. Brock, Darryl.

If I Quit Baseball, Will You Still Love Me? Millar, Jeff, and Bill Hinds.

I'll Tell on You. Lexau, Joan M.

In Shelly's Leg. Vogan, Sara.

In the Year of the Boar and Jackie Robinson. Lord, Betty Bao.

Incomplete Pitcher, The. McCormick, Wilfred.

Indian Softball Summer. Bliss, Ronald G.

Infield Flash. Bowen, Robert Sidney.

Infield Rivals. Barbour, Ralph Henry.

Infield Spark. Bowen, Robert Sidney.

Infield Twins. Barbour, Ralph Henry.

Iowa Baseball Confederacy, The. Kinsella, W. P.

Iron Arm of Michael Glenn, The. Lee, Robert C.

Ironweed. Kennedy, William.

It Had to be a Woman. Newlin, Paul.

It Happens Every Spring. Davies, Valentine.

It Looked Like For Ever. Harris, Mark.

It's Arbor Day, Charlie Brown. Schulz, Charles M.

It's Great to be a Superstar. Schulz, Charles M.

It's Hard Work Being Bitter. Schulz, Charles M.

It's Your Turn at Bat. Aiello, Barbara, and Jeffrey Shulman.

Jack Hall, or, The School Days of an American Boy. Grant, Robert.

Jack Lorimer's Champions. Standish, Winn.

Jack Race's Baseball Nine. Hale, Harry.

Jack Ranger's School Victories. Young, Clarence.

Jack Winters' Baseball Team. Overton, Mark.

Jackson of Hillsdale High. Silvers, Earl Reed.

Jake. Slote, Alfred.

Jason and the Baseball Bear. Elish, Dan.

Jeffrey's Ghost and the Baseball Leftover Team. Adler, David A.

Jimmy Kirkland and the Plot for a Pennant. Fullerton, Hugh.

Jimmy Kirkland of the Cascade College Team. Fullerton, Hugh.

Jimmy Kirkland of the Shasta Boys' Team. Fullerton, Hugh.

Jinx Glove. Christopher, Matthew F.

Jinx: Stories of the Diamond, The. Sangree, Allen.

Jock and Jill. Lipsyte, Robert.

John Henry and Paul Bunyan Play Baseball. Blassingame, Wade.

Johnny Get Your Gun. Ball, John.

Johnny Lee. Honig, Donald.

Johnny No Hit. Christopher, Matthew F.

Johnson of Lansing. Williams, Hawley.

Journal of Leo Smith: Story of a Nineteenth Century Shortstop. Linthurst, Randolph.

Joy in Mudville. McAlpine, Gordon.

Junior Cup, The. French, Allen.

Junk Pitcher. Knott, Bill.

Katie and the Very Little League. Batting, Joan.

Kenton Pines, The. Burleigh, C. B.

Keystone Kelly. Scholz, Jackson.

Keystone Kids. Tunis, John R.

Kid Battery. Kramer, George.

Kid Brother. Keating, Lawrence.

Kid Comes Back, The. Tunis, John R.

Kid from Tomkinsville, The. Tunis, John R.

Kid Who Batted 1.000, The. Allison, Bob, and Frank E. Hill.

Kid Who Beat the Dodgers and Other Sports Stories, The. Miers, Earl Schenck.

Kid Who Only Hit Homers, The. Christopher, Matthew F.

King of the Diamond, The. Verral, Charles Spain.

Kirby's Last Circus. Spencer, Ross H.

Kissyfur of Paddlecab County. Lord, Suzanne.

Knave of Eagles. Wade, Robert.

Ladder: The Story of a Casual Man, The. Curtiss, Philip.

Lady Umpire's Hot Hands, The. Strong, Rod.

Lank of the Little League. Bishop, Curtis K.

Larry Comes Home. Bishop, Curtis K.

Larry Leads Off. Bishop, Curtis K.

Larry of Little League. Bishop, Curtis K.

Larry's Fadeaway. Dawson, Elmer.

Larry's Luck. Urmston, Mary.

Larry's Speedball. Dawson, Elmer.

Last Great Season, The. Honig, Donald.

Last Man Is Out, The. Karlins, Marvin.
Last Man Out. Sherman, Harold.
Last Out, The. Maule, Hamilton "Tex."
Last Put-Out, The. McCormick, Wilfred.
Last Series, The. Higdon, Hal.
Last Sunday. Peck, Robert Newton.
Last Was Lloyd. Smith, Doris Buchanan.
Last Western, The. Klise, Thomas S.
Lead-off Man. Friendlich, Dick.
Left-Handed Shortstop. Giff, Patricia.
Left Hander, The. Kramer, George.
Lefty Finds a Catcher. Carol, Bill J.
Lefty Locke Wins Out. Standish, Burt L.
Lefty Locke, Owner. Standish, Burt L.
Lefty Locke, Pitcher-Manager. Standish, Burt L.
Lefty O' the Big League. Standish, Burt L.
Lefty O' the Blue Stockings. Standish, Burt L.
Lefty O' the Bush. Standish, Burt L.
Lefty O' the Training Camp. Standish, Burt L.
Lefty Plays First. Carol, Bill J.
Lefty's Boy. Drdek, Richard.
Lefty's Long Throw. Carol, Bill J.
Legion Tourney. McCormick, Wilfred.
Lego Lamb, Southpaw. Standish, Burt L.
Let's Go to a Baseball Game. Hood, Robert.
Letters from Lefty. Herskowitz, Mickey.
Lightning Southpaw. Bowen, Robert Sidney.
L'il Wildcat. Scholefield, Edmund.
Line Drive. Hughes, Dean.
Little League Amigo. Bishop, Curtis K.
Little League Ball Hawk. Creighton, Don.
Little League Catcher. Smith, Robert.
Little League Champions. Olgin, Joseph.
Little League Champs. Heuman, William.
Little League Double Play. Bishop, Curtis K.
Little League Family. Wibberley, Leonard P. O.
Little League Giant. Creighton, Don.
Little League Heroes. Bishop, Curtis K.
Little League Hotshots. Heuman, William.
Little League Leader. Lee, S. C.
Little League Little Brother. Bishop, Curtis K.
Little League Old-Timers. Creighton, Don.
Little League Stepson. Bishop, Curtis K.
Little League Tournament. Jackson, C. Paul.
Little League Victory. Bishop, Curtis K.

Little League Visitor. Bishop, Curtis K.
Little League Way, The. Bishop, Curtis K.
Little Leaguer. Bishop, Curtis K.
Little Leaguer's First Uniform. Jackson, C. Paul.
Little Lefty. Christopher, Matthew F.
Little Major Leaguer. Jackson, C. Paul.
Littlest Leaguer, The. Hoff, Syd.
London: The Dog Who Made the Team. Malcolmson, David.
Lonely Mound, The. Gault, William C.
Long Ball to Left Field. Decker, Duane.
Long Gone. Hemphill, Paul.
Long Pitcher, The. McCormick, Wilfred.
Long Stretch at First Base. Christopher, Matthew F.
Look Who's Playing First Base. Christopher, Matthew F.
Lose With a Smile. Lardner, Ring.
Loser's End, The. Heyliger, William.
Lou Gehrig, Boy of the Sand Lots. Van Riper, Guernsey, Jr.
Lovell Leads Off. Barbour, Ralph Henry.
Lucky Baseball Bat, The. Christopher, Matthew F.
Lucky Bat Boy. Waldman, Frank.
Lucky Seven. Christopher, Matthew F.
Lucky Seventh, The. Barbour, Ralph Henry.
Lucky Seventh, The. Van Loan, Charles.
Luke. Winston, Peter.
Lumpy. McGraw, Frank E. "Tug," Jr.
Macklin Brothers, The. Heyliger, William.
Magic Bat, The. Philbrook, Clem.
Magic Mitt, The. Kay, Helen.
Major League Murder. Geller, Michael.
Make-Believe Ballplayer. Slote, Alfred.
Make the Play-offs! Shea, George.
Making of a Big Leaguer, The. Standish, Burt L.
Making the Nine. Dudley, Albertus True.
Making the Team. Hughes, Dean.
Making the Team. Mann, Ted.
Man in a Cage. Scholz, Jackson.
Man on First. Bowen, Robert Sidney.
Man on First, The. Standish, Burt L.
Man on Spikes. Asinof, Eliot.
Man on the Bench, The. McCormick, Wilfred.
Man Who Brought the Dodgers Back to Brooklyn, The. Ritz, David.

Man Who Wanted to Play Centerfield for the New York Yankees, The. Morgenstein, Gary.

Man's Code, A. Ferguson, William Blair Morton.

Matt Gargan's Boy. Slote, Alfred.

Matt's Mitt. Sachs, Marilyn.

Maverick on the Mound. Scholefield, Edmund.

Max. Isadora, Rachel.

"Me and You and a Dog Named Blue." Corcoran, Barbara.

Me, Mop, and the Moondance Kid. Myers, Walter D.

Meg Mackintosh and the Case of the Missing Babe Ruth Baseball. Landon, Lucinda.

Memoirs of a Pussycad. Gold, R. C.

Merritt Leads the Nine. Barbour, Ralph Henry.

Mice at Bat. Oechsli, Kelly.

Mickey Mouse and the Great Lot Plot. Walt Disney Productions.

Midget Blake, Pitcher. Quirk, Leslie.

Midget League Catcher. Jackson, Caary.

Mighty Men of Baseball. Verral, Charles Spain.

Million-Dollar Rookie. Bowen, Robert Sidney.

Minor League Shortstop. Jackson, C. Paul.

Miracle at the Plate. Christopher, Matthew F.

Missing Mitt, The. Chandler, Edna W.

Mister Shortstop. Decker, Duane.

Mitt Maverick. Archibald, Joe.

Money Pitcher. Thurman, A. R.

Monkey Shines. Miers, Earl Schenck.

Monsters in the Outfield. Mooser, Stephen.

Mortal Stakes. Parker, Robert B.

Most Valuable Player. Mullins, Richard.

Mound Menace. Mackellar, William.

Muckaluck. Andersen, Richard.

MVP. Montgomery, Robert.

My Father, the Coach. Slote, Alfred.

My Life in the 7th Grade. Geller, Mark.

Mystery at Raider Stadium. Jenkins, Jerry B.

Mystery at the Ball Game. McVey, R. Parker.

Mystery at the Ball Park, The. Cooper, John R.

Mystery Coach. Christopher, Matthew F.

Mystery Cottage in Left Field, The. Caroselli, Remus F.

Mystery House. Burrough, Ruth J.

Mystery of the Stolen Base, The. Broekel, Ray.

Natural, The. Malamud, Bernard.

Never Come Back. O'Rourke, Frank.

New AToms Bombshell, The. Browne, Robert.

New Boys at Oakdale, The. Scott, Morgan.

New Kid, The. Economos, Chris.

New Klondike, The. Griffith, Peggy.

Nice Guy, Go Home. Weaver, Robert.

Nid and Nod. Barbour, Ralph Henry.

Nine Good Men. O'Rourke, Frank.

Nine Make a Team. Neigoff, Mike.

Ninth Inning Rally. Barbour, Ralph Henry.

Nipper. Turner, Morrie.

No Arm in Left Field. Christopher, Matthew F.

No Fun on Sunday. Manfred, Frederick.

No Hitter. Bowen, Robert Sidney.

No-Hitter. Bee, Clair.

No Place for Baseball. Allen, Alex B.

Noonan: A Novel About Baseball, ESP and Time Warps. Fisher, Leonard Everett.

Norman Plays Second Base. Gault, Clare and Frank.

Northend Wildcats. Davis, Clyde Brion.

Not Bad for a Girl. Taves, Isabella.

Odditorium. Broun, Hob.

Old Iron Glove. Archibald, Joe.

Old Turtle's Baseball Stories. Kessler, Leonard P.

Ollie's Team and the Baseball Computer. Philbrook, Clem.

Ollie's Team and the Million Dollar Mistake. Philbrook, Clem.

Ollie's Team and the 200 Pound Problem. Philbrook, Clem.

Ollie's Team Plays Biddy Baseball. Philbrook, Clem.

On Home Ground. Lelchuk, Alan.

On the Diamond. Greenberg, Martin H., ed.

Once a Slugger. McCormick, Wilfred.

One O'Clock Hitter. McCormick, Wilfred.

Only Game in Town, The. Einstein, Charles.

Opening Day. Gelman, Mitch.

Orange Air, The. Doliner, Roy.

Original Colored House of David, The. Quigley, Martin.

Our Base Ball Club and How It Won the Championship. Brooks, Noah.

Our Jim. Ellis, Edward S.

Out at Home. Mackenzie, Christine B.

Out at Home. Pomeranz, Gary.

Out to Win. Bonner, Mary G.

Outfield Orphan. Archibald, Joe.

Over the Fence is Out. Rhoades, Jonathan.

Partners. Beardslee, Ken.

Paul the Pitcher. Sharp, Paul.

Pay-Off Pitch. Bee, Clair.

Payoff Pitch. Archibald, Joe.

Pee Wee Cook of the Midget League. Jackson, C. Paul.

Pennant, The. Tomlinson, Everett.

Pennant Fever. Bowen, Robert Sidney.

Pennant for the Kremlin, A. Molloy, Paul.

Pennant Stretch Drive. Jackson, C. Paul.

Peppy Learns to Play Baseball. Heller, Pete.

Percy the Parrot Strikes Out. Carley, Wayne.

Perfect Game. Bowen, Robert Sidney.

Perfect Game, The. Scholz, Jackson.

Perfect Pitch, The. Lord, Beman.

Pete's Home Run. Renick, Marion.

Phantom Homer, The. Cooper, John R.

Phantom Shortstop, The. McCormick, Wilfred.

Phyllis. Key, Ted.

Pick-up Nine, The. Dawson, Elmer.

Pinch Hitter. Friendlich, Dick.

Pitcher in Left Field. Waldman, Jeri and Neil.

Pitcher of the Year. Bowen, Robert Sidney.

Pitcher Pollock. Mathewson, Christy.

Pitcher to Center Field. Bunting, A. E.

Pitcher's Choice. Lunemann, Evelyn.

Pitchers' Duel. Bee, Clair.

Pitching for Pawling. Temple, Willard H.

Pizza Pie Slugger, The. Marzollo, Jean.

Play Ball! Freeman, Mark.

Play Ball! Verral, Charles Spain.

Play Ball. Wise, Francis H.

Play Ball, Amelia Bedelia. Parish, Peggy.

Play Ball, Kate! Gordon, Sharon.

Play Ball, McGill. Walden, Amelia Elizabeth.

Play Ball, Snoopy. Schulz, Charles M.

Play-Off Pressure. Freeman, Mark.

Play the Game. Corbert, Mack.

Player-Manager. Bowen, Robert Sidney.

Playing the Game. Quirk, Leslie.

Popp Fly. Cosgrove, Stephen.

Pressure Play. Hughes, Dean.

Pride of the Bimbos. Sayles, John.

Pro Fever. St. Sauver, Dennis.

Professional, The. Honig, Donald.

Prospect. Littlefield, Bill.

Proud Champions, The. McCormick, Wilfred.

Purple Pennant, The. Barbour, Ralph Henry.

Quacky and the Crazy Curve Ball. Oleksy, Walter.

Rabbit Ears. Montgomery, Robert.

Rabbit Ears. Slote, Alfred.

Rachel, the Rabbi's Wife. Tennenbaum, Silvia.

Rambler Club's Ball Nine, The. Sheppard, W. Crispin.

Raymond Benson at Krampton. Burleigh, C. B.

Real Dope, The. Lardner, Ring.

Rebel in Right Field. Decker, Duane.

Rebel Rookie. Bowen, Robert Sidney.

Rebel with a Glove. McCormick, Wilfred.

Redheaded Outfield and Other Baseball Stories, The. Grey, Zane.

Relief Pitcher. Emery, Russell G.

Relief Pitcher. Friendlich, Dick.

Relief Pitcher, The. Barbour, Ralph Henry.

Reluctant Pitcher, The. Christopher, Matthew F.

Rex Kingdon Behind the Bat. Braddock, Gordon.

Rex Kingdon of Ridgewood High. Braddock, Gordon.

Rex Kingdon on Storm Island. Braddock, Gordon.

Rhubarb. Smith, H. Allen.

Rick Goes to Little League. Walker, David G.

Right Field Rookie. Archibald, Joe.

Right Field Runt. Archibald, Joe.

Rigor of the Game, The. Pier, Arthur.

Ring Lardner's You Know Me Al. Lardner, Ring.

Rio Loja Ringmaster, The. Herrin, Lamar.

Rival Pitchers, The. Chadwick, Lester.

Rival Pitchers of Oakdale. Scott, Morgan.

Rivals on the Mound. Barbour, Ralph Henry.

Road Game: A Summer's Tale. Burch, Mark H.

Robbery in Right Field. Molarsky, Osmond.

Rockspur Nine, The. Patten, Gilbert.

Ronald Morgan Goes to Bat. Giff, Patricia.

Rookie Arrives, The. Dygard, Thomas.

Rookie Backstop. Heuman, William.

Rookie Catcher with the Atlanta Braves. Jackson, C. Paul.

Rookie Coach. Fulton, Reed.

Rookie Fights Back, The. Leonard, Burgess.

Rookie First Baseman. Jackson, C. Paul.
Rookie from Junction Flats, The. Webster, Joe.
Rookie of the Year. Tunis, John R.
Rookie on First. McCormick, Wilfred.
Rookie Southpaw. Leonard, Burgess.
Rookie Star. Hughes, Dean.
Rootie Kazootie, Baseball Star. Carlin, Steve.
Roots in the Outfield. Zirpoli, Jane.
Rosie's Double Dare. Harris, Robie H.
Rover Boys at Big Bear Lake, The. Winfield, Arthur M.
Rover Boys at Big Horn Ranch, The. Winfield, Arthur M.
Rover Boys at School, The. Winfield, Arthur M.
Rover Boys Down East, The. Winfield, Arthur M.
Rover Boys in Business, The. Winfield, Arthur M.
Rover Boys in the Land of Luck, The. Winfield, Arthur M.
Rover Boys on a Tour, The. Winfield, Arthur M.
Rover, Jr.'s Baseball Career. Tester, Sylvia.
Rundown, The. Magnuson, James.
Runner Mack. Beckham, Barry.
Rushton Boys at Rally Hall, The. Davenport, Spencer.
Ruth Marini, Dodger Ace. Cebulash, Mel.
Ruth Marini, World Series Star. Cebulash, Mel.
Ruth Marini of the Dodgers. Cebulash, Mel.
Safe! Sherman, Harold M.
Safe on Second. Parks, Edd Winfield.
Sailor Jack and the Ball Game. Wasserman, Selma.
Sam's Legacy. Neugeboren, Jay.
Sand Lot, The. Christian, Mary Blount.
Sandlot Peanuts. Schulz, Charles M.
Sandy Plays Third. Carol, Bill J.
Saturday Night Dead. Rosen, Richard D.
School Team in Camp, The. Earl, John P.
School Team on the Diamond, The. Earl, John P.
Schoolboy Johnson. Tunis, John R.
Score is Tied, The. Barbour, Ralph Henry.
Score by Innings. Van Loan, Charles.
Scram, Kid! McGovern, Ann.
Screwball King Murder, The. Platt, Kin.
Screwballs. Cronley, Jay.
Scroogie. McGraw, Tug, with Mike Witte.
Season of the Owl. Wolff, Miles, Jr.
Seasons Past. Rice, Damon.
Second Base Sloan. Mathewson, Christy.
Second Brother. Guy, David.

Second Time Around Rookie. Jackson, C. Paul.
Second-Season Jinx. Leonard, Burgess.
Secret Baseball Challenge, The. Jenkins, Jerry B.
Secret Little Leaguer, The. Creighton, Don.
Senior Challenge. Keating, Lawrence.
Sensation, The. Keifetz, Norman.
Sensuous Southpaw, The. Rothweiler, Paul R.
Series Showdown. Freeman, Mark.
Seven Games in October. Brady, Charles.
Seventh Babe, The. Charyn, Jerome.
Seventh Game, The. Kahn, Roger.
7th Game, The. Kowett, Don.
She's On First. Gregorich, Barbara.
Shiner Watson. Jenkins, MacGregor.
Shoe Goes to Wrigley Field. MacNelly, Jeff.
Shoeless Joe. Kinsella, W. P.
Short Season. Eller, Scott.
Short Season and Other Stories. Klinkowitz, Jerry.
Short Stop for Romance. Harper, Elaine.
Short-stop, The. Grey, Zane.
Shortstop, The. Maule, Hamilton "Tex."
Shortstop from Tokyo. Christopher, Matthew F.
Shortstop on Wheels. Archibald, Joe.
Shortstop Shadow. Brier, Howard M.
Shorty at Shortstop. Jackson, C. Paul.
Shotgun Shaw: a Baseball Story. Keith, Harold.
Show, The. Montgomery, Robert.
Showboat Southpaw. Decker, Duane.
Simple Suburban Murder, A. Zubro, Mark Richard.
Single to Center. Carol, Bill J.
Sister Beatrice Goes to Bat. Anderson, Catherine Corley.
Skid. Hayes, Florence.
Skinnybones. Park, Barbara.
Sleuth at Shortstop. Coombs, Charles.
Slide, Charlie Brown! Slide! Schulz, Charles M.
Slide, Danny, Slide. Christopher, Matthew F.
Slugger in Right. Maris, Roger, and Jack Ogle.
Slugger Sal's Slump. Hoff, Syd.
Slugging Backstop. Lee, Wayne C.
Smitty at the Ball Game. Berndt, Walter.
Soldiers at Bat. Scholz, Jackson.
Somebody Called Booie. Gardner, Lillian.
Somebody Stole Second. Foley, Louise M.
Something Queer at the Ball Park. Levy, Elizabeth.
Sons of Old Eli. Patten, Gilbert.

Soupbone. Offit, Sidney.

Southpaw. King, Frank.

Southpaw, The. Haines, Donal Hamilton.

Southpaw, The. Harris, Mark.

Southpaw Fly Hawk. Rand, Addison.

Southpaw from San Francisco. Harkins, Philip.

Southpaw from Sonora Mystery, The. Van Steenwyk, Elizabeth.

Southpaw in the Mighty Mite League. Jackson, O. B.

Southpaw Speed. Archibald, Joe.

Southpaw's Secret, The. Cooper, John R.

Southworth Scores. Barbour, Ralph Henry.

Spark Plug at Short. Scholz, Jackson.

Special Season, A. Burksaze, Phil F.

Speed Boy, The. Hart, Frank J.

Spirit of the Leader, The. Heyliger, William.

Spitballs and Holy Water. Donohue, James F.

Spoiler, The. Stansberry, Domenic.

Spray Hitter. Bonner, Mary G.

Spring Training. Freeman, Mark.

Spy on Third Base, The. Christopher, Matthew F.

Squeeze Play. Freeman, Mark.

Squeeze Play. Barbour, Ralph Henry.

Squeeze Play. Benjamin, Paul.

Squeeze Play. Carol, Bill J.

Squeeze Play. Feldspar, Walter.

Squeeze Play. Glenn, Mel.

Squeeze Play. Leavy, Jane.

Squeeze Play. Lochlons, Colin.

Stand-Off. Gray, Genevieve.

Starmaker, The. McCormick, Wilfred.

Starting Pitcher. Decker, Duane.

Stay Loose. Nye, Bud.

Steady. Renick, James and Marion.

Stealing Home. O'Connor, Philip F.

Stirring Baseball Stories. Sainsbury, Noel, Jr.

Stitch in Time Saves the Nine, A. Peck, Wallace.

Stranger City Caper, The. Spencer, Ross H.

Stranger on the Ball Club. Slote, Alfred.

Stretch Bolton Comes Back. Leonard, Burgess.

Stretch Bolton: Mr. Shortstop. Leonard, Burgess.

Stretch Bolton's Rookies. Leonard, Burgess.

Strictly Amateur. McCormack, Tom.

Strictly from Brooklyn. Heuman, William.

Strike Four! Ziefert, Harriet.

Strike Him Out! Sherman, Harold M.

Strike-Out King, The. De Vries, Julian.

Strike Three! Bee, Clair.

Strike Three! Heyliger, William.

Strike Three, Charlie Brown. Schulz, Charles M.

Strike Three You're Dead. Rosen, Richard D.

Strike Two. Shea, George.

Strike Zone, The. Curtis, Richard.

Strikezone. Nighbert, David F.

Striking Out! Dixon, Michael B., and Valerie Smith.

Stubborn Sam. Gault, William C.

Submarine Pitch, The. Christopher, Matthew F.

Suder. Everett, Percival L.

Summer Season. Munn, Vella.

Sun Field, The. Broun, Heywood.

Sunlit Field, The. Kennedy, Lucy.

Superbaby. Mendelsohn, Felix, Jr.

Supercharged Infield. Christopher, Matthew F.

Surfaces of a Diamond. Rubin, Louis D., Jr.

Sweet Swing, The. Friendlich, Dick.

Sweet Valley Twins: Standing Out. Suzanne, Jamie.

Switch Hitter. Decker, Duane.

Switcharound. Lowry, Lois.

Switch-Hitting Big-Leaguer. Author unknown.

Take Me Out to the Ballgame. Morgenstein, Gary.

Take-Charge Guy, The. Weeks, Jack.

Taking the Field. Bowering, George, ed.

Tall at the Plate. McCormick, Wilfred.

Tall Baseball Stories. Amarant, Jiggs.

Team, The. O'Rourke, Frank.

Team First. Silvers, Earl Reed.

Team that Stopped Moving, The. Christopher, Matthew F.

Teen-age Baseball Stories. Owen, Frank, ed.

Teen-Age Stories of the Diamond. Thomas, David, ed.

$10,000 Arm and Other Tales of the Big League, The. Van Loan, Charles.

Terry and Bunky Play Baseball. Fishel, Dick, and Clair Hare.

Thank You, Jackie Robinson. Cohen, Barbara.

That Dodger Horse. Lovelace, Delos W.

That Year at Lincoln High. Gollomb, Joseph.

There Goes the Shutout. Schulz, Charles M.

There's No Base Like Home. Witwer, H. C.

Thine Not Mine. Everett, William.

Things Invisible to See. Willard, Nancy.

Third-Base Rookie. Decker, Duane.

Third Base Thatcher. Scott, Everett "Deacon."

Third Strike, The. Quirk, Leslie.

Those Smith Boys on the Diamond. Garis, Howard Roger.

Three-and-Two Pitcher. Lochlons, Colin.

Three-Base Benson. Barbour, Ralph Henry.

Three-Finger Joe. Heyliger, William.

Three Loves Has Sandy. Walden, Amelia Elizabeth.

Three Men on Third. Olson, Gene.

Three-Two Pitch, The. McCormick, Wilfred.

Thrill of the Grass, The. Kinsella, W. P.

Throwing Catcher, The. McCormick, Wilfred.

Ticket for a Seamstitch. Harris, Mark.

Tied in the Ninth. Allen, Merritt Parmalee.

Tiger Rookie. Scholefield, Edmund.

Time Out! Adams, Phyllis, Eleanore Hartson, and Mark Taylor.

Tiny Dinos Playing Together. Gilchrist, Guy.

To Brooklyn With Love. Green, Gerald.

Tod Hale at Camp. Barbour, Ralph Henry.

Tod Hale on the Nine. Barbour, Ralph Henry.

Today's Game. Quigley, Martin.

Tom Huntner, Sophomore Pitcher. Anderson, Ken.

Tom Mosely—Midget Leaguer. Jackson, C. Paul.

Tommy Tiptop and His Baseball Nine. Stone, Raymond.

Tony and Me. Slote, Alfred.

Too Hot to Handle. Christopher, Matthew F.

Too Steep for Baseball. Stapp, Arthur.

Toot-Toot-Tootsie, Good-bye. Powers, Ron.

Trading Game, The. Slote, Alfred.

Treasure at First Base. Clymer, Eleanor.

Treat 'Em Rough. Lardner, Ring.

Triple Play. Bowen, Robert Sidney.

Triple Play. Lochlons, Colin.

Triple Play! Montgomery, Robert.

Trouble at Second. Gault, William C.

Trouble at Second Base. Cox, William R.

Trouble on the Infield. Napjus, James.

Trouble with Francis, The. Lord, Beman.

Tuesday's Child. Baron, Nancy.

Turning Point, The. Fitzgerald, Ed.

Twin Killing, The. Bagby, George.

Two on First. Neigoff, Mike.

Two Strikes on Johnny. Christopher, Matthew F.

Two Strikes on Lefty. Moore, Joseph A.

Two Strikes, Four Eyes. Delaney, Ned.

Two Time Rookie. Archibald, Joe.

Two-Way Pitcher. Bonner, Mary G.

Underground Skipper, The. Gault, William C.

Uniform for Harry, A. Jackson, Caary.

Universal Baseball Association, Inc., J. Henry Waugh, Prop., The. Coover, Robert.

Varmint, The. Johnson, Owen.

Varsity Double Play. Hirshberg, Al.

Varsity Letter. Reck, Franklin.

Veterans Park. Snyder, Don J.

Viola, Furgy, Bobbi, and Me. Ethridge, Kenneth.

Voices of a Summer Day. Shaw, Irwin.

Ward Hill at College. Tomlinson, Everett.

Ward Hill at Weston. Tomlinson, Everett.

Ward Hill, the Senior. Tomlinson, Everett.

Way to Go, Teddy. Honig, Donald.

Weatherby's Inning. Barbour, Ralph Henry.

What a Catch. Hughes, Dean.

What About Me? Klusmeyer, Joann.

What's So Great About Fourth Grade? Kahaner, Ellen.

Whichaway? Swed, Trebor.

Who Is Felix the Great? Kidd, Ronald.

Who Will Be My Friends? Hoff, Syd.

Why Isn't Becky Twitchell Dead? Zubro, Mark Richard.

Wild on the Bases. McCormick, Wilfred.

Wild Pitch. Christopher, Matthew F.

Wild Pitch. Guthrie, A. B., Jr.

Wild Pitch, The. Cox, William R.

Wild Roses. Paulos, Sheila.

Will You Cross Me? Kaye, Marilyn.

Willy's Raiders. Gantos, Jack, and Nicole Rubel.

Win a Few, Lose a Few, Charlie Brown. Schulz, Charles M.

Win–or Else! Michael, D. J.

Winning His Game. Barbour, Ralph Henry.

Winning Hit, The. Williams, Hawley.

Winning May Not be Everything, But Losing Isn't Anything. Schulz, Charles M.

Winning Pitch, The. Bowen, Robert Sidney.

Winning Pitcher. Porter, Mark.

Winning Run, or, The Baseball Boys of Lakeport, The. Bonehill, Captain Ralph.

Winning Season for the Braves, A. Aaseng, Nate.

Winning Streak. Hughes, Dean.

Winning the Junior Cup. Brainerd, Norman.

Winter Always Comes. Honig, Donald.

Witch, the Cat and the Baseball Bat, The. Hoff, Syd.

With a Name like Lulu, Who Needs More Trouble? Springstubb, Tricia.

With Mask and Mitt. Dudley, Albertus True.

Wobbly Tooth, The. Cooney, Nancy Evans.

Won in the Ninth. Mathewson, Christy.

Wonder Boy. Heuman, William.

Wonderful World Series, The. Verral, Charles Spain.

World Series. Tunis, John R.

World Series Rookie. Jackson, C. Paul.

Worst Team Ever, The. Kessler, Leonard P.

Wrongway Applebaum. Lewis, Marjorie.

Wrong-Way Rookie. Wayne, Richard.

Yachtville Boys, The. Davis, Caroline E. Kelly.

Yank Brown, Pitcher. Stone, David.

Yankee Rookie. Fitzgerald, Ed.

Year I Owned the Yankees, The. Lyle, Sparky, with David Fisher.

Year Mom Won the Pennant, The. Christopher, Matthew F.

Year the Yankees Lost the Pennant, The. Wallop, Douglas.

You Know Me Al. Lardner, Ring.

You're Worth More Than You Think. Johnson, Lois W.

Young Infield Rookie. Coombs, Charles.

Young Pitcher, The. Grey, Zane.

Young Razzle. Tunis, John R.

Young Readers Baseball Mystery. Coombs, Charles.

Young Readers Baseball Stories. Coombs, Charles.

Young Readers Stories of the Diamond. Coombs, Charles.

Zanboomer. Knudson, R. R.

BY TYPE

Adult mysteries

BAGBY, GEORGE. *The Twin Killing.*
BALL, JOHN. *Johnny Get Your Gun.*
BALL, JOHN. *Death for a Playmate.*
BENJAMIN, PAUL. *Squeeze Play.*
BRADY, CHARLES. *Seven Games in October.*
COHLER, DAVID KEITH. *Gamemaker.*
CURTIS, RICHARD. *The Pro #3: Strike Zone.*
DeANDREA, WILLIAM L. *Five O'Clock Lightning.*
DeMARCO, GORDON. *Frisco Blues.*
ENGLEMAN, PAUL. *Dead in Centerfield.*
FISH, ROBERT L. and HENRY ROTHBLATT. *A Handy Death.*
FITZSIMMONS, CORTLAND. *Death on the Diamond.*
GELLER, MICHAEL. *Major League Murder.*
GORDON, ALISON. *The Dead Pull Hitter.*
GRANTHAM, KENNETH L. *Baseball's Darkest Days.*
GUTHRIE, A. B., Jr. *Wild Pitch.*
HOLTON, LEONARD. *The Devil to Play.*
IRVINE, ROBERT. *Gone to Glory.*
JORDAN, PAT. *The Cheat.*
KLEIN, DAVE. *Hit and Run.*
KOWETT, DON. *The 7th Game.*
MAGNUSON, JAMES. *The Rundown.*
McCORMACK, TOM. *Strictly Amateur.*
NIGHBERT, DAVID F. *Strikezone.*
PARKER, ROBERT B. *Mortal Stakes.*
PLATT, KIN. *The Screwball King Murder.*
ROSEN, RICHARD D. *Strike Three You're Dead.*
ROSEN, RICHARD D. *Saturday Night Dead.*
SEAVER, TOM, with HERB RESNICOW. *Beanball: Murder at the World Series.*
SPENCER, ROSS H. *The Stranger City Caper.*
SPENCER, ROSS H. *Kirby's Last Circus.*
STANSBERRY, DOMENIC. *The Spoiler.*
TAPPLY, WILLIAM G. *Follow the Sharks.*
WADE, ROBERT. *Knave of Eagles.*
ZUBRO, MARK RICHARD. *A Simple Suburban Murder.*
ZUBRO, MARK RICHARD. *Why Isn't Becky Twitchell Dead?*

Juvenile mysteries

ADLER, DAVID A. *Cam Jansen and the Mystery of the Babe Ruth Baseball.*
ARCHIBALD, JOE. *Payoff Pitch.*
BONNER, MARY G. *Dugout Mystery.*
BRANDT, KEITH. *The Case of the Missing Dinosaurs.*
BRIER, HOWARD M. *Shortstop Shadow.*
BROEKEL, RAY. *The Mystery of the Stolen Base.*
BROOKS, WALTER R. *Freddy and the Baseball Team from Mars.*
BURROUGH, RUTH J. *Mystery House.*
CAROSELLI, REMUS F. *The Mystery Cottage in Left Field.*
CHAPMAN, ALLEN. *Fred Fenton the Pitcher.*
COHEN, DAN. *The Case of the Battling Ball Clubs.*
COOMBS, CHARLES. *Young Readers Baseball Mystery.*
COOMBS, CHARLES. *Sleuth at Shortstop.*
COOPER, JOHN R. *The Mystery at the Ball Park.*
COOPER, JOHN R. *The Southpaw's Secret.*
COOPER, JOHN R. *The Phantom Homer.*
COOPER, JOHN R. *First Base Jinx.*
COOPER, JOHN R. *The College League Mystery.*
COOPER, JOHN R. *The Fighting Shortstop.*
DIXON, FRANKLIN W. *The Hardy Boys: Danger on the Diamond.*
JENKINS, JERRY B. *Mystery at Raider Stadium.*
JORGENSEN, NELS L. *Dave Palmer's Diamond Mystery.*
LANDON, LUCINDA. *Meg Mackintosh and the Case of the Missing Babe Ruth Baseball.*
LEVY, ELIZABETH. *Something Queer at the Ball Park.*
LUNEMANN, EVELYN. *Pitcher's Choice.*
MAYS, WILLIE, and JEFF HARRIS. *Danger in Center Field.*
McVEY, R. PARKER. *Mystery at the Ballgame.*
MULLER, CHARLES G. *The Baseball Detective.*
PALLAS, NORVIN. *The Baseball Mystery.*
SMITH, CAROLE. *The Hit-and-Run Connection.*
SOBOL, DONALD J. *Encyclopedia Brown and the Case of the Secret Pitch.*
STINE, MEGAN, and H. WILLIAM. *Baseball Card Fever.*

VAN STEENWYK, ELIZABETH. *The Southpaw from Sonora Mystery.*

Adult science fiction

BROWN, ROBERT. *The New AToms Bombshell.*
KARLINS, MARVIN. *The Last Man Is Out.*
McSHERRY, FRANK D., Jr., CHARLES WAUGH, and M. H. GREENBERG, eds. *Baseball 3000.*

Juvenile science fiction

FISHER, LEONARD EVERETT. *Noonan: A Novel About Baseball, ESP and Time Warps.*
RESCINITI, ANGELO. *The Baseball from Outer Space.*

Adult romances

HUDSON, ANNA. *Fun and Games.*
KENNEDY, LUCY. *The Sunlit Field.*
MUNN, VELLA. *Summer Season.*

PAULOS, SHEILA. *Wild Roses.*
STONE, NATALIE. *Double Play.*
TOTH, PAMELA. *Fever Pitch.*

Juvenile romances

ABELS, HARRIETTE. *A Good Sport.*
HARPER, ELAINE. *Short Stop for Romance.*
MICHAELS, RALPH. *The Girl on First Base.*
SUZANNE, JAMIE. *The Sweet Valley Twins: Standing Out.*
WALDEN, AMELIA ELIZABETH. *Three Loves Has Sandy.*
WALDEN, AMELIA ELIZABETH. *Play Ball, McGill.*

Adult horror novels

CONTE, SAL. *Child's Play.*
KING, FRANK. *Southpaw.*

BOOKS ABOUT INTEGRATION AND RACE

Although a black character, and a positive one at that, appears in one of the earliest baseball novels, Brooks's *Fairport Nine* of 1880, books about integration and racial matters didn't begin to appear until after Jackie Robinson. In the early years of the century, blacks appeared occasionally as stereotyped characters. See Mathewson's *Second Base Sloan*, for example. But it was a time when formula boys fiction writing usually included a German boy with a thick accent, an Irish kid who was quick with his fists but not his mind, and a country bumpkin of quaint speech. In the 1960s, more uses of racial and ethnic themes began to appear. Here are some.

The first black player, whether in the majors, on one major league team, or in a minor league

ARCHIBALD, JOE. *Outfield Orphan.*
EDMUNDS, MURREL. *Behold, Thy Brother.*
GRANT, J. JASON. *Dugout Brother.*
HONIG, DONALD. *Johnny Lee.*

Still having troubles in the pros years after Jackie

BECKHAM, BARRY. *Runner Mack.*
GAULT, WILLIAM. *Trouble at Second.*
MAYS, WILLIE. *Danger in Center Field.*

Integration in Little League or youth baseball

BISHOP, CURTIS. *Little League Heroes.*
BISHOP, CURTIS. *Little League Double Play.*
CAIRNS, BOB. *The Comeback Kids.*
CHRISTOPHER, MATT. *No Arm in Left Field.*
COOMBS, CHARLES. *Young Infield Rookie.*
HAYES, FLORENCE. *Skid.*
WIER, ESTER. *Easy Does It.*

Books in which race or ethnicity plays a part

BROOKS, NOAH. *The Fairport Nine.*
COHEN, BARBARA. *Thank You, Jackie Robinson.*
COX, WILLIAM. *Chicano Cruz.*
MATHEWSON, CHRISTY. *Second Base Sloan.*
NEUGEBOREN, JAY. *Sam's Legacy.*
SHEA, GEORGE. *Big Bad Ernie.*
SUMMERS, RICHARD. *Ball-Shy Pitcher.*
WEAVER, ROBERT. *Nice Guy, Go Home.*

Barnstorming black teams

BRASHLER, WILLIAM. *The Bingo Long Traveling All-Stars and Motor Kings.*
CHARYN, JEROME. *The Seventh Babe.*
CRAIG, JOHN. *Chappie and Me.*
DONOHUE, JAMES. *Spitballs and Holy Water.*
QUIGLEY, MARTIN. *The Original Colored House of David.*

BOOKS ABOUT WOMEN, GIRLS, AND THE GAME

This was a genre that didn't sprout until the 1970s.

The first woman in major league ball

BOWEN, MICHAEL. *Can't Miss.*
CEBULASH, MEL. *Ruth Marini* series.
GREGORICH, BARBARA. *She's on First.*
PUECHNER, RAY. *A Grand Slam.*
ROTHWEILER, PAUL. *The Sensuous Southpaw.*
SACHS, MARILYN. *Fleet-Footed Florence.*

Women in the minors

CLIFTON, MERRITT. *Baseball Classic.*
MICHAELS, RALPH. *The Girl on First Base.*

Adult women's softball

BROUN, HOB. *Odditorium.*
COONEY, ELLEN. *All the Way Home.*
PAULOS, SHEILA. *Wild Roses.*
TOTH, PAMELA. *Fever Pitch.*

Juvenile girls softball

CHRISTOPHER, MATT. *Supercharged Infield.*
DESSENT, MICHAEL. *Baseball Becky.*
DUE, LINNEA. *High and Outside.*

HARPER, ELAINE. *Short Stop for Romance.*
WALDEN, AMELIA. *Play Ball, McGill.*
WALDEN, AMELIA. *Three Loves Has Sandy.*

Girls and boys together (usually with some misgiving on the boys' part)

As the 1980s moved along, mixing boys and girls without comment in youth baseball became fairly common. The following list is of those books that deal with problems about girls coming into the game.
CAROL, BILL. *Single to Center.*
CHRISTOPHER, MATT. *Diamond Champs.*
CHRISTOPHER, MATT. *Supercharged Infield.*
CHRISTOPHER, MATT. *Wild Pitch.*
ELLIS, LUCY. *The Girls Strike Back.*
ELLIS, LUCY. *All That Jazz.*
GRAY, GENEVIEVE. *Stand-Off.*
HAYNES, MARY. *The Great Pretender.*
KELLY, JEFFREY. *The Basement Baseball Club.*
PERKINS, AL. *Don and Donna Go to Bat.*
RENICK, MARION. *The Dooleys Play Ball.*
SLOTE, ALFRED. *Matt Gargan's Boy.*
SULLIVAN, SILKY. *Henry and Melinda.*
TAVES, ISABELLA. *Not Bad for a Girl.*
WOODLEY, RICHARD. *The Bad News Bears* series.

BOOKS BY MAJOR LEAGUE AUTHORS OR THOSE WITH OTHER SPORTS CONNECTIONS

Eleven major league players, and a number of minor leaguers or people with other major sports connections, have had baseball novels published under their names.

The first was Frank Chance's *The Bride and the Pennant* in 1910, a year the Cubs he managed were winning their fourth pennant in five years. It contained a brief biography of Husk and an introduction by Charles Comiskey, owner of the crosstown White Sox. Presumably, this book was written by a ghostwriter. I suspect Hugh Fullerton, but I have no proof.

In a similar vein, Christy Mathewson had five novels written under his name by a ghostwriter named John Wheeler. The titles are *Won in the Ninth, Pitcher Pollock, Catcher Craig, First Base Faulkner,* and *Second Base Sloan.* These titles were evidently successful because after Matty was gassed in World War I, another title was issued under the name of Everett "Deacon" Scott, the Red Sox and Yankee shortstop who held the consecutive-games-played record broken by Lou Gehrig. That book, presumably also ghosted by Wheeler, was called *Third Base Thatcher.*

In addition, in 1920 a book called *The Home Run King* was issued under Babe Ruth's name. This presumably also was done by a ghostwriter, but as it was written in the days before Christy Walsh regularized Babe's outside activities, I have no idea who really wrote it. The title celebrated the entirely new dimension the Babe was introducing to the game.

A similar series was produced in the early 1960s, with famous NY baseball players paired as authors with sportswriters. The books contained playing tips in the back.

Yogi Berra and Til Ferdenzi wrote *Behind the Plate.*

Whitey Ford and Jack Lang wrote *The Fighting Southpaw.*

Roger Maris and Jim Ogle wrote *Slugger in Right.*

Willie Mays and Jeff Harris wrote *Danger in Center Field.*

A fifth title in this series, *New Blood at First* by Bill Skowron and Jack Lang, was never published, although it is advertised on dust jackets of others in the series.

In 1989, Tom Seaver shared credit with Herb Resnicow for a thoroughly forgettable mystery called *Beanball: Murder at the World Series.* And Sparky Lyle teamed with David Fisher in 1990's *The Year I Owned The Yankees.*

Mets' and Phillies' reliever Tug McGraw collaborated on a comic strip called *Scroogie* and produced an original cartoon story published as *Lumpy,* the one book by a major leaguer that pretty clearly came solely from the player's brain.

The situation for minor leaguers is somewhat different, as their books were not published because of their fame. Eliot Asinof (of *Eight Men Out* fame) has written two novels, *Man on Spikes* and *The Bedfellow.* Asinof spent a year in the Phillies system.

Zane Grey also played a year in the minors. He did several baseball books—*The Short-stop, The Young Pitcher,* and *The Red Headed Outfield and Other Stories* before settling on westerns.

And Pat Jordan, more famous for his journalism including *False Spring* about his own minor league career, has written one baseball novel, *The Cheat.* Similarly, Donald Honig had a brief minor league career before turning out a large number of baseball books, both fiction and nonfiction.

Robert Dews, a former minor leaguer and father of Braves' coach Bobby Dews, published a strange vanity press book called *Whichaway* under the pseudonym Trebor Swed.

There have also been baseball novels by football people (Walter Camp), nationally known basketball coaches (Clair Bee), Olympic medal winners in track (Jackson Scholz), and the owners of minor league clubs (Miles Wolff and, for one dilettantish season, Roger Kahn).

BOOKS IN WHICH CHEMICAL SUBSTANCES PLAY A ROLE

The most famous chemical substance has to be that invented by Ray Milland in the movie version of Valentine Davies's *It Happens Every Spring*. It repelled wood, and he became a great pitcher. The genre is actually much older, going back to a Ralph Henry Barbour short story called "Billy Mayes' Great Discovery," which was a tropical wood that attracted horsehide.

CORBETT, SCOTT. *The Baseball Trick.*
CORBETT, SCOTT. *The Home Run Trick.*
DAVIES, VALENTINE. *It Happens Every Spring.*
HEUMAN, WILLIAM. *Horace Higby and the Scientific Pitch.*
LEE, ROBERT. *The Iron Arm of Michael Glenn.*
OFFIT, SIDNEY. *Soupbone.*

BOOKS ABOUT PEOPLE CONNECTED TO THE GAME (NOT PLAYERS OR MANAGERS)

Most baseball books inevitably focus on the people on the field. But a number of baseball novels have focused on others connected to the game; herewith, a list.

Scouts

LITTLEFIELD, BILL. *Prospect.*
MAGNUSON, JAMES. *The Rundown.*

Umpires

HOUGH, JOHN. *The Conduct of the Game.*

Broadcasters

POWERS, RON. *Toot-Toot-Tootsie, Good-bye.*
STONE, NATALIE. *Double Play.*

Sportswriters (usually as detectives)

FITZSIMMONS, CORTLAND. *Death on the Diamond.*
JORDAN, PAT. *The Cheat.*
KLEIN, DAVE. *Hit and Run.*
LEAVY, JANE. *Squeeze Play.*
SCHIFFER, MICHAEL. *Ballpark.*
SEAVER, TOM with HERB RESNICOW. *Beanball: Murder at the World Series.*
STANSBERRY, DOMENIC. *The Spoiler.*

Front office types/owners

GILL, CHARLES. *The Boozer Challenge.*
MAGNUSON, JAMES. *The Rundown.*

BOOKS BY NOTED SPORTSWRITERS

This list is limited to sportswriters with a national reputation, those who did nonfiction baseball books, or those who covered a major league team for a long period.

WALTER CAMP
FRANK DEFORD
CHARLES EINSTEIN
ED FITZGERALD
DICK FRIENDLICH
HUGH FULLERTON
AL HIRSHBERG
PAT JORDAN
ROGER KAHN
JACK LANG (*see* Whitey Ford)
TEX MAULE

BOOKS ABOUT VARIOUS MAJOR LEAGUE TEAMS

I don't know how many books I've seen about the St. Louis Redbirds or the St. Louis Robins or even the St. Louis Tanagers. Why are some baseball books set on real major league teams and some on the Hawks, Miners, Phantoms, Cougars, or Gnats?

The answer lies in the courage of the author and publisher. A major league team's name may be used only with the permission of that team, says Sam Fernandez, who is assistant secretary and general counsel for the Los Angeles Dodgers. In the Dodgers' case, that means Brooklyn, too. But, Fernandez says, enforcing this right is often more trouble than it's worth for the team. Legal action would cost money and would force the team to prove that it had been hurt by the use of its name, something unlikely from most baseball fiction.

Thus, we have individual books set on real teams with characters clearly modeled on real players, whether their real names are used or not. Several authors have even produced whole series of books set on a real team and using thinly disguised major leaguers for characters. The most long-lived series were Baseball Joe on the New York Giants and Tunis's books set on the Brooklyn Dodgers and featuring players from well-knowns like Leo Durocher and Dolph Camilli to lesser lights such as Tuck Stainback and Babe Phelps.

Inevitably, some teams have appeared in fiction more than others. These are books that are set on teams called by real major league names or on teams with names changed but where the characters are so clearly modeled after a major league team that there's no doubt.

The Atlanta Braves

JACKSON, C. PAUL. *Rookie Catcher with the Atlanta Braves.*

The Boston Red Sox

PARKER, ROBERT. *Mortal Stakes.*
WALDMAN, FRANK. *Bonus Pitcher.*

The Brooklyn Dodgers (see also Los Angeles)

HONIG, DONALD. *The Last Great Season.*
LARDNER, RING. *Lose with a Smile.*
RICE, DAMON. *Seasons Past.*
RITZ, DAVID. *The Man Who Brought the Dodgers Back to Brooklyn.*
TUNIS, JOHN. *The Kid from Tomkinsville.*
TUNIS, JOHN. *World Series.*
TUNIS, JOHN. *Keystone Kids.*
TUNIS, JOHN. *Rookie of the Year.*
TUNIS, JOHN. *The Kid Comes Back.*
TUNIS, JOHN. *Highpockets.*
TUNIS, JOHN. *Schoolboy Johnson.*
WEBSTER, JOE. *Dodger Doubleheader.*

The Chicago Cubs

KINSELLA, W. P. *The Iowa Baseball Confederacy.*
MacNELLY, JEFF. *Shoe Goes to Wrigley Field.*
MARLOWE, DAN. *The Hitter.*

The Chicago White Sox

GREY, ZANE. *The Red-Headed Outfield.*
HART, FRANK. *The Speed Boy.*
LARDNER, RING. *You Know Me Al.*
McMANUS, JAMES. *Chin Music.*
MOLLOY, PAUL. *A Pennant for the Kremlin.*
SMITH, CAROLE. *The Hit-and-Run Connection.*

The Cincinnati Reds

MARLOWE, DAN. *Double the Glory.*

The Detroit Tigers

JACKSON, C. PAUL. *Clown at Second Base.*
JACKSON, C. PAUL. *Rookie First Baseman.*
WALDMAN, FRANK. *Delayed Steal.*

The Houston Astros

HERSKOWITZ, MICKEY. *Letters from Lefty.*

The Kansas City Royals

DYGARD, THOMAS. *The Rookie Arrives.*
HUGHES, DEAN. *Hopper Haller.*
STONE, NATALIE. *Double Play.*

The Los Angeles Dodgers

PLATT, KIN. *The Screwball King Murder.*

RITZ, DAVID. *The Man Who Brought the Dodgers Back to Brooklyn.*

The New York Giants (see also San Francisco)

CHADWICK, LESTER. *Baseball Joe on the Giants.*

CHADWICK, LESTER. *Baseball Joe in the World Series.*

CHADWICK, LESTER. *Baseball Joe Around the World.*

CHADWICK, LESTER. *Baseball Joe, Home Run King.*

CHADWICK, LESTER. *Baseball Joe, Saving the League.*

CHADWICK, LESTER. *Baseball Joe, Captain of the Team.*

CHADWICK, LESTER. *Baseball Joe, Pitching Wizard.*

GREENBERG, ERIC. *The Celebrant.*

GREY, ZANE. *The Red-Headed Outfield.*

HARKINS, PHILIP. *The Southpaw from San Francisco.*

HOPPER, JAMES. *Coming Back with the Spitball.*

RICE, DAMON. *Seasons Past.*

The New York Mets

HONIG, DONALD. *The Professional.*

PLIMPTON, GEORGE. *The Curious Case of Sidd Finch.*

The New York Yankees

BROUN, HEYWOOD. *The Sun Field.*

FITZGERALD, ED. *The Turning Point.*

FITZGERALD, ED. *Yankee Rookie.*

FITZGERALD, ED. *The Ballplayer.*

GRANT, J. JASON. *Dugout Brother.*

KLEIN, DAVE. *Hit and Run.*

LYLE, SPARKY, with DAVID FISHER. *The Year I Owned the Yankees.*

MAULE, TEX. *The Shortstop.*

MAULE, TEX. *Beatty of the Yankees.*

MAULE, TEX. *The Last Out.*

McCORMICK, WILFRED. *Rookie on First.*

MOORE, JOSEPH. *Hot Shot at Third.*

MORGENSTEIN, GARY. *The Man Who Wanted to Play Centerfield for the New York Yankees.*

RICE, DAMON. *Seasons Past.*

TUNIS, JOHN. *Young Razzle.*

WALDMAN, FRANK. *Delayed Steal.*

The Philadelphia Phillies

KEY, TED. *Phyllis.*

O'ROURKE, FRANK. *The Team.*

O'ROURKE, FRANK. *Bonus Rookie.*

O'ROURKE, FRANK. *Never Come Back.*

The San Francisco Giants (see also New York)

LEE, ROBERT. *The Iron Arm of Michael Glenn.*

The Seattle Mariners

EVERETT, PERCIVAL. *Suder.*

The St. Louis Browns

WEBSTER, JOE. *The Rookie from Junction Flats.*

The St. Louis Cardinals

CHADWICK, LESTER. *Baseball Joe in the Big League.*

The Washington Senators

WALLOP, DOUGLAS. *The Year the Yankees Lost the Pennant.*